Unity Game Optimization
Third Edition

Enhance and extend the performance of all aspects of your
Unity games

Dr. Davide Aversa
Chris Dickinson

BIRMINGHAM - MUMBAI

Unity Game Optimization
Third Edition

Copyright © 2019 Packt Publishing

Commissioning Editor: Pavan Ramchandani
Acquisition Editor: Larissa Pinto
Content Development Editor: Keagan Carneiro
Senior Editor: Martin Whittemore
Technical Editor: Suwarna Patil
Copy Editor: Safis Editing
Project Coordinator: Kinjal Bari
Proofreader: Safis Editing
Indexer: Manju Arasan
Production Designer: Joshua Misquitta

First published: November 2015
Second edition: November 2017
Third edition: November 2019

Production reference: 1281119

Published by Packt Publishing Ltd.
Livery Place
35 Livery Street
Birmingham
B3 2PB, UK.

ISBN 978-1-83855-651-8

www.packt.com

To Gioia, with whom I am writing my most important book.

- Davide Aversa

Packt.com

Subscribe to our online digital library for full access to over 7,000 books and videos, as well as industry leading tools to help you plan your personal development and advance your career. For more information, please visit our website.

Why subscribe?

- Spend less time learning and more time coding with practical eBooks and Videos from over 4,000 industry professionals

- Improve your learning with Skill Plans built especially for you

- Get a free eBook or video every month

- Fully searchable for easy access to vital information

- Copy and paste, print, and bookmark content

Did you know that Packt offers eBook versions of every book published, with PDF and ePub files available? You can upgrade to the eBook version at www.packt.com and as a print book customer, you are entitled to a discount on the eBook copy. Get in touch with us at customercare@packtpub.com for more details.

At www.packt.com, you can also read a collection of free technical articles, sign up for a range of free newsletters, and receive exclusive discounts and offers on Packt books and eBooks.

Contributors

About the authors

Dr. Davide Aversa holds a PhD in artificial intelligence and an MSc in artificial intelligence and robotics from the University of Rome La Sapienza in Italy. He has a strong interest in artificial intelligence for the development of interactive virtual agents and procedural content generation. He served as a Program Committee member of video game-related conferences such as the IEEE conference on computational intelligence and games, and he also regularly participates in game-jam contests. He also writes a blog on game design and game development.

I'd like to thank my family for the stability I needed during this year; the Unity devs on Twitter that helped me clarify the most obscure elements of Unity internals; and, finally, Keagan and the other Packt Publishing editors for helping me during this work and for being understanding of my delays.

Chris Dickinson grew up in a quiet little corner of England with a strong passion for mathematics, science and, in particular, video games. He loved playing them, dissecting their gameplay, and trying to figure out how they worked. Watching his dad hack the hex code of a PC game to get around the early days of copy protection completely blew his mind! His passion for science won the battle at the time; however, after completing a master's degree in physics with electronics, he flew out to California to work in the field of scientific research in the heart of Silicon Valley. Shortly afterward, he had to admit to himself that research work was an unsuitable career path for his temperament. After firing resumes in all directions, he landed a job that finally set him on the correct course in the field of software engineering (this is not uncommon for physics grads, I hear).

His time working as an automated tools developer for IPBX phone systems fit his temperament much better. Now he was figuring out complex chains of devices, helping its developers fix and improve them, and building tools of his own. Chris learned a lot about how to work with big, complex, real-time, event-based, user-input driven state machines (sounds familiar?). Being mostly self-taught at this point, Chris's passion for video games was flaring up again, pushing him to really figure out how video games were built. Once he felt confident enough, he returned to school for a bachelor's degree in game and simulation programming. By the time he was done, he was already hacking together his own (albeit rudimentary) game engines in C++ and regularly making use of those skills during his day job. However, if you want to build games, you should just build games, and not game engines. So, Chris picked his favorite publically available game engine at the time—an excellent little tool called Unity 3D—and started hammering out some games.

After a brief stint of indie game development, Chris regretfully decided that the demands of that particular career path weren't for him, but the amount of knowledge he had accumulated in just a few short years was impressive by most standards, and he loved to make use of it in ways that enabled other developers with their creations. Since then, Chris has authored a tutorial book on game physics (*Learning Game Physics with Bullet Physics and OpenGL*, published by *Packt*) and two editions of a Unity performance optimization book (which you are currently reading). He has married the love of his life, Jamie, and works with some of the coolest modern technology as a software development engineer in Test (SDET) at Jaunt Inc. in San Mateo, CA, a VR/AR startup that focuses on delivering VR and AR experiences, such as 360 videos (and more!).

Outside of work, Chris continues to fight an addiction to board games (particularly Battlestar: Galactica and Blood Rage), an obsession with Blizzard's Overwatch and Starcraft II, cater to the ever-growing list of demands from a pair of grumpy yet adorable cats, and gazing forlornly at the latest versions of Unity with a bunch of game ideas floating around on paper. Someday soon, when the time is right (and when he stops slacking off), his plans may come to fruition

About the reviewer

Vincent Chu is a professional Unity lead developer (a certified expert) who leads multiple game projects across the globe and ranks highly in global algorithm contests. He has expertise in Unity game development, software architecture, 3D modeling and animation, rendering and shaders, networking, and cloud solutions.

Packt is searching for authors like you

If you're interested in becoming an author for Packt, please visit authors.packtpub.com and apply today. We have worked with thousands of developers and tech professionals, just like you, to help them share their insight with the global tech community. You can make a general application, apply for a specific hot topic that we are recruiting an author for, or submit your own idea.

Table of Contents

Section 2: Graphical Optimizations

Section 3: Advance Optimizations

Preface

User experience is a critical component of any game. This not only includes our game's story and its gameplay but also how smoothly the graphics run, how reliably the game connects to multiplayer servers, how responsive it is to user input, and even how large the final application file size is due to the prevalence of mobile devices and cloud downloads. The barrier of entry into game development has been lowered considerably thanks to tools such as Unity, which offer an enormous array of useful development features while still being accessible to individual developers. However, due to the amount of competition in the gaming industry, the level of quality of the final product that our players expect us to provide is increasing with every passing day. We should expect that players and critics can and will scrutinize every facet of our game.

The goals of performance optimization are deeply entwined with user experience. Poorly optimized games can result in low frame rates, freezes, crashes, input lag, long loading times, inconsistent and jittery runtime behavior, physics engine breakdowns, and even excessively high battery power consumption (an often-neglected metric for mobile devices). Having just one of these issues can be a game developer's worst nightmare as reviews will tend to focus on the one thing that we did poorly, ignoring all the things that we did well.

One goal of performance optimization is to make the best use of the available resources, including CPU resources such as the number of cycles consumed, how much main memory space we're using (known as RAM), as well as **Graphics Processing Unit (GPU)** resources, which includes its own memory space (known as VRAM), Fill Rate, Memory Bandwidth, and so on. However, the most important goal of performance optimization is to ensure that no single resource causes a bottleneck at an inappropriate time and that the highest priority tasks get taken care of first. Even small, intermittent hiccups and sluggishness in performance can pull the player out of the experience, breaking the game immersion and limiting our potential to create the experience we intended. Another consideration is that the more resources we can save, the more activity we can afford to implement in our games, allowing us to generate more exciting and dynamic gameplay.

It is also vital to decide when to take a step back and stop making performance enhancements. In a world with infinite time and resources, there will always be another way to make it better, faster, and more efficient. There must be a point during development where we decide that the product has reached an acceptable level of quality. If not, we risk dooming ourselves to repeatedly implementing changes that result in little or no tangible benefit, while each change also risks the chance that we introduce more bugs.

The best way to decide whether a performance issue is worth fixing is to answer the question, *will the user notice it?*. If the answer to this question is *no*, then performance optimization will be a wasted effort. There is an old saying in software development:

> *Premature optimization is the root of all evil.*

Premature optimization is the cardinal sin of reworking and refactoring code to enhance performance without any proof that it is necessary. This can mean either making changes without showing that a performance problem even exists, or making changes because we only believe a performance issue might stem from a particular area before it has been proven to be true.

Of course, the original version of this common saying by Donald Knuth goes on to say that we should still write our code to avoid the more straightforward and obvious performance problems. However, the real performance optimization work toward the end of a project can take a lot of time, and we should plan the time to polish the product properly while avoiding the desire to implement more costly and time-consuming changes without any valid proof. These kinds of mistakes have cost software developers, as a collective whole, a depressing number of work hours for nothing.

This book intends to give you the tools, knowledge, and skills you need to both detect and fix performance issues in a Unity application, no matter where they stem from. These bottlenecks can appear within hardware components such as the CPU, GPU, and RAM, or within software subsystems such as physics, rendering, and the Unity engine itself.

Optimizing the performance of our games will give them a much better chance of succeeding and standing out from the crowd in a marketplace that is inundated with new, high-quality games every single day.

Who this book is for

The book is intended for game developers who want to learn optimization techniques for building high performant games with the latest Unity version.

What this book covers

Chapter 1, *Evaluating Performance Problems*, provides an exploration of the Unity Profiler and a series of methods to profile our application, detect performance bottlenecks, and perform root cause analysis.

Chapter 2, *Scripting Strategies*, deals with the best practices for our Unity C# script code, minimizing MonoBehaviour callback overhead, improving inter-object communication, and more.

Chapter 3, *The Benefits of Batching*, explores Unity's dynamic batching and static batching systems, and how they can be utilized to ease the burden on the rendering pipeline.

Chapter 4, *Optimizing Your Art Assets*, helps you to understand the underlying technology behind art assets and learn how to avoid common pitfalls with importing, compression, and encoding.

Chapter 5, *Faster Physics*, is about investigating the nuances of Unity's internal physics engines for both 3D and 2D games, and how to properly organize our physics objects for improved performance.

Chapter 6, *Dynamic Graphics*, provides an in-depth exploration of the rendering pipeline, and how to improve applications that suffer rendering bottlenecks in the GPU or CPU, how to optimize graphical effects such as lighting, shadows, and particle effects, ways in which to optimize shader code, and some graphics optimization specific for mobile devices.

Chapter 7, *Optimizations for Virtual and Augmented Reality*, focuses on the new entertainment mediums of VR and AR, and includes several techniques for optimizing performance that is unique to apps built for these platforms.

Chapter 8, *Masterful Memory Management*, examines the inner workings of the Unity engine, the Mono framework, and how memory is managed within these components to protect our application from excessive heap allocations and runtime garbage collection.

Chapter 9, *The Data-Oriented Technology Stack*, examines the new Unity optimizations for multithreading intensive games: DOTS. We introduce the new C# Job System, the new Unity ECS, and the burst compiler.

Chapter 10, *Tactical Tips and Tricks*, concludes the book with a multitude of useful techniques used by Unity professionals to improve project workflow and scene management.

To get the most out of this book

The majority of this book will focus on features and enhancements that apply to Unity 2019 and Unity 2020. Many of the techniques explored within this book can be applied to Unity 2018 projects and older, but some features may be different. These differences will be highlighted, where applicable.

It is worth noting that the code it is supposed to work on Unity 2020 but at the time of writing we could only test it on the alpha version. Additional incompatibilities may arise when Unity 2020 comes out of alpha.

Download the example code files

You can download the example code files for this book from your account at `www.packt.com`. If you purchased this book elsewhere, you can visit `www.packtpub.com/support` and register to have the files emailed directly to you.

You can download the code files by following these steps:

1. Log in or register at `www.packt.com`.
2. Select the **Support** tab.
3. Click on **Code Downloads**.
4. Enter the name of the book in the **Search** box and follow the onscreen instructions.

Once the file is downloaded, please make sure that you unzip or extract the folder using the latest version of:

- WinRAR/7-Zip for Windows
- Zipeg/iZip/UnRarX for Mac
- 7-Zip/PeaZip for Linux

The code bundle for the book is also hosted on GitHub at `https://github.com/PacktPublishing/Unity-Game-Optimization-Third-Edition`. In case there's an update to the code, it will be updated on the existing GitHub repository.

We also have other code bundles from our rich catalog of books and videos available at `https://github.com/PacktPublishing/`. Check them out!

Download the color images

We also provide a PDF file that has color images of the screenshots/diagrams used in this book. You can download it here: `https://static.packt-cdn.com/downloads/9781838556518_ColorImages.pdf`.

Conventions used

There are a number of text conventions used throughout this book.

`CodeInText`: Indicates code words in text, database table names, folder names, filenames, file extensions, pathnames, dummy URLs, user input, and Twitter handles. Here is an example: "These can be accessed through the `UnityEngine.Profiling.Profiler` class through its `BeginSample()` and `EndSample()` methods."

A block of code is set as follows:

```
void DoSomethingCompletelyStupid() {
  Profiler.BeginSample("My Profiler Sample");
  List<int> listOfInts = new List<int>();
  for(int i = 0; i < 1000000; ++i) {
    listOfInts.Add(i);
  }
  Profiler.EndSample();
}
```

Bold: Indicates a new term, an important word, or words that you see on screen. For example, words in menus or dialog boxes appear in the text like this. Here is an example: "When a Unity application is compiled in **Development Mode**."

Warnings or important notes appear like this.

Tips and tricks appear like this.

Get in touch

Feedback from our readers is always welcome.

General feedback: If you have questions about any aspect of this book, mention the book title in the subject of your message and email us at `customercare@packtpub.com`.

Errata: Although we have taken every care to ensure the accuracy of our content, mistakes do happen. If you have found a mistake in this book, we would be grateful if you would report this to us. Please visit www.packtpub.com/support/errata, selecting your book, clicking on the Errata Submission Form link, and entering the details.

Piracy: If you come across any illegal copies of our works in any form on the internet, we would be grateful if you would provide us with the location address or website name. Please contact us at copyright@packt.com with a link to the material.

If you are interested in becoming an author: If there is a topic that you have expertise in and you are interested in either writing or contributing to a book, please visit authors.packtpub.com.

Reviews

Please leave a review. Once you have read and used this book, why not leave a review on the site that you purchased it from? Potential readers can then see and use your unbiased opinion to make purchase decisions, we at Packt can understand what you think about our products, and our authors can see your feedback on their book. Thank you!

For more information about Packt, please visit packt.com.

Section 1: Base Scripting Optimization

1

The reader will learn how to identify performance bottleneck using the built-in Profiler and how to fix the most common issues. The chapters in this section as follows:

1
Evaluating Performance Problems

Performance evaluation for most software products is a very scientific process. First, we determine the maximum/minimum supported performance metrics, such as the allowed memory usage, acceptable CPU consumption, and the number of concurrent users. Next, we perform load testing against the application in scenarios with a version of the application built for the target platform, and test it while gathering instrumentation data. Once this data is collected, we analyze and search it for performance bottlenecks. If problems are discovered, we complete a **Root Cause Analysis** (**RCA**), and then make changes in the configuration or application code to fix the issue and repeat it.

Although game development is a very artistic process, it is still exceptionally technical. Our game should have a target audience in mind, which can tell us what hardware limitations our game might be operating under and, perhaps, tell us exactly what performance targets we need to meet (particularly in the case of console and mobile games). We can perform runtime testing on our application, gather performance data from multiple subsystems (CPU, GPU memory, the physics engine, the Rendering Pipeline, and so on), and compare them against what we consider to be acceptable. We can then use this data to identify bottlenecks in our application, perform additional instrumentation measurements, and determine the root cause of the issue. Finally, depending on the type of problem, we should be capable of applying a number of solutions to improve our application's performance.

However, before we spend even a single moment making performance fixes, we will first need to prove that a performance problem exists. It is unwise to spend time rewriting and refactoring code until there is a good reason to do so since pre-optimization is rarely worth the hassle. Once we have proof of a performance issue, the next task is figuring out exactly where the bottleneck is located. It is important to ensure that we understand why the performance issue is happening; otherwise, we could waste even more time applying fixes that are little more than educated guesses. Doing so often means that we only fix a symptom of the issue, not its root cause, and so we risk it manifesting itself in other ways in the future, or in ways we haven't yet detected.

In this chapter, we will explore the following:

- How to gather profiling data using the Unity Profiler
- How to analyze Profiler data for performance bottlenecks
- Techniques to isolate a performance problem and determine its root cause

With a thorough understanding of the problems you're likely to face, you will then be ready for the information presented in the remaining chapters, where you will learn what solutions are available for the types of issue we detect.

Gathering profiling data using the Unity Profiler

The Unity Profiler is built into the Unity Editor itself and provides an expedient way of narrowing down our search for performance bottlenecks by generating usage and statistics reports on a multitude of Unity3D subsystems during runtime. The different subsystems for which it can gather data are listed as follows:

- CPU consumption (per-major subsystem)
- Basic and detailed rendering and GPU information
- Runtime memory allocations and overall consumption
- Audio source/data usage
- Physics engine (2D and 3D) usage
- Network messaging and operation usage
- Video playback usage
- Basic and detailed user interface performance
- **Global Illumination** (**GI**) statistics

There are generally two approaches to making use of a profiling tool: **instrumentation** and **benchmarking** (although, admittedly, the two terms are often used interchangeably).

Instrumentation typically means taking a close look into the inner workings of the application by observing the behavior of targeted function calls, where/how much memory is being allocated, and, generally getting an accurate picture of what is happening with the hope of finding the root cause of a problem. However, this is normally not an efficient way of starting to identify performance problems because profiling of any application comes with a performance cost of its own.

When a Unity application is compiled in **Development Mode** (determined by the **Development Build** flag in the **Build Settings** menu), additional compiler flags are enabled causing the application to generate special events at runtime, which get logged and stored by the Profiler. Naturally, this will cause additional CPU and memory overhead at runtime due to all of the extra workload the application takes on. Even worse, if the application is being profiled through the Unity Editor, then even more CPU and memory use will be incurred, ensuring that the Editor updates its interface, renders additional windows (such as the **Scene** window), and handles background tasks. This profiling cost is not always negligible. In excessively large projects, it can sometimes cause all kinds of inconsistent and unexpected behavior when the Profiler is enabled: Unity can go out of memory, some scripts may refuse to run, physics may stop being updated (the time used for a frame may be so large that the physics engine reaches the maximum allowed updates per frame), and more. This is a necessary price we pay for a deep analysis of our code's behavior at runtime, and we should always be aware of its implications. Therefore, before we get ahead of ourselves and start analyzing every line of code in our application, it would be wiser to do some **benchmarking.**

Benchmarking involves performing a surface-level measurement of the application. We should gather some rudimentary data and perform test scenarios during a runtime session of our game while it runs on the target hardware; the test case could simply be, for example, a few seconds of gameplay, playback of a cutscene, or a partial playthrough of a level. The idea of this activity is to get a general feel for what the user might experience and keep watching for moments when performance becomes noticeably worse. Such problems may be severe enough to warrant further analysis.

The important metrics we're interested in when we carry out a benchmarking process are often the number of **frames per-second** (**FPS**) being rendered, overall memory consumption, how CPU activity behaves (looking for large spikes in activity), and sometimes CPU/GPU temperature. These are all relatively simple metrics to collect and can be used as a go-to first approach to performance analysis for one important reason: it will save us an enormous amount of time in the long run. It ensures that we only spend our time investigating problems that users would notice.

We should dig deeper into instrumentation only after a benchmarking test indicates that further analysis is required. It is also very important to benchmark by simulating actual platform behavior as much as possible if we want a realistic data sample. As such, we should never accept benchmarking data that was generated through Editor mode as being representative of real gameplay, since Editor mode comes with some additional overhead costs that might mislead us, or hide potential race conditions in a real application. Instead, we should hook the profiling tool into the application while it is running in a standalone format on the target hardware.

Many Unity developers are surprised to find that the Editor sometimes calculates the results of operations much faster than a standalone application does. This is particularly common when dealing with serialized data such as audio files, Prefabs, and scriptable objects. This is because the Editor will cache previously imported data and is able to access it much faster than a real application would.

Now, let's cover how to access the Unity Profiler and connect it to the target device so that we can start to make accurate benchmarking tests.

Users who are already familiar with connecting the Unity Profiler to their applications can skip to the section entitled *The Profiler window*.

Launching the Profiler

We will begin with a brief tutorial on how to connect our game to the Unity Profiler within a variety of contexts:

- Local instances of the application, either through the Editor or a standalone instance
- Local instances of a WebGL application running in a browser
- Remote instances of the application on an iOS device (for example, iPhone or iPad)
- Remote instances of the application on an Android device (for example, an Android tablet or phone)
- Profiling the Editor itself

We will briefly cover the requirements for setting up the Profiler in each of these contexts.

Editor or standalone instances

In this instance, the only way to access the Profiler is to launch it through the Unity Editor and connect it to a running instance of our application. We will use the same Profiler windows irrespective of whether we execute our game in **Playmode** within the Editor, running a standalone application on the local or remote device, or wish to profile the Editor itself.

To open **Profiler**, navigate to **Window** | **Analysis** | **Profiler** within the Editor or use *Ctrl + 7* (or *cmd + 7* on macOS):

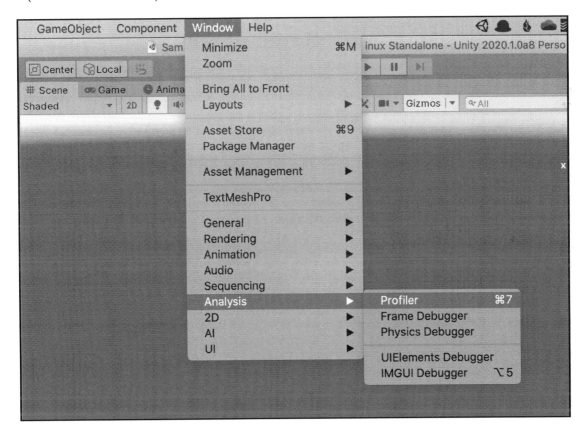

If the Editor is already running in **Playmode**, then we should see profiling data continuously populating the **Profiler** window.

To profile standalone projects, ensure that the **Development Build** and **Autoconnect Profiler** flags are enabled when the application is built.

Choosing whether to profile an Editor-based instance (through the Editor's **Playmode**) or a standalone instance (built and running separately from the Editor) can be achieved through the **Connected Player** option in the **Profiler** window:

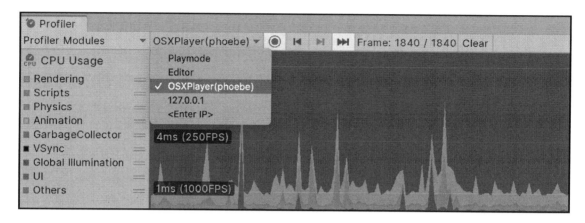

 Note that switching back to the Unity Editor while profiling a separate standalone project will halt all data collection since the application will not be updated while it is in the background.

Connecting to a WebGL instance

The Profiler can also be connected to an instance of the Unity WebGL Player. This can be achieved by ensuring that the **Development Build** and **Autoconnect Profiler** flags are enabled when the WebGL application is built and run from the Editor. The application will then be launched through the operating system's default browser. This enables us to profile our web-based application in a more real-world scenario through the target browser and test multiple browser types for inconsistencies in behavior (although this requires us to keep changing the default browser).

Unfortunately, the Profiler connection can only be established when the application is first launched from the Editor. It currently cannot be connected to a standalone WebGL instance already running in a browser. This limits the accuracy of benchmarking WebGL applications since there will be some Editor-based overhead, but it's the only option we have available for the moment.

Remote connection to an iOS device

The Profiler can also be connected to an active instance of an application running remotely on an iOS device, such as an iPad or iPhone. This can be achieved through a shared Wi-Fi connection.

Note that remote connection to an iOS device is only possible when Unity (and hence the Profiler) is running on an Apple Mac device.

Observe the following steps to connect the Profiler to an iOS device:

1. Ensure that the **Development Build** and **Autoconnect Profiler** flags are enabled when the application is built
2. Connect both the iOS device and macOS device to a local Wi-Fi network, or to an ad hoc Wi-Fi network
3. Attach the iOS device to the macOS via the USB or Lightning Cable
4. Begin building the application with the **Build & Run** option as usual
5. Open the **Profiler** window in the Unity Editor and select the device under **Connected Player**

You should now see the iOS device's profiling data gathering in the **Profiler** window.

The Profiler uses ports 54998 to 55511 to broadcast profiling data. Ensure that these ports are available for outbound traffic if there is a firewall on the network.

To troubleshoot problems with building iOS applications and connecting the Profiler to them, consult the following documentation page: https://docs.unity3d.com/Manual/ TroubleShootingIPhone.html.

Remote connection to an Android device

There are two different methods for connecting an Android device to the Unity Profiler: either through a Wi-Fi connection or by using the **Android Debug Bridge (ADB)** tool. Either of these approaches will work from an Apple macOS, or a Windows PC.

Perform the following steps to connect an Android device over a Wi-Fi connection:

1. Ensure that the **Development Build** and **Autoconnect Profiler** flags are enabled when the application is built
2. Connect both the Android and desktop devices to a local Wi-Fi network
3. Attach the Android device to the desktop device via a USB cable
4. Begin building the application with the **Build & Run** option as usual
5. Open the **Profiler** window in the Unity Editor and select the device under **Connected Player**

The application should then be built and pushed to the Android device through the USB connection, and the Profiler should connect through the Wi-Fi connection. You should then see the Android device's profiling data gathering in the **Profiler** window.

The second option is to use ADB. This is a suite of debugging tools that comes bundled with the Android **Software Development Kit (SDK)**. For ADB profiling, perform the following steps:

1. Ensure that the Android SDK is installed by following Unity's guide for Android SDK/NDK setup: `https://docs.unity3d.com/Manual/android-sdksetup.html`
2. Connect the Android device to your desktop machine via the USB cable
3. Ensure that the **Development Build** and **Autoconnect Profiler** flags are enabled when the application is built
4. Begin building the application with the **Build & Run** option as usual
5. Open the **Profiler** window in the Unity Editor and select the device under **Connected Player**

You should now see the Android device's profiling data gathering in the **Profiler** window.

To troubleshoot problems with building Android applications and connecting the Profiler to them, consult the following documentation page: `https://docs.unity3d.com/Manual/TroubleShootingAndroid.html`.

Editor profiling

We can profile the Editor itself. This is normally used when trying to profile the performance of custom editor scripts. This can be achieved by enabling the **Profile Editor** option in the **Profiler** window and configuring the **Connected Player** option to **Editor**, as shown in the following screenshot:

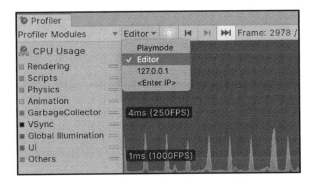

Note that both options must be configured if we want to profile the Editor: if nothing happens in the graph, then it is possible you have not selected the **Profile Editor** button, or you may accidentally be connected to another game build!

The Profiler window

We will now cover the essential features of the Profiler as they can be found within the interface.

The **Profiler** window is split into four main sections:

- **Profiler Controls**
- **Timeline View**
- **Breakdown View Controls**
- **Breakdown View**

These sections are shown in the following screenshot:

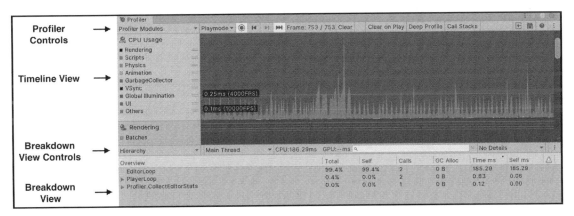

We'll now cover each of these sections in detail.

 Timeline View has a lot of colors, but not everyone sees colors in the same way. Luckily, if you are colorblind, Unity has thought of you! In the top-right hamburger menu, you can enable **Color Blind Mode**:

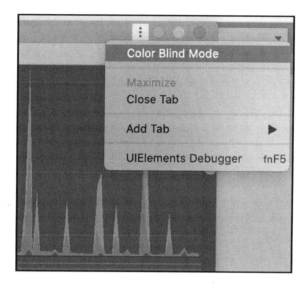

Profiler controls

The top bar in the previous screenshot contains multiple drop-down and toggle buttons we can use to affect what is being profiled and how deeply in the subsystem that data is gathered from. These are covered in the next subsections.

Add Profiler

By default, the Profiler will collect data for several different subsystems that cover the majority of the Unity engine's subsystems in **Timeline View**. These subsystems are organized into various areas containing relevant data. The **Add Profiler** option can be used to add additional areas or restore them if they have been removed. Refer to the **Timeline View** section for a complete list of subsystems we can profile.

Playmode

The **Playmode** drop-down lets us select the target instance of Unity we want to profile. This can be the current Editor application, a local standalone instance of our application, or an instance of our application running on a remote device.

Record

Enabling the **Record** option (the record icon) makes the Profiler record profiling data. This will happen continuously while this option is enabled. Note that runtime data can only be recorded if the application is actively running. For an app running in the Editor, this means that **Playmode** must be enabled and it should not be paused; alternatively, for a standalone app, it must be the active window. If **Profile Editor** is enabled, then the data that appears will be collected for the Editor itself.

Deep Profile

Ordinary profiling will only record the time and memory allocations made by common Unity callback methods, such as `Awake()`, `Start()`, `Update()`, and `FixedUpdate()`. Enabling the **Deep Profile** option recompiles our scripts with a much deeper level of instrumentation, allowing it to measure each and every invoked method. This causes a significantly greater instrumentation cost during runtime than normal, and uses substantially more memory since data is being collected for the entire callstack at runtime. As a consequence, deep profiling may not even be possible in large projects, as Unity may run out of memory before testing even begins, or the application may run so slowly as to make the test pointless.

Note that toggling **Deep Profile** requires the entire project to be completely recompiled before profiling can begin again, so it is best to avoid toggling the option back and forth between tests.

Since this option blindly measures the entire callstack, it would be unwise to keep it enabled during most of our profiling tests. This option is best reserved for when default profiling does not provide sufficient detail to figure out the root cause, or if we're testing the performance of a small test scene, which we're using to isolate certain activities.

If deep profiling is required for larger projects and scenes, but the **Deep Profile** option is too much of a hindrance during runtime, then there are alternative approaches that can be used to perform more detailed profiling; see the upcoming section entitled *Targeted profiling of code segments*.

Allocation Callstack

By activating the **Allocation Callstack** option, Unity Profiler will collect more info about the game's memory allocations without requiring **Deep Profile**:

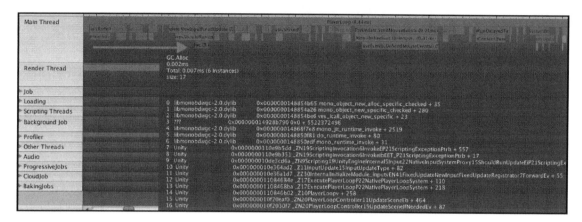

If the option is enabled, you can click on the red boxes representing memory allocations and **Profiler** will show you the origin and the cause of that memory allocation:

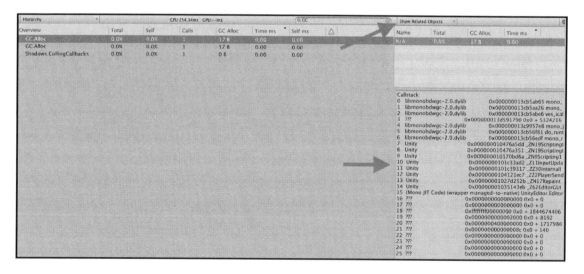

In **Hierarchy** view, instead, you still need to select an allocation call. Then, you need to switch to **Show Related Objects** in the drop-down menu in the upper-right corner and then select one of the **N/A** objects. After that, you'll see **Callstack** info in the box underneath.

We will talk more about memory allocations in `Chapter 8`, *Masterful Memory Management*.

 At the time of writing, in Unity 2019.1, **Allocation Callstack** works only when profiling in the Editor.

Clear

The **Clear** button clears all profiling data from **Timeline View**.

Load

The **Load** icon button will open up a dialog window to load in any previously saved profiling data (by using the **Save** option).

Save

The **Save** icon button saves any Profiler data currently presented in **Timeline View** to a file. Only 300 frames of data can be saved in this fashion at a time, and a new file must be manually created for any more data. This is typically sufficient for most situations, since, when a performance spike occurs, we then have about five to ten seconds to pause the application and save the data for future analysis (such as attaching it to a bug report) before it gets pushed off the left-hand side of **Timeline View**. Any saved Profiler data can be loaded into the Profiler for future examination using the **Load** option.

Frame Selection

The frame selection area is composed of several sub-elements. The **Frame Counter** shows how many frames have been profiled and which frame is currently selected in **Timeline View**. There are two buttons to move the currently selected frame forward or backward by one frame and a third button (the **Current** button) that resets the selected frame to the most recent frame and keeps that position. This will cause **Breakdown View** to always show profiling data for the current frame during runtime profiling; it will display the word **Current**.

Timeline View

Timeline View reveals during runtime,

- A graphical representation of profiling data on the right
- A series of checkboxes (the colored squares in the following screenshot) to enable/disable different activities/data types on the left:

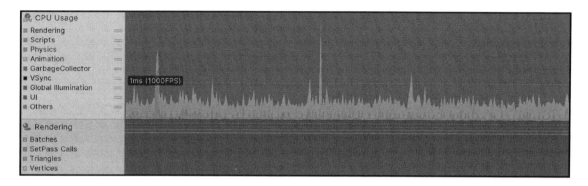

These colored boxes can be toggled, which changes the visibility of the corresponding data types within the graphical section of **Timeline View**.

When an area is selected in **Timeline View**, more detailed information for that subsystem will be revealed in **Breakdown View** (beneath **Timeline View**) for the currently selected frame. The kind of information displayed in **Breakdown View** varies depending on which area is currently selected in **Timeline View**.

Areas can be removed from **Timeline View** by clicking on the **X** in the top-right corner of an area. If you want to show an area that you removed again, you can use the **Add Profiler** option in the **Controls** bar.

At any time, we can click a location in the graphical part of **Timeline View** to reveal information about a given frame. A large vertical white bar will appear (usually with some additional information on either side coinciding with the line graphs), showing us which frame is selected.

Depending on which area is currently selected (determined by which area is currently highlighted in blue), different information will be available in **Breakdown View**, and different options will be available in **Breakdown View Controls**. Changing the area that is selected is as simple as clicking on the relevant box on the left-hand side of **Timeline View** or on the graphical side; however, clicking inside the graphical area might also change which frame has been selected, so be careful clicking in the graphical area if you wish to see **Breakdown View** information for the same frame.

Breakdown View Controls

Different dropdowns and toggle button options will appear within **Breakdown View Controls**, depending on which area is currently selected in **Timeline View**. Different areas offer different controls, and these options dictate what information is available, and how that information is presented in **Breakdown View**.

Breakdown View

The information revealed in **Breakdown View** will vary enormously based on which area is currently selected and which **Breakdown View Controls** options are selected. For instance, some areas offer different modes in a dropdown within **Breakdown View Controls**, which can provide **Simple** or **Detailed** views of the information or even a graphical layout of the same information so that it can be parsed more easily.

Now, let's cover each area and the different kinds of information and options available in **Breakdown View**.

The CPU Usage area

This area shows data for all CPU Usage and statistics. It is perhaps the most complex and useful since it covers a large number of Unity subsystems, such as `MonoBehaviour` components, cameras, some rendering and physics processes, the user interface (including the Editor's interface, if we're running through the Editor), audio processing, the Profiler itself, and more.

There are three different modes for displaying CPU Usage data in **Breakdown View**:

- **Hierarchy** mode
- **Raw Hierarchy** mode
- **Timeline** mode

Let's take a look at each of these modes individually:

- **Hierarchy** mode reveals most callstack invocations, while grouping similar data elements and global Unity function calls together for convenience. For instance, rendering delimiters, such as `BeginGUI()` and `EndGUI()` calls, are combined together in this mode. Hierarchy mode is helpful as an initial first step for determining which function calls take the most CPU time to execute.
- **Raw Hierarchy** mode is similar to Hierarchy mode, except it will separate global Unity function calls into separate entries rather than their being combined into one bulk entry. This will tend to make **Breakdown View** more difficult to read, but may be helpful if we're trying to count how many times a particular global method is invoked, or for determining whether one of these calls is costing more CPU/memory than anticipated. For example, each `BeginGUI()` and `EndGUI()` call will be separated into different entries, making it clearer how many times each is being called compared to the Hierarchy mode.

Perhaps the most useful mode for the **CPU Usage** area is the **Timeline** mode option (not to be confused with the main **Timeline View**). This mode organizes CPU Usage during the current frame in line with how the callstack expanded and contracted during processing.

- **Timeline** mode organizes **Breakdown View** vertically into different sections that represent different threads at runtime, such as **Main Thread**, **Render Thread**, and various background job threads called the **Unity Job System**, used for loading activities such as scenes and other assets. The horizontal axis represents time, so wider blocks are consuming more CPU time than narrower blocks. The horizontal size also represents relative time, making it easy to compare how much time one function call took compared to another. The vertical axis represents the callstack, so deeper chains represent more calls in the callstack at that time.

Under **Timeline** mode, blocks at the top of **Breakdown View** are functions (or, technically, callbacks) called by the Unity Engine at runtime (such as `Start()`, `Awake()`, or `Update()`), whereas blocks beneath them are functions that those functions had called into, which can include functions on other components or regular C# objects.

The **Timeline** mode offers a very clean and organized way to determine which particular method in the callstack consumes the most time and how that processing time measures up against other methods being called during the same frame. This allows us to gauge the method that is the biggest cause of performance problems with minimal effort.

For example, let's assume that we are looking at a performance problem in the following screenshot. We can tell, with a quick glance, that there are three methods that are causing a problem, and they each consume similar amounts of processing time, due to their similar widths:

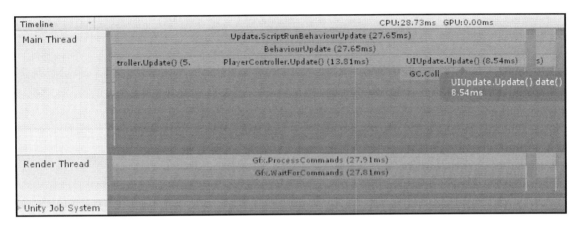

In the previous screenshot, we have exceeded our 16.667 ms budget with calls to three different `MonoBehaviour` components. The good news is that we have three possible methods through which we can find performance improvements, which means lots of opportunities to find code that can be improved. The bad news is that increasing the performance of one method will only improve about one-third of the total processing for that frame. Hence, all three methods may need to be examined and optimized in order get back under budget.

It's a good idea to collapse the **Unity Job System** list when using **Timeline** mode, as it tends to obstruct the visibility of items shown in the **Main Thread** block, which is probably what we're most interested in.

In general, the **CPU Usage** area will be most useful for detecting issues that can be solved by solutions that will be explored in `Chapter 2`, *Scripting Strategies*.

The GPU Usage area

The **GPU Usage** area is similar to the **CPU Usage** area, except that it shows method calls and processing time as it occurs on the GPU. Relevant Unity method calls in this area will relate to cameras, drawing, opaque and transparent geometry, lighting and shadows, and so on.

The **GPU Usage** area offers hierarchical information similar to the **CPU Usage** area and estimates the time spent calling into various rendering functions such as `Camera.Render()` (provided rendering actually occurs during the frame currently selected in **Timeline View**).

The **GPU Usage** area will be a useful tool to refer to when you go through `Chapter 6`, *Dynamic Graphics*.

The Rendering area

The **Rendering** area provides some generic rendering statistics that tend to focus on activities related to preparing the GPU for rendering, which involves a set of activities that occur on the CPU (as opposed to the act of rendering, which is an activity handled within the GPU and is detailed in the **GPU Usage** area). **Breakdown View** offers useful information, such as the number of **SetPass** calls (otherwise known as draw calls), the total number of batches used to render the scene, the number of batches saved from dynamic batching and static batching and how they are being generated, and memory consumed for textures.

The **Rendering** area also offers a button to open **Frame Debugger**, which will be explored more in `Chapter 3`, *The Benefits of Batching*. The remainder of this area's information will prove useful when you go through `Chapter 3`, *The Benefits of Batching*, and `Chapter 6`, *Dynamic Graphics*.

The Memory area

The **Memory** area allows us to inspect the memory usage of the application in **Breakdown View** in the following two modes:

- **Simple** mode
- **Detailed** mode

Simple mode provides only a high-level overview of the memory consumption of subsystems. This include Unity's low-level Engine, the Mono framework (total heap size that is being watched by the garbage collector), graphical assets, audio assets and buffers, and even memory used to store data collected by the Profiler.

Detailed mode shows memory consumption of individual GameObjects and MonoBehaviours for both their native and managed representations. It also has a column explaining the reason why an object may be consuming memory and when it might be deallocated.

The garbage collector is a common feature provided by C#—the Unity's scripting language of choice—that automatically releases any memory we have allocated to store data; but, if it is handled poorly, it has the potential to stall our application for brief moments. This topic, and many more related topics, such as native and managed memory spaces, will be explored in `Chapter 8`, *Masterful Memory Management*.

Note that information only appears in **Detailed** mode through manual sampling by clicking on the **Take Sample <TargetName>** button. This is the only way to gather information when using **Detailed** mode, since performing this kind of analysis automatically for each update would be prohibitively expensive:

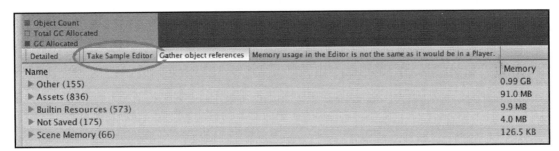

Breakdown View also provides a button labelled **Gather Object References**, which can gather more in-depth memory information pertaining to some objects.

The **Memory** area will be a useful tool to use when we dive into the complexities of memory management, native versus managed memory, and the garbage collector in `Chapter 8`, *Masterful Memory Management*.

The Audio area

The **Audio** area grants an overview of audio statistics and can be used both to measure CPU Usage from the audio system and total memory consumed by audio sources (both for those that are playing or paused) and audio clips.

Breakdown View provides lots of useful insights into how the audio system is operating and how various audio channels and groups are being used.

The **Audio** area may come in handy as we explore art assets in `Chapter 4`, *Optimizing Your Art Assets*.

Audio is often overlooked when it comes to performance optimization, but audio can become a surprisingly large source of bottlenecks if it is not managed properly due to the potential amount of hard disk access and CPU processing required. Don't neglect it!

The Physics 3D and Physics 2D areas

There are two different physics areas, one for **Physics 3D** (NVIDIA 's PhysX), and another for the **Physics 2D** system (**Box2D**). This area provides various physics statistics, such as **Rigidbody**, **Collider**, and **Contact** counts.

The **Breakdown View** for each physics area provides some rudimentary insight into the subsystem's inner workings, but we can gain further insight by exploring the physics debugger, which we will introduce in Chapter 5, *Faster Physics*.

The network messages and network operations areas

These two areas provide information about Unity's networking system, which was introduced during the Unity 5 release cycle. The information present will depend on whether the application is using the **High-Level API (HLAPI)** or **Transport Layer API (TLAPI)** provided by Unity. HLAPI is an easier-to-use system for managing player and GameObject network synchronization automatically, whereas TLAPI is a thin layer that operates just above the socket level, allowing Unity developers to conjure up their own networking system.

Optimizing network traffic is a subject that fills an entire book all by itself, where the right solution is typically very dependent on the particular needs of the application. This will not be a Unity-specific problem, and, as such, the topic of network traffic optimization will not be explored in this book.

The Video area

If our application happens to make use of Unity's VideoPlayer API, then we might find this area useful for profiling video playback behavior.

Optimization of media playback is also a complex, non-Unity-specific topic and will not be explored in this book.

The UI and UI Details areas

These areas provide insight into applications making use of Unity's built-in user interface system. If we're using a custom-built or third-party user interface system (such as the popular Asset Store plugin **Next-Gen UI (NGUI)**), then these areas will probably provide little benefit.

A poorly optimized user interface can often affect one or both of the CPU and GPU, so we will investigate some code optimization strategies for UIs in Chapter 2, *Scripting Strategies*, and graphics-related approaches in Chapter 6, *Dynamic Graphics*.

The Global Illumination area

The **Global Illumination** area gives us a very detailed insight into Unity's GI system. If our application makes use of GI, then we should refer to this area to verify that it is performing properly.

This area may prove useful as we explore lighting and shadowing in Chapter 6, *Dynamic Graphics*.

Best approaches to performance analysis

Good coding practices and project asset management often make finding the root cause of a performance issue relatively simple, at which point the only real problem is figuring out how to improve the code. For instance, if the method only processes a single gigantic for loop, then it will be a pretty safe assumption that the problem is either with how many iterations the loop is performing, whether or not the loop is causing cache misses by reading memory in a non-sequential fashion, how much work is done in each iteration, or how much work it takes to prepare for the next iteration.

Of course, whether we're working individually or in a group setting, a lot of our code is not always written in the cleanest way possible, and we should expect to have to profile some poor coding work from time to time. Sometimes, we are forced to implement a hacky solution for the sake of speed, and we don't always have the time to go back and refactor everything to keep up with our best coding practices. In fact, many code changes made in the name of performance optimization tend to appear very strange or arcane, often making our code base more difficult to read. The common goal of software development is to make code that is clean, feature-rich, and fast. Achieving one of these is relatively easy, but the reality is that achieving two will cost significantly more time and effort, while achieving all three is a near-impossibility.

At its most basic level, performance optimization is just another form of problem solving, and when we overlook the obvious while problem solving, it can be an expensive mistake. Our goal is to use benchmarking to observe our application looking for instances of problematic behavior, and to then use instrumentation to hunt through the code for clues about where the problem originates. Unfortunately, it's often very easy to get distracted by invalid data or jump to conclusions because we're being too impatient or have overlooked a subtle detail. Many of us have run into occasions during software debugging where we could have found the root cause of the problem much faster if we had simply challenged and verified our earlier assumptions. Hunting down performance issues is no different.

A checklist of tasks would be helpful to keep us focused on the issue, and ensure we don't waste time by trying to implement any possible optimization that has no effect on the main performance bottleneck. Of course, every project is different, with its own unique challenges to overcome, but the following checklist is general enough that it should be able to apply to any Unity project:

- Verify that the target script is present in the scene
- Verify that the script appears in the scene the correct number of times
- Verify the correct order of events
- Minimize ongoing code changes
- Minimize internal distractions
- Minimize external distractions

Verifying script presence

Sometimes, there are things we expect to see, but don't. These are usually easy to spot because the human brain is very good at pattern recognition and spotting differences we didn't expect. However, there are also times where we assume that something has been happening, but it didn't. These are generally more difficult to notice, because we're often scanning for the first kind of problem, and we're assuming that the things we don't see are working as intended. In the context of Unity, one problem that manifests itself this way is verifying that the scripts we expect to be operating are actually present in the scene.

Script presence can be quickly verified by typing the following into the **Hierarchy** window textbox:

```
t:<monobehaviour name>
```

For example, typing `t:mytestmonobehaviour` (note that it is not case-sensitive) into the **Hierarchy** textbox will show a shortlist of all GameObjects that currently have at least one `MyTestMonoBehaviour` script attached as a component.

 Note that this shortlist feature also includes any GameObjects with components that derive from the given script name.

We should also double check that the GameObjects they are attached to are still enabled, since we may have disabled them during earlier testing since someone or something may have accidentally deactivated the object.

Verifying script count

If we're looking at our Profiler data and note that a certain `MonoBehaviour` method is being executed more times than expected, or is taking longer than expected, we might want to double-check that it only occurs as many times in the scene as we expect it to. It's entirely feasible that someone created the object more times than expected in the scene file, or that we accidentally instantiated the object more than the expected number of times from code. If so, the problem could be due to conflicting or duplicated method invocations generating a performance bottleneck. We can verify the count using the same shortlist method used in the *Best approaches to performance analysis* section.

If we expected a specific number of components to appear in the scene, but the shortlist revealed more (or fewer!) of these components, then it might be wise to write some initialization code that prevents this from ever happening again. We could also write some custom Editor helpers to display warnings to any level designers who might be making this mistake.

Preventing casual mistakes such as this is essential for good productivity, since experience tells us that, if we don't explicitly disallow something, then someone, somewhere, at some point, for whatever reason, will do it anyway. This is likely to cost us a frustrating afternoon hunting down a problem that eventually turned out to be caused by human error.

Verifying the order of events

Unity applications mostly operate as a series of callbacks from *Native code* to *Managed code*. This concept will be explained in more detail in Chapter 8, *Masterful Memory Management*, but for the sake of a brief summary, Unity's main thread doesn't operate as a simple console application would. In such applications, code would be executed with some obvious starting point (usually a main() function), and we would then have direct control of the game engine, where we initialize major subsystems, and then the game runs in a big while loop (often called the game loop) that checks for user input, updates the game, renders the current scene, and repeats. This loop only exits once the player chooses to quit the game.

Instead, Unity handles the game loop for us, and we expect callbacks such as Awake(), Start(), Update(), and FixedUpdate() to be called at specific moments. The big difference is that we don't have fine-grained control over the order in which events of the same type are called. When a new scene is loaded (whether it's the first scene of the game or a later scene), every MonoBehaviour component's Awake() callback gets called, but there's no way of predicting the order in which this will happen.

So, if we take one set of objects that configure some data in their Awake() callback, and then another set of objects does something with that configured data in its own Awake() callback, some reorganization or recreation of scene objects or a random change in the code base or compilation process (it's unclear what exactly causes it) may cause the order of these Awake() calls to change, and then the dependent objects will probably try to do things with data that wasn't initialized how we expected. The same goes for all other callbacks provided by MonoBehaviour components, such as Start() and Update().

In any sufficiently complex project, there's no way of telling the order in which the same type of callback gets called among a group of MonoBehaviour components, so we should be very careful not to assume that object callbacks are happening in a specific order. In fact, it is essential practice to never write code in a way that assumes these callbacks will need to be called in a certain order because it could break at any time.

A better place to handle late-stage initialization is in a MonoBehaviour component's Start() callback, which is always called after every object's Awake() callback is called and just before its first Update() call. Late-stage updates can also be done in the LateUpdate() callback.

If you're having trouble determining the actual order of events, then this is best handled by either step-through debugging with an IDE (MonoDevelop, Visual Studio, and so on) or by printing simple logging statements with Debug.Log().

Be warned that Unity's logger is notoriously expensive. Logging is unlikely to change the order of the callbacks, but it can cause some unwanted spikes in performance if used too aggressively. Be smart and do targeted logging only on the most relevant parts of the code base.

Coroutines are typically used to script some sequence of events, and when they're triggered will depend on what `yield` types are being used. The most difficult and unpredictable type to debug is perhaps the `WaitForSeconds` yield type. The Unity Engine is non-deterministic, meaning that you'll get a slightly different behavior from one session to the next, even on the same hardware. For example, you might get 60 updates called during the first second of application runtime during one session, 59 in the next, and 62 in the one after that. In another session, you might get 61 updates in the first second, followed by 60, and then 59.

A variable number of `Update()` callbacks will be called between when the coroutine starts and when it ends, and so if the coroutine depends on the `Update()` function of something being called a specific number of times, we will run into problems. It's best to keep a coroutine's behavior dead simple and dependency-free of other behavior once it begins. Breaking this rule may be tempting, but it's essentially guaranteed that some future change is going to interact with the coroutine in an unexpected way, leading to a long, painful debugging session for a game-breaking bug that's very hard to reproduce.

Minimizing ongoing code changes

Making code changes to the application in order to hunt down performance issues is best done carefully, as the changes are easy to forget as time wears on. Adding debug logging statements to our code can be tempting, but remember that it costs us time to introduce these calls, recompile our code, and remove these calls once our analysis is complete. In addition, if we forget to remove them, then they can incur unnecessary runtime overhead in the final build since Unity's debug **Console** window logging can be prohibitively expensive in terms of both CPU and memory.

A good way to combat this problem is to add a flag or comment anywhere we made a change with our name so that it's easy to find and remove it later. Hopefully, we're also wise enough to use a source control tool for our code base, making it easy to differentiate between the content of any modified files and revert them to their original state. This is an excellent way to ensure that unnecessary changes don't make it into the final version. Of course, this is by no means a guaranteed solution if we also applied a fix at the same time and didn't double-check all of our modified files before committing the change.

Making use of breakpoints during runtime debugging is the preferred approach, as we can trace the full callstack, variable data, and conditional code paths (for example, `if-else` blocks), without risking any code changes or wasting time on recompilation. Of course, this is not always an option if, for example, we're trying to figure out what causes something strange to happen in one out of a thousand frames. In this case, it's better to determine a threshold value to look for and add an `if` statement, with a breakpoint inside, which will be triggered when the value has exceeded the threshold.

Minimizing internal distractions

The Unity Editor has its own little quirks and nuances, which can sometimes make it confusing to debug some kinds of problems.

Firstly, if a single frame takes a long time to process, such that our game noticeably freezes, then the Profiler may not be capable of picking up the results and recording them in the **Profiler** window. This can be especially annoying if we wish to catch data during application/scene initialization. The *Custom CPU profiling*, section later will offer some alternatives to explore with a view to solving this problem.

One common mistake (that I have admittedly fallen victim to multiple times during the writing of this book) is that if we are trying to initiate a test with a keystroke and have the **Profiler** window open, we should not forget to click back into the Editor's **Game** window before triggering the keystroke. If the Profiler is the most recently clicked window, then the Editor will send keystroke events to that, instead of the runtime application, and hence, no `GameObject` will catch the event for that keystroke. This can also apply to the GameView for rendering tasks and even coroutines using the `WaitForEndOfFrame` yield type. If the **Game** window is not visible and active in the Editor, then nothing is being rendered to that view, and therefore, no events that rely on **Game** window rendering will be triggered. Be warned!

Vertical sync (otherwise known as **VSync**) is used to match the application's frame rate to the frame rate of the device it is being displayed to; for example, a monitor may run at 60 Hertz (60 cycles per second, about 16 ms). If a rendering loop in our game is running faster than a monitor cycle – for instance, 10 ms – then the game will sit and wait for another 6 ms before outputting the rendered frame. This feature reduces screen tearing, which occurs when a new image is pushed to the monitor before the previous image was finished, and, for a brief moment, part of the new image overlaps the old image.

Executing the Profiler with **VSync** enabled will probably generate a lot of noisy spikes in the **CPU Usage** area under the **WaitForTargetFPS** heading, as the application intentionally slows itself down to match the frame rate of the display. These spikes often appear very large in Editor mode, since the Editor is typically rendering to a very small window, which doesn't take a lot of CPU or GPU work to render.

This will generate unnecessary clutter, making it harder to spot the real issue(s). We should ensure that we disable the **VSync** checkbox under the **CPU Usage** area when we're on the lookout for CPU spikes during performance tests. We can disable the **VSync** feature entirely by navigating to **Edit | Project Settings | Quality** and then to the sub-page for the currently selected platform.

We should also ensure that a drop in performance isn't a direct result of a massive number of exceptions and error messages appearing in the Editor **Console** window. Unity's `Debug.Log()` and similar methods, such as `Debug.LogError()` and `Debug.LogWarning()`, are notoriously expensive in terms of CPU Usage and heap memory consumption, which can then cause garbage collection to occur resulting in even more lost CPU cycles (refer to `Chapter 8`, *Masterful Memory Management*, for more information on these topics).

This overhead is usually unnoticeable to a human being looking at the project in Editor mode, where most errors come from the compiler or misconfigured objects. However, they can be problematic when used during any kind of runtime process, especially during profiling, where we wish to observe how the game runs in the absence of external disruptions. For example, if we are missing an object reference that we were supposed to assign through the Editor, and it is being used in an `Update()` callback, then a single `MonoBehaviour` instance could throw new exceptions every single update. This adds lots of unnecessary noise to our profiling data.

Note that we can hide different log level types with the buttons shown in the next screenshot. The extra logging still costs CPU and memory to execute, even though they are not being rendered, but it does allow us to filter out the junk we don't want. However, it is often good practice to keep all of these options enabled to verify that we're not missing anything important:

Minimizing external distractions

This one is simple, but absolutely necessary. We should double-check that there are no background processes eating away CPU cycles or consuming vast swathes of memory. Being low on available memory will generally interfere with our testing, as it can cause more cache misses, hard drive access for virtual memory page-file swapping, and generally slow responsiveness on the part of the application. If our application is suddenly behaving significantly worse than anticipated, double-check the system's task manager (or equivalent) for any CPU/memory/hard disk activity that might be causing problems.

Targeted profiling of code segments

If our performance problem isn't resolved by the checklist mentioned previously, then we probably have a real issue on our hands that demands further analysis. The **Profiler** window is effective at showing us a broad overview of performance; it can help us find specific frames to investigate and can quickly inform us which `MonoBehaviour` and/or method may be causing issues. We would then need to figure out whether the problem is reproducible, under what circumstances a performance bottleneck arises, and from where exactly within the problematic code block the issue is originating.

To accomplish these, we will need to perform some profiling of targeted sections of our code, and there are a handful of useful techniques we can employ for this task. For Unity projects, they essentially fit into two categories:

- Controlling the Profiler from script code
- Custom timing and logging methods

 Note that the next section focuses on how to investigate scripting bottlenecks through C# code. Detecting the source of bottlenecks in other engine subsystems will be discussed in their related chapters.

Profiler script control

The Profiler can be controlled in script code through the `Profiler` class. There are several useful methods in this class that we can explore within the Unity documentation, but the most important methods are the delimiter methods that activate and deactivate profiling at runtime. These can be accessed through the `UnityEngine.Profiling.Profiler` class through its `BeginSample()` and `EndSample()` methods.

Note that the delimiter methods, `BeginSample()` and `EndSample()`, are only compiled in development builds, and, as such, they will not be compiled or executed in release builds where **Development Mode** is unchecked. This is commonly known as **non-operation**, or **no-op**, code.

The `BeginSample()` method has an overload that allows a custom name for the sample to appear in the **CPU Usage** area's **Hierarchy** mode. For example, the following code will profile invocations of this method and make the data appear in **Breakdown View** under a custom heading, as follows:

```
void DoSomethingCompletelyStupid() {
  Profiler.BeginSample("My Profiler Sample");
  List<int> listOfInts = new List<int>();
  for(int i = 0; i < 1000000; ++i) {
    listOfInts.Add(i);
  }
  Profiler.EndSample();
}
```

You can download the example code files from your account at `http://www.packtpub.com` for all the *Packt Publishing* books you have purchased. If you purchased this book elsewhere, you can visit `http://www.packtpub.com/support` and register to have the files emailed directly to you.

We should expect that invoking this poorly designed method (which generates a `List` containing a million integers, and then does absolutely nothing with it) will cause a huge spike in **CPU Usage**, chew up several megabytes of memory, and appear in the **Profiler Breakdown View** under the **My Profiler Sample** heading, as shown in the following screenshot:

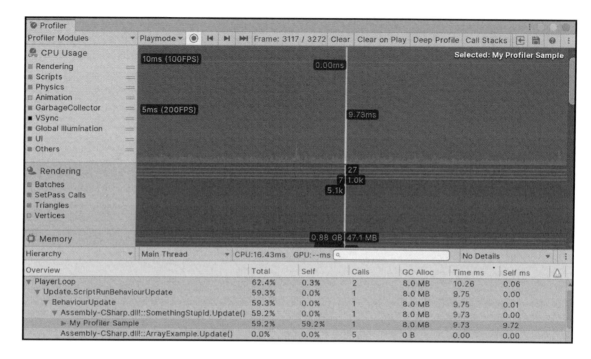

Custom CPU profiling

The Profiler is just one tool at our disposal. Sometimes, we may want to perform customized profiling and logging of our code. Maybe we're not confident that the Unity Profiler is giving us the right answer, maybe we consider its overhead cost too great, or maybe we just like having complete control of every single aspect of our application. Whatever our motivations, knowing some techniques to perform an independent analysis of our code is a useful skill to have. It's unlikely we'll only be working with Unity for the entirety of our game development careers, after all.

Profiling tools are generally very complex, so it's unlikely we would be able to generate a comparable solution on our own within a reasonable time frame. When it comes to testing CPU Usage, all we should really need is an accurate timing system, a fast, low-cost way of logging that information, and some piece of code to test against. It just so happens that the .NET library (or, technically, the Mono framework) comes with a `Stopwatch` class under the `System.Diagnostics` namespace. We can stop and start a `Stopwatch` object at any time, and we can easily acquire a measure of how much time has passed since the `Stopwatch` object was started.

Unfortunately, this class is not perfectly accurate; it is accurate only to milliseconds, or tenths of a millisecond, at best. Counting in a high-precision, real-time manner with a CPU clock can be a surprisingly difficult task when we start to get into it. So, in order to avoid a detailed discussion of the topic, we should try to find a way for the `Stopwatch` class to satisfy our needs.

If precision is important, then one effective way to increase it is by running the same test multiple times. Assuming that the test code block is both easily repeatable and not exceptionally long, we should be able to run thousands, or even millions, of tests within a reasonable time frame and then divide the total elapsed time by the number of tests we just performed to get a more accurate time for a single test.

Before we get obsessed with the topic of high precision, we should first ask ourselves if we even need it. Most games expect to run at 30 FPS or 60 FPS, which means that they only have around 33 ms or 16 ms, respectively, to compute everything for the entire frame. So, hypothetically, if we need to bring only the performance of a particular code block under 10 ms, then repeating the test thousands of times to get microsecond precision is too many orders of magnitude away from the target to be worthwhile.

The following is a class definition for a custom timer that uses a `Stopwatch` object to count time for a given number of tests:

```
using System;
using System.Diagnostics;

public class CustomTimer : IDisposable {
  private string _timerName;
  private int _numTests;
  private Stopwatch _watch;

  // give the timer a name, and a count of the
  // number of tests we're running
  public CustomTimer(string timerName, int numTests) {
    _timerName = timerName;
    _numTests = numTests;
```

```
    if (_numTests <= 0) {
      _numTests = 1;
    }
    _watch = Stopwatch.StartNew();
  }

    // automatically called when the 'using()' block ends
    public void Dispose() {
    _watch.Stop();
    float ms = _watch.ElapsedMilliseconds;
    UnityEngine.Debug.Log(string.Format("{0} finished: {1:0.00} " +
        "milliseconds total, {2:0.000000} milliseconds per-test " +
        "for {3} tests", _timerName, ms, ms / _numTests, _numTests));
    }
  }
```

Adding an underscore before member variable names is a common and useful way of distinguishing a class's member variables (also known as fields) from a method's arguments and local variables.

The following is an example of `CustomTimer` class usage:

```
const int numTests = 1000;
using (new CustomTimer("My Test", numTests)) {
  for(int i = 0; i < numTests; ++i) {
    TestFunction();
  }
} // the timer's Dispose() method is automatically called here
```

There are three things to note when using this approach:

- Firstly, we are only making an average of multiple method invocations. If processing time varies enormously between invocations, then that will not be well represented in the final average.
- Secondly, if memory access is common, then repeatedly requesting the same blocks of memory will result in an artificially higher cache hit rate (where the CPU can find data in memory very quickly because it's accessed the same region recently), which will bring the average time down when compared to a typical invocation.
- Thirdly, the effects of **Just-In-Time (JIT)** compilation will be effectively hidden for similarly artificial reasons, as it only affects the first invocation of the method. JIT compilation is a .NET feature that will be covered in more detail in Chapter 8, *Masterful Memory Management*.

The `using` block is typically used to safely ensure that unmanaged resources are properly destroyed when they go out of scope. When the `using` block ends, it will automatically invoke the object's `Dispose()` method to handle any cleanup operations. In order to achieve this, the object must implement the `IDisposable` interface, which forces it to define the `Dispose()` method.

However, the same language feature can be used to create a distinct code block, which creates a short-term object, which then automatically processes something useful when the code block ends; this is how it is being used in the preceding code block.

Note that the `using` block should not be confused with the `using` statement, which is used at the start of a script file to pull in additional namespaces. It's extremely ironic that the keyword for managing namespaces in C# has a naming conflict with another keyword.

As a result, the `using` block and the `CustomTimer` class give us a clean way of wrapping our test code that makes it obvious when and where it is being used.

Something else to worry about is application warm-up time. Unity has a significant start-up cost when a scene begins, given the amount of data that needs to be loaded from disk, the initialization of complex subsystems, such as the physics and rendering systems, and the number of calls to various `Awake()` and `Start()` callbacks that need to be resolved before anything else can happen. This early overhead might only last a second, but that can have a significant effect on the results of our testing if the code is also executed during this early initialization period. This makes it crucial that, if we want an accurate test, then any runtime testing should begin only after the application has reached a steady state.

Ideally, we would be able to execute the target code block in its own scene after its initialization has completed. This is not always possible; so, as a backup plan, we could wrap the target code block in an `Input.GetKeyDown()` check in order to assume control over it when it is invoked. For example, the following code will execute our test method only when the spacebar is pressed:

```
if (Input.GetKeyDown(KeyCode.Space)) {
    const int numTests = 1000;
    using (new CustomTimer("Controlled Test", numTests)) {
        for(int i = 0; i < numTests; ++i) {
            TestFunction();
        }
    }
}
```

As mentioned previously, Unity's **Console** window logging mechanism is prohibitively expensive. As a result, we should try not to use these logging methods in the middle of a profiling test (or during gameplay, for that matter). If we find ourselves absolutely in need of detailed profiling data that prints out lots of individual messages (such as performing a timing test on a loop to figure out which iteration is costing more time than the rest), then it would be wiser to cache the logging data and print it all out at the end, as the CustomTimer class does. This will reduce runtime overhead, at the cost of some memory consumption. The alternative is that many milliseconds are lost to printing each Debug.Log() message in the middle of the test, which pollutes the results.

The CustomTimer class also makes use of string.Format(). This will be covered in more detail in Chapter 8, *Masterful Memory Management*, but a short explanation is that this method is used because generating a custom string object using the + operator (for example, code such as Debug.Log("Test: " + output);) can result in a surprisingly large number of memory allocations, which attracts the attention of the garbage collector. Doing otherwise would conflict with our goal of achieving accurate timing and analysis and should be avoided.

Final thoughts on profiling and analysis

One way of thinking about performance optimization is *the act of stripping away unnecessary tasks that waste valuable resources*. We can do the same and maximize our own productivity by minimizing any wasted effort. Effective use of the tools we have at our disposal is of paramount importance. It would serve us well to optimize our own workflow by remaining aware of some best practices and techniques.

Most, if not all, advice for using any kind of data-gathering tool properly can be summarized into three different strategies:

- Understanding the tool
- Reducing noise
- Focusing on the issue

Understanding the Profiler

The Profiler is a well-designed and intuitive tool, so understanding the majority of its feature set can be gained by simply spending an hour or two exploring its options with a test project and reading its documentation. The more we know about a tool in terms of its benefits, pitfalls, features, and limitations, the more sense we can make of the information it is giving us, so it is worth spending the time to use it in a playground setting. We don't want to be two weeks away from release, with a hundred performance defects to fix, with no idea how to do performance analysis efficiently.

For example, always remain aware of the relative nature of **Timeline View** graphical display. **Timeline View** does not provide values on its vertical axis and automatically readjusts this axis based on the content of the last 300 frames; it can make small spikes appear to be a bigger problem than they really are because of the relative change. So, just because a spike or resting state in the timeline seems large and threatening does not necessarily mean there is a performance issue.

Several areas in **Timeline View** provide helpful benchmark bars, which appear as horizontal lines with a timing and FPS value associated with them. These should be used to determine the magnitude of the problem. Don't let the Profiler trick us into thinking that big spikes are always bad. As always, it's only important if the user will notice it.

As an example, if a large CPU Usage spike does not exceed the 60 FPS or 30 FPS benchmark bars (depending on the application's target frame rate), then it would be wise to ignore it and search elsewhere for CPU performance issues, since no matter how much we improve the offending piece of code, it will probably never be noticed by the end user, and therefore isn't a critical issue that affects user experience.

Reducing noise

The classical definition of noise (at least in the realm of computer science) is meaningless data, and a batch of profiling data that was blindly captured with no specific target in mind is always full of data that won't interest us. More sources of data take more time to mentally process and filter, which can be very distracting. One of the best methods to avoid this is to simply reduce the amount of data we need to process by stripping away any data deemed non-vital to the current situation.

Reducing the clutter in the Profiler's graphical interface will make it easier to determine which subsystems are causing a spike in resource usage. Remember to use the colored checkboxes in each **Timeline View** area to narrow the search.

Be warned that these settings are autosaved in the Editor, so ensure that you re-enable them for the next profiling session, as this might cause us to miss something important next time.

Also, GameObjects can be deactivated to prevent them from generating profiling data, which will also help to reduce clutter in our profiling data. This will naturally cause a slight performance boost for each object we deactivate. However, if we're gradually deactivating objects and performance suddenly becomes significantly more acceptable when a specific object is deactivated, then clearly that object is related to the root cause of the problem.

Focusing on the issue

This category may seem redundant, given that we've already covered reducing noise. All we should have left is the issue at hand, right? Not exactly. Focus is the skill of not letting ourselves become distracted by inconsequential tasks and wild-goose chases.

You will recall that profiling with the Unity Profiler comes with a minor performance cost. This cost is even more severe when using the **Deep Profile** option. We might even introduce more minor performance costs into our application with additional logging. It's easy to forget when and where we introduced profiling code if the hunt continues for several hours.

We are effectively changing the result by measuring it. Any changes we implement during data sampling can sometimes lead us to chase after non-existent bugs in the application when we could have saved ourselves a lot of time by attempting to replicate the scenario without additional profiling instrumentation. If the bottleneck is reproducible and noticeable without profiling, then it's a candidate for beginning an investigation. However, if new bottlenecks keep appearing in the middle of an existing investigation, then keep in mind that they could be bottlenecks we introduced with our test code and not an existing problem that's been newly exposed.

Finally, when we have finished profiling, completed our fixes, and are now ready to move on to the next investigation, we should make sure to profile the application one last time to verify that the changes have had the intended effect.

Summary

You learned a great deal throughout this chapter on how to detect and analyze performance issues within your applications. You learned about many of the Profiler's features and secrets, explored a variety of tactics to investigate performance issues with a more hands-on approach, and have been introduced to a variety of different tips and strategies to follow. You can use these to improve your productivity immensely, so long as you appreciate the wisdom behind them and remember to exploit them when the situation makes it possible.

This chapter has introduced us to the tips, tactics, and strategies we need in order to identify a performance issue that requires improvement. In the remaining chapters, we will explore methods on how to fix issues and improve performance whenever possible. So, give yourself a pat on the back for getting through the boring part first. We will now move on to best practices for C# development and how to avoid common performance pitfalls in your Unity scripts.

Scripting Strategies

2

Since scripting will consume a great deal of our development time, it will be enormously beneficial to learn some best practices. Scripting is a very broad term, so we will try to limit our exposure in this chapter to situations that are very Unity-specific, focusing on problems surrounding MonoBehaviours, GameObjects, and related functionality.

 We will discuss the nuances and advanced topics of the C# language, .NET library, and Mono framework in Chapter 8, *Masterful Memory Management*.

In this chapter, we will explore ways of applying performance enhancements for the following:

- Obtaining components in other game objects
- Optimizing component callbacks (Update(), Awake(), and so on)
- Using coroutines
- Using GameObject and Transform efficiently
- Exchanging messages between different objects
- Optimizing mathematical calculations
- Serializing/deserializing during scene and Prefab loading

Whether you have some specific problems in mind that you wish to solve or you just want to learn some techniques for future reference, this chapter will introduce you to a wide array of methods that you can use to improve your scripting efforts now and in the future. In each case, we will explore how and why the performance issue arises, an example situation in which the problem occurs, and one or more solutions to combat the issue.

Obtaining components using the fastest method

There are several variations of the GetComponent() method, and they each have a different performance cost, so it is prudent to call the fastest possible version of this method. The three overloads available are GetComponent(string), GetComponent<T>(), and GetComponent(typeof(T)). It turns out that the fastest version depends on which version of Unity we are running since several optimizations have been made to these methods through the years; however, if you are using any version of Unity (from Unity 2017 onward), it is best to use the GetComponent<T>() variant.

Let's prove this with some simple testing:

```
int numTests = 1000000;
TestComponent test;
using (new CustomTimer("GetComponent(string)", numTests)) {
  for (var i = 0; i < numTests; ++i) {
    test = (TestComponent)GetComponent("TestComponent");
  }
}

using (new CustomTimer("GetComponent<ComponentName>", numTests)) {
  for (var i = 0; i < numTests; ++i) {
    test = GetComponent<TestComponent>();
  }
}

using (new CustomTimer("GetComponent(typeof(ComponentName))", numTests)) {
  for (var i = 0; i < numTests; ++i) {
    test = (TestComponent)GetComponent(typeof(TestComponent));
  }
}
```

The preceding code tests each of the GetComponent() overloads a million times. This is far more tests than would be sensible for a typical project, but it helps to make the relative costs clear.

Here is the result we get when the tests complete (of course, the specific numeric values may be different on your machine):

```
(!) GetComponent(string) finished: 6413.00ms total, 0.006413ms per test for 1000000 tests
    UnityEngine.Debug:Log(Object)
(!) GetComponent<ComponentName> finished: 89.00ms total, 0.000089ms per test for 1000000 tests
    UnityEngine.Debug:Log(Object)
(!) GetComponent(typeof(ComponentName)) finished: 95.00ms total, 0.000095ms per test for 1000000 tests
    UnityEngine.Debug:Log(Object)
```

As you can see, the `GetComponent<T>()` method is only a tiny fraction faster than `GetComponent(typeof(T))`, whereas `GetComponent(string)` is significantly slower than the alternatives. Therefore, it is pretty safe to use either of the type-based versions of `GetComponent()` because of the small performance difference. However, we should ensure that we never use `GetComponent(string)` since the outcome is identical, and there are no benefits for the costs incurred. There are some very rare exceptions. Imagine that we were writing a custom debug console for Unity that can parse a user-input `string` to acquire a component. In this case, we would acquire a component by using the expensive `GetComponent(string)` only during debugging and diagnostics situations. In these cases, performance isn't too important. On the contrary, for a production-level application, the use of `GetComponent(string)` is just a needless waste of CPU cycles.

Removing empty callback definitions

The primary means of scripting in Unity is to write callback functions in classes derived from `MonoBehaviour`, which we know Unity will call when necessary. Perhaps the four most commonly used callbacks are `Awake()`, `Start()`, `Update()`, and `FixedUpdate()`.

`Awake()` is called the moment `MonoBehaviour` is first created, whether this occurs during scene initialization or when a new `GameObject` instance containing the `MonoBehaviour` component is instantiated at runtime from a Prefab. `Start()` will be called shortly after `Awake()` but before its first `Update()`. During scene initialization, every `MonoBehaviour` component's `Awake()` callback will be called before any of their `Start()` callbacks are.

After this, `Update()` will be called repeatedly, each time the rendering pipeline presents a new image. `Update()` will continue to be called provided `MonoBehaviour` is still present in the scene, it is still enabled, and its parent `GameObject` is active.

Finally, `FixedUpdate()` is called just before the physics engine updates. Fixed updates are used whenever we want activity similar in behavior to `Update()` but that isn't tied directly to the render frame rate and is called more consistently over time.

 Refer to the following page in the Unity documentation for an accurate picture of when various Unity callbacks are called: `https://docs.unity3d.com/Manual/ExecutionOrder.html`.

Whenever a `MonoBehaviour` component is first instantiated in our scene, Unity will add any defined callbacks to a list of function pointers, which it will call at key moments. However, it is important to realize that Unity will hook into these callbacks even if the function body is empty. The core Unity Engine has no awareness that these function bodies may be empty and only knows that the method has been defined and, therefore, that it must acquire it and then call it when necessary. Consequently, if we leave empty definitions of these callbacks scattered throughout the code base, then they will waste a small amount of CPU due to the overhead cost of the engine invoking them.

This can be a problem since, anytime we create a new `MonoBehaviour` script file in Unity, it will automatically generate two boilerplate callback stubs for us for `Start()` and `Update()`:

```
// Use this for initialization
void Start () {

}

// Update is called once per-frame
void Update () {

}
```

It can be easy to accidentally leave these empty definitions on scripts that don't actually need them. An empty `Start()` definition is liable to cause any object to initialize a little more slowly, for no good reason. This effect may not be particularly noticeable for a handful of MonoBehaviours, but as development on the project continues and we populate our scenes with thousands of custom MonoBehaviours with lots of empty `Start()` definitions, it could start to become a problem, causing slow scene initialization and wasting CPU time whenever a new Prefab is created via `GameObject.Instantiate()`.

Such calls typically happen during key gameplay events; for instance, when two objects collide, we might spawn a particle effect, create some floating damage text, play a sound effect, and so on. This can be a critical moment for performance because we've suddenly requested that the CPU makes a lot of complicated changes, but with only a finite amount of time to complete them before the current frame ends. If this process takes too long, then we would experience a frame drop as the Rendering Pipeline isn't allowed to present a new frame until all of the Update() callbacks—counted across all MonoBehaviours in the scene—have finished. Ergo, a bunch of empty Start() definitions being called at this time is a needless waste and could potentially cut into our tight time-budget at a critical moment.

Meanwhile, if our scene contains thousands of MonoBehaviours with these empty Update() definitions, then we would be wasting a lot of CPU cycles every frame, potentially causing havoc on our frame rate.

Let's prove all of this with a simple test. Our test scene should have GameObjects with two types of component, EmptyClassComponent, with no methods defined at all, and EmptyCallbackComponent, with an empty Update() callback defined:

```
public class EmptyClassComponent : MonoBehaviour {
}

public class EmptyCallbackComponent : MonoBehaviour {
  void Update () {}
}
```

The following are the test results for 30,000 components of each type. If we enable all GameObjects with attached EmptyClassComponents during runtime, then nothing interesting happens under the **CPU Usage** area of the **Profiler**. There will be a small amount of background activity, but none of this activity will be caused by EmptyClassComponents. However, as soon as we enable all objects with EmptyCallbackComponent, we will observe a huge increase in CPU usage:

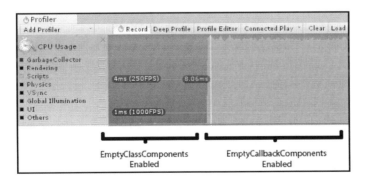

It's hard to imagine a scene with more than 30,000 objects in it, but keep in mind that MonoBehaviours contain the `Update()` callback, not GameObjects. A single `GameObject` instance can contain multiple MonoBehaviours at once, and each of their children can contain even more MonoBehaviours, and so on. A few thousand or even a hundred empty `Update()` callbacks will inflict a noticeable impact on frame rate budget, for zero potential gain. This is particularly common with Unity UI components, which tend to attach a lot of different components in a very deep hierarchy.

The fix for this is simple: delete the empty callback definitions. Unity will have nothing to hook into, and nothing will be called. Finding such empty definitions in an expansive code base may be difficult, but if we use some basic regular expressions (known as *regex*), we should be able to find what we're looking for relatively easily.

All common code-editing tools for Unity, such as MonoDevelop, Visual Studio, and even Notepad++, provide a way to perform a regex-based search on the entire code base. Check out the tool's documentation for more information, since the method can vary greatly depending on the tool and its version.

The following regex search should find any empty `Update()` definitions in our code:

```
void\s*Update\s*?\(\s*?\)\s*?\n*?\{\n*?\s*?\}
```

This regex checks for a standard method definition of the `Update()` callback, while including any surplus whitespace and newline characters that can be distributed throughout the method definition.

Naturally, all of the preceding is also true for the non-boilerplate Unity callbacks, such as `OnGUI()`, `OnEnable()`, `OnDestroy()`, and `LateUpdate()`. The only difference is that only `Start()` and `Update()` are defined automatically in a new script.

Check out the `MonoBehaviour` Unity Documentation page for a complete list of these callbacks at `http://docs.unity3d.com/ScriptReference/MonoBehaviour.html`.

It might also seem unlikely that someone generated so many empty versions of these callbacks in our code base, but never say never. For example, if we use a common base class, `MonoBehaviour`, throughout all of our custom components, then a single empty callback definition in that base class will permeate the entire game, which can cost us dearly. Be particularly careful of the `OnGUI()` method, as it can be invoked multiple times within the same frame or UI event.

Perhaps the most common source of performance problems in Unity scripting is to misuse the Update() callback by doing one or more of the following things:

- Repeatedly recalculating a value that rarely or never changes
- Having too many components perform work for a result that could be shared
- Performing work far more often than is necessary

It's worth getting into the habit of remembering that literally every single line of code we write in an Update() callback, and functions called by those callbacks, will eat into our frame rate budget. To hit 60 fps, we have 16.667 milliseconds to complete all of the work in all of our Update() callbacks, every frame. This seems like plenty of time when we start prototyping, but somewhere in the middle of development, we will probably start noticing things getting slower and less responsive because we've gradually been eating away at that budget, due to an unchecked desire to cram more stuff into our project.

Let's cover some tips that directly address these problems.

Caching component references

Repeatedly recalculating a value is a common mistake when scripting in Unity, and particularly when it comes to the GetComponent() method. For example, the following script code is trying to check a creature's health value, and if its health goes below 0, it will disable a series of components to prepare it for a death animation:

```
void TakeDamage() {

    Rigidbody rigidbody = GetComponent<Rigidbody>();
    Collider collider = GetComponent<Collider>();
    AIControllerComponent ai = GetComponent<AIControllerComponent>();
    Animator anim = GetComponent<Animator>();

    if (GetComponent<HealthComponent>().health < 0) {
        rigidbody.enabled = false;
        collider.enabled = false;
        ai.enabled = false;
        anim.SetTrigger("death");
    }
}
```

Each time this poorly optimized method executes, it will reacquire five different component references. This is not very friendly on CPU usage. This is particularly problematic if the main method was called during Update(). Even if it is not, it still might coincide with other important events, such as creating particle effects, replacing an object with a Ragdoll (hence invoking various activity in the Physics Engine), and so on. This coding style can seem harmless, but it can cause a lot of long-term problems and runtime work for very little benefit.

It costs us a small amount of memory space (only 32 or 64 bits each time—Unity version, platform, and fragmentation permitting) to cache these references for future use. So, unless you're extremely bottlenecked on memory, a better approach would be to acquire the references during initialization and keep them until they are needed:

```
private HealthComponent _healthComponent;
private Rigidbody _rigidbody;
private Collider _collider;
private AIControllerComponent _ai;
private Animator _anim;

void Awake() {
  _healthComponent = GetComponent<HealthComponent>();
  _rigidbody = GetComponent<Rigidbody>();
  _collider = GetComponent<Collider>();
  _ai = GetComponent<AIControllerComponent>();
  _anim = GetComponent<Animator>();
}

void TakeDamage() {
  if (_healthComponent.health < 0) {
    _rigidbody.detectCollisions = false;
    _collider.enabled = false;
    _ai.enabled = false;
    _anim.SetTrigger("death");
  }
}
```

Caching component references in this way spares us from reacquiring them each time they're needed, saving us some CPU overhead each time. The cost is a small amount of additional memory consumption, which is very often worth the price.

The same tip applies to literally any piece of data we decide to calculate at runtime. There's no need to ask the CPU to keep recalculating the same value every `Update()` callback when we can just store it in memory for future reference.

Sharing calculation output

Performance can be saved by having multiple objects share the result of some calculation; of course, this only works if all of them generate the same result. Such situations are often easy to spot but can be tricky to refactor, and so exploiting this would be very implementation-dependent.

Some examples might include finding an object in a scene, reading data from a file, parsing data (such as XML or JSON), finding something in a big list or deep dictionary of information, calculating pathing for a group of **Artificial Intelligence (AI)** objects, complex mathematics-like trajectories, raycasting, and so on.

Think about each time an expensive operation is undertaken, and consider whether it is being called from multiple locations but always results in the same output. If this is the case, then it would be wise to restructure things so that the result is calculated once and then distributed to every object that needs it to minimize the amount of recalculation. The biggest cost is typically just a small loss in code simplicity, although we may inflict some extra overhead by moving the value around.

Note that it's often easy to get into the habit of hiding some big complex function in a base class, and then we define derived classes that make use of that function, completely forgetting how costly that function is because we rarely glance at that code again. It's best to use the Unity Profiler to tell us how many times that expensive function may be called, and as always, don't preoptimize those functions unless it's been proven to be a performance issue. No matter how expensive it may be, if it doesn't cause us to exceed performance restrictions (such as frame rate and memory consumption), then it's not really a performance problem.

Update, coroutines, and InvokeRepeating

Another habit that's easy to fall into is to call something repeatedly in an `Update()` callback way more often than is needed. For example, we may start with a situation like this:

```
void Update() {
  ProcessAI();
}
```

In this case, we're calling some custom `ProcessAI()` subroutine every single frame. This may be a complex task, requiring the AI system to check some grid system to figure out where it's meant to move or determine some fleet maneuvers for a group of spaceships or whatever our game needs for its AI.

If this activity is eating into our frame rate budget too much, and the task can be completed less frequently than every frame with no significant drawbacks, then a good trick to improve performance is to simply reduce the frequency at which that `ProcessAI()` gets called:

```
private float _aiProcessDelay = 0.2f;
private float _timer = 0.0f;

void Update() {
  _timer += Time.deltaTime;
  if (_timer > _aiProcessDelay) {
    ProcessAI();
    _timer -= _aiProcessDelay;
  }
}
```

In this case, we've reduced the `Update()` callback's overall cost by only invoking `ProcessAI()` about five times every second, which is an improvement over the previous situation, at the expense of code that can take a bit of time to understand at first glance, and a little extra memory to store some floating-point data—although, at the end of the day, we're still having Unity call an empty callback function more often than not.

This function is a perfect example of a function, which can be converted into a coroutine to make use of their delayed invocation properties. As mentioned previously, coroutines are typically used to script a short sequence of events, either as a one-time or repeated action. They should not be confused with threads, which would run on a completely different CPU core concurrently, and multiple threads can be running simultaneously. Instead, coroutines run on the main thread in a sequential manner such that only one coroutine is handled at any given moment, and each coroutine decides when to pause and resume via `yield` statements. The following code is an example of how we might rewrite the preceding `Update()` callback in the form of a coroutine:

```
void Start() {
  StartCoroutine(ProcessAICoroutine ());
}

IEnumerator ProcessAICoroutine () {
  while (true) {
    ProcessAI();
    yield return new WaitForSeconds(_aiProcessDelay);
  }
}
```

The preceding code demonstrates a coroutine that calls `ProcessAI()`, then pauses at the `yield` statement for the given number of seconds (the value of `_aiProcessDelay`) before the main thread resumes the coroutine again, at which point, it will return to the start of the loop, call `ProcessAI()`, pause on the `yield` statement again, and repeat forever (via the `while(true)` statement) until asked to stop.

The main benefit of this approach is that this function will only be called as often as dictated by the value of `_aiProcessDelay`, and it will sit idle until that time, reducing the performance hit inflicted in most of our frames. However, this approach has its drawbacks.

For one, starting a coroutine comes with an additional overhead cost relative to a standard function call (around three times as slow), as well as some memory allocations to store the current state in memory until it is invoked the next time. This additional overhead is also not a one-time cost because coroutines often constantly call `yield`, which inflicts the same overhead cost again and again, so we need to ensure that the benefits of reduced frequency outweigh this cost.

In a test of 1,000 objects with empty `Update()` callbacks, it took 1.1 milliseconds to process, whereas 1,000 coroutines yielding on `WaitForEndOfFrame` (which has an identical frequency to `Update()` callbacks) took 2.9 milliseconds. So, the relative cost is almost three times as much.

Secondly, once initialized, coroutines run independently of the triggering MonoBehaviour component's Update() callback and will continue to be invoked regardless of whether the component is disabled or not, which can make them unwieldy if we're performing a lot of GameObject construction and destruction.

Thirdly, the coroutine will automatically stop the moment the GameObject instance that contains it is made inactive for whatever reason (whether it was set inactive or one of its parents was) and will not automatically restart if GameObject is set to active again.

Finally, by converting a method into a coroutine, we may have reduced the performance hit inflicted during most of our frames, but if a single invocation of the method body causes us to break our frame rate budget, then it will still be exceeded no matter how rarely we call the method. Therefore, this approach is best used for situations where we are only breaking our frame rate budget because of the sheer number of times the method is called in a given frame, not because the method is too expensive on its own. In those cases, we have no option but to either dig into and improve the performance of the method itself or reduce the cost of other tasks to free up the time it needs to complete its work.

There are several yield types available to us when generating coroutines. WaitForSeconds is fairly self-explanatory; the coroutine will pause at the yield statement for a given number of seconds. It is not really an exact timer, however, so expect a small amount of variation when this yield type actually resumes.

WaitForSecondsRealTime is another option and is different from WaitForSeconds only in that it uses unscaled time. WaitForSeconds compares against scaled time, which is affected by the global Time.timeScale property while WaitForSecondsRealTime is not, so be careful about which yield type you use if you're tweaking the time scale value (for example, for slow-motion effects).

There is also WaitForEndOfFrame, which would continue at the end of the next Update() callback, and then there's WaitForFixedUpdate, which would continue at the end of the next FixedUpdate() invocation. Lastly, Unity 5.3 introduced WaitUntil and WaitWhile, where we provide a delegate function, and the coroutine will pause until the given delegate returns true or false, respectively. Note that the delegates provided to these yield types will be executed for each Update() until they return the Boolean value needed to stop them, which makes them very similar to a coroutine using WaitForEndOfFrame in a while loop that ends on a certain condition. Of course, it is also important that the delegate function we provide is not too expensive to execute.

Delegate functions are incredibly useful constructs in C# that allow us to pass local methods around as arguments to other methods and are typically used for callbacks. Check out the MSDN *C# Programming Guide* for more information on delegates at `https://docs.microsoft.com/en-us/dotnet/csharp/programming-guide/delegates/`.

The way that some `Update()` callbacks are written could probably be condensed down into simple coroutines that always call `yield` on one of these types, but we should be aware of the drawbacks mentioned previously. Coroutines can be tricky to debug since they don't follow normal execution flow; there's no caller in the callstack we can directly blame for why a coroutine triggered at a given time, and if coroutines perform complex tasks and interact with other subsystems, then they can result in some impossibly difficult bugs because they happened to be triggered at a moment that some other code didn't expect, which also tend to be the kinds of bugs that are painstakingly difficult to reproduce. If you do wish to make use of coroutines, the best advice is to keep them simple and independent of other complex subsystems.

Indeed, if our coroutine is simple enough that it can be boiled down to a `while` loop that always calls `yield` on `WaitForSeconds` or `WaitForSecondsRealtime`, as in the preceding example, then we can usually replace it with an `InvokeRepeating()` call, which is even simpler to set up and has a slightly lower overhead cost. The following code is functionally equivalent to the previous implementation that used a coroutine to regularly invoke a `ProcessAI()` method:

```
void Start() {
    InvokeRepeating("ProcessAI", 0f, _aiProcessDelay);
}
```

An important difference between `InvokeRepeating()` and coroutines is that `InvokeRepeating()` is completely independent of the states of both `MonoBehaviour` and `GameObject`. The only two ways to stop an `InvokeRepeating()` call is to either call `CancelInvoke()`, which stops all `InvokeRepeating()` callbacks initiated by the given `MonoBehaviour` (note that they cannot be canceled individually) or to destroy the associated `MonoBehaviour` or its parent `GameObject`. Disabling either `MonoBehaviour` or `GameObject` does not stop `InvokeRepeating()`.

A test of 1,000 `InvokeRepeating()` calls was processed in about 2.6 milliseconds; this is slightly faster than 1,000 equivalent coroutine `yield` calls, which took 2.9 milliseconds.

That covers most of the useful information related to the Update() callback. Let's look into some other useful scripting tips.

Faster GameObject null reference checks

It turns out that performing a null reference check against a GameObject will result in some unnecessary performance overhead. GameObjects and MonoBehaviours are special objects compared to a typical C# object, in that they have two representations in memory: one exists within the memory managed by the same system managing the C# code we write (managed code), whereas the other exists in a different memory space, which is handled separately (native code). Data can move between these two memory spaces, but each time this happens will result in some additional CPU overhead and possibly an extra memory allocation.

This effect is commonly referred to as crossing the Native-Managed Bridge. If this happens, it is likely to generate an additional memory allocation for an object's data to get copied across the bridge, which will require the garbage collector to eventually perform some automatic cleanup of memory for us. This subject will be explored in much more detail in Chapter 8, *Masterful Memory Management*, but for the time being, just consider that there are many subtle ways to accidentally trigger this extra overhead, and a simple null reference check against GameObject is one of them:

```
if (gameObject != null) {
  // do stuff with gameObject
}
```

An alternative that generates a functionally equivalent output that operates around twice as quickly (although it does obfuscate the purpose of the code a little) is System.Object.ReferenceEquals():

```
if (!System.Object.ReferenceEquals(gameObject, null)) {
  // do stuff with gameObject
}
```

This applies to both GameObjects and MonoBehaviours, as well as other Unity objects, which have both native and managed representations such as the WWW class. However, some rudimentary testing reveals that either null reference check approach still consumes mere nanoseconds on an Intel Core i5 3570K processor. So, unless you are performing massive amounts of null reference checks, the gains might be marginal at best. However, this is a warning worth keeping in mind for the future, as it will come up a lot.

Avoid retrieving string properties from GameObjects

Ordinarily, retrieving a `string` property from an object is the same as retrieving any other reference type property in C#; it should be acquired with no additional memory cost. However, retrieving `string` properties from GameObjects is another subtle way of accidentally crossing over the Native-Managed Bridge.

The two properties of `GameObject` affected by this behavior are `tag` and `name`. Therefore, it is unwise to use either property during gameplay, and you should only use them in performance-inconsequential areas, such as editor scripts. However, the tag system is commonly used for the runtime identification of objects, which can make this a significant problem for some teams.

For example, the following code would cause an additional memory allocation during every iteration of the loop:

```
for (int i = 0; i < listOfObjects.Count; ++i) {
    if (listOfObjects[i].tag == "Player") {
      // do something with this object
    }
}
```

It is often a better practice to identify objects by their components and class types and to identify values that do not involve `string` objects, but sometimes we're forced into a corner. Maybe we didn't know any better when we started, we inherited someone else's code base, or we're using it as a workaround for something. Let's assume that, for whatever reason, we're stuck with the tag system, and we want to avoid the Native-Managed Bridge overhead cost.

Fortunately, the `tag` property is most often used in comparison situations, and `GameObject` provides the `CompareTag()` method, which is an alternative way to compare `tag` properties that avoids the Native-Managed Bridge entirely.

Let's perform a simple test to prove how this simple change can make all the difference:

```
void Update() {

  int numTests = 10000000;

  if (Input.GetKeyDown(KeyCode.Alpha1)) {
    for(int i = 0; i < numTests; ++i) {
      if (gameObject.tag == "Player") {
        // do stuff
```

```
        }
      }
    }

    if (Input.GetKeyDown(KeyCode.Alpha2)) {
      for(int i = 0; i < numTests; ++i) {
        if (gameObject.CompareTag ("Player")) {
          // do stuff
        }
      }
    }
  }
}
```

We can execute these tests by pressing the *1* and *2* keys to trigger the respective for loops. Here are the results:

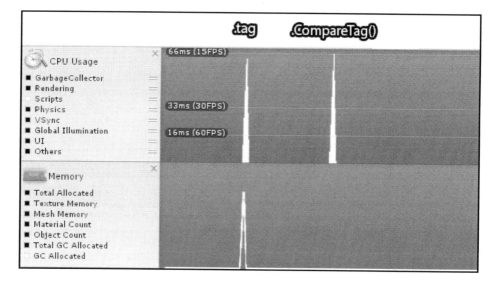

Looking at the breakdown view for each spike, we can see two completely different outcomes:

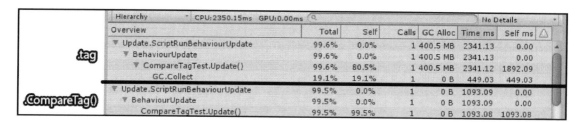

It's worth noting how the two spikes in the Timeline View appear relatively the same height, and yet one operation took twice as long as the other. The Profiler doesn't have the vertical resolution necessary to generate relatively accurate peaks when we go beyond the 15FPS marker. Both would result in a poor gameplay experience anyway, so the accuracy doesn't really matter.

Retrieving the `tag` property 10 million times (way more than makes sense in reality, but this is useful for comparison) results in about 400 megabytes of memory being allocated just for `string` objects alone. We can see this memory allocation happening in the spike within the **GC Allocated** element in the Memory Area of the Timeline View. Also, this process takes around 2,000 milliseconds to process, where another 400 milliseconds are spent on garbage collection once the `string` objects are no longer needed.

Meanwhile, using `CompareTag()` 10 million times costs around 1,000 milliseconds to process and causes no memory allocations, and hence no garbage collection. This is made apparent from the lack of a spike in the **GC Allocated** element in the Memory Area. This should make it abundantly clear that we must avoid accessing the `name` and `tag` properties whenever possible. If `tag` comparison becomes necessary, then we should make use of `CompareTag()`. Unfortunately, there is no equivalent for the `name` property, so we should stick to using tags where possible.

Note that passing in a `string` literal, such as `"Player"`, into `CompareTag()` does not result in a runtime memory allocation since the application allocates hardcoded strings like this during initialization and merely references them at runtime.

Using appropriate data structures

C# offers many different data structures in the `System.Collections` namespace and we shouldn't become too accustomed to using the same ones over and over again. A common performance problem in software development is making use of an inappropriate data structure for the problem we're trying to solve simply because it's convenient. The two most commonly used are perhaps lists (`List<T>`) and dictionaries (`Dictionary<K,V>`).

If we want to iterate through a set of objects, then a list is preferred, since it is effectively a dynamic array where the objects and/or references reside next to one another in memory, and therefore iteration causes minimal cache misses. Dictionaries are best used if two objects are associated with one another and we wish to acquire, insert, or remove these associations quickly. For example, we might associate a level number with a particular scene file, or an `enum` representing different body parts on a character, with `Collider` components for those body parts.

However, it's fairly common that we want a data structure that handles both scenarios; we want to quickly figure out which object maps to another, while also being able to iterate through the group. Typically, the developer of this system will use a dictionary and then iterate over it. However, this process is unfortunately very slow, compared to iterating over a list, since it must check every potential hash in the dictionary to iterate over it fully.

In these cases, it is often better to store data in both a list and a dictionary to better support this behavior. This will cost additional memory overhead to maintain multiple data structures, and insertion and deletion will require adding and removing objects from both data structures each time, but the benefits of iteration on the list (which tends to happen way more often) will be a stark contrast compared to iterating over a dictionary.

Avoiding re-parenting transforms at runtime

In earlier versions of Unity (version 5.3 and older), the references to `Transform` components would be laid out in memory in a generally random order. This meant that iteration over multiple `Transform` components was fairly slow due to the likelihood of cache misses. The upside was that re-parenting `GameObject` to another one wouldn't really cause a significant performance hit since the `Transforms` operated a lot like a heap data structure, which tend to be relatively fast at insertion and deletion. This behavior wasn't something we could control, and so we simply lived with it.

However, since Unity 5.4 and beyond, the `Transform` component's memory layout has changed significantly. Since then, a `Transform` component's parent-child relationships have operated more like dynamic arrays, whereby Unity attempts to store all `Transforms` that share the same parent sequentially in memory inside a pre-allocated memory buffer and are sorted by their depth in the **Hierarchy** window beneath the parent. This data structure allows for much, much faster iteration across the entire group, which is particularly beneficial to multiple subsystems such as physics and animation.

The downside of this change is that if we re-parent GameObject to another one, the parent must fit the new child within its pre-allocated memory buffer as well as sorting all of these Transforms based on the new depth. Also, if the parent has not pre-allocated enough space to fit the new child, then it must expand its buffer to be able to fit the new child, and all of its children, in depth-first order. This could take some time to complete for deep and complex GameObject structures.

When we instantiate a new GameObject through GameObject.Instantiate(), one of its arguments is the Transform component we wish to parent GameObject to, which is null by default and which would place Transform at the root of the **Hierarchy** window. All Transforms at the root of the **Hierarchy** window need to allocate a buffer to store its current children as well as those that might be added later (child Transforms do not need to do this). But, if we then re-parent Transform to another one immediately after instantiation, then it discards the buffer we just allocated! To avoid this, we should provide the parent Transform argument into the GameObject.Instantiate() call, which skips this buffer allocation step.

Another way to reduce the costs of this process is to make root Transform pre-allocate a larger buffer before we need it so that we don't need to both expand and re-parent another GameObject instance into the buffer in the same frame. This can be accomplished by modifying a Transform component's hierarchyCapacity property. If we can estimate the number of child Transforms the parent will contain, then we can save a lot of unnecessary memory allocations.

Considering caching transform changes

The Transform component stores data only relative to its own parent. This means that accessing and modifying a Transform component's position, rotation, and/or scale properties could potentially result in a lot of unanticipated matrix multiplication calculations to generate the correct Transform representation for the object through its parent Transforms. The deeper the object is in the **Hierarchy** window, the more calculations are needed to determine the final result.

However, this also means that using `localPosition`, `localRotation`, and `localScale` has a relatively trivial cost associated with it since these are the values stored directly in the given `Transform` component and they can be retrieved without any additional matrix multiplication. Therefore, these local property values should be used whenever possible.

Unfortunately, changing our mathematical calculations from world-space to local-space can over-complicate what were originally simple (and solved) problems, so making such changes risks breaking our implementation and introducing a lot of unexpected bugs. Sometimes, it's worth absorbing a minor performance hit to solve a complex 3D mathematical problem more easily.

Another problem with constantly changing a `Transform` component's properties is that it also sends internal notifications to components such as `Collider`, `Rigidbody`, `Light`, and `Camera`, which must also be processed since the physics and rendering systems both need to know the new value of `Transform` and update accordingly.

It is not uncommon, during a complex event chain, that we replace a `Transform` component's properties multiple times in the same frame (although this is probably a warning sign of over-engineered design). This would cause the internal messages to fire each and every time this happens, even if they occur during the same frame or even the same function call. Ergo, we should consider minimizing the number of times we modify `Transform` properties by caching them in a member variable and committing them only at the end of the frame, as follows:

```
private bool _positionChanged;
private Vector3 _newPosition;

public void SetPosition(Vector3 position) {
  _newPosition = position;
  _positionChanged = true;
}

void FixedUpdate() {
  if (_positionChanged) {
    transform.position = _newPosition;
    _positionChanged = false;
  }
}
```

This code will only commit changes to `position` in the next `FixedUpdate()` method.

Note that changing the `Transform` component in this manner does not result in strange-looking behavior or teleporting objects during gameplay. The whole purpose of those internal events is to make sure the physics and rendering systems are always synchronized with the current `Transform` state. Hence, Unity doesn't skip a beat and fires the internal events every time changes come through the `Transform` component, just to be sure nothing gets missed.

Avoiding Find() and SendMessage() at runtime

The `SendMessage()` method and family of `GameObject.Find()` methods are notoriously expensive and should be avoided at all costs. The `SendMessage()` method is about 2,000 times slower than a simple function call, and the cost of the `Find()` method scales very poorly with scene complexity since it must iterate through every `GameObject` in the scene. It is sometimes forgivable to call `Find()` during the initialization of a scene, such as during an `Awake()` or `Start()` callback. Even in this case, it should only be used to acquire objects that we know for certain already exist in the scene and for scenes that have only a handful of GameObjects in them. Regardless, using either of these methods for inter-object communication at runtime is likely to generate a very noticeable overhead and, potentially, dropped frames.

Relying on `Find()` and `SendMessage()` is typically symptomatic of poor design, inexperience in programming with C# and Unity, or just plain laziness during prototyping. Their usage has become something of an epidemic among beginner-level and intermediate-level projects, so much so that Unity Technologies feels the need to keep reminding users to avoid using them in a real game over and over again in their documentation and at their conferences. They only exist as a less *programmer-y* way to introduce new users to inter-object communication, and for some special cases where they can be used in a responsible way (which are few and far between). In other words, they're so ridiculously expensive that they break the rule of not pre-optimizing our code, and it's worth going out of our way to avoid using them if our project is going beyond the prototyping stage (which is a distinct possibility since you're reading this book).

To be fair, Unity targets a wide demographic of users, from hobbyists to students and professionals, to individual developers, to hundreds of people on the same team. This results in an incredibly wide range of software development ability. When you're starting out with Unity, it can be difficult to figure out on your own what you should be doing differently, especially given how the Unity engine does not adhere to the design paradigms of many other game engines we might be familiar with. It has some foreign and quirky concepts relating to scenes and Prefabs and does not have a built-in God class entry point, nor any obvious raw data storage systems to work with.

A God class is a fancy name for the first object we might create in our application and whose job would be to create everything else we need based on the current context (what level to load, which subsystems to activate, and so on). These can be particularly useful if we want a single centralized location that controls the order of events as they happen during the entire lifecycle of our application.

Understanding how to exchange messages between intricate software architecture components is not useful just for Unity's performance, but also for the design of any real-time event-driven system (including, but not limited to games), so it is worth exploring the subject in some detail, evaluating some alternative methods for inter-object communication.

Let's start by examining a worst-case example, which uses both `Find()` and `SendMessage()` to communicate between objects, and then look into ways to improve upon it.

The following is a class definition for a simple `EnemyManagerComponent` instance that tracks a list of GameObjects representing enemies in our game and provides a `KillAll()` method to destroy them all when needed:

```
using UnityEngine;
using System.Collections.Generic;

class EnemyManagerComponent : MonoBehaviour {
  List<GameObject> _enemies = new List<GameObject>();

  public void AddEnemy(GameObject enemy) {
    if (!_enemies.Contains(enemy)) {
      _enemies.Add(enemy);
    }
  }

  public void KillAll() {
    for (int i = 0; i < _enemies.Count; ++i) {
      GameObject.Destroy(_enemies[i]);
```

```
    }
    _enemies.Clear();
  }
}
```

We would then place a `GameObject` instance in our scene containing this component, and name it `EnemyManager`.

The following example method attempts to instantiate several enemies from a given Prefab, and then notifies the `EnemyManager` object of their existence:

```
public void CreateEnemies(int numEnemies) {
  for(int i = 0; i < numEnemies; ++i) {
    GameObject enemy = (GameObject)GameObject.Instantiate(_enemyPrefab,
                        5.0f * Random.insideUnitSphere,
                        Quaternion.identity);
    string[] names = { "Tom", "Dick", "Harry" };
    enemy.name = names[Random.Range(0, names.Length)];
    GameObject enemyManagerObj = GameObject.Find("EnemyManager");
    enemyManagerObj.SendMessage("AddEnemy",
                        enemy,
                        SendMessageOptions.DontRequireReceiver);
  }
}
```

Initializing data and putting method calls inside any kind of loop, which always outputs to the same result, is a big red flag for poor performance, and when we're dealing with expensive methods, such as `Find()`, we should always look for ways to call them as few times as possible. Ergo, one improvement we can make is to move the `Find()` call outside of the `for` loop and cache the result in a local variable so that we don't need to keep reacquiring the `EnemyManager` object over and over again.

 Moving the initialization of the `names` variable outside of the `for` loop is not necessarily critical since the compiler is often smart enough to realize it doesn't need to keep reinitializing data that isn't being changed elsewhere. However, it does often make the code easier to read.

Another big improvement we can implement is to optimize our usage of the `SendMessage()` method by replacing it with a `GetComponent()` call. This replaces a very costly method with an equivalent and much cheaper alternative.

This gives us the following result:

```
public void CreateEnemies(int numEnemies) {
  GameObject enemyManagerObj = GameObject.Find("EnemyManager");
  EnemyManagerComponent enemyMgr =
enemyManagerObj.GetComponent<EnemyManagerComponent>();
  string[] names = { "Tom", "Dick", "Harry" };

  for(int i = 0; i < numEnemies; ++i) {
    GameObject enemy = (GameObject)GameObject.Instantiate(_enemyPrefab,
                        5.0f * Random.insideUnitSphere,
                        Quaternion.identity);
    enemy.name = names[Random.Range(0, names.Length)];
    enemyMgr.AddEnemy(enemy);
  }
}
```

If this method is called during the initialization of the scene, and we're not overly concerned with loading time, then we can probably consider ourselves finished with our optimization work.

However, we will often need new objects that are instantiated at runtime to find an existing object to communicate with. In this example, we want new enemy objects to register with our EnemyManagerComponent so that it can do whatever it needs to do to track and control the enemy objects in our scene. We would also like EnemyManager to handle all enemy-related behavior so that objects calling its functions don't need to perform work on its behalf. This will improve the coupling (how well our code base separates related behavior) and encapsulation (how well our classes prevent outside changes to the data they manage) of our application. The ultimate aim is to find a reliable and fast way for new objects to find existing objects in the scene without unnecessary usage of the Find() method so that we can minimize complexity and performance costs.

There are multiple approaches we can take to solving this problem, each with their own benefits and pitfalls:

- Assign references to preexisting objects
- Static classes
- Singleton components
- A global messaging system

Assigning references to pre-existing objects

A simple approach to the problem of inter-object communication is to use Unity's built-in serialization system. Software design purists tend to get a little combative about this feature since it breaks encapsulation; it makes any field (the C# term for a member variable) marked `private` act in a way that treats it like a `public` field. However, it is a very effective tool for improving development workflow. This is particularly true when artists, designers, and programmers are all tinkering when the same product, where each has wildly varying levels of computer science and software programming knowledge, and with some of whom would prefer to stay away from modifying code files. Sometimes, it's worth bending a few rules in the name of productivity.

Whenever we create a `public` field in `MonoBehaviour`, Unity automatically serializes and exposes the value in the **Inspector** window when the component is selected. However, `public` fields are always dangerous from a software design perspective. These variables can be changed through code at anytime from anywhere, making it hard to keep track of the variable and it's liable to introduce a lot of unexpected bugs.

A better solution is to take any `private` or `protected` member variable of a class and expose it to the **Inspector** window with the `[SerializeField]` attribute. The value will then behave like a `public` field with respect to the **Inspector** window, allowing us to change it through the Editor interface for convenience, but will keep the data safely encapsulated from other parts of our code base.

For example, the following class exposes three `private` fields to the **Inspector** window:

```
using UnityEngine;

public class EnemyCreatorComponent : MonoBehaviour {
    [SerializeField] private int _numEnemies;
    [SerializeField] private GameObject _enemyPrefab;
    [SerializeField] private EnemyManagerComponent _enemyManager;

    void Start() {
        for (int i = 0; i < _numEnemies; ++i) {
            CreateEnemy();
        }
    }

    public void CreateEnemy() {
        _enemyManager.CreateEnemy(_enemyPrefab);
    }
}
```

Note that the `private` access specifiers shown in the preceding code are redundant keywords in C# since fields and methods default to `private` unless specified otherwise. However, it is often best practice to be explicit about the intended access level.

Looking at this component in the **Inspector** window reveals three values, initially given default values of 0 or `null`, which can be modified through the Editor interface:

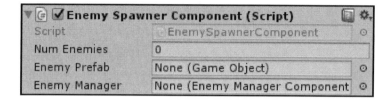

We can drag and drop a Prefab reference from the **Project** window into the **Enemy Prefab** field revealed in the **Inspector** window.

Note how Unity automatically takes a camel-cased field name and creates a convenient **Inspector** window name for it. `_numEnemies` becomes **Num Enemies**, `_enemyPrefab` becomes **Enemy Prefab**, and so on.

Meanwhile, the `_enemyManager` field is interesting because it is a reference to a specific `MonoBehaviour` class type. If a `GameObject` is dragged and dropped into this field, then it will refer to the component on the given object as opposed to the `GameObject` itself. Note that if `GameObject` does not contain the expected `MonoBehaviour`, instance, then nothing will be assigned to the field.

A common usage of this component reference technique is to obtain references to other components attached to the very same `GameObject` a component is attached to. This is an alternative means of caching components with zero cost, as discussed in the section entitled *Cache component references*, earlier in this chapter.

There is some danger to using this method. Much of our code would assume that a Prefab is assigned to a field that is used like a Prefab and `GameObject` is assigned to a field that refers to an instance of `GameObject`. However, since Prefabs are essentially GameObjects, any Prefab or `GameObject` can be assigned to a serialized `GameObject` reference field, which means we could assign the wrong type by accident.

If we do assign the wrong type, then we could accidentally instantiate a new `GameObject` instance from an existing one that was previously modified, or we could make changes to a Prefab, which would then change the state of all GameObjects instantiated from it. To make matters worse, any accidental changes to a Prefab become permanent since Prefabs occupy the same memory space whether Playmode is active or not. This is the case even if the Prefab is only modified during Playmode.

Therefore, this approach is a very team-friendly way of solving the problem of inter-object communication, but it is not ideal due to all of the risks involved with team members accidentally leaving `null` references in place, assigning Prefabs to references that expect an instance of `GameObject` from the scene or vice versa.

It is also important to note that not all objects can be serialized and revealed in the **Inspector** window. Unity can serialize all primitive data types (`int`, `float`, `string`, and `bool`), various built-in types (`Vector3`, `Quaternion`, and so on), `enum`, `class`, `struct`, and various data structures containing other serializable types such as `List`. However, it is unable to serialize `static` fields, `readonly` fields, properties, and dictionaries.

> Some Unity developers like to implement the pseudo-serialization of dictionaries via two separate lists for keys and values, along with a Custom Editor script, or via a single list of `struct` objects, which contain both keys and values. Both of these solutions are a little clumsy, and are rarely as performant as a proper dictionary, but they can still be useful.

Another solution to the problem of inter-object communication is to try and make use of globally accessible objects to minimize the number of custom assignments we need to make.

Static classes

This approach involves creating a class that is globally accessible to the entire code base at anytime. Any kind of global manager class is often frowned upon in software engineering circles, partly since the name manager is vague and doesn't say much about what it's meant to do, but mostly because problems can be difficult to debug. Changes can occur from anywhere and at any point during runtime, and such classes tend to maintain state information that other systems rely upon. It is also perhaps the most difficult approach to change or replace since many of our classes might contain direct function calls into it, requiring each to be modified at a future date if it were to be replaced. Despite all of these drawbacks, it is by far the easiest solution to understand and implement.

The singleton design pattern is a common way of ensuring only one instance of a certain object type ever exists in memory. This design pattern is implemented by giving the class a private constructor, a static variable is maintained to keep track of the object instance, and the class can only be accessed through a static property it provides. Singletons can be useful for managing shared resources or heavy data traffic, such as file access, downloads, data parsing, and messaging. A singleton ensures that we have a single entry point for such activities, rather than having tons of different subsystems competing for shared resources and potentially bottlenecking one another.

Singletons don't necessarily have to be globally accessible objects—their most important feature is that only a single instance of the object exists at a time. However, the way that singletons are primarily used in most projects is to be a global access point to some shared functionality, and they are designed to be created once during application initialization, persist through the entire lifecycle of the application, and only be destroyed during application shutdown. As such, a simpler way of implementing this kind of behavior in C# is to use a static class. In other words, implementing the typical singleton design pattern in C# just provides the same behavior as a static class, but takes more time and code to implement.

A static class that functions in much the same way as EnemyManagerComponent, as demonstrated in the previous example, can be defined as follows:

```
using System.Collections.Generic;
using UnityEngine;

public static class StaticEnemyManager {
  private static List<Enemy> _enemies;

  public static void CreateEnemy(GameObject prefab) {
    string[] names = { "Tom", "Dick", "Harry" };
    GameObject enemy = GameObject.Instantiate(prefab, 5.0f *
    Random.insideUnitSphere, Quaternion.identity);
    Enemy enemyComp = enemy.GetComponent<Enemy>();
    enemy.gameObject.name = names[Random.Range(0, names.Length)];
    _enemies.Add(enemyComp);
  }

  public static void KillAll() {
    for (int i = 0; i < _enemies.Count; ++i) {
      _enemies[i].Die();
      GameObject.Destroy(_enemies[i].gameObject);
    }
    _enemies.Clear();
  }
}
```

Note that every method, property, and field in a static class must have the `static` keyword attached, which implies that only one instance of this object will ever reside in memory. This also means that its `public` methods and fields are accessible from anywhere. Static classes, by definition, do not allow any non-`static` fields to be defined.

If static class fields need to be initialized (such as the `_enemies` field, which is initially set to `null`), then static class fields can be initialized inline like so:

```
private static List<Enemy> _enemies = new List<Enemy>();
```

However, if object construction needs to be more complicated than this, then static classes can be given a `static` constructor, instead. The static class constructor is automatically called the moment the class is first accessed through any of its fields, properties, or methods and can be defined like so:

```
static StaticEnemyManager() {
  _enemies = new List<Enemy>();
  // more complicated initialization activity goes here
}
```

This time, we have implemented the `CreateEnemy()` method so that it handles much of the activity for creating an enemy object. However, the static class must still be given a reference to a Prefab from which it can instantiate an enemy object. A static class can only contain `static` member variables, and therefore cannot easily interface with the **Inspector** window in the same way that MonoBehaviours can, therefore requiring the caller to provide some implementation-specific information to it. To solve this problem, we could implement a companion-component for our static class to keep our code properly *decoupled*. The following code demonstrates what this class might look like:

```
using UnityEngine;

public class EnemyCreatorCompanionComponent : MonoBehaviour {
  [SerializeField] private GameObject _enemyPrefab;

  public void CreateEnemy() {
    StaticEnemyManager.CreateEnemy(_enemyPrefab);
  }
}
```

Despite these drawbacks, the `StaticEnemyManager` class illustrates a simple example of how a static class might be used to provide information or communication between external objects, providing a better alternative than using `Find()` or `SendMessage()`.

Singleton components

As mentioned previously, static classes have difficulty interfacing with Unity-related functionality and cannot directly make use of MonoBehaviour features, such as event callbacks, coroutines, hierarchical design, and Prefabs. Also, since there's no object to select in the **Inspector** window, we lose the ability to inspect the data of a static class at runtime through the **Inspector** window, which can make debugging difficult. These are features that we may wish to make use of in our global classes.

A common solution to this problem is to implement a component that acts as a singleton—it provides static methods to grant global access, and only one instance of MonoBehaviour is ever allowed to exist at any given time.

The following is the definition for a SingletonComponent class:

```
using UnityEngine;

public class SingletonComponent<T> : MonoBehaviour where T :
SingletonComponent<T> {
  private static T __Instance;

  protected static SingletonComponent<T> _Instance {
    get {
      if(!__Instance) {
        T[] managers = GameObject.FindObjectsOfType(typeof(T)) as T[];
        if (managers != null) {
          if (managers.Length == 1) {
            __Instance = managers[0];
            return __Instance;
          } else if (managers.Length > 1) {
            Debug.LogError("You have more than one " +
                          typeof(T).Name +
                          " in the Scene. You only need " +
                          "one - it's a singleton!");
            for(int i = 0; i < managers.Length; ++i) {
              T manager = managers[i];
              Destroy(manager.gameObject);
            }
          }
        }
        GameObject go = new GameObject(typeof(T).Name, typeof(T));
        __Instance = go.GetComponent<T>();
        DontDestroyOnLoad(__Instance.gameObject);
      }
      return __Instance;
    }
```

```
        set {
            __Instance = value as T;
        }
    }
}
```

This class works by creating GameObject containing a component of itself the first time it is accessed. Since we wish this to be a global and persistent object, we will need to call DontDestroyOnLoad() shortly after GameObject is created. This is a special function that tells Unity that we want the object to persist between scenes for as long as the application is running. From that point onward, when a new scene is loaded, the object will not be destroyed and will retain all of its data.

This class definition assumes two things. Firstly, because it is using *generics* to define its behavior, we must derive it to create a concrete class. Secondly, a method must be defined to assign the _Instance property (which, in turn, sets the private __Instance field) and cast it to/from the correct class type.

For example, the following is the minimum amount of code that is needed to successfully generate a new SingletonComponent derived class called EnemyManagerSingletonComponent:

```
public class EnemyManagerSingletonComponent : SingletonComponent<
EnemyManagerSingletonComponent > {
    public static EnemyManagerSingletonComponent Instance {
        get { return ((EnemyManagerSingletonComponent)_Instance); }
        set { _Instance = value; }
    }

    public void CreateEnemy(GameObject prefab) {
        // same as StaticEnemyManager
    }

    public void KillAll() {
        // same as StaticEnemyManager
    }
}
```

This class can be used at runtime by having any other object access the Instance property at anytime. If the component does not already exist in our scene, then the SingletonComponent base class will instantiate its own GameObject and attach an instance of the derived class to it as a component. From that point forward, access through the Instance property will reference the component that was created, and only one instance of that component will exist at a time.

Note that this means we don't need to implement `static` methods in a singleton component class definition. For example, we could simply call `EnemyManagerSingletonComponent.Instance.KillAll()` to access the `KillAll()` method.

Note that it is possible to place an instance of `SingletonComponent` in a **Hierarchy** window since it derives from `MonoBehaviour`. Although, be warned, the `DontDestroyOnLoad()` method would never be called, which would prevent the singleton component's `GameObject` from persisting when the next scene is loaded. We will perhaps need to call `DontDestroyOnLoad()` in the `Awake()` callback of the derived class to make this work, unless, of course, we actually want destructible singletons. Sometimes, it makes sense to allow such singletons to be destroyed between scenes so that it can start fresh each time; it all depends on our particular use cases.

In either case, the shutdown of a singleton component can be a little convoluted because of how Unity tears down scenes. An object's `OnDestroy()` callback is called whenever it is destroyed during runtime. The same method is called during application shutdown, whereby every component on each `GameObject` has its `OnDestroy()` callback called by Unity. The same activities take place when we end Playmode in the Editor, hence returning to edit mode. However, the destruction of objects occurs in a random order, and we cannot assume that the `SingletonComponent` object will be the last object destroyed.

Consequently, if any object attempts to do anything with the singleton component in the middle of their `OnDestroy()` callback, then they may be calling the `SingletonComponent` object's `Instance` property. However, if the singleton component has already been destroyed before this moment, then a new instance of `SingletonComponent` will be created in the middle of the application shutdown. This can corrupt our scene files, as instances of our singleton components will be left behind in the scene. If this happens, then Unity will throw the following error message:

"Some objects were not cleaned up when closing the scene. (Did you spawn new GameObjects from OnDestroy?)"

The obvious workaround is to simply never call into a `SingletonComponent` object during any `MonoBehaviour` component's `OnDestroy()` callback. However, there are some legitimate reasons we may wish to do so: most notable is that singletons are often designed to make use of the observer design pattern. This design pattern allows other objects to register/deregister with them for certain tasks, similar to how Unity latches onto callback methods, such as `Start()` and `Update()`, but in a more strict fashion.

With the observer design pattern, objects will typically register with the system when they are created, will make use of it during runtime, and then either deregister from it during runtime when they are finished using it or deregister during their own shutdown for the sake of cleanup. We will see an example of this design pattern in the upcoming section, *A global messaging system*, but if we imagine MonoBehaviour making use of such a system, then the most convenient place to perform shutdown deregistration would be within an OnDestroy() callback. Consequently, such objects are likely to run into the aforementioned problem, where a new GameObject instance for SingletonComponent is accidentally created during application shutdown.

To solve this problem, we will need to make three changes. Firstly, we need to add an additional flag to SingletonComponent, which keeps track of its active state and disables it at the appropriate times. This includes the singleton's own destruction, as well as application shutdown (OnApplicationQuit() is another useful Unity callback for MonoBehaviours, which is called during this time):

```
private bool _alive = true;
void OnDestroy() { _alive = false; }
void OnApplicationQuit() { _alive = false; }
```

Secondly, we should implement a way for external objects to verify the singleton's current state:

```
public static bool IsAlive {
  get {
    if (__Instance == null)
      return false;
    return __Instance._alive;
  }
}
```

Finally, any object that attempts to call into the singleton during its own OnDestroy() method must first verify the state using the IsAlive property before calling Instance, as follows:

```
public class SomeComponent : MonoBehaviour {
  void OnDestroy() {
    if (MySingletonComponent.IsAlive) {
      MySingletonComponent.Instance.SomeMethod();
    }
  }
}
```

This will ensure that nobody attempts to access the singleton instance during destruction. If we don't follow this rule, then we will run into problems where instances of our singleton object will be left behind in the scene after returning to Edit Mode.

The irony of the `SingletonComponent` approach is that we are using a `Find()` call to determine whether or not one of these `SingletonComponent` objects already exists in the scene before we attempt to assign the `__Instance` reference variable. Fortunately, this will only happen when the singleton component is first accessed, which is usually not a problem if there aren't too many GameObjects in the scene, but it's possible that the initialization of the singleton component may not necessarily occur during scene initialization and can, therefore, cost us a performance spike at a bad time during gameplay when an instance is first acquired and `Find()` gets called. The workaround for this is to have some `God` class confirm that the important singletons are instantiated during scene initialization by simply accessing the `Instance` property on each one.

Another downside to this approach is that if we later decide that we want more than one of these singletons executing at once or we wish to separate out its behavior to be more modular, then there would be a lot of code that needs to change.

The final approach we will explore will attempt to solve many of the problems revealed by the previous solutions and provide a way to gain all of their benefits, by combining ease of implementation, ease of extension, and strict usage that also reduces the likelihood of human error during configuration.

A global messaging system

The final suggested approach to solve the problem of interobject communication is to implement a global messaging system that any object can access and send messages through to any object that may be interested in listening to that specific type of message. Objects can send messages or listen for them (sometimes both!), and the responsibility is on the listener to decide what messages they are interested in. The message sender can broadcast the message without caring at all who is listening, and a message can be sent through the system regardless of the specific contents of the message. This approach is by far the most complex and may require some effort to implement and maintain, but it is an excellent long-term solution to keep our object communication modular, decoupled, and fast as our application gets more and more complex.

The kinds of message we wish to send can take many forms, including data values, references, instructions for listeners, and more, but they should all have a common, basic definition that our messaging system can use to determine what the message is and who it is intended for.

The following is a simple class definition for a `Message` object:

```
public class Message {
  public string type;
  public Message() { type = this.GetType().Name; }
}
```

The `Message` class constructor caches the message's `type` in a local `string` property to be used later for cataloging and distribution purposes. Caching this value is important, as each call to `GetType().Name` will result in a new string being allocated, and we've previously learned that we want to minimize this activity as much as possible.

Any custom messages can contain whatever superfluous data they wish so long as they derive from this base class, which will allow it to be sent through our messaging system. Take note that despite acquiring `type` from the object during its base class constructor, the `name` property will still contain the name of the derived class, not the base class.

Moving on to our `MessagingSystem` class, we should define its features by what kind of requirements we need it to fulfill:

- It should be globally accessible
- Any object (`MonoBehaviour` or not) should be able to register/deregister as listeners to receive specific message types (that is, the observer design pattern)
- Registering objects should provide a method to call when the given message is broadcasted from elsewhere
- The system should send the message to all listeners within a reasonable time frame, but not choke on too many requests at once

A globally accessible object

The first requirement makes the messaging system an excellent candidate for a singleton object, since we would only ever need one instance of the system. Although, it is wise to think long and hard as to whether this is truly the case before committing to implementing a singleton.

If we later decide that we want multiple instances of this object to exist, wish to allow the systems to be created/destroyed during runtime, or even wish to create test cases that allow us to fake or create/destroy them in the middle of a test, then it can be a difficult task to refactor a singleton out of our code base. This is due to all of the dependencies we will gradually introduce to our code as we use the system more and more.

If we wish to avoid singletons due to the above drawbacks, then it may be easier to create a single instance of the messaging system during initialization and then pass it around from subsystem to subsystem as needed, or we might wish to go further and explore the concept of dependency injection, which attempts to solve problems like these. However, for the sake of simplicity, we will assume that a singleton fits our needs and design our `MessagingSystem` class accordingly.

Registration

The second and third requirements can be achieved by offering some public methods that allow registration with the messaging system. If we force the listening object to provide us a delegate function to call when the message is broadcast, then this allows listeners to customize which method is called for which message. We can make our code base very easy to understand if we name the delegate after the message it is intended to process.

In some cases, we might wish to broadcast a general notification message and have all listeners do something in response, such as an *Enemy Created* message. Other times, we might be sending a message that specifically targets a single listener among a group. For example, we might want to send an *Enemy Health Value Changed* message that is intended for a specific health bar object that is attached to the enemy that was damaged. However, we may have many health bar objects in the scene, all of which are interested in this message type, but each is only interested in hearing health update messages for the enemy they're providing health information for. So, if we implement a way for the system to stop checking after it has been handled, then we can probably save a good number of CPU cycles when many listeners are waiting for the same message type.

The delegate we define should, therefore, provide a way to retrieve the message via an argument and return a response that determines whether or not processing for the message should stop if and when the listener is done with it. The decision on whether to stop processing or not can be achieved by returning a simple Boolean, where `true` implies that this listener has handled the message and the processing for the message must stop, and `false` implies that this listener has not handled the message and the messaging system should try the next listener.

Here is the definition for the delegate:

```
public delegate bool MessageHandlerDelegate(Message message);
```

Listeners must define a method of this form and pass a delegate reference to the messaging system during registration, hence providing a means for the messaging system to tell the listening object when the message is being broadcast.

Message processing

The final requirement for our messaging system is that this object should have some kind of timing-based mechanism built in to prevent it from choking on too many messages at once. This means that, somewhere in the code base, we will need to make use of MonoBehaviour event callbacks to tell our messaging system to perform work during Unity's Update(), essentially enabling it to count time.

This could be achieved with the static class singleton (which we defined earlier), which would require some other MonoBehaviour-based God class to call into it, informing it that the scene has been updated. Alternatively, we can use the singleton component to achieve the same thing, which has its own means of determining when Update() is called and hence handle its workload independently of any God class. The most notable difference between the two approaches is whether or not the system is dependent on the control of other objects and the various pros and cons of managing a singleton component (such that it won't get destroyed between scenes; we don't want to accidentally recreate it during shutdown).

The singleton component approach is probably the best since there aren't too many occasions where we wouldn't want this system acting independently, even if much of our game logic depends upon it. For example, even if the game was paused, we wouldn't want the game logic to pause our messaging system. We would still want the messaging system to continue receiving and processing messages so that we could, for example, keep UI-related components communicating with one another while the gameplay is in a paused state.

Implementing the messaging system

Let's define our messaging system by deriving from the SingletonComponent class and provide a method for objects to register with it:

```
using System.Collections.Generic;
using UnityEngine;

public class MessagingSystem : SingletonComponent<MessagingSystem> {
  public static MessagingSystem Instance {
    get { return ((MessagingSystem)_Instance); }
    set { _Instance = value; }
  }

  private Dictionary<string,List<MessageHandlerDelegate>> _listenerDict =
new Dictionary<string,List<MessageHandlerDelegate>>();
```

```
    public bool AttachListener(System.Type type, MessageHandlerDelegate
handler) {
        if (type == null) {
           Debug.Log("MessagingSystem: AttachListener failed due to having no "
+
                     "message type specified");
          return false;
        }

        string msgType = type.Name;
        if (!_listenerDict.ContainsKey(msgType)) {
          _listenerDict.Add(msgType, new List<MessageHandlerDelegate>());
        }

        List<MessageHandlerDelegate> listenerList = _listenerDict[msgType];
        if (listenerList.Contains(handler)) {
          return false; // listener already in list
        }

        listenerList.Add(handler);
        return true;
    }
}
```

The `_listenerDict` field is a dictionary of strings mapped to lists
containing `MessageHandlerDelegate`. This dictionary organizes our listener delegates
into lists by which message type they wish to listen to. Hence, if we know what message
type is being sent, then we can quickly retrieve a list of all delegates that have been
registered for that message type. We can then iterate through the list, querying each listener
to check whether one of them wants to handle it.

The `AttachListener()` method requires two parameters: a message type in the form of its
`System.Type` and `MessageHandlerDelegate` to send the message to when the given
message type comes through the system.

Message queuing and processing

To process messages, our messaging system should maintain a queue of incoming message
objects so that we can process them in the order they were broadcast:

```
private Queue<Message> _messageQueue = new Queue<Message>();

public bool QueueMessage(Message msg) {
    if (!_listenerDict.ContainsKey(msg.type)) {
       return false;
```

```
    }
    _messageQueue.Enqueue(msg);
    return true;
}
```

The QueueMessage() method simply checks whether the given message type is present in our dictionary before adding it to the queue. This effectively tests whether or not an object actually cares to listen to the message before we queue it to be processed later. We have introduced a new private field, _messageQueue, for this purpose.

Next, we'll add a definition for Update(). This callback will be called regularly by the Unity Engine. Its purpose is to iterate through the current contents of the message queue, one message a time; verify whether or not too much time has passed since we began processing; and if not, pass them along to the next stage in the process:

```
private const int _maxQueueProcessingTime = 16667;
private System.Diagnostics.Stopwatch timer = new
System.Diagnostics.Stopwatch();

void Update() {
  timer.Start();
  while (_messageQueue.Count > 0) {
    if (_maxQueueProcessingTime > 0.0f) {
      if (timer.Elapsed.Milliseconds > _maxQueueProcessingTime) {
        timer.Stop();
        return;
      }
    }

    Message msg = _messageQueue.Dequeue();
    if (!TriggerMessage(msg)) {
      Debug.Log("Error when processing message: " + msg.type);
    }
  }
}
```

The time-based safeguard is in place to make sure that it does not exceed a processing time limit threshold. This prevents the messaging system from freezing our game if too many messages get pushed through the system too quickly. If the total time limit is exceeded, then all message processing will stop, leaving any remaining messages to be processed during the next frame.

Note that we use the full namespace when creating the `Stopwatch` object. We could have added `using System.Diagnostics`, but this would lead to a namespace conflict between `System.Diagnostics.Debug` and `UnityEngine.Debug`. Omitting it allows us to continue to call Unity's debug logger with `Debug.Log()`, without having to explicitly call `UnityEngine.Debug.Log()` each time.

Lastly, we will need to define the `TriggerMessage()` method, which distributes messages to listeners:

```
public bool TriggerMessage(Message msg) {
  string msgType = msg.type;
  if (!_listenerDict.ContainsKey(msgType)) {
    Debug.Log("MessagingSystem: Message \"" + msgType + "\" has no
listeners!");
    return false; // no listeners for message so ignore it
  }

  List<MessageHandlerDelegate> listenerList = _listenerDict[msgType];

  for(int i = 0; i < listenerList.Count; ++i) {
    if (listenerList[i](msg)) {
      return true; // message consumed by the delegate
    }
    return true;
  }
}
```

The preceding method is the main workhorse behind the messaging system. The `TriggerEvent()` method's purpose is to obtain the list of listeners for the given message type and give each of them an opportunity to process it. If one of the delegates returns `true`, then the processing of the current message ceases and the method exits, allowing the `Update()` method to process the next message.

Normally, we would want to use `QueueEvent()` to broadcast messages, but we also provide direct access to `TriggerEvent()` as an alternative. Using `TriggerEvent()` directly allows message senders to force their messages to be processed immediately without waiting for the next `Update()` event. This bypasses the throttling mechanism, which might be necessary for messages that need to be sent during critical moments of gameplay, where waiting an additional frame might result in strange-looking behavior.

For example, if we intend for two objects to be destroyed and create a **Particle Effect** the moment they collide with one another, and this work is handled by another subsystem (hence an event needs to be sent for it), then we would want to send the message via `TriggerEvent()` to prevent the objects from continuing to exist for one frame before the event is handled. Conversely, if we wanted to do something less frame-critical, such as create a pop-up message when the player walks into a new area, we could safely use a `QueueEvent()` call to handle it.

Try to avoid habitually using `TriggerEvent()` for all events, as we could end up handling too many calls simultaneously in the same frame, causing a sudden drop in frame rate. Decide which events are frame-critical, and which are not, and use the `QueueEvent()` and `TriggerEvent()` methods appropriately.

Implementing custom messages

We've created the messaging system, but an example of how to use it would help us to wrap our heads around the concept. Let's start by defining a pair of simple classes that derive from `Message`, which we can use to create a new enemy, as well as to notify other parts of our code base that an enemy was created:

```
public class CreateEnemyMessage : Message {}

public class EnemyCreatedMessage : Message {

   public readonly GameObject enemyObject;
   public readonly string enemyName;

   public EnemyCreatedMessage(GameObject enemyObject, string enemyName) {
     this.enemyObject = enemyObject;
     this.enemyName = enemyName;
   }
}
```

`CreateEnemyMessage` is the simplest form of message that contains no special data, while `EnemyCreatedMessage` will contain a reference to the enemy's `GameObject` as well as its name. Good practice for message objects is to make their member variables not only `public` but also `readonly`. This ensures that the data is easily accessible but cannot be changed after the object's construction. This safeguards the content of our messages against being altered, as they're passed between one listener and another.

Message sending

To send one of these message objects, we simply need to call either `QueueEvent()` or `TriggerEvent()` and pass it an instance of the message we wish to send. The following code demonstrates how we would broadcast a `CreateEnemyMessage` object when the spacebar is pressed:

```
public class EnemyCreatorComponent : MonoBehaviour {
  void Update() {
    if (Input.GetKeyDown(KeyCode.Space)) {
      MessagingSystem.Instance.QueueMessage(new CreateEnemyMessage());
    }
  }
}
```

If we were to test this code right now, nothing would happen, because even though we are sending a message through the messaging system, there are no listeners for this message type. Let's cover how to register listeners with the messaging system.

Message registration

The following code contains a pair of simple classes that register with the messaging system, each requesting to have one of their methods called whenever certain types of messages have been broadcast from anywhere in our code base:

```
public class EnemyManagerWithMessagesComponent : MonoBehaviour {
  private List<GameObject> _enemies = new List<GameObject>();
  [SerializeField] private GameObject _enemyPrefab;

  void Start() {
    MessagingSystem.Instance.AttachListener(typeof(CreateEnemyMessage),
                                            this.HandleCreateEnemy);
  }

  bool HandleCreateEnemy(Message msg) {
    CreateEnemyMessage castMsg = msg as CreateEnemyMessage;
    string[] names = { "Tom", "Dick", "Harry" };
    GameObject enemy = GameObject.Instantiate(_enemyPrefab,
                       5.0f * Random.insideUnitSphere,
                       Quaternion.identity);
    string enemyName = names[Random.Range(0, names.Length)];
    enemy.gameObject.name = enemyName;
    _enemies.Add(enemy);
    MessagingSystem.Instance.QueueMessage(new EnemyCreatedMessage(enemy,
enemyName));
```

```
      return true;
   }
}

public class EnemyCreatedListenerComponent : MonoBehaviour {
   void Start () {
      MessagingSystem.Instance.AttachListener(typeof(EnemyCreatedMessage),
                                    HandleEnemyCreated);
   }
   bool HandleEnemyCreated(Message msg) {
      EnemyCreatedMessage castMsg = msg as EnemyCreatedMessage;
      Debug.Log(string.Format("A new enemy was created! {0}",
                        castMsg.enemyName));
      return true;
   }
}
```

During initialization, the EnemyManagerWithMessagesComponent class registers to receive messages of the CreateEnemyMessage type, and will process the message through its HandleCreateEnemy() delegate. During this method, it can typecast the message into the appropriate derived message type and resolves the message in its own unique way. Other classes can register for the same message and resolve it differently through its own custom delegate method (assuming that an earlier listener didn't return true from its own delegate).

We know what type of messages will be provided by the msg argument of the HandleCreateEnemy() method, because we defined it during registration through the AttachListener() call. Due to this, we can be certain that our typecasting is safe, and we can save time by not having to do a null reference check although, technically, nothing is stopping us using the same delegate to handle multiple message types. In these cases, though, we will need to implement a way to determine which message object is being passed and treat it accordingly. However, the best approach is to define a unique method for each message type to keep things appropriately decoupled. There really is little benefit in trying to use one monolithic method to handle all message types.

Note how the HandleEnemyCreated() method definition matches the function signature of MessageHandlerDelegate (that is, it has the same return type and argument list), and that it is being referenced in the AttachListener() call. This is how we tell the messaging system what method to call when the given message type is broadcast and how delegates ensure type-safety.

If the function signature had a different return value or a different list of arguments, then it would be an invalid delegate for the `AttachListener()` method, and we would get compiler errors. Also, note that `HandleEnemyCreated()` is a `private` method, and yet our `MessagingSystem` class can call it. This is a useful feature of delegates in that we can allow only systems we give permission to call this message handler. Exposing the method publicly might lead to some confusion in our code's API, and developers may think that they're meant to call the method directly, which is not its intended use.

The beautiful part is that we're free to give the delegate method whatever name we want. The most sensible approach is to name the method after the message that it handles. This makes it clear to anyone reading our code what the method is used for and what message object type must be sent to call it. This makes the future parsing and debugging of our code much more straightforward since we can follow the chain of events by the matching names of the messages and their handler delegates.

During the `HandleCreateEnemy()` method, we also queue another event, which broadcasts `EnemyCreatedMessage` instead. The second class, `EnemyCreatedListenerComponent`, registers to receive these messages and then prints out a message containing that information. This is how we would implement a way for subsystems to notify other subsystems of changes. In a real application, we might register a UI system to listen for these types of messages and update a counter on the screen to show how many enemies are now active. In this case, the enemy management and UI systems are appropriately *decoupled* such that neither needs to know any specific information about how the other operates to do their assigned tasks.

If we now add `EnemyManagerWithMessagesComponent`, `EnemyCreatorComponent`, and `EnemyCreatedListenerComponent` to our scene, and press the spacebar several times, we should see log messages appear in the **Console** window, informing us of a successful test:

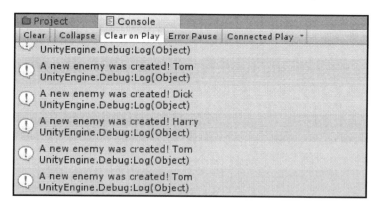

Note that a `MessagingSystem` singleton object will be created during scene initialization, when either the `EnemyManagerWithMessagesComponent` or `EnemyCreatedListenerComponent` object's `Start()` methods are called (whichever happens first), since that is when they register their delegates with the messaging system, which accesses the `Instance` property, and hence creates the necessary `GameObject` instance containing the singleton component. No additional effort is required on our part to create the `MessagingSystem` object.

Message cleanup

Since message objects are classes, they will be created dynamically in memory and will be disposed of shortly afterward when the message has been processed and distributed among all listeners. However, as you will learn in `Chapter 8`, *Masterful Memory Management*, this will eventually result in garbage collection, as memory accumulates over time. If our application runs for long enough, it will eventually result in occasional garbage collection, which is the most common cause of unexpected and sudden CPU performance spikes in Unity applications. Therefore, it is wise to use the messaging system sparingly and avoid spamming messages too frequently on every update.

The more important cleanup operation to consider is the deregistration of delegates if an object needs to be destroyed. If we don't handle this properly, then the messaging system will hang on to delegate references that prevent objects from being fully destroyed and freed from memory.

Essentially, we will need to pair every `AttachListener()` call with an appropriate `DetachListener()` call when the object is destroyed or disabled or we otherwise decide that we no longer need it to be queried when messages are being sent.

The following method definition in the `MessagingSystem` class will detach a listener for a specific event:

```
public bool DetachListener(System.Type type, MessageHandlerDelegate
handler) {
  if (type == null) {
    Debug.Log("MessagingSystem: DetachListener failed due to having no " +
              "message type specified");
    return false;
  }

  string msgType = type.Name;

  if (!_listenerDict.ContainsKey(type.Name)) {
    return false;
```

```
  }

  List<MessageHandlerDelegate> listenerList = _listenerDict[msgType];
  if (!listenerList.Contains (handler)) {
    return false;
  }
  listenerList.Remove(handler);
  return true;
}
```

Here is an example usage of the `DetachListener()` method added to our `EnemyManagerWithMessagesComponent` class:

```
void OnDestroy() {
  if (MessagingSystem.IsAlive) {
    MessagingSystem.Instance.DetachListener(typeof(EnemyCreatedMessage),
                                            this.HandleCreateEnemy);
  }
}
```

Note how this definition makes use of the `IsAlive` property declared in the `SingletonComponent` class. This safeguards us against the aforementioned problem of accidentally creating a new `MessagingSystem` class during application shutdown since we can never guarantee that the singleton gets destroyed last.

Wrapping up the messaging system

Congratulations are in order, as we have finally built a fully functional global messaging system that any and all objects can interface with and use it to send messages between one another. A useful feature of this approach is that it is `Type`-agnostic, meaning that the message senders and listeners do not even need to derive from any particular class in order to interface with the messaging system; it just needs to be a class that provides a message type and a delegate function of the matching function signature, which makes it accessible to both ordinary classes and MonoBehaviours.

As far as benchmarking the `MessagingSystem` class goes, we will find that it is capable of processing hundreds, if not thousands, of messages in a single frame with minimal CPU overhead (depending on the CPU, of course). The CPU usage is essentially the same, whether one message is being distributed to 100 different listeners or 100 messages are distributed to just one listener. Either way, it costs about the same.

Even if we're predominantly sending messages during UI or gameplay events, this probably has far more power than we need. So, if it does seem to be causing performance problems, then it's far more likely to be caused by what the listener delegates are doing with the message than the messaging system's ability to process those messages.

There are many ways to enhance the messaging system to provide more useful features we may need in the future, as follows:

- Allow message senders to suggest a delay (in time or frame count) before a message is delivered to its listeners.
- Allow message listeners to define a priority for how urgently it should receive messages compared to other listeners waiting for the same message type. This is a means for a listener to skip to the front of the queue if it was registered later than other listeners.
- Implement some safety checks to handle situations where a listener gets added to the list of message listeners for a particular message while a message of that type is still being processed. Currently, C# will throw `EnumerationException` at us since the delegate list will be changed by `AttachListener()`, while it is still being iterated through in `TriggerEvent()`.

At this point, we've probably explored the messaging system enough, so these tasks will be left as an academic exercise for you to undertake if you become comfortable using this solution in your games. Let's continue to explore more ways to improve performance through script code.

Disabling unused scripts and objects

Scenes can get pretty busy sometimes, especially when we're building large, open worlds. The more objects there are invoking code in an `Update()` callback, the worse it will scale and the slower the game becomes. However, much of what is being processed may be completely unnecessary if it is outside of the player's view or simply too far away to matter. This may not be a possibility in large city-building simulation games, where the entire simulation must be processed at all times, but it is often possible in first-person and racing games since the player is wandering around a large expansive area, where non-visible objects can be temporarily disabled without having any noticeable effect on gameplay.

Disabling objects by visibility

Sometimes, we may want components or GameObjects to be disabled when they're not visible. Unity comes with built-in rendering features to avoid rendering objects that are not visible to the player's camera view (through a technique known as **Frustum Culling,** which is an automatic process) and to avoid rendering objects that are hidden behind other objects (**Occlusion Culling,** which will be discussed in Chapter 6, *Dynamic Graphics*), but these are only rendering optimizations. Frustum and Occlusion Culling do not affect components that perform tasks on the CPU, such as AI scripts, user interface, and gameplay logic. We must control their behavior ourselves.

A good solution to this problem is using the OnBecameVisible() and OnBecameInvisible() callbacks. As the names imply, these callback methods are invoked when a renderable object has become visible or invisible with respect to any cameras in our scene. Also, when there are multiple cameras in a scene (for example, a local multiplayer game), the callbacks are only invoked if the object becomes visible to any one camera and becomes invisible to all cameras. This means that the aforementioned callbacks will be called at exactly the right times we expect; if nobody can see it, OnBecameInvisible() gets called, and if at least one player can see it, OnBecameVisible() gets called.

Since the visibility callbacks must communicate with the rendering pipeline, GameObject must have a renderable component attached, such as MeshRenderer or SkinnedMeshRenderer. We must ensure that the components we want to receive the visibility callbacks from are also attached to the same GameObject instance as the renderable object and are not a parent or child GameObject; otherwise, they won't be invoked.

Note that Unity also counts the hidden camera of the **Scene** window toward the OnBecameVisible() and OnBecameInvisible() callbacks. If we find that these methods are not being invoked properly during Playmode testing, ensure that you turn the **Scene** window camera away from everything or disable the **Scene** window entirely.

To enable/disable individual components with the visibility callbacks, we can add the following methods:

```
void OnBecameVisible() { enabled = true; }
void OnBecameInvisible() { enabled = false; }
```

Also, to enable/disable the entire `GameObject` the component is attached to, we can implement the methods this way instead:

```
void OnBecameVisible() { gameObject.SetActive(true); }
void OnBecameInvisible() { gameObject.SetActive(false); }
```

Although, be warned that disabling the `GameObject` containing the renderable object, or one of its parents, will make it impossible for `OnBecameVisible()` to be called since there's now no graphical representation for the camera to see and trigger the callback with. We should place the component on a child `GameObject`, and have the script disable that instead, leaving the renderable object always visible (or find another way to re-enable it later).

Disabling objects by distance

In other situations, we may want components or GameObjects to be disabled after they are far enough away from the player such that they may be barely visible, but too far away to matter. A good candidate for this type of activity is roaming Non-Player Character creatures: we want to see them at a distance, but where we don't need them to process anything, and therefore they can sit idle until we get closer.

The following code is a simple coroutine that periodically checks the total distance from a given target object and disables itself if it strays too far away from it:

```
[SerializeField] GameObject _target;
[SerializeField] float _maxDistance;
[SerializeField] int _coroutineFrameDelay;

void Start() {
  StartCoroutine(DisableAtADistance());
}

IEnumerator DisableAtADistance() {
  while(true) {
    float distSqrd = (transform.position -
_target.transform.position).sqrMagnitude;
    if (distSqrd < _maxDistance * _maxDistance) {
      enabled = true;
    } else {
      enabled = false;
    }

    for (int i = 0; i < _coroutineFrameDelay; ++i) {
      yield return new WaitForEndOfFrame();
```

```
    }
  }
}
```

We should assign the player's character object (or whatever object we want it to compare with) to the `_target` field in the **Inspector** window, define the maximum distance in `_maxDistance`, and modify the frequency with which the coroutine is invoked using the `_coroutineFrameDelay` field. Anytime the object goes further than `_maxDistance` distance away from the object assigned to `_target`, it will be disabled. It will be re-enabled if it returns within that distance.

A subtle performance-enhancing feature of this implementation is comparing against distance-squared instead of the raw distance. This leads us conveniently to our next section.

Using distance-squared over distance

It is safe to say that CPUs are relatively good at multiplying floating-point numbers together, but relatively dreadful at calculating square roots from them. Every time we ask `Vector3` to calculate a distance with the `magnitude` property or with the `Distance()` method, we're asking it to perform a square root calculation (as per Pythagorean theorem), which can cost a lot of CPU overhead compared to many other types of vector math calculations.

However, the `Vector3` class also offers a `sqrMagnitude` property, which provides the same result as distance, only the value is squared. This means that if we also square the value we wish to compare distance against, then we can perform essentially the same comparison without the cost of an expensive square-root calculation.

For example, consider the following code:

```
float distance = (transform.position -
other.transform.position).Distance();
if (distance < targetDistance) {
  // do stuff
}
```

This can be replaced with the following and achieve a nearly identical result:

```
float distanceSqrd = (transform.position -
other.transform.position).sqrMagnitude;
if (distanceSqrd < (targetDistance * targetDistance)) {
  // do stuff
}
```

The reason the result is nearly identical is because of the floating-point precision. We're likely to lose some of the precision that we would have had from using the square root values, since the value will be adjusted to an area with a different density of representable numbers; it could land exactly on, or closer to, a more accurate representable number, or, more likely, it will land on a number with less accuracy. As a result, the comparison is not exactly the same, but, in most cases, it is close enough to be unnoticeable, and the performance gain can be quite significant for each instruction we replace in this manner.

If this minor precision loss is not important, then this performance trick should be considered. However, if precision is very important (such as running an accurate large-scale galactic space simulation), then you may want to give this tip a pass.

Note that this technique can be used for any square-root calculations, not just for distance. This is simply the most common example you might come across, and it brings to light the important `sqrMagnitude` property of the `Vector3` class. This is a property that Unity Technologies intentionally exposed for us to make use of in this manner.

Minimizing deserialization behavior

Unity's serialization system is mainly used for scenes, Prefabs, ScriptableObjects, and various asset types (which tend to derive from ScriptableObject). When one of these object types is saved to disk, it is converted into a text file using the **Yet Another Markup Language (YAML)** format, which can be deserialized back into the original object type at a later time. All GameObjects and their properties get serialized when a Prefab or scene is serialized, including `private` and `protected` fields and all of their components, as well as child GameObjects and their components and so on.

When our application is built, this serialized data is bundled together in large binary data files internally called serialized files in Unity. Reading and deserializing this data from disk at runtime is an incredibly slow process (relatively speaking) and so all deserialization activity comes with a significant performance cost.

This kind of deserialization takes place anytime we call `Resources.Load()` for a file path found under a folder named `Resources`. Once the data has been loaded from disk into memory, then reloading the same reference later is much faster, but disk activity is always required the first time it is accessed. Naturally, the larger the dataset we need to deserialize, the longer this process takes. Since every component of a Prefab gets serialized, then the deeper the hierarchy is, the more data needs to be deserialized.

This can be a problem for Prefabs with very deep hierarchies, Prefabs with many empty GameObjects (since every `GameObject` always contains at least a `Transform` component), and particularly problematic for **User Interface (UI)** Prefabs, since they tend to house many more components than a typical Prefab.

Loading in large serialized datasets like these could cause a significant spike in CPU the first time they are loaded, which tends to increase loading time if they're needed immediately at the start of the scene. More importantly, they can cause frame drops if they are loaded at runtime. There are a couple of approaches we can use to minimize the costs of deserialization.

Reducing serialized object size

We should aim to make our serialized objects as small as possible or partition them into smaller data pieces we combine together piece by piece so that they can be loaded one piece at a time over time. This can be tricky to manage for Prefabs since Unity does not inherently support nested Prefabs, and so we would be implementing such a system ourselves, which is a notoriously difficult problem to solve in Unity. UI Prefabs are good candidates for separating into smaller pieces since we don't normally need the entire UI at any given moment, and so we can usually afford to load them in one piece at a time.

Loading serialized objects asynchronously

Prefabs and other serialized content can be loaded in asynchronously via `Resources.LoadAsync()`, which will offload reading from disk onto a worker thread that eases the burden on the main thread. It will take some time for the serialized object to become available, which can be checked by calling the `isDone` property on the `ResourceRequest` object returned by the previous method call.

This is not ideal for Prefabs we need immediately at the start of the game, but all future Prefabs are good candidates for asynchronous loading if we're willing to create systems that manage this behavior.

Keeping previously loaded serialized objects in memory

As previously mentioned, once a serialized object has been loaded into memory, then it remains there and can be copied if we need it again later, such as instantiating more copies of a Prefab. We can free this data later with explicit calls to `Resources.Unload()`, which will release the memory space to be reused later. But if we have a lot of surplus memory in the application's budget, then we could choose to keep this data in memory, which would reduce the need to reload it again from disk later. This naturally consumes a lot of memory with more and more serialized data, making it a risky strategy for memory management, and so we should only do this when necessary.

Moving common data into ScriptableObjects

If we have a lot of different Prefabs with components that contain a lot of properties that tend to share data, such as game design values such as hit points, strength, and speed, then all of this data will be serialized into every Prefab that uses them. A better approach is to serialize this common data in a `ScriptableObject`, which they load and use instead. This reduces the amount of data stored within the serialized file for the Prefab and could significantly reduce the loading time of our scenes by avoiding too much repetitive work.

Loading scenes additively and asynchronously

Scenes can be loaded either to replace the current scene or can be loaded additively to add its contents to the current scene without unloading the preceding one. This can be toggled via the `LoadSceneMode` argument of the `SceneManager.LoadScene()` family of functions.

Another mode of scene loading is to complete it either synchronously or asynchronously, and there are good reasons to use both. Synchronous loading is the typical means of loading a scene by calling `SceneManager.LoadScene()`, where the main thread will block until the given scene completes loading. This normally results in poor user experience, as the game appears to freeze as the contents are loaded in (whether as a replacement or additively). This is best used if we want to get the player into the action as soon as possible, or we have no time to wait for scene objects to appear. This would normally be used if we're loading into the first level of the game or returning to the main menu.

For future scene loading, however, we may wish to reduce the performance impact so that we can continue to keep the player in action. Loading a scene can take a lot of work, and the larger the scene, the longer it will take. However, the option of asynchronous additive loading offers a huge benefit: we can let the scene gradually load in the background without causing a significant impact on the user experience. This can be accomplished with `SceneManager.LoadSceneAsync()` combined with passing in `LoadSceneMode.Additive` for the loading mode argument.

It's important to realize that scenes do not strictly follow the concept of a game level. In most games, players are normally trapped in one level at a time, but Unity can support multiple scenes being loaded simultaneously through additive loading, allowing each scene to represent a small chunk of a level. Ergo, we could initialize the first scene for the level (*Scene-1-1a*), and as the player nears the next section, asynchronously and additively load in the next (*Scene-1-1b*), and repeat this continuously as the player travels through the level.

Exploiting this feature would require a system that either constantly checks the player's position in the level until they get close or uses trigger volumes to broadcast a message that the player is nearing the next section and begin asynchronous loading at the appropriate time. Another important consideration is that the scene's contents won't appear immediately since asynchronous loading effectively spreads the loading out over a handful of frames to cause as little visible impact as possible. We need to make sure that we trigger asynchronous scene loading with more than enough time to spare so that the player won't see objects popping into the game.

Scenes can also be unloaded to clear them out of memory. This will save some memory or runtime performance in the form of removing any components making use of `Update()` that we no longer need. Again, this can be done both synchronously and asynchronously with `SceneManager.UnloadScene()` and `SceneManager.UnloadSceneAsync()`. This can be an enormous performance benefit because we're only using what we need due to the player's location in the level, but note that it is not possible to unload small chunks of a monolithic scene. If the original scene file was enormous, then unloading it would unload everything. The original scene would have to be broken up into smaller scenes and then loaded and unloaded as needed. Similarly, we should only begin to unload a scene if we're certain the player can no longer see its constituent objects; otherwise, they would witness objects disappearing out of nowhere. One last consideration is that scene unloading would trigger the destruction of many objects, which is likely to free up a lot of memory and trigger the garbage collector. The efficient use of memory is also important when making use of this tip.

This approach would require a significant amount of scene redesign work, scriptwriting, testing, and debugging, which is not to be underestimated, but the benefits of improving user experience are exceptional. Having seamless transitions between areas in a game is a benefit that is often praised by players and critics because it doesn't take the player out of the action. If we use it appropriately, it can save a significant amount of runtime performance, improving the user experience further.

Creating a custom Update() layer

Earlier in this chapter, in the *Update, coroutines, and InvokeRepeating* section, we discussed the relative pros and cons of using these Unity Engine features as a means of avoiding excessive CPU workload during most of our frames. Regardless of which of these approaches we might adopt, there is an additional risk of having lots of MonoBehaviours written to periodically call some function, which is having too many methods triggering in the same frame simultaneously.

Imagine thousands of MonoBehaviours that initialized together at the start of a scene, each starting a coroutine at the same time that will process their AI tasks every 500 milliseconds. It is highly likely that they would all trigger within the same frame, causing a huge spike in its CPU usage for a moment, which settles down temporarily and then spikes again a few moments later when the next round of AI processing is due. Ideally, we would want to spread these invocations out over time.

The following are the possible solutions to this problem:

- Generating a random amount of time to wait each time the timer expires or a coroutine triggers
- Spreading out coroutine initialization so that only a handful of them are started at each frame
- Passing the responsibility of calling updates to some God class that places a limit on the number of invocations that occur each frame

The first two options are appealing since they're relatively simple and we know that coroutines can potentially save us a lot of unnecessary overhead. However, as we discussed, there are many dangers and unexpected side effects associated with such drastic design changes.

A potentially better approach to optimize updates is to not use Update() at all—or, more accurately, to use it only once. When Unity calls Update(), and in fact, any of its callbacks, it crosses the aforementioned Native-Managed Bridge, which can be a costly task. In other words, the processing cost of executing 1,000 separate Update() callbacks will be more expensive than executing one Update() callback, which calls into 1,000 regular functions. As we witnessed in the *Remove empty callback definitions* section, calling Update() thousands of times is not a trivial amount of work for the CPU to undertake, primarily because of the bridge. We can, therefore, minimize how often Unity needs to cross the bridge by having a God class MonoBehaviour use its own Update() callback to call our own custom update-style system used by our custom components.

In fact, many Unity developers prefer implementing this design right from the start of their projects, as it gives them finer control over when and how updates propagate throughout the system; this can be used for things such as menu pausing, cool-time manipulation effects, or prioritizing important tasks and/or suspending low-priority tasks if we detect that we're about to reach our CPU budget for the current frame.

All objects wanting to integrate with such a system must have a common entry point. We can achieve this through an Interface class with the interface keyword. An Interface is a code construct used to essentially set up a contract whereby any class that implements the Interface class must provide a specific series of methods. In other words, if we know the object implements an Interface class, then we can be certain about what methods are available. In C#, classes can only derive from a single base class, but they can implement any number of Interface classes (this avoids the *deadly diamond of death* problem that C++ programmers will be familiar with).

The following Interface class definition will suffice, which only requires the implementing class to define a single method called OnUpdate():

```
public interface IUpdateable {
  void OnUpdate(float dt);
}
```

It's common practice to start an Interface class definition with an uppercase "I" to make it clear that it is an Interface class we're dealing with. The beauty of Interface classes is that they improve the decoupling of our code base, allowing huge subsystems to be replaced, and as long as the Interface class is adhered to, we will have greater confidence that it will continue to function as intended.

Next, we'll define a custom `MonoBehaviour` type that implements this `Interface` class:

```
public class UpdateableComponent : MonoBehaviour, IUpdateable {
  public virtual void OnUpdate(float dt) {}
}
```

Note that we're naming the method `OnUpdate()` rather than `Update()`. We're defining a custom version of the same concept, but we want to avoid name collisions with the built-in `Update()` callback.

The `OnUpdate()` method of the `UpdateableComponent` class retrieves the current delta time (`dt`), which spares us from a bunch of unnecessary `Time.deltaTime` calls, which are commonly used in `Update()` callbacks. We've also created the `virtual` function to allow derived classes to customize it.

This function will never be called as it's currently being written. Unity automatically grabs and invokes methods defined with the `Update()` name, but has no concept of our `OnUpdate()` function, so we will need to implement something that will call this method when the time is appropriate. For example, some kind of `GameLogic` God class could be used for this purpose.

During the initialization of this component, we should do something to notify our `GameLogic` object of both its existence and its destruction so that it knows when to start and stop calling its `OnUpdate()` function.

In the following example, we will assume that our `GameLogic` class is `SingletonComponent`, as defined earlier, in the *Singleton components* section, and has appropriate `static` functions defined for registration and deregistration. Bear in mind that it could just as easily use the aforementioned `MessagingSystem` to notify `GameLogic` of its creation/destruction.

For MonoBehaviours to hook into this system, the most appropriate place is within their `Start()` and `OnDestroy()` callbacks:

```
void Start() {
  GameLogic.Instance.RegisterUpdateableObject(this);
}

void OnDestroy() {
  if (GameLogic.Instance.IsAlive) {
    GameLogic.Instance.DeregisterUpdateableObject(this);
  }
}
```

It is best to use the `Start()` method for the task of registration, since using `Start()` means that we can be certain all other pre-existing components will have at least had their `Awake()` methods called prior to this moment. This way, any critical initialization work will have already been done on the object before we start invoking updates on it.

Note that because we're using `Start()` in a `MonoBehaviour` base class, if we define a `Start()` method in a derived class, it will effectively override the base class definition, and Unity will grab the derived `Start()` method as a callback instead. It would, therefore, be wise to implement a virtual `Initialize()` method so that derived classes can override it to customize initialization behavior without interfering with the base class's task of notifying the `GameLogic` object of our component's existence.

The following code provides an example of how we might implement a virtual `Initialize()` method:

```
void Start() {
    GameLogic.Instance.RegisterUpdateableObject(this);
    Initialize();
}

protected virtual void Initialize() {
    // derived classes should override this method for initialization code,
and NOT reimplement Start()
}
```

Finally, we will need to implement the `GameLogic` class. The implementation is effectively the same whether it is `SingletonComponent` or `MonoBehaviour`, and whether or not it uses `MessagingSystem`. Either way, our `UpdateableComponent` class must register and deregister as `IUpdateable` objects, and the `GameLogic` class must use its own `Update()` callback to iterate through every registered object and call their `OnUpdate()` function.

Here is the definition for our `GameLogic` class:

```
public class GameLogicSingletonComponent :
SingletonComponent<GameLogicSingletonComponent> {
    public static GameLogicSingletonComponent Instance {
        get { return ((GameLogicSingletonComponent)_Instance); }
        set { _Instance = value; }
    }

    List<IUpdateable> _updateableObjects = new List<IUpdateable>();

    public void RegisterUpdateableObject(IUpdateable obj) {
        if (!_updateableObjects.Contains(obj)) {
```

```
        _updateableObjects.Add(obj);
      }
    }
    public void DeregisterUpdateableObject(IUpdateable obj) {
      if (_updateableObjects.Contains(obj)) {
        _updateableObjects.Remove(obj);
      }
    }

    void Update()
    {
      float dt = Time.deltaTime;
      for (int i = 0; i < _updateableObjects.Count; ++i) {
        _updateableObjects[i].OnUpdate(dt);
      }
    }
  }
}
```

If we make sure that all of our custom components inherit from the
UpdateableComponent class, then we've effectively replaced N invocations of
the Update() callback with just one Update() callback, plus N virtual function calls. This
can save us a large amount of performance overhead because even though we're calling
virtual functions (which cost a small overhead more than non-virtual function calls because
they need to redirect the call to the correct place), we're still keeping the overwhelming
majority of update behavior inside our managed code and avoiding the Native-Managed
Bridge as much as possible. This class can even be expanded to provide priority systems, to
skip low-priority tasks if it detects that the current frame has taken too long, and many
other possibilities.

Depending on how deep you already are into your current project, such changes can be
incredibly daunting, time-consuming, and likely to introduce a lot of bugs as subsystems
are updated to make use of a completely different set of dependencies. However, the
benefits can outweigh the risks if time is on your side. It would be wise to do some testing
on a group of objects in a scene that is similarly designed to your current scene files to
verify that the benefits outweigh the costs.

Summary

This chapter introduced you to many methods that will improve your scripting practices in the Unity Engine and to improve performance if (and only if) you have already proven some scripts are the cause of a performance problem. Some of these techniques demand some forethought and profiling investigation before being implemented since they often come with introducing additional risks or obfuscating our code base. Workflow is often just as important as performance and design, so before you make any performance changes to the code, you should consider whether or not you're sacrificing too much on the altar of performance optimization.

We will investigate more advanced scripting improvement techniques later, in Chapter 8, *Masterful Memory Management*, but let's take a break from staring at code and explore some ways to improve graphics performance using a pair of built-in Unity features known as dynamic batching and static batching.

Section 2: Graphical Optimizations

The readers will learn how to optimize the graphical stack of a Unity game/application. The chapters in this section are as follows:

The Benefits of Batching 3

In 3D graphics and games, batching is a very general term used to describe the process of grouping a large number of wayward pieces of data together and processing them as a single, large block of data. This situation is ideal for CPUs, and particularly GPUs, which can handle the simultaneous processing of multiple tasks with their multiple cores. Having a single core switching back and forth between different locations in memory takes time, so the less this needs to be done, the better.

In some cases, the act of batching refers to large sets of meshes, vertices, edges, UV coordinates, and other different data types that are used to represent a 3D object; however, the term could just as easily refer to the act of batching audio files, sprites, texture files, and other large datasets.

So, just to clear up any confusion, when the topic of batching is mentioned in Unity, it is usually referring to the two primary mechanisms it offers for batching mesh data: **dynamic batching** and **static batching**. These methods are essentially two different forms of geometry merging, where we combine the mesh data of multiple objects together and render them all in a single instruction, as opposed to preparing and drawing each one separately.

The process of batching together multiple meshes into a single mesh is possible because there is no reason why a mesh object must fill a contiguous volume of 3D space. The Rendering Pipeline is perfectly happy with accepting a collection of vertices that are not attached together with edges, and so we can take multiple separate meshes that might have resulted in multiple render instructions and combine them together into a single mesh, thereby rendering it using a single instruction.

There has been a lot of confusion over the years surrounding the conditions under which the dynamic batching and static batching systems activate and where we might even see an improvement in performance. After all, in some cases, batching can actually degrade performance if it is not used wisely. A proper understanding of these systems will give us the knowledge we need to improve the graphics performance of our application in significant ways.

This chapter intends to dispel much of the misinformation floating around about these systems. We will see, via explanation, exploration, and examples, just how these two batching methods operate. This will enable us to make informed decisions, using most of them to improve our application's performance.

We will cover the following topics in this chapter:

- A brief introduction to the Rendering Pipeline and the concept of draw calls
- How Unity's materials and shaders work together to render our objects
- Using the Frame Debugger to visualize rendering behavior
- How dynamic batching works, and how to optimize it
- How static batching works, and how to optimize it

Draw calls

Before we discuss dynamic batching and static batching, let's first learn about the problems that they are both trying to solve within the Rendering Pipeline. We will try to keep our analysis fairly light on the technicalities as we will explore this topic in greater detail in Chapter 6, *Dynamic Graphics*.

The primary goal of these batching methods is to reduce the number of draw calls required to render all objects in the current view. At its most basic form, a draw call is a request sent from the CPU to the GPU asking it to draw an object.

 Draw call is the common industry vernacular for this process, although they are sometimes referred to as **SetPass Calls** in Unity since some low-level methods are named as such. Think of this as configuring options before initiating the current rendering pass. We will refer to them as draw calls throughout the remainder of this book.

Before a draw call can be requested, the system needs to perform several operations. The complete list is too long for this book, and depends on the specific features enabled on Unity; however, we can categorize them into two significant steps:

1. Upload assets and meshes to the GPU
2. Set up the rendering of the meshes using the uploaded assets.

In the first step, mesh and texture data must be pushed from the CPU memory (RAM) into GPU memory (VRAM), which typically takes place during the initialization of the scene, but only for textures and meshes that the scene file knows about. If we dynamically instantiate objects at runtime using texture and mesh data that hasn't appeared in the scene yet, then they must be loaded at the time we instantiate them. The scene cannot know ahead of time which Prefabs we're planning to instantiate at runtime, as many of them are hidden behind conditional statements and much of our application's behavior depends upon user input.

In the second step, the CPU must prepare the GPU by configuring the options and rendering features that are needed to process the object that is the target of the draw call.

To handle all these interactions between the CPU and GPU, we use the underlying graphics API, which could be DirectX, OpenGL, OpenGLES, Metal, WebGL, or Vulkan, depending on the platform we're targeting and the specific graphical settings we are using. These API calls go through a library—called a **driver**—which maintains a long series of complex and interrelated settings, state variables, and datasets that can be configured and executed from our application. The available features change enormously based on the graphics card we're using and the version of the graphics API we're targeting. More advanced graphics cards support more advanced features, which would need to be supported by newer versions of the API, so updated drivers would be needed to enable them. The sheer number of settings, features, and compatibility levels between one version and another that have been created over the years (particularly for older APIs such as DirectX and OpenGL) is nothing short of mind boggling. Thankfully, at a certain level of abstraction, all of these APIs tend to operate similarly, which means that Unity can support many different graphics APIs through a common interface.

To refer to this utterly massive array of settings that must be configured to prepare the Rendering Pipeline just before rendering an object, we often use a single term: **Render State**. Until these **Render State** options remain the same, the GPU maintains the last **Render State** settings for all incoming objects and renders them accordingly.

Changing any of the **Render State** settings can be a time-consuming process. For example, if we set the **Render State** to use a blue texture file, and then we try to render one gigantic mesh, it would be rendered very rapidly, with the whole mesh appearing blue. At this point, we could render nine more completely different meshes, and they would all be rendered blue since we haven't changed which texture the GPU should use in **Render State**. If, however, we wanted to render 10 meshes using 10 different textures, then this would take longer because we would need to prepare **Render State** with the new texture for each mesh just before sending the draw call instruction.

The texture used to render the current object is effectively a global variable in the graphics API, and changing a global variable within a parallel system is much easier said than done. In a massively parallel system such as a GPU, we must effectively wait until all of the current jobs have reached the same synchronization point (in other words, the fastest cores need to stop and wait for the slowest ones to catch up, wasting processing time could be used on other tasks) before we can make **Render State** change, at which point we will need to spin up all of the parallel jobs again. This continuous waiting can waste a lot of time, and therefore the less we need to ask **Render State** to change, the faster the graphics API will be able to process our requests.

Things that can trigger **Render State** synchronization include—but are not limited to—an immediate push of a new texture to the GPU and changing a shader, lighting information, shadows, transparency, and pretty much any graphical setting we can think of.

Once we configure **Render State**, the CPU must decide what mesh to draw, what textures and shader it should use, and where to draw the object based on its position, rotation, and scale (all represented within a 4 x 4 matrix known as a **transform**, which is where the Transform component gets its name from), and then send an instruction to the GPU to draw it. To keep the communication between the CPU and GPU very dynamic, Unity pushes new instructions into a queue known as the **command buffer**. This queue contains instructions that the CPU has created, from which the GPU pulls a new command each time it finishes the preceding one.

The trick to how batching improves the performance of this process is that a new draw call does not necessarily mean that we need to configure a new **Render State**. If two objects share the exact same **Render State** information, then the GPU can immediately begin rendering the new object since the same **Render State** is maintained after the last object is finished. This eliminates the time wasted because of **Render State** synchronization. It also reduces the number of instructions that need to be pushed into the command buffer, reducing the workload on both the CPU and GPU.

Materials and shaders

Render State in Unity is essentially exposed to us via **materials**. Materials are containers around shaders, short programs that define how the GPU should render incoming vertex and texture data. A shader on its own does not have the necessary knowledge of the state to accomplish anything of value. A shader requires input such as diffuse textures, normal maps, and lighting information, and effectively dictates what **Render State** variables need to be set in order to render the incoming data.

Shaders are named this way because, many years ago, their original implementation was to only handle the lighting and shading of an object (applying shadows where originally there were none). Their purpose has grown enormously since then, and now they have the much more generic purpose of being a programmable access point to many different kinds of parallel tasks, but the old name still remains.

Every shader needs a material, and every material must have a shader. Even newly imported meshes introduced into the scene without an assigned material are automatically assigned a default (hidden) material, which gives them a basic diffuse shader and a white coloration, so there is no way of getting around this relationship.

Note that a single material can only support a single shader. The use of multiple shaders on the same mesh requires separate materials to be assigned to different parts of the same mesh.

Therefore, if we want to minimize how often **Render State** changes, then we can do so by reducing the number of materials we use during a scene. This would result in two performance improvements simultaneously: the CPU will spend less time generating and transmitting instructions to the GPU during each frame and the GPU won't need to stop and resynchronize state changes as often.

Let's begin with a simple scene in order to visualize the behavior of materials and batching. However, before we start, we should disable a few rendering options, as they will contribute some extra draw calls, which might be distracting:

1. Navigate to **Edit | Project Settings | Quality** and set **Shadows** to **Disable Shadows** (or select the default **Fastest** quality level)
2. Navigate to **Edit | Project Settings | Player**, open the **Other Settings** tab, and disable **Static Batching** and **Dynamic Batching**, if they are enabled

Next, we'll create a scene that contains a single directional light with four cubes and four spheres, where each object has its own unique material, position, rotation, and scale, as shown in the following screenshot:

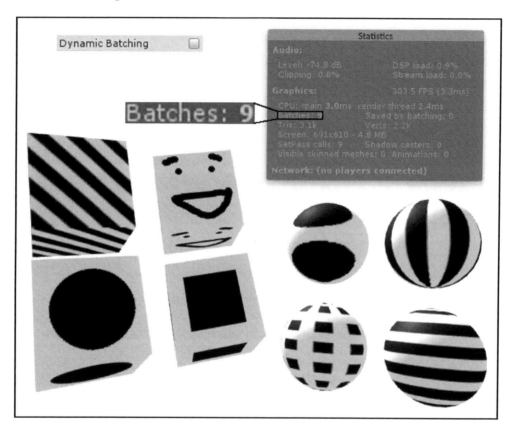

In the preceding screenshot, we can see 9 total batches in the **Batching** value in the **Game** window's **Stats** popup. This value closely represents the number of draw calls used to render the scene. The current view will consume one of these batches that renders the background of the scene, which could be set to **Skybox** or **Solid Color**. This is determined by the camera object's **Clear Flags** settings.

The remaining eight batches are used to draw our eight objects. In each case, the draw call involves preparing the Rendering Pipeline using the material's properties and asking the GPU to render the given mesh at its current transform. We have ensured that each material is unique by giving them each a unique texture file to render. So, each mesh requires a different **Render State**, and, therefore, each of our eight meshes requires a unique draw call.

As previously mentioned, we can theoretically minimize the number of draw calls by reducing how often we cause the system to change **Render State** information; so, part of the goal is to reduce the number of materials we use. However, if we configure all objects to use the same material, we still won't see any benefit, and the number of batches will remain at nine:

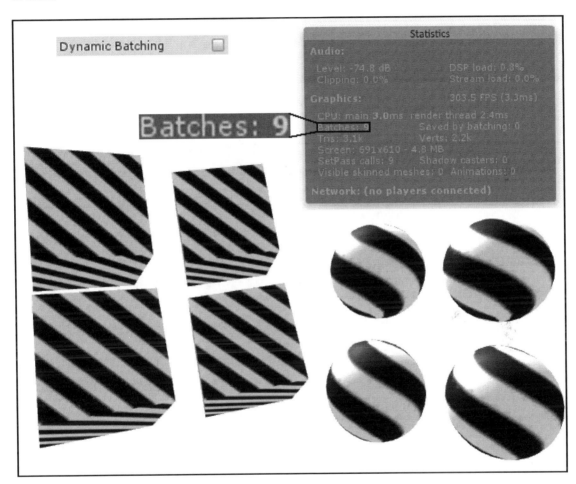

This is because we're not actually reducing the number of **Render State** changes, nor are we efficiently grouping mesh information. Unfortunately, the Rendering Pipeline is not smart enough to realize we're overwriting the exact same **Render State** values and then asking it to render the same meshes over and over again.

The Frame Debugger

Before we dive into how batching can save us draw calls, let's explore a useful tool that can help us to determine how batching is affecting our scene—the Frame Debugger.

We can open **Frame Debugger** by selecting **Window** | **Analysis** | **Frame Debugger** from the main window or clicking on the **Frame Debugger** button in **Breakdown View Options** in the rendering area of the Profiler. Either approach will open the **Frame Debug** window.

Clicking on the **Enable** button in the **Frame Debug** window will allow us to observe how our scene is being constructed, one draw call at a time. The following screenshot shows the user interface of the Frame Debugger, with a list of GPU instructions in the left-hand panel and more detailed information in the right-hand panel:

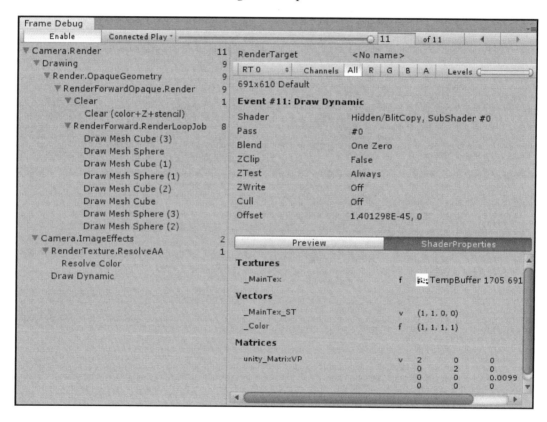

There is a lot of information in this window that can provide us with useful information if we want to debug the behavior of a single draw call, but the most useful area to look at is the **Drawing** section in the left-hand panel, which lists all of the draw calls in our scene.

Each item in this section represents a unique draw call and what was rendered by it. An amazingly useful feature of this tool is the ability to click on any one of these items and immediately observe only the draw calls needed to render the scene up to that point in the **Game** window. This lets us see visually the differences between two sequential draw calls. This can make it easy to spot exactly which object(s) were rendered by a given draw call. This can help determine whether or not a set of objects were batched together by looking at how many of them appear during that draw call.

 A weird bug with the Frame Debugger (which still exists in early builds of Unity 2019) is that if we are observing a scene that is making use of a skybox and click on various items under the **Drawing** section, then only the final scene presentation can be observed in the **Game** window. We would need to temporarily disable the skybox via the camera's **Clear Flags** setting to look at how the draw call progression appears in the **Game** window by setting it to **Solid Color** instead.

As we can see in the preceding Frame Debugger screenshot, one draw call is being consumed to clear the screen (the item labeled **Clear**), and then our eight meshes are being rendered in eight separate draw calls (the item labeled `RenderForward.RenderLoopJob`).

 Note that the number next to each item in the left-hand panel actually represents a graphics API call, of which a draw call is but one type of API call. These can be seen in the `Camera.Render`, `Camera.ImageEffects`, and `RenderTexture.ResolveAA` items. Any API call can be just as costly as a draw call, but the overwhelming majority of API calls we will make in a complex scene will be in the form of draw calls, so it is often best to focus on minimizing draw calls before worrying about the API communication overhead of things such as post processing effects.

Dynamic batching

Dynamic batching has the following three important qualities:

- Batches are generated at runtime (batches are dynamically generated)
- The objects that are contained within a batch can vary from one frame to the next, depending on what meshes are currently visible to the **Main Camera** view (batch contents are dynamic)
- Even objects that can move around the scene can be batched (it works on dynamic objects)

These attributes lead us to the name **Dynamic Batching**.

If we return to the **Player Settings** page and enable **Dynamic Batching,** we should see that the number of batches drops from nine down to six. **Dynamic Batching** automatically recognizes that our objects share material and mesh information and, therefore, combines some of them into a larger batch for processing. We should also see a different list of items in the Frame Debugger, demonstrating that meshes are now being dynamically batched:

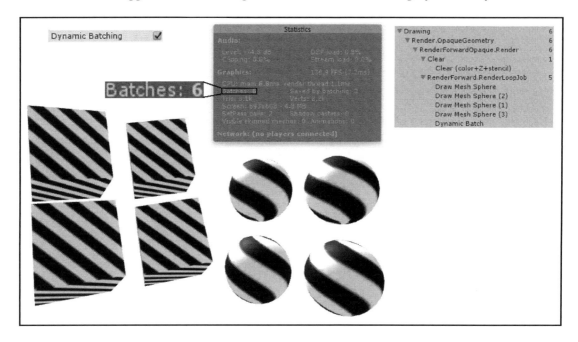

As we can see from the Frame Debugger, our four boxes have been combined into a single draw call named **Dynamic Batch,** but our four spheres are still being rendered with four separate draw calls. This is because the four spheres do not fit the requirements of dynamic batching, despite the fact that they all use the same material. There are many more requirements we must fulfill.

You can find the list of the requirements needed to successfully dynamically batch a mesh in the Unity documentation at this address: `http://docs.unity3d.com/Manual/DrawCallBatching.html`.

The following list covers the requirements to enable dynamic batching for a given mesh:

- All mesh instances must use the same material reference.
- Only `ParticleSystem` and `MeshRenderer` components are dynamically batched. The `SkinnedMeshRenderer` components (for animated characters) and all other renderable component types cannot be batched.

- There is a limit of 300 vertices per mesh; however, the total number of vertex attributes used by the shader must be no greater than 900. This means that for complex shaders, the maximum number of vertices per mesh may be less than 300 (see the *Vertex attributes* section for more details).
- The objects must not contain mirroring on the transform (that is, a `GameObject` A with a positive scale and a `GameObject` B with a negative scale cannot be batched together).
- Mesh instances should refer to the same lightmap file.
- The material's shader should not depend on multiple passes.
- Mesh instances must not receive real-time shadows.
- There is an upper limit on the total number of mesh indices in the entire batch, which varies for the graphics API and platform used, which is around 32,000–64,000 indices (check out the documentation/previously mentioned blog post for specifics).

It is important to note the term **material references** because, if we happen to use two different materials with identical settings, the Rendering Pipeline is not smart enough to realize that, and they will be treated as different materials and, therefore, will be disqualified from dynamic batching. Most of the rest of these requirements have already been explained; however, a couple of these requirements are not completely intuitive or clear from their description, which merits some additional explanation.

Vertex attributes

A vertex attribute is simply a piece of information contained within a mesh file on a per-vertex basis, and each is normally represented as a group of multiple floating-point values. This includes, but is not limited to, a vertex's position (relative to the root of the mesh), a normal vector (a vector pointing away from the object's surface, most often used in lighting calculations), one or more sets of texture UV coordinates (used to define how one or more textures wrap around the mesh), and possibly even color information per vertex (normally used in custom lighting or for a flat shaded, low poly style object). Only meshes with fewer than 900 total vertex attributes used by the shader can be included in dynamic batching.

Note that looking into a mesh's raw data file may contain less vertex attribute information than what Unity loads into memory because of how the engine converts mesh data from one of several raw data formats into an internal format, so don't assume that the number of attributes our 3D modeling tool tells us the mesh uses will be the final count. The best way to verify the attribute count is to drill down into the mesh object in the **Project** window until you find the `MeshFilter` component and look at the **verts** value that appears in the **Preview** subsection of the **Inspector** window.

Using more attribute data per vertex within the accompanying shader will consume more from our 900-attribute budget, and therefore reduce the number of vertices the mesh is allowed to have before it can no longer be used in dynamic batching. For example, a simple diffuse shader might only use three attributes per vertex: position, normal, and a single set of UV coordinates. Dynamic watching would, therefore, be able to support meshes using this shader, which has a combined total of 300 vertices; however, a more complex shader, requiring 5 attributes per vertex, would only be able to support dynamic batching with meshes using no more than 180 vertices. Also, note that even if we are using less than 3 vertex attributes per vertex in our shader, dynamic batching still only supports meshes with a maximum of 300 vertices, so only relatively simple objects are candidates for dynamic batching.

These restrictions are why our scene saves only 3 draw calls with dynamic batching enabled, despite having all objects share the same material reference. The cube mesh that is autogenerated by Unity contains a mere 8 vertices, each with position, normal, and UV data, for 24 attributes in total. This is far less than the 300-vertex limit and 900-vertex attribute limit. However, an autogenerated sphere mesh contains 515 vertices, and therefore has 1,545 total vertex attributes. These meshes clearly exceed both the 300-vertex and 900-vertex attribute limits and, therefore, cannot be dynamically batched.

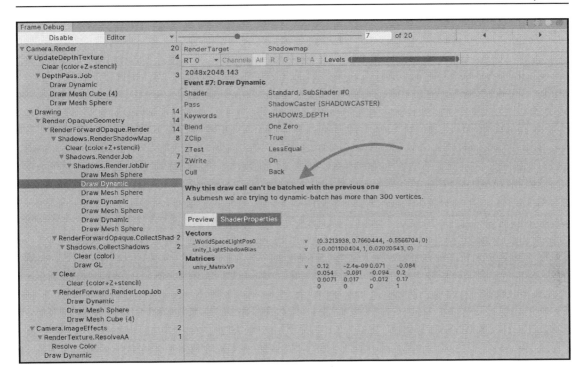

If we click on one of the draw call items in the Frame Debugger, a section labeled **Why this draw call can't be batched with the previous one** will appear. Most of the time, the explanation text beneath tells us which requirement we failed (or at least the first one it detected) and which ones can be useful for debugging batching behavior.

Mesh scaling

The documentation clearly states that using negative scaling has a strange effect on dynamic batching. Negative scaling is often a quick way to mirror a mesh in our scene, which can save us from having to create and import a completely different mesh for something that's only flipped on one axis. This trick is commonly used for pairs of doors, or just to make a scene look more varied. However, if we only negatively scale the mesh on one or three axes, then it will be placed into a different dynamic batch than meshes that are negatively scaled on zero or two axes. It does not matter which of the three values (x, y, or z) are negative, only whether the total number of negative values is odd or even.

Another strange property of how batch-splitting works behind the scene is that the rendering order of the objects can determine what gets batched together. If the previous object would have appeared in a different batch group than the current one, then it cannot be batched. Again, this is best explained by an example. Consider that we have five objects again: *V* scaled at (1, 1, 1), *W* scaled at (-1, 1, 1), *X* scaled at (-1, -1, 1), *Y* scaled at (-1, -1, -1), and finally *Z* scaled similarly to *V* at (1, 1, 1). Objects *V* and *Z* share a common uniform scale, so we might expect them to be batched together. However, if all of these objects were rendered to the scene in the preceding order, then object *V* will be rendered and Unity will test to check whether objects *W* and *V* could share a batch. They cannot because of object *W*'s odd negative scaling, so no batching will take place. Unity will then compare object *X* with object *W* to check whether they can be batched, which they cannot because *W* has an odd negative scaling and *X* has an even negative scaling. The next comparisons between objects *W-Y* and *Y-Z* fail for the same reason. The end result is that all five objects will be rendered with five separate draw calls, and there was no opportunity to combine objects *V* and *Z*. Note that this weird effect comes into play only when negative scaling is used.

Presumably, this is all a by-product of the algorithm used to detect valid batchable groups, since mirroring a mesh in two dimensions is mathematically equivalent to rotating the mesh by 180 degrees around the mirroring axis, while there is no rotational equivalent to mirroring a mesh on one or three axes. Therefore, the behavior we observe is perhaps just the dynamic batching system automatically transforming the object for us, although this isn't completely clear. Regardless, hopefully this prepares us for many of the weird situations we might run into when it comes to generating dynamic batches.

Dynamic batching summary

Dynamic batching is a very useful tool when we want to render very large groups of simple meshes. The design of the system makes it ideal to use when we're making use of large numbers of simple meshes, which are nearly identical in appearance. Some possible use cases to apply dynamic batching could be as follows:

- We want to render a large forest filled with rocks, trees, and bushes
- We want to render a building, factory, or space station with many simple, common elements (computers, corridor pieces, pipes, and so on)
- We want to build a game featuring many dynamic, non-animated objects with simple geometry and particle effects (a game such as *Geometry Wars* springs to mind)

If the only requirement preventing two objects from being dynamically batched together is the fact that they use different texture files, be aware that it only takes a bit of development time and effort to combine textures and regenerate mesh UVs so that they can be dynamically batched together (commonly known as **atlasing**). This may cost us in texture quality or the overall size of a texture file (which can have drawbacks that we will understand once we dive into the topic of GPU memory bandwidth in `Chapter 6`, *Dynamic Graphics*), but it is worth considering.

Perhaps the only situation where dynamic batching may hinder performance is if we were to set up a scene with hundreds of simple objects, where only a few objects are put into each batch. In these cases, the overhead cost of detecting and generating so many small batches might cost more time than we'd save by just making a separate draw call for each mesh. Even so, this is unlikely.

If anything, we're far more likely to inflict performance losses on our application by simply assuming that dynamic batching is taking place when we've actually forgotten one of the essential requirements. We can accidentally break the vertex limit by pushing a new version of a mesh, and in the process of Unity converting a raw object (with the `.obj` extension) file into its own internal format, it will generate more vertex attributes than we expected. We could also exceed it by tweaking some shader code or adding additional passes without realizing that this would disqualify it from dynamic batching. We might even set up the object to enable shadows or light probes, which breaks another requirement.

There will be no warning sign when these accidents occur, save for the number of draw calls increasing after changes are made and causing graphic performance to degrade further and further. Maintaining a healthy amount of dynamic batching in our scenes requires constant vigilance in checking our draw call count and looking at Frame Debugger data to make sure that we didn't accidentally disqualify objects from dynamic batching during our latest changes. However, as always, we only need to worry about our draw call performance if we've already proven that it's causing a performance bottleneck.

Ultimately, every situation is unique, so it is worth experimenting with our mesh data, materials, and shaders to determine what can and cannot be dynamically batched, as well as performing tests on our scene from time to time to ensure that the number of draw calls we're using remains reasonable.

Static batching

Unity offers a second batching mechanism known as **static batching**. This batching feature is similar to dynamic batching in a couple of ways, in that the objects that are to be batched are determined at runtime based on what's visible to the camera, and the contents of these batches will vary from frame to frame. However, there is one very important difference: it only works on objects that are marked **Static**, hence the name static batching.

The static batching system has its own set of requirements:

- As the name implies, the meshes must be flagged as **Static** (specifically, **Batching Static**)
- Additional memory must be set aside for each mesh that is being statically batched
- There is an upper limit on the number of vertices that can be combined in a static batch that varies per graphics API and platform, which is around 32,000–64,000 vertices (check out the documentation/previously mentioned blog post for specifics)
- The mesh instances can come from any source mesh, but they must share the same material reference

Let's cover some of these requirements in more detail.

The Static flag

Static batching can only be applied to objects with the **Static** flag enabled, or, more specifically, the **Batching Static** subflag (these subflags are known as **StaticEditorFlags**). Clicking on the small down arrow next to the **Static** option for a `GameObject` will reveal a drop-down list of **StaticEditorFlags**, which can alter the object's behavior for various **Static** processes.

An obvious side effect of this is that the object's transform cannot be changed, and, hence, any object wishing to make use of static batching cannot be moved, rotated, or scaled in any way.

Memory requirements

The additional memory requirement for static batching will vary, depending on the amount of replication occurring within the batched meshes. Static batching works by copying the data for all flagged and visible meshes into a single, large mesh data buffer, and passing it into the Rendering Pipeline through a single draw call while ignoring the original mesh. If all of the meshes being statically batched are unique, then this would cost us no additional memory usage compared to rendering the objects normally, as the same amount of memory space is required to store the meshes.

However, since the data is effectively copied, these statically batched duplicates cost us additional memory equal to the number of meshes, multiplied by the size of the original mesh. Ordinarily, rendering one, ten, or a million clones of the same object costs us the same amount of memory, because they're all referencing the same mesh data. The only difference between objects, in this case, is the transform of each object; however, because static batching needs to copy the data into a large buffer, this referencing is lost, since each duplicate of the original mesh is copied into the buffer with a unique set of data with a hardcoded transform baked into the vertex positions.

Therefore, using static batching to render 1,000 identical tree objects will cost us 1,000 times more memory than rendering the same trees without static batching. This causes some significant memory consumption and performance issues if static batching is not used wisely.

Material references

We are already aware that sharing material references is a means of reducing **Render State** changes, so this requirement is fairly obvious. In addition, sometimes, we statically batch meshes that require multiple materials. In this case, all meshes using a different material will be grouped together in their own static batch for each unique material being used.

The downside to this requirement is that, at best, static batching can only render all of the static meshes using a number of draw calls equal to the number of materials they need.

Static batching caveats

Because of how it approaches the batching solution (by combining meshes into a single greater mesh), the static batching system has a few caveats that we need to be aware of. These concerns range from minor inconveniences to major drawbacks, depending on the Scene:

- Draw call savings are not immediately visible from the **Stats** window until runtime
- Objects marked **Batching Static** introduced in the Scene at runtime will not be automatically included in static batching

Let's explore these problems in a little more detail.

Edit Mode debugging of static batching

Trying to determine the overall effect that static batching will have on our Scene can be a little tricky since nothing is being statically batched while in **Edit Mode**. All of the magic happens during runtime, which can make it difficult to determine what benefits static batching would provide without manual testing. We should use the Frame Debugger to verify that our static batches are being properly generated and that they contain the expected objects.

This can be especially problematic if we leave implementing this feature until late in the project life cycle, where we can spend a lot of time launching, tweaking, and relaunching our Scene to ensure that we're getting the draw call savings we're expecting. Consequently, it is best to start working on static batching optimization early in the process of building a new Scene.

It goes without saying that static batch creation work is not completely trivial, and it may also massively inflate Scene initialization time if there are many batches to create and/or many large objects to batch.

Instantiating static meshes at runtime

Any new objects we add into the Scene at runtime will not be automatically combined into any existing batch by the static batching system, even if they were marked as **Batching Static**. To do so would cause an enormous runtime overhead between recalculating the mesh and synchronizing with the Rendering Pipeline, so Unity does not even attempt to do it automatically.

For the most part, we should try to keep any meshes we want to be statically batched present in the original Scene file; however, if dynamic instantiation is necessary, or we are making use of additional Scene loading, then we can control static batch eligibility with the `StaticBatchUtility.Combine()` method. This utility method has two overloads: either we provide a root `GameObject`, in which case all child `GameObject` instances with meshes will be turned into new static batch groups, or we provide a list of `GameObject` instances and a root `GameObject`, and it will automatically attach them as children to the root and generate new static batch groups in the same manner.

We should profile our usage of this function, as it can be quite an expensive operation if there are many vertices to combine. It will also not combine the given meshes with any preexisting statically batched groups, even if they share the same material. This means that we will not be able to save draw calls by instantiating or additively loading **Static** meshes that use the same material as other statically batched groups already present in the Scene (it can only combine with meshes it was grouped with in the `Combine()` call).

Note that if any of the GameObjects we batch with the `StaticBatchUtility.Combine()` method are not marked as **Static** before batching, the GameObjects will remain non-static, but the mesh itself will be **Static**. This means that we could accidentally move the `GameObject` instance, its `Collider` component, and any other important objects, but the mesh will remain in the same location. Be careful about accidentally mixing **Static** and non-static states in statically batched objects.

Static batching summary

Static batching is a powerful, but dangerous, tool. If we don't use it wisely, we can very easily inflict enormous performance losses because of memory consumption (potentially leading to application crashes) and rendering costs on our application. It also takes a good amount of manual tweaking and configuration to ensure that batches are being properly generated and that we aren't accidentally introducing any unintended side effects of using various **Static** flags. However, it does have a significant advantage in that it can be used on meshes of different shapes and enormous sizes, which dynamic batching cannot provide.

Summary

It is clear that the dynamic batching and static batching systems are not a silver bullet. We cannot blindly apply them to any given Scene and expect improvements. If our application and Scene happen to fit a particular set of parameters, then these methods are very effective at reducing CPU load and rendering bottlenecks. However, if they do not, then some additional work is required to prepare our Scene to meet batching feature requirements. Ultimately, only a good understanding of these batching systems and how they function can help us determine where and when this feature can be applied, and, hopefully, this chapter has given us all of the information we need to make informed decisions.

You will learn more about the Rendering Pipeline and performance improvement techniques in Chapter 6, *Dynamic Graphics*. But now, let's move onto a different topic and look into some of the more subtle performance improvements that we can achieve through managing our art assets in intelligent ways.

4
Optimizing Your Art Assets

Art is a famously subjective discipline, dominated by personal opinion and preference. It can be challenging to say whether, and why, one piece of art is better than another. Oftentimes, our opinions won't be able to find a complete consensus. The technical aspects behind art assets that support a game's artistry can also be very subjective. Multiple workarounds can be implemented to improve performance, but these tend to result in a loss of quality for the sake of speed. If we're trying to reach peak performance, then we must consult with our team members whenever we decide to make any changes to our art assets, as it is primarily a balancing act, which can be an art form in itself.

Whether we're trying to minimize our runtime memory footprint, keep the smallest possible executable size, maximize loading speed, or maintain consistency in frame rate, there are plenty of options to explore. Some methods are clearly always ideal, but most require a little more care and forethought before being adopted, as they would result in reduced quality or could increase the chances of developing bottlenecks in other subsystems.

In this chapter, we will explore how to improve performance for the following asset types:

- Audio files
- Texture files
- Mesh and animation files
- Asset bundles and resources

In each case, we will investigate how Unity stores, loads, and manipulates these assets both during application build time and runtime. We will also examine our options in the event of performance issues, and what we can do to avoid behavior that might generate performance bottlenecks.

Audio

As a framework, Unity can be used to build anything from small applications that require only a handful of sound effects and a single background track to huge role-playing games that need millions of lines of spoken dialog, music tracks, and ambient sound effects. Regardless of the actual scope of the application, audio files are often a significant contributor to the application size after it is built (sometimes called its *disk footprint*). Moreover, many developers are surprised to find that runtime audio processing can turn into a significant source of CPU and memory consumption.

Audio is often neglected on both sides of the gaming industry: developers tend not to commit many resources to it until the last minute and users rarely pay attention to it. Nobody notices when audio is handled well, but we all know what lousy audio sounds like—it's instantly recognizable, jarring, and guaranteed to draw unwanted attention. This makes it crucial not to sacrifice too much audio clarity in the name of performance.

Audio bottlenecks can come from a variety of sources. Excessive compression, too much audio manipulation, too many active audio components, inefficient memory storage methods, and access speeds all lead to poor memory and CPU performance.

Fortunately, you can learn to avoid such issues with just a little effort and understanding. In the following sections, we will learn some useful tricks to save us from a user experience disaster. We will learn how to choose among the different audio loading options, how to choose the right audio format for our game, and some other relevant performance tweaks.

Importing audio files

When we select an imported audio file in the **Project** window, the **Inspector** window will reveal multiple **Import Settings**. These settings dictate everything from loading behavior, compression behavior, quality, sample rate, and (in later versions of Unity) whether to support ambisonic audio (multichannel audio, which combines tracks via spherical harmonics to create more realistic audio experiences).

Many of the audio import options can be configured on a per-platform basis, allowing us to customize behavior between different target platforms.

Loading audio files

The following are the three settings that dictate how an audio file is loaded:

- **Preload Audio Data**
- **Load In Background**
- **Load Type**

What we see when we look at an imported file in the inspector.

Our audio files are initially packaged as binary data files that are bundled with our application, which reside on the hard disk of the device (although in some cases they are downloaded from somewhere on the internet). *Loading* audio data simply means pulling it into main memory (RAM) so that it can be later processed by audio decoders, which then convert the data into audio signals to our headphones or speakers. However, how loading happens will vary enormously based on the previous three settings, which are as follows:

- The first setting, **Preload Audio Data**, determines whether audio data will be automatically loaded during scene initialization or at a later time.
- When the loading of audio data does occur, the second setting, **Load In Background**, determines whether this activity blocks the main thread until it is finished or loads it asynchronously in the background.
- Finally, the **Load Type** setting defines what kind of data gets pulled into memory and how much data gets pulled at a time.

All three of these settings can have a dramatically negative effect on performance if they are not used wisely.

The typical use case of an audio file is to assign it to the **AudioClip** property of an AudioSource component, which will wrap it in an AudioClip object. We can then trigger playback via AudioSource.Play() or AudioSource.PlayOneShot(). Each audio clip assigned in this way would be loaded into memory during scene initialization as the scene contains immediate references to these files, which it must resolve before they are needed. This is the default behavior when **Preload Audio Data** is enabled.

Disabling **Preload Audio Data** tells the Unity engine to skip audio file asset loading during scene initialization, which defers loading activity to the first moment it is needed—that is, when Play() or PlayOneShot() are called. Disabling this option will speed up scene initialization, but it also means that the first time we play the file, the CPU will need to immediately access the disk, retrieve the file, load it into memory, decompress it, and play it. This is a synchronous operation and will block the main thread until it is completed. We can prove this with a simple test:

```
public class PreloadAudioDataTest : MonoBehaviour {
  [SerializeField] AudioSource _source;

  void Update() {
    if (Input.GetKeyDown(KeyCode.Space)) {
        using (new CustomTimer("Time to play audio file", 1)) {
        _source.Play();
    }
  }
}
```

If we add an AudioSource object to our scene, assign a large audio file to it, and assign it to the _source field of the PreloadAudioDataTest component, we can press the spacebar and take a look at a printout of how long the Play() function took to complete. A simple test of this code against a 10-MB audio file with **Preload Audio Data** enabled will reveal that the call was practically instantaneous; however, disabling **Preload Audio Data**, applying the changes to the file, and repeating the test shows that it takes significantly longer (around 700 ms on a desktop PC with an Intel i5 3570K). This completely blows past our budget for a single frame, so to use this toggle responsibly, we will need to load the majority of our audio assets into memory ahead of time.

This can be achieved by calling `AudioClip.LoadAudioData()` (which can be acquired through an `AudioSource` component's `clip` property). However, this activity will still block the main thread for the same amount of time it takes to load it in the previous example, and so loading our audio file will still cause frame drops, regardless of whether we choose to load it ahead of time. Data can also be unloaded through `AudioClip.UnloadAudioData()`.

This is where the **Load In Background** option comes in. This changes audio loading into an asynchronous task, which means that loading will not block the main thread. With this option enabled, the actual call to `AudioClip.LoadAudioData()` will complete instantly, but keep in mind that the file won't be ready to play until loading completes on a separate thread. We can double-check an `AudioClip` component's current loading state through the `AudioClip.loadState` property. If **Load In Background** is enabled and we call `AudioSource.Play()` without loading the data first, Unity will still require the file to be loaded into memory before it can be played, and so there will be a delay between when we called `AudioSource.Play()` and when the audio file begins playback. This risks introducing jarring behavior if we try to access a sound file before it is fully loaded, causing it to be out of sync with other tasks, such as animations.

Modern games typically implement convenient stopping points in levels to perform tasks such as loading or unloading audio data—for example, an elevator between floors, or long corridors where minimal action is taking place. Solutions involving custom loading and unloading of audio data via these methods would need to be tailor-made to the particular game, depending on when audio files are required, how long they're needed for, how scenes are put together, and how players traverse them.

This can require a significant number of special case changes, testing, and asset management tweaks, so it is recommended that you save this approach as a *nuclear option* to be used late in production, in the event that all other techniques have not succeeded as well as we hoped.

Finally, there is the **Load Type** option, which dictates how audio data loads when it occurs. There are three options available:

- **Decompress On Load**
- **Compressed In Memory**
- **Streaming**

These three options are explained in detail in the following list:

- **Decompress On Load**: This setting compresses the file on disk to save space and decompresses it into memory when it is first loaded. This is the standard method of loading an audio file and should be used in most cases. It takes some time to decompress the file, which leads to a little extra overhead during loading, but reduces the amount of work required when the audio file is played.

- **Compressed In Memory**: This setting copies the compressed file straight from disk into memory when it is loaded. It will only decompress the audio file during runtime when it is being played. This will sacrifice runtime CPU when the audio clip is played, but improves loading speed and reduces runtime memory consumption while the audio clip remains dormant. Hence, this option is best used for very large audio files that are used relatively frequently, or if we're incredibly bottlenecked on memory consumption and are willing to sacrifice some CPU cycles to play the audio clip.

- **Streaming**: Finally, this setting (also known as *Buffered*) will load, decode, and play files on the fly at runtime by gradually pushing the file through a small buffer where only one small piece of the overall file is present in memory at a time. This method uses the least amount of memory for a particular audio clip, but the largest amount of runtime CPU. Since each instance of playback of the file will need to generate its buffer, this setting comes with the unfortunate drawback of referencing the audio clip more than once, which leads to multiple copies of the same audio clip in memory that must all be processed separately, resulting in a runtime CPU cost if used recklessly. Consequently, this option is best reserved for single-instance audio clips that play regularly and never need to overlap with other instances of themselves or even with other streamed audio clips—for example, this setting is best used with background music and ambient sound effects that need to be played during the majority of a scene's lifetime.

So, let's recap. The default case, with **Preload Audio Data** enabled, **Load In Background** disabled, and a **Load Type** of **Decompress On Load**, causes a long scene loading time, but ensures that every audio clip we reference in the scene is ready immediately when we need it. There will be no loading delays when the audio clip is needed, and the audio clip will play back the moment we call `Play()`.

A good compromise to improve scene loading time is to enable **Load In Background** for audio clips we won't need until later, but this should not be used for audio clips we need shortly after scene initialization. We then control when our audio data is loaded manually through `AudioClip.LoadAudioData()` and `AudioClip.UnloadAudioData()`. We should be willing to use all of these methods in a single scene to reach optimal performance.

Encoding formats and quality levels

Unity supports three general case encoding formats for audio clips, which are determined by the **Compression Format** option when we view an audio clip's properties in the **Inspector** window:

- **Compressed** (the actual text for this option can appear differently, depending on the platform)
- **PCM**
- **ADPCM**

The audio files we import into the Unity engine can be one of many popular audio file formats, such as Ogg Vorbis, MPEG-3 (MP3), and Wave, but the actual encoding that is bundled into the executable will be converted into a different format.

The compression algorithm used with the **Compressed** setting will depend on the platform being targeted. Standalone applications and other nonmobile platforms will convert the file into Ogg Vorbis format, whereas mobile platforms use MP3.

 There are a few platforms that always use a specific type of compression, such as HEVAG for the PS Vita, XMA for Xbox One, and AAC for WebGL.

Statistics are provided in the **Inspector** window for the currently selected format in the area following the **Compression Format** option, giving you an idea of how much disk space the compression is saving. Note that the first value displays the original file size and the second displays the size cost on disk. How much memory the audio file will consume at runtime once loaded will be determined by how efficient the chosen compression format is—for example, the Ogg Vorbis compression will generally decompress to about ten times its compressed size, whereas ADPCM will decompress to about four times the compressed size.

 The cost savings displayed in the **Inspector** window for an audio file only apply for the currently selected platform and most recently used settings. Ensure that the editor is switched to the correct platform in **File | Build Settings**, and that you click on **Apply** after making changes in order to see the actual cost savings (or cost inflation) for the current configuration. This is particularly important for WebGL applications since the AAC format generally leads to very inflated audio file sizes.

The encoding/compression format used can have a dramatic effect on the quality, file size, and memory consumption of the audio file during runtime, and only the **Compressed** setting gives us the ability to alter the quality without affecting the sampling rate of the file. Meanwhile, the **PCM** and **ADPCM** settings do not provide this luxury, and we're stuck with whatever file size those compression formats decide to give us—that is, unless we're willing to reduce audio quality for the sake of file size by reducing the sampling rate.

In the following table, you can take a glance at the differences and use cases for each format:

Format	Lossless	Size	Quality	Usage
PCM	Yes	Large	High	Very short sound effects that require a lot of clarity where any compression would otherwise distort the experience.
ADPCM	No	Very Small	Poor	Compression results in a fair amount of noise, and therefore it is used for short sound effects with a lot of chaos, such as explosions, collisions, and impact sounds.
Compressed	No	Small/Medium	Variable	This consumes more CPU for decoding and should be used in most cases. This option allows us to customize the resulting quality level of the compression algorithm to tweak the quality against the file size.

Do not forget that any additional audio effects applied to the file at runtime will not play through the editor in *Edit Mode*, so any changes should be thoroughly tested through the application in *Play Mode*.

Now that we have a better understanding of audio file formats, loading methods, and compression modes, let's explore some approaches that we can use to improve performance by tweaking audio behavior.

Audio performance enhancements

In this section, we explore some other small but important enhancements you can add to your game's sound architecture to improve the overall player experience. We will see why it is important to minimize the audio sources in a scene, in which situation we should prefer mono sounds over stereo sounds, when we should prefer streaming over preloading, and much more.

Minimizing active audio source count

Since each actively playing audio source consumes a particular amount of CPU, it stands to reason that we can save CPU cycles by disabling redundant audio sources in our scene. One approach is to limit how many instances of an audio clip can be played simultaneously. This involves sending audio playback requests through an intermediary that controls our audio sources in such a way that it puts a hard cap on how many instances of an audio clip can be played simultaneously.

Almost every audio management asset available in the Unity Asset Store implements an audio-throttling feature of some kind (often known as *audio pooling*), and for good reason: it's the best trade-off in minimizing excessive audio playback with the least cost in quality—for example, having 20 footstep sounds playing simultaneously won't sound too much different to playing 10 of them simultaneously, and is less likely to become distracting by being too loud. For this reason, and because these tools often provide many more subtle performance-enhancing features, it is recommended that you use a preexisting solution rather than rolling out your own, as there is a lot of complexity to consider from audio file types, stereo/3D audio, layering, compression, filters, cross-platform capability, efficient memory management, and so on.

When it comes to ambient sound effects, they still need to be placed at specific locations in the scene to make use of the logarithmic volume effect, which gives it a pseudo-3D effect, so an audio pooling system would probably not be an ideal solution. Limiting playback on ambient sound effects is best achieved by reducing the total number of audio sources. The best approach is to either remove some of them or reduce them down to one larger, louder audio source. Naturally, this approach affects the quality of the user experience since it would appear that the sound is coming from a single source and not multiple sources; therefore, it should be used with care.

Enabling Force to Mono for 3D sounds

Enabling the **Force to Mono** setting on a stereo audio file will mix together the data from both audio channels into a single channel, saving 50 percent of the file's total disk and memory space usage effectively. Enabling this option is generally not a good idea for some 2D sound effects, where the stereo effect is often used to create a specific audio experience; however, we can enable this option for some good space savings on 3D positional audio clips, where the two channels are effectively identical. These audio source types will let the direction between the audio source and the player determine how the audio file gets played into the left/right ear, and playing a stereo effect in this case is generally meaningless.

Forcing 2D sounds (sounds that play into the player's ears at full volume, regardless of distance/direction to the audio source) to mono might also make sense if there is no need for a stereo effect.

Resampling to lower frequencies

Resampling imported audio files to lower frequencies will reduce the file size and runtime memory footprint. This can be achieved by setting an audio file's **Sample Rate Setting** to **Override Sample Rate**, at which point we can configure the sample rate through the **Sample Rate** option. Some files require high sample rates to sound reasonable, such as files with high pitches and most music files; however, lower settings can reduce the file's size without noticeable quality degradation in most cases. Most use a 22,050 Hertz sampling rate for sources that involve human speech and classical music; some sound effects may be able to get away with even lower frequency values. However, each sound effect will be affected by this setting in a unique way, so it would be wise to spend some time running a few tests before we finalize our decision on the sampling rate.

Considering all compression formats

Each of the **Compressed**, **PCM**, and **ADPCM** compression formats have their own benefits and drawbacks, as explained previously. It's possible to make some compromises in memory footprint, disk footprint, CPU usage, and audio quality using different encoding formats for different files where appropriate. We should be willing to use all of them in the same application and come up with a system that works for the kinds of audio files we're using so that we don't need to treat each file individually; otherwise, we would need to do a prohibitive amount of testing to ensure that audio quality hasn't been degraded for each file.

Being cautious of streaming

The upside of the **Streaming** loading type is a low runtime memory cost, since a small buffer is allocated and the file is continuously pushed through it like a data queue. This can seem quite appealing, but streaming files from the disk should be restricted to large, single-instance files only, as it requires runtime hard disk access, which is one of the slowest forms of data access available to us (second only to pulling a file through a network). Layered or transitioning music clips may run into major hiccups using the **Streaming** option, at which point it would be wise to consider using a different **Load Type** and control loading/unloading manually.

We should also avoid streaming more than one file at a time, as it's likely to inflict a lot of cache misses on the disk that will interrupt gameplay. This is why this option is primarily used for background music/ambient sound effects, since we only need one at a time.

Applying filter effects through mixer groups to reduce duplication

Filter effects can be used to modify the sound effect playing through an audio source, and can be accomplished through `FilterEffect` components. Each individual filter effect will cost a certain amount of both memory and CPU, and can be a good way to achieve disk space savings while maintaining a lot of variety in audio playback since one file could be tweaked by a different set of filters to generate completely different sound effects.

Because of the additional overhead, overusing filter effects in our scene can result in dire consequences in performance. A better approach is to make use of Unity's audio mixer utility (**Window** | **Audio** | **Audio Mixer**) to generate common filter effect templates that multiple audio sources can reference to minimize the amount of memory overhead.

The official tutorial on audio mixers at `https://learn.unity.com/tutorial/audio-mixing` covers the topic in excellent detail.

Using remote content streaming responsibly

It is possible to dynamically load game content via the web through Unity, which can be an effective means of reducing an application's disk footprint since fewer data files need to be bundled into the executable. This also provides a means to present dynamic content using web services to determine what is presented to the user at runtime. Asset streaming can be accomplished through the `UnityWebRequest` class in Unity 2017 and later.

The `UnityWebRequest` class makes use of the new HLAPI and LLAPI networking layers. This class provides various utilities to download and access what are primarily text files. Multimedia-based requests should go through the `UnityWebRequestMultimedia` helper class. So, if an `AudioClip` is requested, we should call `UnityWebRequestMultimedia.GetAudioClip()` to create the request and `DownloadHandlerAudioClip.GetContent()` to retrieve it once the download is complete.

This new version of the API is designed to be more efficient at storing and providing the data we requested, and so reacquiring an `AudioClip` multiple times through `DownloadHandlerAudioClip.GetContent()` will not lead to additional allocations. Instead, it will merely return a reference to the originally downloaded `AudioClip`.

Consider using audio module files for background music

Audio module files, also known as **tracker modules**, are an excellent means of saving a significant amount of space without any noticeable quality loss. Supported file extensions in Unity are `.it`, `.s3m`, `.xm`, and `.mod`. Unlike the common audio formats, which are read like streams of bits that must be decoded at runtime to generate a specific sound, tracker modules contain lots of small, high-quality samples and organize the entire track similar to a music sheet, defining when, where, how loud, with what pitch, and with what special effects each sample should be played with. This can provide significant size savings while maintaining high-quality sampling, so if the opportunity is available for us to make use of tracker module versions of our music files, then it is worth exploring.

Texture files

The terms *texture* and *sprite* often get confused in game development, so it's worth making the distinction: a texture is simply an image file, a big list of color data telling the interpreting program what color each pixel of the image should be, whereas a sprite can be seen as the 2D equivalent of a mesh—it defines how and where the image will appear in the game scene. Usually, a sprite is just a single *quad* (a pair of triangles combined to make a rectangular mesh) that renders flat against the current camera.

There are also things called sprite sheets, which are large collections of individual images contained within a larger texture file, commonly used to contain the animations of a 2D character. These files can be split apart by tools, such as Unity's Sprite Atlas tool, to form individual textures for the character's animated frames.

 Of course, you can render a 2D sprite in a 3D environment; however, in essence, a sprite is still a 2D element in the same way a playing card is still a flat card, even when it is used to build a house of cards.

Both meshes and sprites use textures to render an image onto its surface. Texture image files are typically generated in tools such as Adobe Photoshop or GIMP and then imported into our project in much the same way as audio files. At runtime, these files are loaded into memory, pushed to the GPU's VRAM, and rendered by a shader over the target sprite or mesh during a given draw call.

Texture compression formats

Much like audio files, Unity will import texture files with a default list of settings that tend to keep things simple and work okay in the general case, but there are many import settings available, allowing us to improve a texture's quality and performance with some custom tweaking. Of course, making changes is just as likely to reduce quality and performance if we blindly make changes without fully understanding the internal processes going on.

The first option is the file's **Texture Type**. This setting will determine what other options are available, particularly under the **Advanced** dropdown. Not all importing options are available to all types, so it is best to configure this option for the texture's intended purpose, whether it is set to **Normal Map**, **Sprite**, **Lightmap**, and so on, as this will reveal the options appropriate for that type:

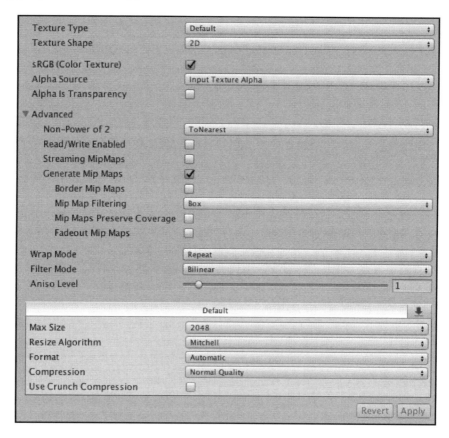

Similar to audio files, we can import texture files in multiple common formats (such as .jpg and .png), but the actual compression format built into the application could be one of many different texture compression formats ideally suited for GPUs of the given platform. These formats represent different ways of organizing the texture's color information, which includes the following:

- Different numbers of bits used to represent each channel (the more bits that are used, the more colors that can be represented)
- Different numbers of bits per channel (for example, the red channel may use more bits than the green channel)

- Different total number of bits used for all channels (more bits naturally mean larger textures and more disk and memory consumption)
- Whether or not an alpha channel is included
- Perhaps the most important, different ways of packing the data together, which can allow for efficient memory access for the GPU (or incredibly inefficient access if the wrong packing type is chosen!)

The simple way of altering compression is to use the **Compression** texture import option to select one of the following options:

- **None**
- **Low Quality**
- **Normal Quality**
- **High Quality**

Selecting **None** means that no compression will be applied. In this case, the final texture will still change the format from the file type we imported, but it will select a format that makes no attempt at compression, and so we should see little or no quality loss at the expense of large texture files. The other three settings will pick a compression format, which, again, will vary depending on the platform, and Unity will try to pick a compression format that matches the option. For instance, selecting **Low Quality** will mean that Unity picks a compression format that greatly reduces the texture size, but will generate some compression artifacts, whereas selecting **High Quality** will consume more memory with much larger texture sizes and minimal artifacts. Again, this is an automatic selection made by Unity.

 The exact formats Unity picks for each platform for each of these **Compression** settings can be found at `https://docs.unity3d.com/Manual/class-TextureImporterOverride.html`.

The exact compression format Unity chooses can be overridden, although the available options vary per platform since practically every platform has its own custom formats that work best for it. If we click on one of the platform-specific tabs beside the **Default** tab (just above the **Max Size** option), we will expose the settings for a specific platform and can choose the exact compression format we want Unity to use.

There is also the **Crunch Compression** setting, which will apply an additional level of lossy compression on top of the DXT compression format. This option is only revealed if the other compression settings result in a DXT level of compression. This setting can save even more space at the cost of potentially glaring compression artifacts, depending on the **Compressor Quality** setting.

Several of a texture's import settings are fairly mundane, such as determining whether the file contains an alpha channel, how to wrap the texture at its extents, the filtering method, and the maximum possible resolution of the file (a global limit so that we don't accidentally overscale the texture beyond its original size on certain platforms). However, there are several other interesting options in these import settings, which we will cover in other sections where appropriate.

Texture performance enhancements

Let's explore some changes that we can make to our texture files, which might help improve performance, depending on the situation and the content of the files we're importing. In each case, we'll explore the changes that need to be made and the overall effect they have, whether this results in a positive or negative impact on memory or CPU, an increase or decrease in the texture quality, and under what conditions we can expect to make use of these techniques.

Reducing texture file size

The larger a given texture file, the more GPU memory bandwidth will be consumed, pushing the texture when it is needed. If the total memory pushed per second exceeds the graphics card's total memory bandwidth, then we will have a bottleneck, as the GPU must wait for all textures to be uploaded before the next rendering pass can begin. Smaller textures are naturally easier to push through the pipeline than larger textures, so we will need to find a good middle ground between high quality and performance.

A simple test to find out whether we're bottlenecked in memory bandwidth is to reduce the resolution of our game's largest and most abundant texture files and relaunch the scene. If the frame rate suddenly improves, then the application was most likely bound by texture throughput. If the frame rate does not improve or improves very little, then either we still have some memory bandwidth to make use of or there are bottlenecks elsewhere in the rendering pipeline, preventing us from seeing any further improvement.

Using mipmaps wisely

There would be no point rendering small, distant objects, such as rocks and trees, with a high-detail texture if there's no way the player would ever be able to see that detail. Of course, they may see some slight improvement, but the performance cost may not be worth the minor detail increase. Mipmaps were invented as a way to solve this problem (as well as to help eliminate aliasing problems that were plaguing video games at around the same time) by pregenerating lower-resolution alternatives of the same texture and keeping them together in the same memory space. At runtime, the GPU picks the appropriate mipmap level based on how large the surface appears within the perspective view (essentially based on the texel-to-pixel ratio when the object is rendered).

By enabling the **Generate Mip Maps** setting, Unity automatically handles the generation of these lower-resolution copies of the texture. These alternatives are generated using high-quality resampling and filtering methods within the editor rather than during runtime. There are several other options available for mipmap generation that can affect the quality of the generated levels, so some tweaking may be required to get a high-quality set of mipmaps. We will need to decide whether the time spent tweaking these values is worth it since the whole purpose of mipmaps is to intentionally reduce quality to save performance in the first place.

The following image shows how a 1024 x 1024 image that has been mipmapped into multiple lower-resolution images duplicates:

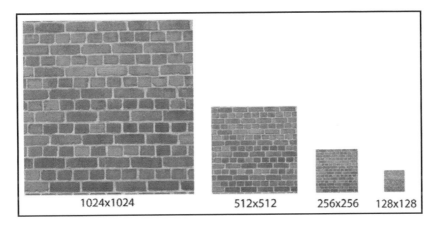

These images will be packed together to save space, essentially creating a final texture file that will be about 33 percent larger than the original image. This will cost some disk space and GPU memory bandwidth to upload.

Since Unity 2018.2, there is another way to load mipmaps: streaming. As in the audio case, mipmap streaming is used to reduce the memory needed to keep in memory the multiple textures of a mipmap without sacrificing the quality. In fact, if we enable mipmap streaming, then Unity will try to load on the fly from disk only the correct resolution of a texture on the basis of the camera position in the scene. This can save up to 30% of texture memory depending on the scene (and the player's position).

However, this comes at a price. First of all, streaming a mipmap is slower than generation; therefore, if you have instantaneous camera cuts or you move quickly, you can start noticing the texture quality change as the mipmaps are loaded. This can be mitigated by using the mipmap streaming API in order to preload the mipmaps in the destination location.

Second, mipmap streaming may not be supported on all platforms at the moment. If you want to be sure that mipmap streaming is supported on your platform, you can check the `SystemInfo.supportsMipStreaming` property.

 If you want more information on texture streaming, you can check the detailed page in the manual at `https://docs.unity3d.com/Manual/TextureStreaming-API.html`.

It's possible to see which mipmap levels are being used by our application at certain points by changing the **Draw Mode** setting of the **Scene** window to **Mipmaps**. This will highlight textures in red if they are larger than they should be, given the player's current view (the extra detail is wasted), whereas being highlighted blue means that they are too small (the player is observing a low-quality texture with a poor texel-to-pixel ratio).

Remember that mipmapping is only useful if we have textures that need to be rendered at varying distances from the camera. If we have textures that always render at a common distance from the main camera in such a way that the mipmapped alternatives are never used, then enabling mipmaps is just a waste of space. Similarly, if we happen to have a texture that always resolves to the same mipmap level because the player's camera never gets too close/far away to switch levels, then it would be wiser to simply downscale the original texture.

Good examples of this would be any texture file used in a 2D game, textures used by UI systems, or those used in a Skybox or distant background, since, by design, these textures will always be about the same distance from the camera, so mipmapping would be essentially pointless. Other good examples include objects that only appear near the player, such as player-centric particle effects, characters, objects that only appear near the player, and objects that only the player can hold/carry.

Managing resolution downscaling externally

Unity puts a lot of effort into making things as easy to use as possible and provides us with the ability to place the project files from external tools to our project workspace, such as .PSD and .TIFF files, which are often large and split into multiple layered images. Unity automatically generates a texture file from the file's contents for the rest of the engine to make use of, which can be very convenient, as we only need to maintain a single copy of the file through source control, and the Unity copy is automatically updated when an artist makes changes.

The problem is that the aliasing introduced by Unity's autotexture generation and compression techniques from these files may not be as good as what the texture-editing tools we use could generate for us. Unity is very feature-rich and, first and foremost, focuses on being a game-development platform, which means that it can have difficulty competing in areas that other software developers work on full time. Unity may be introducing artifacts through aliasing as a result of downscaling the image for us, and so we might find ourselves working around it by importing image files with a higher resolution than necessary just to keep the intended quality level; however, had we downscaled the image through the external application first, we might have suffered much less aliasing. In these cases, we may achieve an acceptable level of quality with a lower resolution, while consuming less overall disk and memory space.

We can either avoid using .PSD and .TIFF files within our Unity project as a matter of habit (storing them elsewhere and importing the downscaled version into Unity) or just perform some occasional testing to ensure that we're not wasting file size, memory, and GPU memory bandwidth using larger resolution files than necessary. This costs us some convenience in project file management, but can provide some significant savings for some textures if we're willing to spend the time comparing the different downscaled versions.

Adjusting anisotropic filtering levels

Anisotropic filtering is a feature that improves the image quality of textures when they are viewed at very oblique (shallow) angles. The following screenshot shows the classic example of painted lines on a road with and without anisotropic filtering applied:

In either case, the painted lines close to the camera appear fairly clear, but things change as they get further away from the camera. Without anisotropic filtering, the distant painted lines get more and more blurry and distorted, whereas these lines remain crisp and clear with anisotropic filtering applied.

The strength of anisotropic filtering applied to the texture can be hand modified on a per-texture basis with the **Aniso Level** setting, as well as globally enabled/disabled using the **Anisotropic Textures** option within the **Edit** | **Project** | **Quality** settings.

Much like mipmapping, this effect can be costly and, sometimes, unnecessary. If there are textures in our scene that we are certain will never be viewed at an oblique angle (such as distant background objects, UI elements, and billboard particle effect textures), then we can safely disable anisotropic filtering for them to save runtime overhead. We can also consider adjusting the strength of the anisotropic filtering effect on a per-texture basis to find the magic spot between quality and performance.

Consider atlasing

Atlasing is the technique of combining lots of smaller, isolated textures together into a single, large texture file in order to minimize the number of materials, and therefore draw calls, we need to use. This is effectively a means to exploit dynamic batching. Conceptually, this technique is very similar to the approaches of minimizing material usage that you learned in `Chapter 3`, *The Benefits of Batching*.

Each unique material will require an additional draw call, but each material only supports a single primary texture. Of course, they can also support multiple secondary textures, such as normal maps and emission maps. However, by combining multiple primary textures into a single large texture file, we can minimize the number of draw calls used to render objects that share this texture:

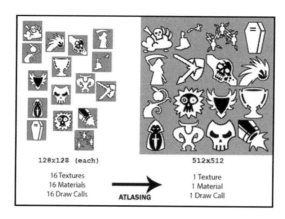

Extra work is required to modify the UV coordinates used by the mesh or sprite object to only sample the portion of the larger texture file that it needs, but the benefits are clear: reducing draw calls results in the reduction of CPU workload and improvement in the frame rate if our application is bottlenecked on the CPU. Assuming that the merged texture file's resolution is equivalent to that of all of the combined images, there will be no loss of quality, and memory consumption will be essentially identical. Note that atlasing does not result in reduced memory bandwidth consumption since the amount of data being pushed to the GPU would also be identical. It just happens to be bundled together in one bigger texture file.

Atlasing is only an option when all of the given textures require the same shader. If some of the textures need unique graphical effects applied through shaders, then they must be isolated into their own materials and atlased in separate groups.

Atlasing is a common tactic applied to UI elements and in games that feature a lot of 2D graphics. Atlasing becomes practically essential when developing mobile games with Unity since draw calls tend to be the most common bottleneck on those platforms. However, we would not want to generate these atlas files manually. Life would be much simpler if we could continue to edit our textures individually and automate the task of combining them into a larger file.

Many GUI-related tools in the Unity Asset Store provide an automated texture-atlasing feature. There are some standalone programs scattered across the internet that can handle this work, and Unity can generate atlases for sprites in the form of assets. These can be created by going to **Asset** | **Create** | **Sprite Atlas**.

Check out the Unity documentation to discover more about this useful feature at `https://docs.unity3d.com/Manual/class-SpriteAtlas.html`.

Note that the sprite atlas feature effectively supplants the sprite packer tool from older versions of Unity.

Atlasing does not need to be applied to 2D graphics and UI elements either. We can apply this technique to 3D meshes if we happen to be creating a lot of low-resolution textures. 3D games that feature simple texture resolutions or a flat-shaded, low-poly art style are ideal candidates for atlasing in this way.

However, because dynamic batching affects only nonanimated meshes (that is, `MeshRenderer`, but not `SkinnedMeshRenderer`), there is no reason to combine texture files for animated characters into an atlas. Since they are animated, the GPU needs to multiply each object's bones by the transform of the current animation state. This means that a unique calculation is needed for each character, and they will result in an extra draw call regardless of any attempts we make to have them share materials.

As a result, combining textures for animated characters should be done only as a matter of convenience and space-saving; for example, in a flat-shaded, low-poly art style game, where everything happens to use a common color palette, we can make some space savings using a single texture for the entire game world, objects, and characters.

The disadvantages of atlasing are mostly in terms of development time and workflow costs. It requires a lot of effort to overhaul an existing project to make use of atlasing, which can be a lot of work just to figure out whether it is worth the effort or not. In addition, we need to be aware of generating texture files that are too large for the target platform.

Some devices (specifically mobile devices) have a relatively low limit on the size of the textures that can be pulled into the lowest memory cache of the GPU. If the atlased texture file is too large, then it must be broken up into smaller textures in order to fit the target memory space. If the device's GPU happens to need textures from different pieces of the atlas every other draw call, then not only will we inflict a lot of cache misses, but we also might find that we choke the memory bandwidth, as textures are constantly pulled from VRAM and the lower-level cache.

We would probably not have this problem if the atlas was left as individual textures. The same texture swapping will occur, but will result in much smaller files being swapped at the cost of additional draw calls. Our best options at this stage would be to lower the Atlas resolution or generate multiple smaller atlases to have better control over how they will be dynamically batched.

Atlasing is clearly not a perfect solution, and if it is not clear whether it would result in a performance benefit, then we should be careful not to waste too much time on its implementation. Speaking very generally, mobile games with a very simplistic 2D art style probably won't need to make use of atlasing; however, mobile games attempting to compete with high-quality assets or use any kind of 3D graphics should probably start integrating atlasing from the very beginning of development, since it is likely that the project will reach texture throughput limits very quickly. They may even need to apply many per-platform and per-device optimizations in order to reach a wide audience.

Meanwhile, we should consider applying atlasing to high-quality desktop games only if our draw call count exceeds reasonable hardware expectations, since we will want many of our textures to maintain high resolutions for maximum quality. Low-quality desktop games can probably afford to avoid atlasing since draw calls are unlikely to be the biggest bottleneck.

Of course, no matter what the product is, if we're ever limited in CPU by too many draw calls and have already exhausted many of the alternative techniques, then atlasing is a very effective performance enhancement in most cases.

Adjusting compression rates for nonsquare textures

Texture files are normally stored in a square, power-of-two format, meaning that their height and width are equal in length, and its size is a power of two—for example, some typical sizes are 256 x 256 pixels, 512 x 512, and 1024 x 1024, and so on.

It is possible to provide rectangular power-of-two textures (such as 256 x 512) or those with a non-power-of-two format (such as 192 x 192), but creating textures such as these is not recommended. Some GPUs require square texture formats, so Unity will compensate by automatically expanding the texture to include additional empty space in order to fit the form factor that the GPU expects, which will result in additional memory bandwidth costs, pushing what is essentially unused and useless data to the GPU. Other GPUs may support non-power-of-two textures, but this is likely to result in slower sampling than a square texture.

So the first recommendation is to avoid nonsquare and/or non-power-of-two textures altogether. If the image can be placed within a square, power-of-two texture and does not result in too much quality degradation due to squeezing/stretching, then we should apply those changes just to keep the CPU and GPU happy. As a second option, we can customize this scaling behavior in Unity through the texture file's `Non Power of 2` import setting, though because this is an automated process, it might not give us the graphical quality we expect.

Sparse textures

Sparse textures, also known as **mega-textures** or **tiled-textures**, provide a way of effectively streaming texture data from disk at runtime. Relatively speaking, if the CPU performs operations in the order of seconds, then the disk would operate in the order of days. So the common advice is that hard-disk access during gameplay should be avoided as much as possible since any such technique risks inflicting more disk access than available, causing our application to grind to a halt.

However, sparse texturing offers some interesting performance-saving techniques if we're smart about starting data transfer for portions of the texture before we need them. Sparse texturing is prepared by combining many textures into an enormous texture file that would be far too large to load into graphics memory as a single texture file. This is similar to the concept of atlasing, except the file containing the textures is incredibly large—for example, 32,768 x 32,768 pixels—and would contain considerable color detail, such as 32 bits per pixel (this would result in a texture file that consumes 4 GBs of disk space). The idea is to save large amounts of runtime memory and memory bandwidth by hand-picking small subsections of the texture to load from the disk dynamically, pulling them from the disk moments before they are needed in the game. The main cost of this technique is the file size requirement and the potentially continuous disk access. Other costs for this technique can be overcome, but normally take a great deal of scene preparation work.

The game world needs to be created in such a way that it minimizes the amount of texture swapping taking place. In order to avoid very noticeable *texture popping* problems, texture subsections must be pulled from a disk into RAM with just enough time to spare that the GPU does not need to wait before the transfer to VRAM can begin (in much the same way that it normally doesn't need to wait for ordinary texture files that are preloaded into RAM). This takes place in the design of the texture file itself by keeping common elements for a given scene in the same general area of the texture, and the design of the scene, by triggering new texture subsection loading at key moments during gameplay and making sure that disk access of the new tile is quickly located by the disk without extreme cache misses. If it is handled with care, then sparse texturing can result in impressive benefits in both scene quality and memory savings.

It is a highly specialized technique in the gaming industry and has not yet been widely adopted, partly because it requires specialized hardware and platform support and partly because it is difficult to pull it off well. The Unity documentation on sparse texturing has improved somewhat over time and provides an example scene showing the effect at work, which can be found at `http://docs.unity3d.com/Manual/SparseTextures.html`.

For Unity developers who consider themselves advanced enough to experiment with sparse texturing, it might be worth taking the time to perform some research to check whether sparse texturing is right for their project since it promises some significant performance savings.

Procedural materials

Procedural materials, also known as **substances**, are a means of procedurally generating textures at runtime by combining small, high-quality texture samples with custom mathematical formulas. The goal of procedural materials is to greatly minimize the application disk footprint at the cost of additional runtime memory and CPU processing during initialization to generate the texture via mathematical operations rather than static color data.

Texture files are, sometimes, the biggest disk space consumer of a game project, and it's fairly common knowledge that download times have a tremendous negative impact on the completed download rate and getting people to try our game (even if it's free). Procedural materials offer us the ability to sacrifice some initialization and runtime processing power for much faster downloads. This is very important for mobile games that are trying to compete via graphical fidelity.

As for Unity 2019, procedural materials are no longer part of Unity. Instead, they are offered as a separate plugin. You can check more about substances on the official page at `https://www.substance3d.com/integrations/substance-in-unity`.

Asynchronous texture uploading

The last texture import option we haven't covered is the read/write enabled option. By default, this option is disabled, which is good, because this allows textures to make use of the asynchronous texture uploading feature, which has two benefits: the texture will be uploaded asynchronously from disk to RAM, and when the texture data is needed by the GPU, the transfer happens on the render thread, not the main thread. Textures will be pushed into a circular buffer, which pushes data to the GPU continuously so long as the buffer contains new data. If not, then it early-exits the process and waits until new texture data is requested.

Ultimately, this reduces the time spent preparing the render states for each frame and allows more CPU resources to be spent on gameplay logic, the physics engine, and so on. Of course, some time is still spent on the main thread preparing the render state, but moving the texture uploading task to a separate thread saves a significant chunk of CPU time on the main thread.

However, enabling read/write access to the texture essentially tells Unity that we might be reading and editing this texture at any time. This implies that the GPU will need fresh access to it every time, so it will disable asynchronous texture uploading for that texture; all uploading must occur on the main thread. We might want to enable this option for things such as simulating painting colors onto a canvas or writing image data from the internet into a premade texture, but the downside is that the GPU must always wait for any changes to be made to the texture before it can be uploaded since it cannot predict when those changes will happen.

In addition, asynchronous texture uploading only works for textures we explicitly imported into the project and that were present during build time since the feature only works if the texture was packed together into special streamable assets. Therefore, any textures generated via `LoadImage(byte[])`, texture assets imported/downloaded from external locations, or loaded from a *resources* folder via `Resources.Load()` (which all implicitly call `LoadImage(byte[])` themselves) will not be converted into streamable content, and therefore will be unable to make use of asynchronous texture uploading.

It is possible to tweak both the upper limit of the maximum allowed time so that it can be spent on asynchronous texture uploads, and the total circular buffer size Unity should use to push the textures we want to upload. These settings can be tweaked under **Edit | Project Settings | Quality | Other** and are named **Async Upload Time Slice** and **Async Upload Buffer Size**, respectively. We should set the **Async Upload Time Slice** value to the maximum number of milliseconds we want Unity to spend on asynchronous texture uploads on the render thread. It might be wise to set the **Async Upload Buffer Size** value to the largest texture file we might need to use, plus a little extra buffer if multiple fresh textures are needed in the same frame. The circular buffer that texture data is copied into will expand as needed, but this is often costly. Since we probably already know ahead of time how large we need that circular buffer to be, we might as well set it to the maximum expected size to avoid potential frame drops when it needs to resize the buffer. We now move on to our next topic— the mesh and animation file types.

Mesh and animation files

The mesh and animation file types are essentially large arrays of vertex and skinned bone data, and there are a variety of techniques we can apply to minimize file size while keeping similar, if not identical, appearances. There are also ways to lower the cost of rendering large groups of these objects through batching techniques. Let's take a look at a series of performance-enhancing techniques that we can apply to such files.

Reducing the polygon count

Reducing the polygon count is the most obvious way to gain performance and should always be considered. In fact, since we cannot batch objects using skinned mesh renderers, it's one of the good ways of reducing CPU and GPU runtime overhead for animated objects.

Reducing the polygon count is simple, straightforward, and provides both CPU and memory cost savings for the time required for artists to clean up the mesh. In this day and age, much of an object's detail is almost entirely based on detailed texturing and complex shading, so we can often get away with stripping away a lot of vertices on modern meshes, and most users would be unable to tell the difference.

Tweaking mesh compression

Unity offers four different **Mesh Compression** settings for imported mesh files: **Off**, **Low**, **Medium**, and **High**. Increasing this setting will convert floating-point data into fixed values, reducing the accuracy in the vertex position/normal direction, simplifying vertex color information, and so on. This can have a noticeable effect on meshes that contain lots of small parts near one another, such as a fence or grate. If we're generating meshes procedurally, we can achieve the same type of compression by calling the `Optimize()` method of a `MeshRenderer` component (of course, this will take some time to complete).

There are also two global settings found in **Edit** | **Project Settings** | **Player** | **Other Settings** that can affect how mesh data is imported. They are as follows:

- **Vertex Compression**: We can use this option to configure the type of data that will be optimized when we import a mesh file with **Mesh Compression** enabled, so if we want accurate normal data (for lighting), but are less worried about positional data, then we can configure it here. Unfortunately, this is a global setting, and will affect all imported meshes (although it can be configured on a per-platform basis since it is a **Player** setting).
- **Optimize Mesh Data**: Enabling **Optimize Mesh Data** will strip away any data from the mesh that isn't required by the material(s) assigned to it. So, if the mesh contains tangent information, but the shader never requires it, then Unity will ignore it during build time.

In each case, the benefits reduce the application's disk footprint at the cost of extra time loading the mesh, since extra time must be spent decompressing the data before it's needed.

The 3D mesh-building/animation tools often provide their own built-in ways of automated mesh optimization in the form of estimating the overall shape and stripping the mesh down to fewer total polygons. This can cause a significant loss of quality and should be tested vigorously if used.

Using Read-Write Enabled appropriately

The **Read-Write Enabled** flag allows changes to be made to the mesh at runtime either via scripting or automatically by Unity during runtime, similar to how it is used for texture files. Internally, this means that it will keep the original mesh data in memory until we want to duplicate it and make changes dynamically. Disabling this option will allow Unity to discard the original mesh data from memory once it has determined the final mesh to use, since it knows it will never change.

If we use only a uniformly scaled version of a mesh throughout the entire game, then disabling this option will save runtime memory since we will no longer need the original mesh data to make further rescaled duplicates of the mesh (incidentally, this is how Unity organizes objects by scale factor when it comes to dynamic batching). Unity can, therefore, discard this unwanted data early since we won't need it again until the next time the application is launched.

However, if the mesh often reappears at runtime with different scales, then Unity needs to keep this data in memory so that it can recalculate a new mesh more quickly; therefore, it would be wise to enable the **Read-Write Enabled** flag. Disabling it will require Unity to not only reload the mesh data each time the mesh is reintroduced, but also make the rescaled duplicate at the same time, causing a potential performance hiccup.

Unity tries to detect the correct behavior for this setting at initialization time, but when meshes are instantiated and scaled in a dynamic fashion at runtime, we must force the issue by enabling this setting. This will improve the instantiation speed of the objects, but cost some memory overhead since the original mesh data is kept around until it's needed.

Note that this potential overhead cost also applies when using the **Generate Colliders** option.

Considering baked animations

Using baked animations will require changes in the asset by using the 3D rigging and animation tool that we are using, since Unity does not provide such tools itself. Animations are normally stored as keyframe information, which it uses to keep track of specific mesh positions and interpolate between them at runtime using skinning data (bone shapes, assignments, animation curves, and so on). Baking animations means effectively sampling and hardcoding each position of each vertex into the mesh/animation file per frame without the need for interpolation and skinning data.

Using baked animations can sometimes result in much smaller file sizes and memory overhead than blended/skinned animations for some objects since skinning data can take up a surprisingly large amount of space to store. This is most likely to be the case for relatively simple objects or objects with short animations since we would effectively be replacing procedural data with a hardcoded series of vertex positions. So if the mesh's polygon count is low enough where storing lots of vertex information is cheaper than skinning data, then we may see some significant savings through this simple change.

In addition, how often the baked sample is taken can usually be customized by the exporting application. Different sample rates should be tested to find a good value where the key moments of the animation still shine through what is essentially a simplified estimate.

Combining meshes

Forcefully combining meshes into a large, single mesh can be a convenient option to reduce draw calls, particularly if the meshes are too large for dynamic batching and don't play well with other statically batched groups. This is essentially the equivalent of static batching, but it is performed manually, so sometimes it's a wasted effort if static batching could take care of the process for us.

Be aware that if any single vertex of the mesh is visible in the scene, then the entire object will be rendered together as one whole. This can lead to a lot of wasted processing if the mesh is only partially visible most of the time. This technique also comes with the drawback that it generates a whole new mesh asset file that we must deposit into our scene, which means that any changes we make to the original meshes will not be reflected in the combined one. This results in a lot of tedious workflow effort every time changes need to be made, so if static batching is an option, it should be used instead.

There are several tools available online that can combine mesh files together for us in Unity. They are only an Asset Store or Google search away.

Asset bundles and resources

We touched upon the topic of resources and serialization in Chapter 2, *Scripting Strategies*, and it should be fairly clear that the resource system can be a great benefit during prototyping, as well as during the early stages of our project, and can be used relatively effectively in games of limited scope.

However, professional Unity projects should instead favor the asset bundle system. There are a number of reasons for this. Firstly, the resource system is not very scalable when it comes to builds. All resources are merged together into a single massive serialized file binary data blob with an index list of where various assets can be found within it. This can be hard to manage, and take a long time to build as we add more data to the list.

Secondly, the resource system's ability to acquire data from the serialized file scales in an $Nlog(N)$ fashion, which should make us very wary of increasing the value of N. Thirdly, the resource system makes it unwieldy for our application to provide different asset data on a per-device basis, whereas asset bundles tend to make this matter trivial. Finally, asset bundles can be used to provide small, periodic custom content updates to the application, while the resource system would require updates that completely replace the entire application to achieve the same effect.

Asset bundles share a lot of common functionality with resources, such as loading from files, loading data asynchronously, and unloading data we no longer need. However, they also offer much more functionality, such as content streaming, content updates, and content generation and sharing. These can all be used to improve the performance of our application to great effect. We can deliver applications with much smaller disk footprints and have the user download additional content before or during gameplay, stream assets at runtime to minimize the initial loading time of the application, and provide more optimized assets to the application on a per-platform basis without the need to push a complete application to overwrite to the user.

Of course, there are downsides to asset bundles. They are much more complicated to set up and maintain than resources, they're more complicated to understand since they use a much more sophisticated system for accessing asset data than the resources system, and making full use of their functionality (such as streaming and content updates) would require a lot of additional QA testing to make sure that the server is delivering content properly, and that the game is reading and updating its content to match. Ergo, asset bundles are best used only when our team size is able to support the extra workload they require.

A tutorial on the asset bundle system is beyond the scope of this book, but there are dozens of useful guides online and in the Unity documentation.

Check out the Unity tutorial at `https://learn.unity.com/tutorial/assets-resources-and-assetbundles` to find out more about the asset bundle system.

If you require further convincing, then a Unity blog post from April 2017 should help reveal how the asset bundle system can use memory more efficiently during runtime in ways that the resources system cannot provide through memory pooling. You can find this blog at `https://blogs.unity3d.com/2017/04/12/asset-bundles-vs-resources-a-memory-showdown/`.

Summary

There are many different opportunities that we can explore to achieve performance gains for our application just by tinkering with our imported assets. Alternatively, from another perspective, there are plenty of ways to ruin our application's performance through asset mismanagement. Almost every single import configuration opportunity is a trade-off between one performance metric or workflow task and another. Typically, this means saving the disk footprint via compression at the expense of CPU at runtime to decompress the data, or faster access while reducing the quality level of the final presentation. So we must remain vigilant and only pick the right techniques for the right assets for the right reasons.

This concludes our exploration of improving performance through art asset manipulation. In the next chapter, we will be investigating how to improve our usage of Unity's physics engine.

5
Faster Physics

Each of the performance-enhancing suggestions we've explored so far has been primarily centered on reducing resource costs and avoiding frame rate issues. However, at its most fundamental level, seeking peak performance means improving the user experience. This is because every frame rate hiccup, every crash, and every system requirement that is too costly for a given market ultimately detracts from the quality of the product. Physics engines are a unique category of subsystems whose behavior and consistency contributes a significant factor toward product quality. Spending the time to improve their behavior is often worth the cost.

If important collision events get missed, the game freezes while it calculates a complex physics event, or the player falls through the floor, these scenarios have an obvious and significant negative impact on the quality of gameplay. A few glitches are often bearable, but continuous problems will get in the way of gameplay. This often results in pulling the player out of the experience, and it's a coin-toss whether the user finds it inconvenient, obnoxious, or hilarious. Unless our game is explicitly targeting the Comedy Physics genre (games such as *QWOP* or *Goat Simulator*), these are situations we should strive to avoid.

Some games may not use physics at all, whereas others require the physics engine to handle a considerable number of tasks during gameplay, such as collision detection between hundreds of objects, trigger volumes to initiate cutscenes, raycasting for player attacks and UI behavior, gathering lists of objects in a given region, or even just using physics as eye candy with lots of physical particles flying around. Its importance also varies depending on the type of game being created. For example, it is essential in platformer and action games to tune the physics properly—how the player character reacts to input and how the world reacts to the player character are two of the most critical aspects that make the game feel responsive and fun, whereas accurate physics may be somewhat less important in **Massively Multiplayer Online (MMO)** games, which tend to have limited physics interaction.

Therefore, in this chapter, we will cover ways to reduce CPU spikes, overhead, and memory consumption through Unity's physics engine, but also include ways to alter physics behavior to improve, or at least maintain, gameplay quality while optimizing performance. In this chapter, we will cover the following areas:

- Understanding how Unity's physics engine works:
    - Timesteps and fixed updates
    - Collider types
    - Collisions
    - Raycasting
    - Rigidbody active states
- Physics performance optimizations:
    - How to structure scenes for optimal physics behavior
    - Using the most appropriate types for a collider
    - Optimizing the Collision Matrix
    - Improving physics consistency and avoiding error-prone behavior
    - Ragdolls and other joint-based objects

Understanding the physics engine

Unity technically features two different physics engines: Nvidia's PhysX for 3D physics and the open source project Box2D for 2D physics. However, their implementations are highly abstracted, and from the perspective of the higher-level Unity API that we configure through the main Unity engine, both physics engine solutions operate in a functionally identical fashion.

In either case, the more we understand about Unity's physics engines, the more sense we can make of possible performance enhancements. So, first, we'll cover the theory about how Unity implements these systems.

Physics and time

Physics engines generally operate under the assumption that time advances by fixed values, and both of Unity's physics engines operate in this manner. Each of these iterations is known as a **timestep**. The physics engine will only resolve each timestep using precise values of time, which is independent of how much time it took to render the previous frame. This is known in Unity as the **fixed update timestep**, and it is set to a value of 20 milliseconds by default (50 updates per second).

It can be challenging to generate consistent results for collisions and forces between two different computers if a physics engine uses a variable timestep due to differences in architecture (in how floating-point values are represented) as well as the latency between clients. Such physics engines tend to generate very inconsistent results between multiplayer clients or during recorded replays.

The following diagram shows an important snippet of the Unity order of execution diagram:

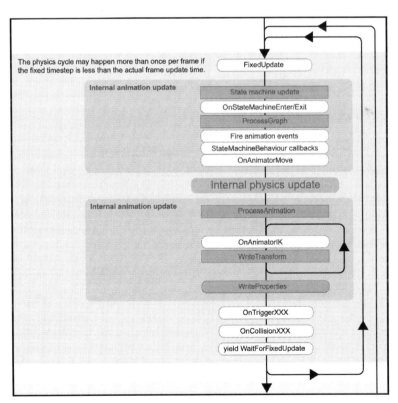

The full execution order diagram can be found at `http://docs.unity3d.com/Manual/ExecutionOrder.html`.

As we can see in the preceding diagram, fixed updates are processed just before the physics engine performs its update, and the two are inextricably linked. The process begins with determining whether enough time has passed to start the next fixed update. Once this is determined, the outcome will vary depending on how much time has passed since the last fixed update.

If enough time has passed, then the fixed update processes will invoke all `FixedUpdate()` callbacks defined across all active MonoBehaviours in the scene, followed by any coroutines tied to fixed updates (specifically those that `yield` to `WaitForFixedUpdate`). Note that there is no guarantee of execution order for methods invoked during either of these processes, so we should never write code under this assumption. Once these tasks are done, the physics engine can begin to process the current timestep and invoke any necessary trigger and collider callbacks.

Conversely, if too little time has passed since the last fixed update (that is, less than 20 milliseconds), then the current fixed update is skipped, and all of the tasks listed previously don't happen during the current iteration. At this point, input, gameplay logic, and rendering will be allowed to happen as normal. Once this activity is complete, Unity checks whether the next fixed update is required.

At high frame rates, rendering updates are likely to complete multiple times before the physics engine gets a chance to update itself. As a consequence, fixed updates and the physics engine get a higher priority over rendering while also forcing the physics simulation into a fixed frame rate.

To ensure that objects move smoothly between fixed updates, physics engines (including Unity's) interpolate the visible location of each object between where it was during the previous state and where it should be after resolving the current state based on how much time remains until the next fixed update. This interpolation ensures that objects appear to move smoothly even though their physical positions, velocities, and so on are being updated less frequently than the render frame rate.

The `FixedUpdate()` callback is a useful place to define any gameplay behavior that we want to be frame-rate independent. AI calculations are commonly resolved in fixed updates since they tend to be easier to work with if we assume a fixed update frequency.

Maximum Allowed Timestep

It is important to note that if a lot of time has passed since the last fixed update (for example, the game froze momentarily), then fixed updates will continue to be calculated within the same fixed update loop until the physics engine has caught up with the current time. For example, if the previous frame took 100 ms to render (for example, a sudden CPU spike caused the main thread to block for a long time), then the physics engine will need to be updated five times. The `FixedUpdate()` method will, therefore, be called five times before `Update()` can be called again due to the default fixed update timestep of 20 ms. Of course, if there is a lot of physics activity to process during these five fixed updates, such that it takes more than 20 ms to resolve them all, then the physics engine will need to invoke a sixth update.

Consequently, it's possible during moments of heavy physics activity that the physics engine takes more time to process a fixed update than the amount of time it is simulating. For example, if it took 30 ms to process a fixed update simulating 20 ms of gameplay, then it has fallen behind, requiring it to handle more timesteps to try and keep up, but this could cause it to fall back even further, requiring it to process even more timesteps, and so on. In these situations, the physics engine is never able to escape the fixed update loop and allow another frame to render. This problem is often known as the **spiral of death**. However, to prevent the physics engine from locking up our game during these moments, there is a maximum amount of time that the physics engine is allowed to process each fixed update loop. This threshold is called the **Maximum Allowed Timestep**, and if the current batch of fixed updates takes too long to process, then it will simply stop and forgo further processing until the next render update completes. This design allows the Rendering Pipeline to at least render the current state and allow for user input and gameplay logic to make some decisions during rare moments where the physics engine has gone ballistic (pun intended).

This setting can be accessed through **Edit** | **Project Settings** | **Time** | **Maximum Allowed Timestep**.

Physics updates and runtime changes

When the physics engine processes a given timestep, it must move any active `Rigidbody` objects (GameObjects with a `Rigidbody` component), detect any new collisions, and invoke the collision callbacks on the corresponding objects. The Unity documentation makes an explicit note that changes to `Rigidbody` objects should be handled within `FixedUpdate()` and other physics callbacks for precisely this reason. These methods are tightly coupled with the update frequency of the physics engine as opposed to other parts of the game loop, such as `Update()`.

This means that callbacks such as `FixedUpdate()` and `OnTriggerEnter()` are safe places to make `Rigidbody` changes, whereas methods such as `Update()` and coroutines yielding on `WaitForSeconds` or `WaitForEndOfFrame` are not. Ignoring this advice could cause unexpected physics behavior, as multiple changes may be made to the same object before the physics engine is given a chance to catch and process all of them.

It's particularly dangerous to apply forces or impulses to objects in `Update()` callbacks without taking into account the frequency of those calls. For instance, imagine applying a 10 Newton force in the `Update` function while the player holds down a key: the resultant velocity will be completely different between two different devices than if we did the same thing in a fixed update. In fact, we can't rely on the number of `Update()` calls being consistent. However, doing so in a `FixedUpdate()` callback will be much more consistent. Therefore, we must ensure that all physics-related behavior is handled in the appropriate callbacks, or we will risk introducing some especially confusing gameplay bugs that are very hard to reproduce.

It logically follows that the more time we spend in any given fixed update iteration, the less time we have for the next gameplay and rendering pass. Most of the time this results in minor, unnoticeable background processing tasks, since the physics engine barely has any work to do, and the `FixedUpdate()` callbacks have a lot of time to complete their work. However, in some games, the physics engine could be performing a lot of calculations during each fixed update. This bottlenecking in physics processing time will affect our frame rate, causing it to plummet as the physics engine is tasked with greater and higher workloads. Essentially, the Rendering Pipeline will try to proceed as usual, but whenever it's time for a fixed update, in which the physics engine takes a long time to process, the Rendering Pipeline would have very little time to generate the current display before the frame is due, causing a sudden stutter. This is in addition to the visual effect of the physics engine stopping early because it hit **Maximum Allowed Timestep**. All of this together would generate an inferior user experience.

Hence, to keep a smooth and consistent frame rate, we will need to free up as much time as we can for rendering by minimizing the amount of time the physics engine takes to process any given timestep. This applies in both the best-case scenario (nothing moving) and worst-case scenario (everything smashing into everything else at once). There are several time-related features and values we can tweak within the physics engine to avoid performance pitfalls such as these.

Static colliders and dynamic colliders

There is a rather extreme namespace conflict with the terms **static** and **dynamic** in Unity. When static is used, it usually means that the object or process under discussion is not moving, remains unchanged, or exists in only one location, whereas dynamic means the opposite—objects or processes that tend to move or change. However, it's important to remember that each of these is a separate topic, and usage of the terms static and dynamic means something different in each case. We have already introduced the **Static** sub flags for GameObjects, the dynamic batching and static batching systems, and the concepts of static classes, static variables, and static functions in the C# language. So, just to be extra-confusing, Unity also has the concept of static and dynamic colliders.

Dynamic colliders mean GameObjects that contain both a `Collider` component (which could be one of several types) and a `Rigidbody` component. By attaching `Rigidbody` to the same object as a collider, the physics engine will treat that collider as the bounding volume of a physical object that must react to outside forces (such as gravity) and collisions with other Rigidbodies. If we collide one dynamic collider into another, they will both react based on Newton's laws of motion (or at least as best as a computer using floating-point arithmetic is capable of).

We can also have colliders that do not have a `Rigidbody` component attached, and these are called static colliders. These effectively work as invisible barriers that dynamic colliders can collide into, but the static collider will not react in response. To think of it another way, imagine objects without a `Rigidbody` component as having infinite mass. No matter how hard you throw a rock into an object of infinite mass, it will never move, but you can still expect the rock to react like it just hit a solid wall. This makes static colliders ideal for world barriers and other obstacles that must not move.

The physics engine automatically separates dynamic and static colliders into two different data structures, each optimized to handle the types of collider present. This helps to simplify future processing tasks since, for example, there's no point in resolving collisions and impulses between two static colliders.

Collision detection

There are three settings for collision detection in Unity, which can be configured in a `RigidBody` component's **Collision Detection** property: **Discrete**, **Continuous**, and **ContinuousDynamic**.

The **Discrete** setting enables **Discrete Collision Detection**, which effectively teleports objects a small distance every timestep based on their velocity and how much time has passed. Once all of the objects have been moved, it then performs a bounding volume check for any overlaps, treats them as collisions, and resolves them based on their physical properties and how they overlap. This method risks collisions being missed if small objects move too quickly.

The following diagram shows how **Discrete Collision Detection** works to catch two objects as they teleport from one location to the next:

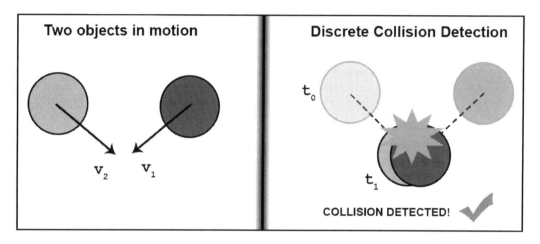

Either of the remaining settings will enable **Continuous Collision Detection**, which works by interpolating colliders from their starting and ending positions for the current timestep and checking for any collisions along the way. This reduces the risk of missed collisions and generates a more accurate simulation at the expense of a significantly higher CPU overhead compared to **Discrete Collision Detection**.

The **Continuous** setting enables **Continuous Collision Detection** only between the given collider and static colliders. Collisions between the same collider and dynamic colliders will still make use of **Discrete Collision Detection**.

Meanwhile, the **ContinuousDynamic** setting enables **Continuous Collision Detection** between the collider and all static and dynamic colliders, making it the most expensive in terms of resources.

The following diagram shows how the **Discrete Collision Detection** and **Continuous Collision Detection** methods work for a pair of small, fast-moving objects:

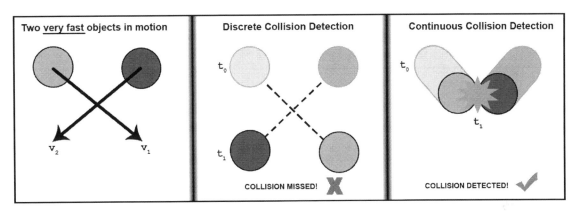

This is an extreme example for the sake of illustration. In the case of **Discrete Collision Detection**, we can observe that the objects are teleporting a distance around four times their size in a single timestep, which would typically only happen with very small objects with very high velocities, and is, hence, very rare if our game is running optimally. In the overwhelming majority of cases, the distances the objects travel in a single 20 ms timestep are much smaller relative to the size of the object, and so the collision is easily caught by **Discrete Collision Detection** methods.

Collider types

There are four different types of 3D colliders in Unity. In order of the lowest performance cost to the greatest, they are as follows:

- Sphere
- Capsule
- Box
- Mesh

The first three collider types are often called **primitives** and maintain precise shapes, although they can generally be scaled in different directions to meet specific needs. Mesh Colliders can, however, be customized to a particular shape depending on the assigned mesh. There are also three types of 2D Collider—Circle, Box, and Polygon—that are functionally similar to Sphere, Box, and Mesh Colliders, respectively. All of the following information is mostly transferable to the equivalent 2D shape.

Note that we can also generate cylindrical 3D objects in Unity, but this is only for its graphical representation. Auto-generated cylinder shapes use Capsule Colliders to represent their physical bounding volume, which may not create the expected physics behavior.

Also, there are two varieties of Mesh Collider: **Convex** and **Concave**. The difference is that a Concave shape features at least one internal angle (an angle between two inside edges of the shape) of greater than 180 degrees. To illustrate this, the following diagram shows the difference between **Convex** and **Concave** shapes:

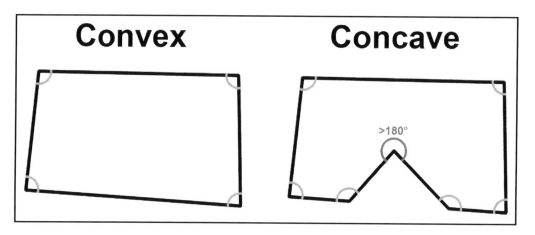

An easy way to remember the difference between a Convex and Concave shape is that a Concave shape has at least one cave within it.

Both Mesh Collider types use the same component (a `MeshCollider` component). The type of Mesh Collider that gets generated is toggled using the **Convex** checkbox. Enabling this option will allow the object to collide with all primitive shapes (Spheres, Boxes, and so on) as well as other Mesh Colliders with **Convex** enabled.

Also, if the **Convex** checkbox is enabled for a Mesh Collider with a Concave shape, then the physics engine will automatically simplify it, generating a collider with the nearest Convex shape it can.

In the preceding example, if we imported the Concave mesh on the right and enable the **Convex** checkbox, it would generate a collider shape closer to the Convex shape on the left. In either case, the physics engine will attempt to generate a collider that matches the shape of the attached mesh with an upper limit of 255 vertices. If the target mesh has more vertices than this, it will throw an error during mesh generation.

`Collider` components also contain the `IsTrigger` property, allowing them to be treated as nonphysical objects but still invoke physics events when other colliders enter or leave them. These are called **trigger volumes**. Normally, a collider's `OnCollisionEnter()`, `OnCollisionStay()`, and `OnCollisionExit()` callbacks are called when another collider touches, keeps touching (each timestep), or stops touching it, respectively. However, when the collider is used as a trigger volume, the `OnTriggerEnter()`, `OnTriggerStay()`, and `OnTriggerExit()` callbacks will be used instead.

Note that due to the complexity of resolving inter-object collisions, Concave Mesh Colliders cannot also be dynamic colliders. Concave shapes can only be used as static colliders or trigger volumes. If we attempt to add a `Rigidbody` component to a Concave Mesh Collider, Unity will ignore it.

What if you *really* need a Concave Mesh Collider acting as a `Rigidbody` component? The solution is to divide the object into a composition of separate Convex Mesh Colliders: for instance, you may want to compose an L-shaped `Rigidbody` by combining two convex boxes. Unfortunately, because this is a delicate decision, there is no automatic way to do that, and you need to perform such decomposition by hand.

The Collision Matrix

The physics engine features a Collision Matrix that defines which objects are allowed to collide with which other objects. Objects that do not fit this matrix are automatically ignored by the physics engine when the time comes to resolve bounding volume overlaps and collisions. This saves on physics processing during collision detection stages and allows the objects to move through one another without any collisions taking place.

The Collision Matrix can be accessed through **Edit | Project Settings | (Physics / Physics2D) | Layer Collision Matrix**.

The Collision Matrix system works through Unity's Layer system. The matrix represents every possible Layer-to-Layer combination that might be possible, and enabling a checkbox means that colliders in both of those Layers will be checked during the collision detection phase. Note that there's no way to allow only one of the two objects to respond to the collision. If one Layer can collide with another, then they must both respond to the collision. However, static colliders are an exception since they aren't allowed to react physically to collisions (although they still receive the `OnCollision...()` callbacks).

Note that we are limited to only 32 total Layers for our entire project (since the physics engine uses a 32-bit bitmask to determine inter-Layer collision opportunities), so we must organize our objects into sensible Layers that will extend throughout the entire lifetime of the project. If for whatever reason, 32 Layers are not enough for our project, then we might need to find cunning ways to reuse Layers or remove Layers that aren't necessary.

Rigidbody active and sleeping states

Every modern physics engine shares a standard optimization technique, where by objects that have come to rest have their internal state changed from an active state to a sleeping state. While `Rigidbody` is in the sleeping state, little to no processor time will be spent during fixed updates to update the object until an external force or collision event has awoken it.

The value of measurement that is used to determine what at rest means tends to vary among different physics engines; it could be calculated using linear and rotational speed, kinetic energy, momentum, or some other physical properties of `Rigidbody`. Both of Unity's physics engines work by evaluating the object's mass-normalized kinetic energy, which essentially boils down to the magnitude of its velocity, squared.

If the object's velocity has not exceeded some threshold value after a short time, then the physics engine will assume that the object will no longer need to move again until it has undergone a new collision, or a new force has been applied to it. Until then, the sleeping object will maintain its current position. Setting the threshold value too low would mean objects are much less likely to go to sleep, so we will keep paying a small processing cost within the physics engine every fixed update, even though it is not doing anything important. Meanwhile, setting the threshold value too high would mean slow-moving objects will appear to jerk to a sudden stop once the physics engine decides that they need to go to sleep. The threshold value that controls the sleeping state can be modified under **Edit** | **Project Settings** | **Physics** | **Sleep Threshold**. We can also get a count of the total number of active `Rigidbody` objects from the **Physics Area** of the **Profiler** window.

Note that sleeping objects are not removed entirely from the simulation. If a moving `Rigidbody` approaches the sleeping object, then it must still perform checks to see whether nearby objects have collided with it, which would reawaken the sleeping object, reintroducing it to the simulation for processing.

Ray and object casting

Another common feature of physics engines is the ability to cast a ray from one point to another and generate collision information with one or more of the objects in its path. This is known as **raycasting**. It is pretty common to implement several gameplay mechanics through raycasting, such as firing a gun. This is typically implemented by performing raycasts from the player to the target location and finding any viable targets in its path (even if it's just a wall).

We can also obtain a list of targets within a finite distance of a fixed point in space using a `Physics.OverlapSphere()` check. This is typically used to implement area-of-effect gameplay features, such as grenade or fireball explosions. We can even cast entire objects forward in space using `Physics.SphereCast()` and `Physics.CapsuleCast()`. These methods are often used to simulate wide laser beams, or if we want to see what would be in the path of a moving character.

Debugging physics

Physics bugs usually fall into two categories: an object pair collided/didn't collide when it shouldn't have/should have, or the objects collided but something unexpected happened after the fact. The former case is generally easier to debug; it is often either due to mistakes in the Collision Matrix, incorrect Layers used in raycasting, or object colliders being the wrong size or shape. The latter case is often much more challenging to resolve because of three big problems:

- Determining which collided objects caused the issue
- Determining the conditions of the collision just before the resolution
- Reproducing the collision

Any of these three pieces of information would make resolution much easier, but they can all be difficult to obtain in some circumstances.

The Profiler provides some measure of information in the **Physics** and **Physics (2D) Areas** (for 3D and 2D physics, respectively), which can be moderately useful. We can get a measure of how much CPU activity is being spent on all Rigidbodies and groups of Rigidbodies isolated to different types such as dynamic colliders, static colliders, kinematic objects, trigger volumes, constraints (used to simulate hinges and other connected physics objects), and contacts.

The **Physics 2D Area** contains a little more information such as the number of sleeping and active Rigidbodies and how long processing the Timestep took. The **Detailed Breakdown View** provides even more information in both cases. This information helps us to keep an eye on the physics performance, but it doesn't tell us much about what went wrong in the event we find a bug in our physics behavior.

A tool that is better suited to the task of helping us to debug physics issues is the **Physics Debugger**, which can be opened via **Window | Analysis | Physics Debugger**. This tool can help us to filter out different types of colliders from the **Scene** window to give us a better idea of which objects collide with one another. Of course, this does not help too much in determining the conditions of the problem and reproducing issues.

 Note that settings in the Physics Debugger do not affect object visibility in the **Game** window.

Unfortunately, there isn't much secret advice to be given for the remaining problems. Catching information about collisions before or when they happen involves typically a lot of targeted breakpoints in an `OnCollisionEnter()` or `OnTriggerEnter()` callback to catch the problem in the act and using step-through debugging until the source of the issue becomes apparent. As a last resort, we can add `Debug.Log()` statements to log important information just before the problem occurs, although this can be a frustrating exercise because we sometimes don't know what information we need to log or which objects to log from, and so we end up adding logs to everything.

Another frequent source of headaches is trying to reproduce physics problems. Reproducing collisions is always a challenge due to the non-deterministic nature between user input (typically handled in `Update()`) and physics behavior (processed in `FixedUpdate()`). Even though physics timesteps occur with relative regularity, the simulation will have different timings on each `Update()` between one session and the next, so also, if we recorded user input timings and automatically replayed the scene, trying to apply the recorded inputs at the moments they were applied isn't going to be precisely the same every time, and so we may not get the same result.

Moving user input handling to `FixedUpdate()` is possible, and helpful if user input controls `Rigidbody` behavior such as applying forces in different directions while the player holds down certain keys. However, this will tend to lead to input latency or *lag*, since it will be anywhere from 0 to 20 ms (based on the fixed update timestep frequency) before the physics engine can respond to the key being pressed. Instantaneous inputs, such as jumping or activating an ability, are always best handled in `Update()` to avoid missing keystrokes.

Helper functions such as `Input.GetKeyDown()` would only return `true` for the frame the player presses the given key and will return `false` during the next `Update()`. If we tried to read a key-down event during `FixedUpdate()`, we would never know that the user pressed the key, unless a physics timestep just happens to occur between these two frames. This can be worked around with an input buffering/tracking system, but this is certainly more trouble than its worth if we're implementing it merely to replicate a physics bug.

Ultimately, experience and persistence are the only right ways to debug most physics problems. The more knowledge we have with the physics engine, the more intuition we will have to find the source of the problem, but unfortunately they almost always take a lot of time to resolve due to their limited reproducibility and sometimes nebulous behavior, and so we should expect physics issues to take longer than most logic bugs to fix and plan extra time before it can be resolved.

Now that we have an understanding of the majority of features of the Unity physics engine, we can cover several optimization techniques to improve our game's physics performance.

Physics performance optimizations

In this section, we will go over several techniques, optimizations, tricks, and settings that will allow your game to extract every drop of physics performance from your game. This includes how to set up your scene, learn when to use static colliders, how to configure the Collision Matrix, when to use triggers instead of Rigidbodies, and much more. Let's go over all of these, one by one.

Scene setup

Firstly, there are several best practices we can apply to our scenes to improve the consistency of the physics simulation. Note that several of these techniques will not necessarily improve CPU or memory usage, but they will result in a reduced likelihood of instability from the physics engine.

Scaling

We should try to keep all physics object scales in the world as close to (1,1,1) as we possibly can. By default, Unity assumes that we are trying to simulate gameplay equivalent to being on the surface of the Earth. The force of gravity at the surface of the Earth is 9.81 meters-per-second squared, and hence the default gravity value is set to -9.81 to match. One unit in Unity's world space is equivalent to 1 meter, and the negative sign means that it will pull the object downward. Our object sizes should reflect our effective world scale since scaling them too large will cause gravity to appear to move the objects much more slowly than we would expect. If all of our objects are scaled five times too big, then gravity will appear to be five times weaker. The converse is also true; scaling objects too small will make them look to fall too quickly and will not seem realistic.

We can tweak the world's implied scale by modifying the strength of gravity under **Edit | Project Settings | Physics / Physics 2D | Gravity**. However, note that any floating-point arithmetic will be more accurate with values closer to 0, so if we have some objects that have scale values far above (1,1,1), even if they match the implied world scale, then we could still observe erratic physics behavior. So, early in the project, we should import and scale our most common physics objects around a scale value of (1,1,1) and then adjust the value of gravity to match. This will give us a reference point to work with as we introduce new objects.

Positioning

Similarly, keeping all objects close to (0,0,0) in the world-space position will result in better floating-point accuracy, improving the consistency of the simulation. Space simulator and free-running games try to simulate incredibly large spaces and typically use a trick of either secretly teleporting the player back toward the center of the world or fixing their position there, in which case, either volumes of space are compartmentalized so that physics calculations are always calculated with values close to 0, or everything else is moved to simulate travel, and the player's motion is only an illusion.

Most games are not at risk of introducing floating-point inaccuracy, since most game levels tend to last around 10 to 30 minutes, which doesn't give the player much time to travel absurdly long distances, but if we're working with exceptionally large scenes or asynchronously loading scenes throughout the course of the entire game to the point that the player travels tens of thousands of meters, then we may start to notice some strange physics behavior the further they go.

So, unless we're already far too deep into our project so that changing and retesting everything at a late stage would be too much hassle, we should try to keep all of our physics objects close to (0,0,0). Plus, this is good practice for our project workflow, as it makes it much quicker to find objects and tweak things in our game world.

Mass

Mass is stored as a floating-point value under a `Rigidbody` component's mass property, and documentation on its usage has changed a fair amount over the years due to updates in its physics engine. Since late Unity 5, we are essentially free to choose whatever we want the 1.0 value to represent and then scale other values appropriately.

Traditionally, a mass value of 1.0 is used to represent a mass of 1 kilogram, but we could decide that a human being has a mass of 1.0 (~80 kilograms), in which case, a car would be given a mass value of 15.0 (~1,200 kilograms), and physics collisions will resolve similarly to what we expect. The most important part is the relative difference in mass, which allows collisions between these objects to look believable without stressing the engine too much. Floating-point precision is also a concern, so we don't want to use large mass values that are too ridiculous.

 Note that if we intend to use Wheel Colliders, their design assumes that a mass of 1.0 represents 1 kilogram, so we should assign our mass values appropriately.

Ideally, we would maintain mass values around 1.0 and ensure a maximum relative mass-ratio of around 100. If two objects collide with a mass ratio much higher than this, then large momentum differences can turn into sudden, immense velocity changes from the impulse, resulting in some unstable physics and potential loss of floating-point precision. Object pairs that have a significant scale difference should probably be culled with the Collision Matrix to avoid problems (more on this shortly).

 Improper mass ratios are the most common cause of physics instability and erratic behavior in Unity. This is particularly true when using joints for objects such as ragdolls.

Note that the force of gravity at the center of the Earth affects all objects equally, regardless of their mass, so it does not matter if we consider a mass property value of 1.0 to be the mass of a rubber ball or the mass of a warship. There's no need to adjust the force of gravity to compensate. What does matter, however, is the amount of air resistance the given object undergoes while falling (which is why a parachute falls slowly). So, to maintain realistic behavior, we may need to customize the drag property for such objects or customize the force of gravity on a per-object basis. For example, we could disable the **Use Gravity** checkbox and apply our custom gravitational force during fixed updates.

Using static colliders appropriately

As mentioned previously, the physics engine automatically generates two separate data structures to contain static colliders separately from dynamic colliders. Unfortunately, if new objects are introduced into the static collider data structure at runtime, then it must be regenerated, similar to calling `StaticBatchingUtility.Combine()` for static batching. This is likely to cause a significant CPU spike. This makes it vital that we avoid instantiating new static colliders during gameplay.

Also, merely moving, rotating, or scaling static colliders triggers this regeneration process and should be avoided. If we have colliders that we wish to move around without physically reacting to other objects colliding with them, then we should attach `Rigidbody` to make it a dynamic collider and enable the **Kinematic** flag. This flag prevents the object from reacting to external impulses from inter-object collisions, similar to static colliders, except the object can still be moved through its `transform` component or through forces applied to its `Rigidbody` component (preferably during fixed updates). Since a kinematic object won't respond to other objects hitting it, it will tend to push other dynamic colliders out of its way as it moves.

 It's for this reason that player character objects are often made into Kinematic Colliders.

Using trigger volumes responsibly

As mentioned previously, we can treat our physics objects as normal colliders or as trigger volumes. An important distinction between these two types is that the `OnCollider...()` callbacks provide a `Collision` object as a parameter to the callback, which contains useful information such as the exact location of collision (helpful to position a particle effect) and the contact normal (useful if we want to move the object after the collision manually). However, the `OnTrigger...()` callbacks do not provide this kind of information.

As a result, we should not try to use trigger volumes for collision-reactive behavior since we won't have enough information to make the collision appear accurate. trigger volumes are best used for their intended purpose of tracking when an object enters/exits a specific area, such as dealing with damage while a player stays in a lava pit, triggering a cutscene when a player enters a building, and initiating asynchronous loading/unloading of a scene when the player approaches/moves far enough away from another major area.

If the contact information is absolutely needed for a trigger volume collision, then common workarounds are to do any of the following:

- Generate a rough estimate for the contact point by halving the distance between the trigger volume and colliding objects' centers of mass (this assumes that they're of roughly equal size).
- Perform a raycast upon collision from the center of the trigger volume to the center of mass of the colliding object (works best if both of the objects are spherical).
- Create a non-trigger volume object, give it an infinitesimally small mass (so that its presence barely affects the colliding object), and immediately destroy it upon collision (since a collision with such a large mass differential will probably send this small object into orbit).

Of course, each of these approaches has its drawbacks—limited physical accuracy, extra CPU overhead during the collision, and/or additional scene setup (and rather hacky-looking collision code)—but they can be useful in a pinch.

Optimizing the Collision Matrix

As we know, the physics engine's Collision Matrix defines which objects assigned to specific Layers are allowed to collide with objects assigned to other Layers. To put it more succinctly, which object collision pairs are even considered viable by the physics engine. Every other object-Layer pair is simply ignored by the physics engine, which makes this an important avenue for minimizing physics engine workload since it reduces the number of bounding volume checks that must be performed every fixed update and how many collisions would ever need to be processed during the life cycle of the application (which would save on battery life for a mobile device).

 Note that the Collision Matrix can be accessed through **Edit** | **Project Settings** | **Physics (or Physics2D)** | **Layer Collision Matrix.**

The following screenshot shows a standard Collision Matrix for an arcade shooter game:

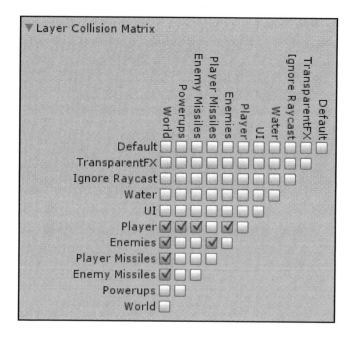

In the preceding example, we have objects flagged as **Player**, **Enemies**, **Player Missiles**, **Enemy Missiles**, and **Powerups**, and we have minimized the number of possible inter-object collisions for the physics engine to check.

Starting with the first row of checkmarks labeled **Player**, we want the **Player** object to be able to collide with **World** objects, pick up **Powerups**, get hit by **Enemy Missiles**, and collide with **Enemies**. However, we do not want them to collide with their **Player Missiles** or themselves (although there would probably only be one object in this Layer, anyway). Hence, the enabled checkboxes in the **Player** row reflect these requirements. We only want **Enemies** to collide with **World** objects and **Player Missiles**, so these are checked in the **Enemies** row. Note that the **Player**-to-**Enemies** collision pair would have been handled already by the previous row; hence, there is no need for it to appear in the **Enemies** row. We also want both **Player Missiles** and **Enemy Missiles** to explode when they hit **World** objects, so these are marked, and finally we don't care about **Powerups** colliding with anything but the **Player**, nor do we want **World** objects to collide with other **World** objects, so no checkboxes are marked on the final two rows.

At any given moment, we might have a single **Player** object, 2 **Powerups**, 7 **Player Missiles**, 10 **Enemies**, and 20 **Enemy Missiles**, which is 780 potential collision pairs (this is calculated as each of 40 different objects could collide with 39 other ones, giving us 1,560 likely collision pairs, but then we divide the total by 2 to ignore duplicate pairs). By merely optimizing this matrix, we have reduced this to less than 100, for an almost 90% reduction in potential collision checks. Of course, the Unity physics engine efficiently culls away many of these object pairs if they are too far apart from one another. Hence, there is little to no chance that they could collide (this is calculated during a hidden process known as **Broadphase culling**), so the actual savings will probably never be this good, but it will free up some CPU cycles with next to no effort. Another significant benefit is that it simplifies our game logic coding; there's no need to figure out what's supposed to happen if **Powerups** and **Enemy Missiles** collide if we tell the physics engine to ignore collisions between them.

We should perform logical sanity checks like this for all potential Layer combinations in the Collision Matrix to see whether we're wasting precious time checking for inter-object collisions between object pairs that aren't necessary.

Preferring discrete collision detection

Discrete collision detection is relatively cheap since teleporting objects once and performing a single overlap check between nearby object pairs is a relatively trivial amount of work to perform in a single timestep. The amount of calculation required to perform continuous collision detection is significantly higher since it involves interpolating both objects between their starting and ending positions while analyzing for any slight bounding volume overlaps between these points as they might occur during the timestep.

Consequently, the **Continuous** collision detection option is an order of magnitude more expensive than the **Discrete** detection method, whereas the **ContinuousDynamic** collision detection setting is an order of magnitude even more costly than **Continuous**. Having too many objects configured to use either of the continuous collision detection types will cause severe performance degradation in complex scenes. In both cases, the cost for collision detection grows exponentially with the number of objects that need to be compared during any given frame with a steep increase if the collider is dynamic instead of static.

Ergo, we should favor the **Discrete** collision detection setting for the overwhelming majority of our objects, while using either of the continuous collision detection settings only in extreme circumstances. The **Continuous** setting should be used when important collisions are frequently missed with the more static parts of our game world. For instance, if we wish to be sure that the player characters never fall through the game world or never accidentally teleport through walls if they move too quickly, then we might want to apply continuous collision detection only for those objects. Finally, the **ContinuousDynamic** setting should only be used if the same situation applies, and we wish to catch collisions between pairs of very fast-moving dynamic colliders.

Modifying the fixed update frequency

In some cases, **Discrete** collision detection might not work well enough on a large scale. Perhaps our entire game revolves around a lot of small physics objects, and discrete collision detection simply isn't catching enough collisions to maintain product quality. However, applying one of the continuous collision detection settings to everything would be far too prohibitive on performance. In this case, there is one option we can try: we can customize the physics timestep to give the **Discrete** collision detection system a better chance of catching such collisions by modifying how frequently the engine checks for fixed updates.

As mentioned previously, fixed updates and physics timestep processing are strongly coupled; so, by modifying the frequency of fixed update checks, we not only change the rate that the physics engine will calculate and resolve the next callback, but we also change how frequently the `FixedUpdate()` callbacks and coroutines are being invoked. Consequently, changing this value can be risky if we're deep into our project and have a lot of behavior that depends on these callbacks since we will be changing a fundamental assumption about how often these methods are invoked.

Altering the fixed update frequency can be accomplished using the **Edit | Project Settings | Time | Fixed Timestep** property in the Editor or through the `Time.fixedDeltaTime` property in script code.

Reducing this value (increasing the frequency) will force the physics engine to process more frequently, giving it a better chance of catching collisions with discrete collision detection. Naturally, this comes with an added CPU cost since we're invoking more `FixedUpdate()` callbacks and asking the physics engine to update more frequently, having it move objects and verify collisions more often.

Conversely, increasing this value (decreasing the frequency) provides more time for the CPU to complete other tasks before it must handle physics processing again, or, looking at it from another perspective, it gives the physics engine more time to process the last timestep before it begins processing the next one. Unfortunately, lowering the fixed update frequency would necessarily reduce the maximum velocity at which objects can move before the physics engine can no longer capture collisions with discrete collision detection (depending on the objects' sizes). We might also start to see objects changing velocities in strange ways because it is essentially becoming a weaker approximation of real-world physics behavior.

This makes it vital to perform a significant amount of testing each time the Fixed Timestep value is changed. Even with a complete understanding of how this value works, it is difficult to predict the overall outcome during gameplay and whether the result is passable for quality purposes. Hence, changes to this value should be made early in the project's life cycle and then made infrequently to get a sufficient amount of testing against as many physics situations as possible.

It might help to create a test scene that flings some of our high-velocity objects at one another to verify that the results are acceptable and run through this scene whenever Fixed Timestep changes are made. However, actual gameplay tends to be rather complicated, with many background tasks and unanticipated player behavior that causes additional work for the physics engine or gives it less time to process the current iteration. Actual gameplay conditions are impossible to replicate in a vacuum. Also, there's no substitute for the real thing, so the more testing we can accomplish against the current value of the Fixed Timestep, the more confident we can be that the changes meet acceptable quality standards.

Take it from someone who's in the career of developing software automation tools: automation of software testing is helpful in a lot of situations, but when it comes to real-time event- and user input-driven applications that synchronize with multiple hardware devices and complex subsystems such as physics engines and tend to change rapidly due to iterations on feedback, the support and maintenance costs of automated testing often becomes more effort than its worth, making manual testing the most sensible approach.

We always have continuous collision detection as a last resort to offset some of the resulting instability we're observing. Unfortunately, even if the changes are targeted, it is more likely that this will cause further performance issues than we started with due to the overhead costs of continuous collision detection. It would be wise to profile our scene before and after enabling continuous collision detection to verify that the benefits are outweighing the costs.

Adjusting the Maximum Allowed Timestep

If we're regularly exceeding the Maximum Allowed Timestep (which, as a reminder, determines how much time the physics engine has to resolve a timestep before it must exit early), then it will result in some pretty bizarre-looking physics behavior. Rigidbodies will appear to slow down or jerk to a stop since the physics engine needs to keep exiting timestep calculations early before it has fully resolved its entire time quota. In this case, it is a clear sign that we need to optimize our physics behavior from other angles. However, at the very least, we can be confident that the threshold will prevent the game from completely locking up from a spike in the middle of physics processing.

 Reminder: this setting can be accessed through **Edit** | **Project Settings** | **Time** | **Maximum Allowed Timestep**.

The default setting is to consume a maximum of 0.333 seconds, which would manifest itself as a very noticeable drop in frame rate (a mere 3 FPS) if it were exceeded. If you ever feel the need to change this setting, then you obviously have some big problems with your physics workload, so it is recommended that you only tweak this value if you have exhausted all other approaches.

Minimizing raycasting and bounding-volume checks

All of the raycasting methods are incredibly useful, but they are relatively expensive, particularly `CapsuleCast()` and `SphereCast()`. We should avoid calling these methods regularly within the `Update()` callbacks or coroutines, saving them only for critical events in our script code.

If we're making use of persistent line, ray, or area-of-effect collision areas in our scene (examples include security lasers, continuously burning fires, and beam weapons), and the object remains relatively stationary, then they would perhaps be better simulated using a simple trigger volume.

If such replacements are not possible, and we truly need persistent casting checks using these methods, we should minimize the amount of processing each raycast makes by exploiting LayerMasks. This is particularly true if we're making use of Physics.RaycastAll(). For example, a poorly optimized usage of this kind of raycasting would look as follows:

```
void PerformRaycast() {
 RaycastHit[] hits;
  hits = Physics.RaycastAll(transform.position, transform.forward,
  100.0f);
  for (int i = 0; i < hits.Length; ++i) {
    RaycastHit hit = hits[i];
    EnemyComponent e = hit.transform.GetComponent<EnemyComponent>();
    if (e.GetType() == EnemyType.Orc) {
       e.DealDamage(10);
    }
  }
}
```

In the preceding example, we're collecting raycast collision data for every object in the path of this ray, but we're only processing its effects on objects that hold a specific EnemyComponent instance. Consequently, we're asking the physics engine to complete much more work than is necessary.

A better approach will be to use a different overload of RaycastAll(), which accepts a LayerMask value as an argument. This will filter collisions for the ray in much the same way as the Collision Matrix so that it only tests against objects in the given Layer(s). The following code contains a subtle improvement by providing an additional LayerMask property; we would configure LayerMask through the **Inspector** window for this Component, and it will filter the list much faster and only contain hits for objects matching the mask:

```
[SerializeField] LayerMask _layerMask;

void PerformRaycast() {
  RaycastHit[] hits;
  hits = Physics.RaycastAll(transform.position, transform.forward, 100.0f,
 _layerMask);
  for (int i = 0; i < hits.Length; ++i) {
    // as before ...
```

```
        }
    }
```

This optimization doesn't work as well for the `Physics.RaycastHit()` function since that version only provides ray collision information for the first object the ray collides with, regardless of whether we're using `LayerMask` or not.

 Note that because the `RaycastHit` and `Ray` classes are managed by the native memory space of the Unity engine, they don't result in memory allocations that draw the attention of the garbage collector. We will learn more about such activity in `Chapter 8`, *Masterful Memory Management*.

Avoiding complex Mesh Colliders

In order of collision detection efficiency, the various colliders are Spheres, Capsules, Boxes, Convex Mesh Colliders, and Concave Mesh Colliders, the last being far and away the most expensive. Collisions always involve pairs of objects, and the amount of work (math) needed to resolve the collision will depend on the complexity of both objects. Detecting collisions between two primitive objects can be reduced down to a relatively simple set of mathematical equations that are highly optimized. Performing comparisons against a pair of Convex Mesh Colliders is a much more complex equation, making them an order of magnitude more expensive than collisions between two primitives. Then, there are collisions between two Concave Mesh Colliders, which are so complex that they cannot be reduced down to a simple formula and require collision checks to be resolved between each pair of triangles across both meshes, easily making them orders of magnitude more expensive than collisions between other collider types. The amount of work involved scales similarly when we resolve collisions between shapes of different groups. For example, a collision between a primitive and Concave Mesh Collider would be slower than a collision between two primitives, but faster than a collision between two Concave Mesh Colliders.

There is also the question of whether one—or both—of the objects involved in the collision is moving (one of the objects being a static collider is easier to process than both objects being dynamic colliders). There is also the matter of how many of these objects are within our scene since the total processing costs of collision detection will snowball if we're not careful with how many shapes we introduce into the simulation.

A great irony between representing physics and graphics in 3D applications is how difficult it is to handle spherical and cube objects between the two of them. The perfect spherical mesh would require an infinite number of polygons to be generated, making such an object impossible to represent graphically.

However, handling collisions between two spheres in a physics engine is perhaps the most straightforward problem to solve for contact points and collisions (the contact point is always at the edge of either of the sphere's radius, and the contact normal is always the vector between their centers of mass). Conversely, a cube is one of the simplest objects to represent graphically (as little as 8 vertices and 12 triangles) and yet takes significantly more mathematics and processing power to find contact points and resolve collisions for (and the mathematics to resolve it depends on whether the collision occurred between faces, edges, corners, or a mixed pairing). Anecdotally, this implies that the most efficient way of creating the largest number of objects would be to populate our world with cube objects that use spherical colliders. However, this would make absolutely no sense to a human observer, as they would witness cubes rolling around like balls.

The previous anecdote serves as a reminder that the physical representation of an object does not necessarily need to match its graphical representation. This is beneficial, as a graphical mesh can often be condensed down into a much simpler shape, while still generating very similar physics behavior and simultaneously removing the need to use an overly complex Mesh Collider.

This separation of representations between graphics and physics allows us to optimize the performance of one system without (necessarily) negatively affecting the other. So long as there are no noticeable repercussions on gameplay (or we're willing to make the sacrifice), then we are free to represent complex graphical objects with much simpler physics shapes without players noticing. Also, if the player never notices, then no harm is done.

So, we can solve this problem in one of the two ways: either by approximating the physics behavior of the complex shape using one (or more) of the standard primitives or by using a much simpler Mesh Collider.

Using simpler primitives

Most shapes can be approximated using one of the three primitive colliders. In fact, we do not need to represent the object using only a single collider. We are free to use several colliders if they serve our needs for creating a complex collision shape by attaching additional child GameObjects with their colliders. This is almost always less expensive than using a single Mesh Collider and should be preferred.

The following screenshot shows a handful of complex graphical objects represented by one or more simpler primitive collider shapes:

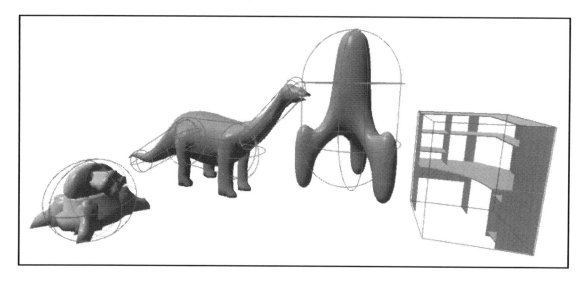

Using a Mesh Collider for any one of these objects would be significantly more expensive than the primitive colliders shown here due to the number of polygons they contain. It is worth exploring all opportunities to simplify our objects down using these primitives as much as we can, as they can provide significant performance gains.

For example, Concave Mesh Colliders are unique in that they can feature gaps or holes that allow other meshes to fall into or even through them, which introduces opportunities for the objects to fall through the world if such colliders are used for world collision areas. It is often better to place Box Colliders in strategic locations for this purpose.

Using simpler Mesh Colliders

Similarly, the mesh assigned to a Mesh Collider does not necessarily need to match the graphical representation of the same object (Unity simply picks it as the default). This allows us to assign a simpler mesh to the Mesh Collider's `mesh` property, which is different from the one we use for its graphical representation.

The following screenshot shows an example of a sophisticated graphical mesh that has been given a much more simplified mesh for its Mesh Collider:

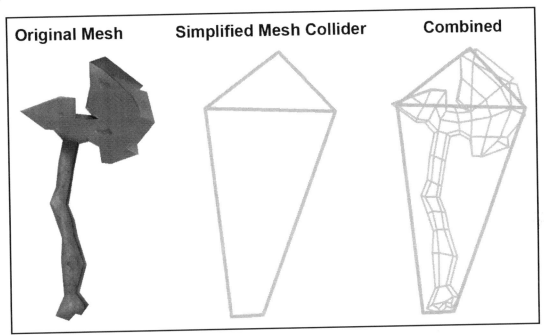

Simplifying the rendered mesh into convex shapes with lower polygon counts in this way will significantly reduce the overhead needed to determine bounding volume overlaps with other colliders. Depending on how well the original object is estimated, there should be minimal noticeable gameplay differences, especially in the case of this ax, which we expect to be moving quickly as creatures swing it during attacks, making it unlikely that players will notice the difference between the two meshes as colliders. In fact, the simplified mesh is much less likely to be missed by discrete collision detection and is preferable for that reason.

Avoiding complex physics components

Certain special physics `Collider` components, such as `TerrainCollider`, `Cloth`, and `WheelCollider`, are orders of magnitude more expensive than all primitive colliders and even Mesh Colliders in some cases. We should not include such components in our Scenes unless they are absolutely necessary. For instance, if we have terrain objects in the distance that the player will never approach, there's little reason to include an attached `TerrainCollider` component.

Games featuring `Cloth` components should consider instantiating different objects without them when running in lower-quality settings or simply animating cloth behavior (although it is totally understandable if the team has grown attached to and fallen in love with how the stuff moves around).

Games using `WheelCollider` components should simply try to use fewer Wheel Colliders. Large vehicles, with more than four wheels, may be able to simulate similar behavior using only four wheels, while faking the graphical representation of additional wheels.

Letting physics objects sleep

The physics engine's sleep feature can pose several problems for our game. Firstly, some developers don't realize that many of their Rigidbodies are sleeping during most of the lifetime of their application. This tends to lead developers to assume that they can get away with (for example) doubling the number of Rigidbodies in their game, and the overall costs would simply double to match it. This is unlikely. The frequency of collisions and the total accumulated time of active objects is more likely to increase in an exponential fashion rather than a linear one. This leads to unexpected performance costs every time new physics objects are introduced into the simulation. We should keep this in mind when we decide to increase the physical complexity of our scenes.

Secondly, changing any properties on a `Rigidbody` component at runtime, such as mass, drag, and useGravity, will also reawaken an object. If we're regularly changing these values (such as a game where object sizes and masses change over time), then they will remain active for more extended periods than usual. This is also the case for applying forces, so if we're using a custom gravity solution (such as suggested in the mass section), we should try to avoid applying the gravitational force every fixed update; otherwise, the object will be unable to fall asleep. We could check its mass-normalized kinetic energy (just take the value of `velocity.sqrMagnitude`) and manually disable our custom gravity when we detect that it is very low.

Thirdly, there is the danger of islands of sleeping physics objects being generated. Islands are created when a large number of Rigidbodies are touching one another and have gradually gone to sleep once the kinetic energy of the system has fallen low enough. However, because they're all still touching one another, as soon as one of these objects is awoken, it will start a chain reaction, awakening all other nearby Rigidbodies. Suddenly, we have a large spike in CPU usage because dozens of objects have re-entered the simulation. Even worse, because the objects are so close together, there will be many potential collision pairs that must keep being resolved until the objects fall asleep again.

Avoiding these situations is best done by reducing the complexity of our scenes, but if we find ourselves unable to do so, we could look for ways to detect that islands are forming, and then strategically destroy/despawn some of them to prevent too many large islands from being generated. However, performing regular distance comparisons between all of our Rigidbodies is not a cheap task to accomplish and could be costly. The physics engine already performs such checks itself, during Broadphase culling, but, unfortunately, Unity doesn't expose this data through the physics engine API. Any workarounds for this problem will be dependent on how the game is designed; for example, a game that requires the player to move lots of physics objects into an area (for example, a game that involves herding sheep into a pen) could choose to remove the sheep's collider as soon as the player moves it into position, locking the object to its final destination, easing the workload on the physics engine and preventing islands from becoming a problem.

Sleeping objects can be a blessing and a curse. They can save us a lot of processing power, but if too many of them reawaken at the same time or our simulation is too busy to allow enough of them to fall asleep, then we could be incurring some unfortunate performance costs during gameplay. We should strive to limit these situations as much as possible by letting our objects enter the sleeping state as much as possible and avoiding grouping them in large clusters.

Note that the sleep threshold can be modified under **Edit** | **Project Settings** | **Physics** | **Sleep Threshold**.

Modifying the solver iteration count

Using joints, springs, and other ways to connect Rigidbodies are fairly complex simulations in physics engines. Owing to the codependent interactivity (internally represented as movement constraints) that occurs due to joining two objects together, the system must often make several attempts at solving the necessary mathematical equations. This multi-iteration approach is required to calculate an accurate result whenever there is a change in velocity to any single part of the object chain.

It, therefore, becomes a balancing act of limiting the maximum number of attempts the solver makes to resolve a particular situation versus how accurate a result we can get away with. We don't want the solver to spend too much time on a single collision because there are a lot of other tasks that the physics engine has to complete within the same iteration. However, we also don't want to reduce the maximum number of iterations too far, as it will only approximate what the final solution would have been, making its motion look much less believable than if it had been given more time to calculate the result.

 The same solver also gets involved when resolving inter-object collisions and contacts. It can almost always determine the correct result for simple collisions with a single iteration, except for some very rare and complex collision situations with Mesh Colliders. It is mostly when attached objects will be affected through joints that the solver requires additional effort to integrate the final result.

The maximum number of iterations the solver is allowed to attempt is called the **solver iteration count**, which can be modified under **Edit | Project Settings | Physics | Default Solver Iterations**. In most cases, the default value of six iterations is perfectly acceptable. However, games that include very complex joint systems may wish to increase this count to suppress any erratic (or downright explosive) `CharacterJoint` behaviors, whereas some projects may be able to get away with reducing this count. Testing must be performed after changing this value to check whether the project still maintains the intended levels of quality. Note that this value is the default solver iteration count—the value that gets applied to any newly created Rigidbodies. We can change this value at runtime through the `Physics.defaultSolverIterations` property, but this still won't affect preexisting Rigidbodies. If necessary, we can modify their solver iteration count after they are constructed through the `Rigidbody.solverIterations` property.

If we find our game regularly runs into jarring, erratic, and physics-breaking situations with complex joint-based objects (such as ragdolls), then we should consider gradually increasing the solver iteration count until the problems are suppressed. These problems typically occur if our ragdolls absorb too much energy from colliding objects, and the solver is unable to iterate the solution down to something reasonable before it is asked to give up. At this point, one of the joints goes supernova, dragging the rest of them into orbit along with it. Unity has a separate setting for this problem, which can be found under **Edit | Project Settings | Physics | Default Solver Velocity Iterations**. Increasing this value will give the solver more opportunity to calculate a sensible velocity during joint-based object collisions and help to avoid the above scenario. Again, this is a default value; hence, it is only applied to newly created Rigidbodies. The value can be modified at runtime through the `Physics.defaultSolverVelocityIterations` property and can be customized on specific Rigidbodies through the `Rigidbody.solverVelocityIterations` property.

In either case, increasing the number of iterations will consume more CPU resources during every fixed update where the joint objects remain active.

 Note that the Physics 2D settings for solver iterations are named **Position Iterations** and **Velocity Iterations**.

Optimizing ragdolls

Speaking of joint-based objects, ragdolls are incredibly popular features for a good reason; they're tons of fun! Ignoring the morbidity of flinging corpses around a game world for the moment, there's something about watching a complex chain of objects flail around and smash into things that hits a lot of fun psychological buttons. This makes it very tempting to allow many ragdolls to coexist within our scene at the same time, but as we quickly discover, this risks an enormous performance hit when too many ragdolls are in motion and/or collide with other objects due to the amount of iterations the solver would need to resolve them all. So, let's explore some ways to improve the performance of ragdolls.

Reducing joints and colliders

Unity provides a simple ragdoll-generation tool (the Ragdoll Wizard) under **GameObject | 3D Object | Ragdoll...**. This tool can be used to create ragdolls from a given object by selecting the appropriate child GameObjects to attach `Joint` and `Collider` components for any given body part or limb. This tool always creates 13 different colliders and associated joints (pelvis, chest, head, two colliders per arm, and three colliders per leg).

 Note that a bug causes the Ragdoll Wizard not to complain if nothing is assigned to **Left Foot** or **Right Foot** `transform` component references as it does for the rest of them, but Unity will throw `NullReferenceException` if we try to create the mesh without them assigned. Ensure that all 13 `transform` component references have been assigned when we try to create a ragdoll.

However, it's possible to use only seven colliders (pelvis, chest, head, and one collider per limb) to greatly reduce the overhead cost at the expense of ragdoll realism. This can be achieved by deleting unwanted colliders and manually reassigning the character joint's `connectedBody` properties to the proper parent joints (connect the arm colliders to the chest, and connect the leg colliders to the pelvis).

Note that we assign a mass value during ragdoll creation using the Ragdoll Wizard. This mass value is spread across the various joints as appropriate and, therefore, represents the total mass of the object. We should ensure that we don't apply a mass value too high or too low compared to other objects in our game to avoid potential instability.

Avoiding inter-ragdoll collisions

The performance cost of ragdolls grows exponentially when they are allowed to collide with other ragdolls. In fact, any joint collision requires the solver to calculate the resultant velocity applied to all of the joints connected to it, and then each of the joints connected to the other ragdoll. That means, in practice, that both ragdolls must be resolved entirely multiple times. Moreover, it gets significantly more complicated if various parts of the ragdolls are likely to collide with one another during the same collision.

This is a tough task for the solver to handle, so we should avoid it. The best way to do this is to use the Collision Matrix. It is wise to assign all ragdolls to their own Layer and uncheck the corresponding checkbox in the Collision Matrix so that objects in the given Layer cannot collide with objects in the same Layer.

Replacing, deactivating, or removing inactive ragdolls

In some games, once a ragdoll has reached its final destination, we no longer need it to remain in the game world as an interactable object. We could then either deactivate, destroy, or replace the ragdoll with a more straightforward alternative when they are no longer needed (a good trick is to replace them with the simpler version that uses only seven joints as suggested earlier). Such simplifications are often implemented as a means of reducing overhead for weaker hardware/lower quality settings or as a compromise to allow more ragdolls to coexist in our scene. It could even be used dynamically if a particular number of ragdolls is already present.

We would need some object to keep track of all of our ragdolls, being notified any time a ragdoll is created, keeping track of how many ragdolls currently exist, watching each of them until they fall asleep through `RigidBody.IsSleeping()` and then do something appropriate with them. The same object could also choose to instantiate simpler ragdoll variations if the scene already contains more ragdolls than is reasonable. This would be another good opportunity to make use of the messaging system we explored in `Chapter 2`, *Scripting Strategies*.

Whichever approach we choose to improve the performance of our ragdolls will no doubt result in limiting ragdolls as a gameplay feature, either by instantiating fewer of them, giving them less complexity, or giving them a shorter lifetime, but these are reasonable compromises to make given the performance-saving opportunities.

Knowing when to use physics

The most obvious method to improve the performance of a feature is to avoid using it as much as possible. For all movable objects in our game, we should take a moment to ask ourselves if getting the physics engine involved is even necessary. If not, we should look for opportunities to replace them with something simpler and less costly.

Perhaps we're using physics to detect whether the player fell into a kill-zone (water, lava, a death-plummet, and so on), but our game is simple enough that we only have kill-zones at a specific height. In this case, we could avoid physics colliders altogether and get away with only checking whether the player's *y*-position falls below a particular value.

Consider the following example—we're trying to simulate a meteor shower, and our first instinct was to have many falling objects that move via physics Rigidbodies, detect collisions with the ground via colliders, and then generate an explosion at the point of impact. However, perhaps the ground is consistently flat, or we have access to the Terrain's heightmap for some rudimentary collision detection. In this case, object travel could be simplified by manually tweening the objects' `transform.position` over time to simulate the same traveling behavior without requiring any physics components. In both cases, we can reduce the physics overhead by simplifying the situation and pushing the work into the script code.

 Tweening is a common shorthand term for in-betweening, which is the act of interpolating variables from one value to another gradually over time. There are many useful (and free) tweening libraries available on the Unity Asset Store that can provide a lot of useful functionality. Although, be careful of potentially poor optimization in these libraries.

The reverse is also possible. There might be occasions where we're performing a great deal of calculation through script code that could be handled through physics relatively simply. For example, we might have implemented an inventory system with many objects that can be picked up. When the player hits the pick up Object key, each of these objects might be compared against the player's position to figure out which object is the closest.

We could consider replacing all of the script code with a single `Physics.OverlapSphere()` call to get nearby objects when the key is pressed, and then figure out the closest pickup object from the result (or, better yet, just automatically pick up all of them. Why make the player repeatedly click more than necessary?). This could greatly reduce the total number of objects that must be compared each time the key is pressed although comparisons should be made to ensure that this is the case.

Ensure that you seek to remove unnecessary physics grunt work from your scenes or use physics to replace behavior that is costly when performed through script code. The opportunities are as wide and far-reaching as your own ingenuity. The ability to recognize opportunities like this takes experience but is a vital skill that will serve you well when saving performance in current and future game development projects.

Summary

We've covered numerous methods to improve our game's physics simulation both in terms of performance and consistency. The best technique when it comes to costly systems such as physics engines is simply avoidance. The less we need to use the system, the less we need to worry about it generating bottlenecks. In the worst-case scenario, we may need to reduce the scope of our game to condense physics activity down to only the essentials, but as we've learned, there are plenty of ways to reduce physics complexity without causing any noticeable gameplay effects.

In the next chapter, we will immerse ourselves in Unity's Rendering Pipeline and discover how to maximize the graphical fidelity of our application, by making use of all of the CPU cycles we've freed up using the performance enhancements from earlier chapters.

6
Dynamic Graphics

There is no question that the Rendering Pipeline of a modern graphics device is complicated. Even rendering a single triangle to the screen requires a multitude of graphics API calls. This includes tasks such as creating a buffer for the camera view that hooks into the operating system (usually via some kind of windowing system), allocating buffers for vertex data, setting up data channels to transfer vertex and texture data from RAM to VRAM, configuring each of these memory spaces to use a specific set of data formats, determining the objects that are visible to the camera, setting up and initiating a draw call for the triangle, waiting for the Rendering Pipeline to complete its task(s), and finally, presenting the rendered image to the screen. However, there's a simple reason for this seemingly convoluted and over-engineered way of drawing such a simple object—rendering often involves repeating the same tasks over and over again, and all of this initial setup makes future rendering tasks very fast.

CPUs are designed to handle virtually any computational scenario, but can't handle too many tasks simultaneously, whereas GPUs are designed for incredibly large amounts of parallelism, but they are limited in the complexity they can handle without breaking that parallelism. Their parallel nature requires immense amounts of data to be copied around very rapidly. During the setup of the Rendering Pipeline, we configure memory data channels for our graphics data to flow through. So, if these channels are properly configured for the types of data we will be passing, then they will operate more efficiently. However, setting them up poorly will result in the opposite.

Both the CPU and GPU are used during all graphics rendering, making it a high-speed dance of processing and memory management that spans software; hardware; multiple memory spaces, programming languages (each suited to different optimizations), processors, and processor types; and a large number of special-case features that can be thrown into the mix.

To make matters even more complicated, every rendering situation we will come across is different in its own way. Running the same application against two different GPUs often results in an apples-versus-oranges comparison due to the different capabilities and APIs they support.

It can be challenging to determine where a bottleneck resides within such a complex web of hardware and software systems, and it can take a lifetime of industry work in 3D graphics if we want to have a strong and immediate intuition about the source of performance issues in modern Rendering Pipelines.

Thankfully, profiling comes to the rescue once again, which makes becoming a Rendering Pipeline wizard less of a necessity. If we can gather data about each device, use multiple performance metrics for comparison, and tweak our scenes to observe how different rendering features affect their behavior, then we should have sufficient evidence to find the root cause of an issue and make appropriate changes. So, in this chapter, you will learn how to gather the right data, dig just deep enough into the Rendering Pipeline to find the real source of the problem, and explore various solutions and workarounds for a multitude of potential issues.

There are many topics to be covered when it comes to improving rendering performance. So, in this chapter, we will explore the following topics:

- A brief exploration of the Rendering Pipeline, focusing on the parts where the CPU and GPU come into play
- General techniques on how to determine whether our rendering is limited by the CPU or GPU
- A series of performance optimization techniques and features, such as:
  - Using GPU instancing
  - Taking advantage **of Level of Detail (LOD)** and other culling groups
  - Using Occlusion Culling
  - Optimizing Particle Systems
  - Improve Unity UI
  - Optimize your Shaders
  - Optimize lighting and shadow with lightmaps
  - Applying mobile-specific rendering enhancements

Exploring the Rendering Pipeline

Poor rendering performance can manifest itself in several ways, depending on whether the device is limited by CPU activity (we are CPU bound) or by GPU activity (we are GPU bound). Investigating a CPU-bound application can be relatively simple since all of the CPU work is wrapped up in loading data from disk/memory and calling graphics API instructions.

However, a GPU-bound application can be more difficult to analyze since the root cause could originate from one of a large number of potential places within the Rendering Pipeline. We might find that we need to rely on a little guesswork or *process of elimination* to determine the source of a GPU bottleneck. In either case, once the problem is discovered and resolved, we can expect significant improvements since small fixes tend to reap big rewards when it comes to fixing issues in the Rendering Pipeline.

We briefly touched on the Rendering Pipeline in `Chapter 3`, *The Benefits of Batching*. To briefly summarize the essential points, we know that the CPU sends rendering instructions through the graphics API that funnels through the hardware driver to the GPU device, which results in a list of rendering instructions being accumulated in a queue known as the command buffer. The GPU processes these commands one by one until the command buffer is empty. So long as the GPU can keep up with the rate and complexity of instructions before the next frame is due to begin, we will maintain our frame rate. However, if the GPU falls behind, or the CPU spends too much time generating commands, the frame rate will start to drop.

The following is a greatly simplified diagram of a typical Rendering Pipeline on a modern GPU (which can also vary based on device, technology support, and custom optimizations), showing a broad view of the steps that take place:

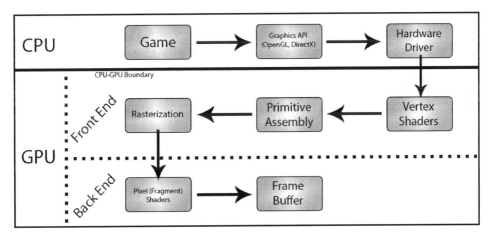

The top row represents the work that takes place in the CPU, which includes both the act of calling into the graphics API through the hardware driver and pushing commands into the GPU. The next two rows represent the steps that take place in the GPU. Owing to the GPU's complexity, its internal processes are often split into two different sections—the **Frontend** and the **Backend**, which require a little added explanation.

The GPU frontend

The frontend refers to the part of the rendering process where the GPU handles vertex data. Let's understand how it works:

1. The frontend will receive mesh data from the CPU (a big bundle of vertex information), and a draw call will be issued.
2. The GPU then gathers all pieces of vertex information from the mesh data and passes them through vertex shaders, which are allowed to modify them and output them in a *1-to-1* manner.
3. From this, the GPU now has a list of primitives to process (triangles—the most primitive shapes in 3D graphics).
4. Next, the rasterizer takes these primitives and determines which pixels of the final image will need to be drawn on to create the primitive based on the positions of its vertices and the current camera view. The list of pixels generated from this process is known as **fragments**, which will be processed in the backend.

Vertex shaders are small C-like programs that determine the input data that they are interested in and the way that they will manipulate it, and then will output a set of information for the rasterizer to generate fragments with. It is also home to the process of tessellation, which is handled by geometry shaders (sometimes called **tessellation shaders**), similar to a vertex shader in that they are small scripts uploaded to the GPU, except that they are allowed to output vertices in a *1-to-many* manner, hence, generating additional geometry programmatically.

 The term **shader** is an anachronism from back when these scripts primarily handled lighting and shading tasks before their role was expanded to include all of the tasks they are used for today.

The GPU backend

The backend represents the part of the Rendering Pipeline where fragments are processed. Let's see how it works:

1. Each fragment will pass through a fragment shader (also known as a **pixel shader**). These shaders tend to involve a lot more complex activity compared to vertex shaders, such as depth testing, alpha testing, colorization, texture sampling, lighting, shadows, and various post-processing effects, to name but a few of the possibilities.

2. This data is then drawn onto the frame buffer, which holds the current image that will eventually be sent to the display device (our monitor) once rendering tasks for the current frame are complete. There usually are two Frame Buffers in use by graphics APIs by default (although more could be generated for custom rendering scenarios).

3. At any given moment, one of the frame buffers contains the data from the frame we rendered to and is being presented to the screen, while the other is actively being drawn to by the GPU while it completes commands from the command buffer.

4. Once the GPU reaches a `swap buffers` command (the final instruction the CPU asks it to complete for the given frame), the frame buffers are flipped around so that the new frame is presented.

5. The GPU will then use the old frame buffer to draw the next frame.

6. This process repeats each time a new frame is rendered; hence, the GPU only needs two Frame Buffers to handle this task.

This entire process, from making graphics API calls to swapping Frame Buffers, repeats continuously for every mesh, vertex, fragment, and frame, so long as our application is still rendering.

Two metrics tend to be the source of bottlenecks in the backend—Fill Rate and memory bandwidth. Let's explore them a little.

Fill Rate

Fill Rate is an inclusive term referring to the speed at which the GPU can draw fragments. However, this only includes fragments that have survived all of the various conditional tests we might have enabled within the given fragment shader. A fragment is merely a *potential pixel*, and if it fails any of the enabled tests, then it is immediately discarded. This can be an enormous performance-saver, as the Rendering Pipeline can skip the costly drawing step and begin working on the next fragment instead.

One such example of a test that might cull a fragment is *Z-testing*, which checks whether the fragment from a closer object has already been drawn to the same fragment location (the Z refers to the depth dimension from the point of view of the camera). If so, the current fragment is discarded. If not, then the fragment is pushed through the fragment shader and drawn over the target pixel, which consumes exactly one fill from our Fill Rate. Now, imagine multiplying this process by thousands of overlapping objects, each of which generates hundreds or thousands of possible fragments (higher screen resolutions require more fragments to be processed). This could easily lead to millions of fragments to process every frame due to all of the possible overlaps of the main camera. On top of this, we're trying to repeat this process dozens of times every second. This is why performing so much initial setup in the Rendering Pipeline is important, and it should be reasonably obvious that skipping as many of these draws as we can results in significant rendering cost savings.

Graphics card manufacturers typically advertise a particular Fill Rate as a feature of the card, usually in the form of gigapixels per second, but this is a bit of a misnomer, as it would be more accurate to call it gigafragments per second; however, this argument is mostly academic. Either way, larger values tell us that the device can potentially push more fragments through the Rendering Pipeline. So, with a budget of 30 gigapixels per second and a target frame rate of 60 Hz, we can afford to process $30,000,000,000/60 = 500$ *million fragments* per frame before being bottlenecked on Fill Rate. With a resolution of 2,560 x 1,440 and a best-case scenario where each pixel is drawn over only once, we could theoretically draw the entire scene about 125 times without any noticeable problems.

Sadly, this is not a perfect world. Fill Rate is also consumed by other advanced rendering techniques, such as shadows and post-processing effects, that need to take the same fragment data and perform their passes on the Frame Buffer. Even so, we will always end up with some amount of redraw over the same pixels due to the order in which objects are rendered. This is known as **Overdraw**, and it is a useful metric to measure how efficiently we are making use of our Fill Rate.

Overdraw

How much Overdraw we have can be represented visually by rendering all objects with additive alpha blending and a flat coloration. Areas of high Overdraw will show up more brightly, as the same pixel is drawn over with additive blending multiple times. This is precisely how the **Scene** window's **Overdraw** shading mode reveals how much Overdraw our scene is undergoing.

The following screenshot shows a scene with several thousand boxes drawn normally (left) versus the **Scene** window's **Overdraw** shading mode (right):

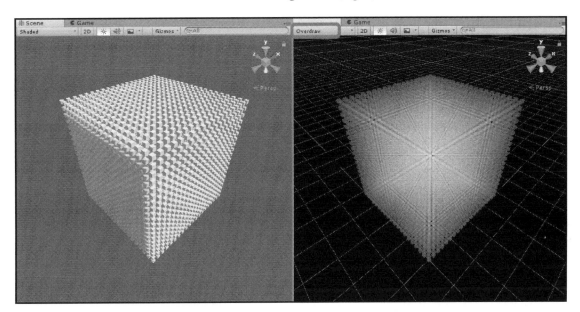

The more Overdraw we have, the more Fill Rate we are wasting by overwriting fragment data. There are several techniques we can apply to reduce Overdraw, which we will explore later.

Note that there are several different queues used for rendering, which can be separated into two types: **opaque queues** and **transparent queues**.

Objects rendered in one of the opaque queues can cull away fragments via Z-testing, as explained previously. However, objects rendered in a transparent queue cannot do so since their transparent nature means we can't assume that they won't need to be drawn no matter how many other objects are in the way, which leads to a lot of overdraws.

All Unity UI objects always render in a transparent queue, making them a significant source of Overdraw.

Memory bandwidth

The other potential source of bottlenecks in the backend comes from memory bandwidth. memory bandwidth is consumed whenever a texture must be pulled from a section of the GPU's VRAM down into the lower memory levels. This typically happens when a texture is sampled, where a fragment shader attempts to pick the matching texture pixel (or *texel*) to draw for a given fragment at a given location. The GPU contains multiple cores that each have access to the same area of VRAM, but they also each contain a much smaller, local texture cache that stores the texture(s) the GPU has been most with most recently. This is similar in design with the multitude of CPU memory cache levels that allow memory transfer up and down the chain. This is a hardware design workaround for the fact that faster memory will, invariably, be more difficult and expensive to produce. So, rather than having a giant, expensive block of VRAM, we have a large, cheap block of VRAM, but use a smaller, very fast, lower-level texture cache to perform sampling with, which gives us the best of both worlds; that is, fast sampling with lower costs.

If a texture is needed that is already within the core's local texture cache, then sampling often becomes lightning fast and is barely perceivable. If not, then the texture must be pulled in from VRAM before it can be sampled. This is effectively a cache miss for the texture cache since it will now take time to find and pull the required texture from VRAM. This transfer consumes a certain amount of our available memory bandwidth, specifically an amount equal to the total size of the texture file stored within VRAM (which may not be the exact size of the original file or the size in RAM, due to GPU-level compression techniques).

If we are bottlenecked in memory bandwidth, the GPU will keep fetching the necessary texture files, but the entire process will be throttled, as the texture cache keeps waiting for data to appear before it can process a given batch of fragments. The GPU won't be able to push data back to the Frame Buffer in time to be rendered onto the screen, blocking the whole process and culminating in a poor frame rate.

Proper usage of memory mandwidth is another budgeting concern. For example, with a memory bandwidth of 96 GBs per second per core and a target frame rate of 60 frames per second, the GPU can afford to pull roughly 1.6 GBs (*96/60*) worth of texture data every frame before being bottlenecked in memory bandwidth. This is not an exact budget, of course, because of the potential for cache misses, but it does give us a rough value to work with.

 Memory bandwidth is normally listed on a per-core basis, but some GPU manufacturers may try to mislead by multiplying memory bandwidth by the number of cores to list a bigger, but less practical number. Due to this, research may be necessary to compare apples with apples.

Note that this value is not the maximum limit on the amount of texture data that our game can contain in the project, nor in CPU RAM, nor even in VRAM. It is a metric that essentially limits how much texture swapping can occur during one frame. The same texture could be pulled back and forth multiple times in a single frame, depending on how many shaders need to use the texture, the order that the objects are rendered, and how often texture sampling must occur. Only a handful of objects can consume whole GBs of memory bandwidth since there is only a finite amount of texture cache space available. Having a shader that needs a lot of large textures is more likely to cause cache misses, hence causing a bottleneck on Memory Bandwidth. This is surprisingly easy to trigger if we consider multiple objects requiring different high-quality textures and multiple secondary texture maps (normal maps, emission maps, and so on), which are not batched together. In this case, the texture cache will be unable to hang on to a single texture file long enough to immediately sample it during the next rendering pass.

We have now covered the GPU front and backend and will now move on to our next section in exploring our Rendering Pipeline: lighting and shadowing.

Lighting and shadowing

In modern games, a single object rarely finishes rendering completely in a single step, primarily due to lighting and shadowing. These tasks are often handled in multiple *passes* of a fragment shader, once for each of the several light sources, and the final result is combined so that multiple lights are given a chance to be applied. The result appears much more realistic, or, at least, more visually appealing.

Several passes are required to gather shadowing information. So, let's begin:

1. We will first set up our scene to have shadow casters and shadow receivers, which will create or receive shadows, respectively.
2. Then, each time a shadow receiver is rendered, the GPU renders any shadow caster objects from the point of view of the light source into a texture to collect distance information for each of their fragments.
3. It then does the same for the shadow receiver, except now that it knows which fragments the shadow casters would overlap from the light source, it can render those fragments darker since they will be in the shadow created by the light source bearing down on the shadow caster.
4. This information then becomes an additional texture known as a **shadow map** and is blended with the surface for the Shadow Receiver when it is rendered from the point of view of the main camera. This will make its surface appear darker in certain spots where other objects stand between the light source and the given object.

A similar process is used to create lightmaps, which are pre-generated lighting information for the more static parts of our scene.

Lighting and shadowing tend to consume a lot of resources throughout all parts of the Rendering Pipeline. We need each vertex to provide a normal direction (a vector pointing away from the surface) to determine how lighting should reflect off that surface, and we might need additional vertex color attributes to apply some extra coloring. This gives the CPU and frontend more information to pass along. Since multiple passes of fragment shaders are required to complete the final rendering, the backend is kept busy, both in terms of Fill Rate (lots and lots of pixels to draw, redraw, and merge) and in terms of memory bandwidth (extra textures to pull in or out for lightmaps and shadow maps). This is why real-time shadows are exceptionally expensive compared to most other rendering features and will inflate draw call counts dramatically when enabled.

However, lighting and shadowing are perhaps two of the most important parts of game art and design to get right, often making the extra performance requirements worth the cost. Good lighting and shadowing can turn a mundane scene into something spectacular, as there is something magical about professional coloring that makes it visually appealing. Even a low-poly art style (for example, the mobile game, *Monument Valley*) relies heavily on a good lighting and shadowing profile to allow the player to distinguish one object from another and create a visually pleasing scene.

Unity offers multiple features that affect lighting and shadows, from real-time lighting and shadows (of which there are multiple types of each) to static lighting called **lightmapping**. There are a lot of options to explore and, of course, a lot of things that can cause performance issues if we're not careful.

The Unity documentation covers all of the various lighting features in an excellent amount of detail. Start with the following pages and work through them. Doing so will be well worth the time since these systems affect the entire Rendering Pipeline. Refer to the following:

- `https://docs.unity3d.com/Manual/LightingOverview.html`

- `https://learn.unity.com/tutorial/introduction-to-lighting-and-rendering`

There are two different rendering formats, which can greatly affect our lighting performance, known as **Forward Rendering** and **Deferred Rendering**. The setting for these **Rendering** options can be found under **Edit** | **Project Settings** | **Player** | **Other Settings** | **Rendering** and configured on a per-platform basis.

Forward Rendering

Forward Rendering is the traditional form of rendering lights in our scene, as explored previously. During Forward Rendering, each object will be rendered in multiple passes through the same shader. How many passes are required will be based on the number, distance, and brightness of light sources. Unity will try to prioritize the `DirectionalLight` component that is affecting the object the most and render the object in a *base* pass as a starting point. It will then take several of the most powerful `PointLight` components nearby and re-render the same object multiple times through the same fragment shader. Each of these light points will be processed on a per-vertex basis, and all remaining lights will be condensed into an *average* color using a technique called spherical harmonics.

Some of this behavior can be simplified by setting a light's **Render Mode** to values such as **Not Important** and changing the value of **Edit** | **Project Settings** | **Quality** | **Pixel Light Count**. This value limits the number of lights that will be gathered for Forward Rendering but is overridden by any lights with a **Render Mode** set to **Important**. It is, therefore, up to us to use this combination of settings responsibly.

As we might imagine, using Forward Rendering can utterly explode our draw call count very quickly in scenes with a lot of light points present due to the number of Render States being configured and shader passes required.

 More information on Forward Rendering can be found in the Unity documentation at `http://docs.unity3d.com/Manual/RenderTech-ForwardRendering.html`.

Deferred Shading

Deferred Rendering, or Deferred Shading as it is sometimes known, is a technique that has been available on GPUs for about a decade or so, but it has not resulted in a complete replacement of the Forward Rendering method due to the caveats involved and somewhat limited support on mobile devices.

Deferred Shading is named as such because actual shading does not occur until much later in the process, that is, it is deferred until later. It works by creating a geometry buffer (called a *G-Buffer*), where our scene is initially rendered without any lighting applied. With this information, the Deferred Shading system can generate a lighting profile within a single pass.

From a performance perspective, the results are quite impressive as it can generate very good per-pixel lighting with little draw call effort. One disadvantage is that effects such as anti-aliasing, transparency, and applying shadows to animated characters cannot be managed through Deferred Shading alone. In this case, the Forward Rendering technique is applied as a fallback to cover those tasks, hence requiring extra draw calls to complete it. A bigger issue with Deferred Shading is that it often requires more powerful and more expensive hardware and is not available for all platforms, so fewer users will be able to make use of it.

 The Unity documentation contains an excellent source of information on the Deferred Shading technique, along with its benefits and pitfalls, which can be found at `http://docs.unity3d.com/Manual/RenderTech-DeferredShading.html`.

Vertex-Lit shading (legacy)

Technically, there are more than two lighting methods. The remaining two are Vertex-Lit shading and a very primitive, feature-lax version of Deferred Rendering (in the Unity documentation, this is called the Legacy Deferred lighting Rendering Path). Vertex-Lit shading is a massive simplification of lighting, as lighting will only be considered per-vertex and not per-pixel. In other words, entire faces are colored the same based on the incoming light color rather than blending lighting colors across the face through individual pixels.

It is not expected that many, or really any, 3D games will make use of this legacy technique, since a lack of shadows and proper lighting make visualizations of depth very difficult. It is mostly used by simple 2D games that don't need to make use of shadows, normal maps, and various other lighting features.

Global Illumination

Global Illumination (**GI**) is an implementation of baked lightmapping. Lightmapping is similar to the shadow maps created by shadowing techniques in that one or more textures are generated for each object that represents extra lighting information and is later applied to the object during its lighting pass of a fragment shader to simulate static lighting effects.

The main difference between these lightmaps and other forms of lighting is that lightmaps are pre-generated (or baked) in the Editor and packaged into the game build. This ensures that we don't need to keep regenerating this information at runtime, saving numerous draw calls and significant GPU activity. Since we can bake this data, we have the luxury of time to generate very high-quality lightmaps (at the expense of larger generated texture files we need to work with, of course).

Since this information is baked ahead of time, it cannot respond to real-time activity during gameplay, and so, by default, any lightmapping information will only be applied to static objects that were present in the scene when the lightmap was generated and at the exact location they were placed. However, light probes can be added to the scene to generate an additional set of lightmap textures that can be applied to nearby dynamic objects that move, allowing such objects to benefit from pre-generated lighting. This won't have pixel-perfect accuracy and will cost disk space for the extra light probe maps and memory bandwidth at runtime to swap them around, but it does generate a more believable and pleasant lighting profile.

There have been several techniques for generating lightmaps developed throughout the years, and Unity has used a couple of different solutions since its initial release. Global Illumination is simply the latest generation of the mathematical techniques behind lightmapping, which offers very realistic coloring by calculating not only how lighting affects a given object, but also how light reflects off nearby surfaces, allowing an object to affect the lighting profile of those around it. This effect is calculated by an internal system called **enlighten**. This tool is used both to create static lightmaps, as well as create something called **Precomputed Realtime GI**, which is a hybrid of real-time and static shading and allows us to simulate effects such as time-of-day (where the direction of light from the sun changes over time) without relying on expensive real-time lighting effects.

A typical issue with generating lightmaps is the length of time it can take to generate them and get visual feedback on the current settings because the lightmapper is often trying to generate full-detail lightmaps in a single pass. If the user attempts to modify its configuration, then the entire job must be canceled and started over. To solve this problem, Unity Technologies implemented Progressive Lightmapper, which performs lightmapping tasks more gradually over time, but also allows them to be modified while they are being calculated. This makes lightmaps of the scene appear to get progressively more detailed as it works in the background while also allowing us to change certain properties when it is still working and without having to restart the entire job. This provides almost immediate feedback and improves the workflow of generating lightmaps immensely.

Multithreaded Rendering

Multithreaded Rendering is enabled by default on most systems, such as desktop and console platforms whose CPUs provide multiple cores. Other platforms still support many low-end devices to enable this feature by default, so it is a toggleable option for them. For Android, it can be enabled via a checkbox under **Edit** | **Project Settings** | **Player** | **Other Settings** | **Multithreaded Rendering**, whereas, for iOS, Multithreaded Rendering can be enabled by configuring the application to make use of Apple's Metal API under **Edit** | **Project Settings** | **Player** | **Other Settings** | **Graphics API**. At the time of writing this book, WebGL does not support Multithreaded Rendering.

For each object in our scene, there are three tasks to complete: determine whether the object needs to be rendered (through a technique known as **Frustum Culling**), and if so, generate commands to render the object (since rendering a single object can result in dozens of different commands), and then send the command to the GPU using the relevant graphics API. Without Multithreaded Rendering, all of these tasks must happen on the main thread of the CPU; hence, any activity on the main thread becomes part of the critical path for all rendering. When Multithreaded Rendering is enabled, the task of pushing commands into the GPU is handled by a render thread, whereas other tasks, such as culling and generating commands, get spread across multiple worker threads. This setup can save an enormous number of CPU cycles for the main thread, which is where the overwhelming majority of other CPU tasks take place, such as physics and script code.

Enabling this feature will affect what it means to be CPU bound. Without Multithreaded Rendering, the main thread is performing all of the work necessary to generate instructions for the command buffer, meaning that any performance we can save elsewhere will free up more time for the CPU to generate commands. However, when Multithreaded Rendering is taking place, a good portion of the workload is pushed onto separate threads, meaning that improvements to the main thread will have less of an impact on rendering performance via the CPU.

Note that being GPU bound is the same regardless of whether Multithreaded Rendering is taking place. The GPU always performs its tasks in a multithreaded fashion.

Low-level rendering APIs

Unity exposes a rendering API to us through their `CommandBuffer` class. This allows us to control the Rendering Pipeline directly through our C# code by issuing high-level rendering commands, such as `render this object,` with `this Material,` using `this Shader,` or `draw N instances of this piece of procedural geometry.` This customization is not as powerful as having direct graphics API access, but it is a step in the right direction for Unity developers to customize unique graphical effects.

Check out the Unity documentation on `CommandBuffer` to make use of this feature at `http://docs.unity3d.com/ScriptReference/Rendering.CommandBuffer.html`.

If an even more direct level of rendering control is needed, such as we wish to make direct graphics API calls to OpenGL, DirectX, and Metal, then be aware that it is possible to create a native plugin (a small library written in C++ code that is compiled specifically for the architecture of the target platform) that hooks into the Unity's Rendering Pipeline, setting up callbacks for when particular rendering events happen, similar to how `MonoBehaviours` hook into various callbacks of the main Unity Engine. This is certainly an advanced topic for most Unity users, but useful to know for the future as our knowledge of rendering techniques and graphics APIs matures.

Unity provides some good documentation on generating a rendering interface in a native plugin at `https://docs.unity3d.com/Manual/NativePluginInterface.html`.

It should be obvious that, due to the number of complex processes involved, there are a lot of different ways in which the GPU can become bottlenecked. Now that we have a thorough understanding of the Rendering Pipeline and how bottlenecks may occur, let's explore how to detect these problems.

Detecting performance issues

When you start looking at issues in your game, lighting is often neglected. That's a novice mistake. In the following sections, we will see how to detect and solve lighting-related performance issues.

Profiling rendering issues

The Profiler can be used to quickly narrow down which of the two devices used in the Rendering Pipeline we are bottlenecked within—whether it is the CPU or GPU. We must examine the problem using both the **CPU Usage** and **GPU Usage Areas** of the **Profiler** window, as this can tell us which device is working the hardest.

The following screenshot shows **Profiler** data for a CPU-bound application. The test involved creating thousands of simple cube objects, with no batching or shadowing techniques taking place. This resulted in an extremely large draw call count (around 32,000) for the CPU to generate commands for, but giving the GPU relatively little work to do due to the simplicity of the objects being rendered:

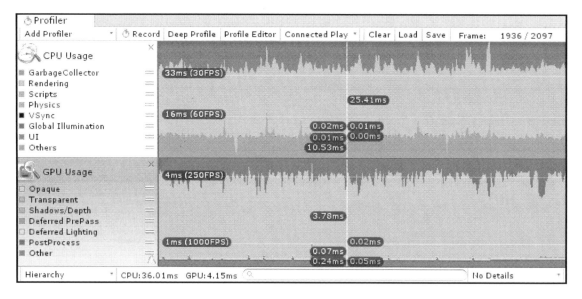

This example shows that the CPU's **Rendering** task is consuming a large number of cycles (around 25 ms per frame), whereas the GPU is processing for less than 4 milliseconds, indicating that the bottleneck resides in the CPU. Note that this profiling test was performed against a standalone app, not within the Editor. We now know that our rendering is CPU bound and can begin to apply some CPU-saving performance improvements (being careful not to introduce rendering bottlenecks elsewhere by doing so).

Meanwhile, profiling a GPU-bound application via the **Profiler** is a little trickier. This time, the test involves creating a simple object requiring minimal draw calls, but using a very expensive shader that samples a texture thousands of times to create an absurd amount of activity in the backend.

> To perform fair GPU-bound profiling tests, you should ensure that you disable vertical sync through **Edit | Project Settings | Quality | Other | V Sync Count**; otherwise, it is likely to pollute our data.

The following screenshot shows Profiler data for this test when it is run in a standalone application:

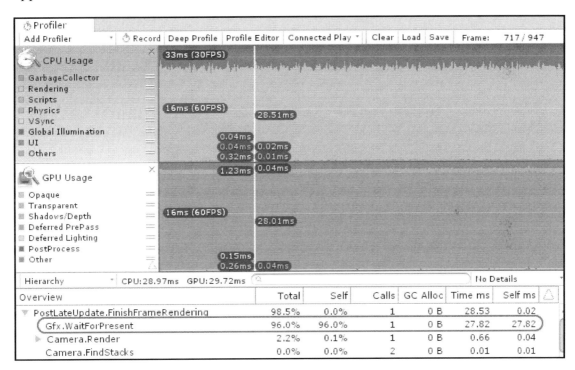

As we can see in the preceding screenshot, the rendering task of the **CPU Usage Area** matches closely with the total rendering costs of the **GPU Usage Area**. We can also see that the CPU and GPU time costs at the bottom of the image are relatively similar (about 29 milliseconds each). This is somewhat confusing as we seem to be bottlenecked equally in both devices, where we would expect the GPU to be working much harder than the CPU.

In actuality, if we drill down into the **Breakdown View** of the **CPU Usage Area** using the **Hierarchy Mode**, we will note that most of the CPU time is spent on the task labeled **Gfx.WaitForPresent**. This is the amount of time that the CPU is wasting while it waits for the GPU to finish the current frame. Hence, we are, in fact, bottlenecked by the GPU despite appearing as though we are bound by both. Even if Multithreaded Rendering is enabled, the CPU must still wait for the Rendering Pipeline to finish before it can begin the next frame.

 Gfx.WaitForPresent is also used to signal that the CPU is waiting on Vertical Sync to complete, hence the need to disable it for this test.

Brute force testing

If we're poring over our profiling data and still not sure where the source of the problem resides, or we're GPU bound and need to determine where we're bottlenecked in the Rendering Pipeline, we should try the brute-force method, that is, cull a specific activity from the scene and check whether it results in greatly improved performance. If a small change results in a significant speed improvement, then we have a strong clue about where the bottleneck lies. There's no harm in this approach if we eliminate enough unknown variables to ensure that the data is leading us in the right direction.

The obvious brute-force test for CPU bounding will be to reduce draw calls to check whether performance suddenly improves. However, this is often not possible since, presumably, we've already been reducing our draw calls to a minimum through techniques such as static batching, dynamic batching, and atlasing. This would mean that we have a very limited scope for reducing them further.

What we can do, however, is intentionally increase our draw call count by a small number, either by introducing more objects or disabling draw call-saving features, such as static and dynamic batching, and observe whether the situation gets significantly worse than before. If so, then we have evidence that we're either very close to being CPU bound or have already become so.

There are two good brute-force tests we can apply to a GPU-bound application to determine whether we're bound by Fill Rate or by memory bandwidth: reducing screen resolution or reducing texture resolution, respectively.

By reducing screen resolution, we will ask the rasterizer to generate significantly fewer fragments and transpose them over a smaller canvas of pixels for the backend to process. This will reduce the Fill Rate consumption of the application, giving this key part of the Rendering Pipeline some additional breathing room. Ergo, if performance suddenly improves with a screen resolution reduction, then Fill Rate should be our primary concern.

 A reduction from a resolution of 2560 x 1440 to 800 x 600 is an improvement factor of about eight, which is often more than enough to reduce Fill Rate costs sufficiently to make the application perform well again.

Similarly, if we're bottlenecked on memory bandwidth, then reducing texture quality is likely to result in significant performance improvement. By doing so, we have shrunk the size of our textures, greatly reducing the memory bandwidth costs of our fragment shaders, allowing the GPU to fetch the necessary textures much more quickly. Globally reducing texture quality can be achieved by going to **Edit** | **Project Settings** | **Quality** | **Texture Quality** and setting the value to **Half Res**, **Quarter Res**, or **Eighth Res**.

An application bound by the CPU has ample opportunities for performance enhancements through practically every performance-enhancing tip in this book. If we free up CPU cycles from other activities, then we can afford to render more objects through more draw calls, keeping in mind, of course, that each will cost us more activity in the GPU. There are, however, additional opportunities to make some indirect improvements in draw call count while we try to improve other parts of the Rendering Pipeline. This includes Occlusion Culling, tweaking our lighting and shadowing behavior, and modifying our shaders. These will be explained in the following sections as we investigate various performance enhancements.

Meanwhile, we will probably need to apply a little brute-force testing and guesswork to determine how a GPU-bound application is bottlenecked. Most applications are bottlenecked by Fill Rate or memory bandwidth, so we should start there. It is rare to find performance bottlenecks in the frontend, at least on desktop applications, so it is worth checking only after we've verified that the other sources are not the problem. Vertex shaders are often trivial compared to fragment shaders, and so the only real opportunity to cause problems with frontend processing is either to push too much geometry or to have overly complex geometry shaders.

Ultimately, this investigation should help us to determine whether we are CPU bound or GPU bound, and, in the latter case, whether we are bound by the frontend or backend, and again in the latter case, whether we are bound by Fill Rate or memory bandwidth. With this knowledge, there are several techniques we can apply to improve performance.

Rendering performance enhancements

We should now have all of the information we need to make sense of performance bottlenecks so that we can start to apply fixes. For the remainder of this chapter, we will cover a series of techniques to improve Rendering Pipeline performance for CPU-bound and GPU-bound applications.

Enabling/disabling GPU skinning

The first tip involves a setting that eases the burden on the CPU or GPU frontend at the expense of the other, that is, GPU Skinning. Skinning is the process where mesh vertices are transformed based on the current location of their animated bones. The animation system, working on the CPU, transforms the object's bones that are used to determine its current pose, but the next important step in the animation process is wrapping the mesh vertices around those bones to place the mesh in the final pose. This is achieved by iterating over each vertex and performing a weighted average against the bones connected to those vertices.

This vertex processing task can either take place on the CPU or within the frontend of the GPU, depending on whether the **GPU Skinning** option is enabled. This feature can be toggled under **Edit** | **Project Settings** | **Player Settings** | **Other Settings** | **GPU Skinning**. Enabling this option pushes skinning activity to the GPU, although bear in mind that the CPU must still transfer the data to the GPU and will generate instructions on the command buffer for the task, so it doesn't remove the CPU's workload entirely. Disabling this option eases the burden on the GPU by making the CPU resolve the mesh's pose before transferring mesh data across and simply asking the GPU to draw it as is. Obviously, this feature is useful if we have lots of animated meshes in our scenes and can be used to help either bounding case by pushing the work onto the least busy device.

Reducing geometric complexity

This tip concerns the GPU frontend. We have already covered some techniques on mesh optimization in `Chapter 4`, *Optimizing Your Art Assets*, which can help to reduce our mesh's vertex attributes. As a quick reminder, it is not uncommon to use a mesh that contains a lot of unnecessary UV and normal vector data, so our meshes should be double-checked for this kind of superfluous fluff. We should also let Unity optimize the structure for us, which minimizes cache misses as vertex data is read within the frontend.

The goal is simply to reduce actual vertex counts. There are three solutions to this:

- First, we can simplify the mesh by either having the art team manually tweak and generate meshes with lower polycounts or using a mesh decimation tool to do this for us.
- Second, we could simply remove meshes from the scene, but this should be a last resort.
- The third option is to implement automatic culling through features such as LOD, which will be explained later in this chapter.

Reducing tessellation

Tessellation through geometry shaders can be a lot of fun, as it is a relatively underused technique that can really make our graphical effects stand out from among the crowd of games that use only the most common effects. However, it can contribute enormously to the amount of processing work taking place in the frontend.

There aren't really any simple tricks we can exploit to improve tessellation, besides improving our tessellation algorithms or easing the burden caused by other frontend tasks to give our tessellation tasks more room to breathe. Either way, if we have a bottleneck in the frontend and are making use of tessellation techniques, we should double-check that they are not consuming the lion's share of the frontend's budget.

Employing GPU instancing

GPU Instancing is a means to render multiple copies of the same mesh quickly by exploiting the fact that they will have identical Render States, hence require minimal draw calls. This is practically identical to dynamic batching, except that it is not an automatic process. In fact, we can think of dynamic batching as a poor man's *GPU instancing* since GPU instancing can enable even better savings and allows for more customization by allowing parameterized variations.

GPU Instancing is applied at the Material level with the **Enable Instancing** checkbox, and variations can be introduced by modifying shader code. This way, we can give different instances of different rotations, scales, colors, and so on. This is useful for rendering scenes such as forests and rocky areas where we want to render hundreds or thousands of different copies of a mesh with some slight variation.

Note that Skinned Mesh Renderers cannot be instanced for similar reasons that they cannot be dynamically batched, and not all platforms and APIs support GPU Instancing.

The following screenshot shows the benefits of GPU Instancing on a group of 512 cube objects (with some extra lighting and shadowing applied to increase the total draw call count):

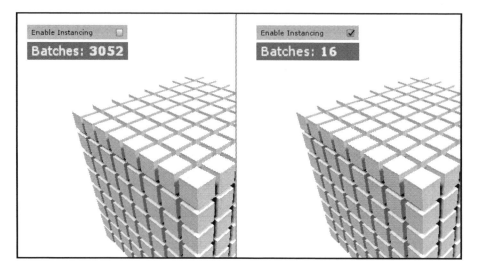

This system is much more versatile than dynamic batching since we have more control over how objects are batched together. Of course, there are more opportunities for mistakes if we batch things in inefficient ways, so we should be careful to use them wisely.

Check out the Unity documentation for more information on GPU Instancing at `https://docs.unity3d.com/Manual/GPUInstancing.html`.

Using mesh-based LOD

LOD is a broad term referring to the dynamic replacement of features based on their distance from the camera and/or how much space they take up in the camera's view. Since it can be difficult to tell the difference between a low- and high-quality object at great distances, there is very little reason to render the high-quality version, and so we may as well dynamically replace distant objects with something more simplified. The most common implementation of LOD is mesh-based LOD, where meshes are dynamically replaced with lower detailed versions as the camera gets farther and farther away.

Making use of mesh-based LOD can be achieved by placing multiple objects in the scene and making them children of `GameObject` with an attached `LODGroup` component. The LOD group's purpose is to generate a bounding box from these objects and decide which object should be rendered based on the size of the bounding box within the camera's field of view. If the object's bounding box consumes a large area of the current view, then it will enable the mesh(es) assigned to lower LOD groups, and if the bounding box is very small, it will replace the mesh(es) with those from higher LOD groups. If the mesh is too far away, it can be configured to hide all child objects. So, with the proper setup, we can have Unity replace meshes with simpler alternatives, or cull them entirely, which eases the burden on the rendering process.

Check out the Unity documentation for more detailed information on the mesh-based LOD feature at `http://docs.unity3d.com/Manual/LevelOfDetail.html`.

This feature can cost us a large amount of development time to fully implement; artists must generate lower polygon count versions of the same object, and level designers must generate LOD groups, configure them, and test them to ensure that they don't cause jarring transitions as the camera moves closer or farther away.

> Note that some game development middleware companies offer third-party tools for automated LOD mesh generation. These might be worth investigating to compare their ease of use versus quality loss versus cost-effectiveness.

Mesh-based LOD will also cost us in disk footprint as well as RAM and CPU; the alternative meshes need to be bundled, loaded into RAM, and the `LODGroup` component must routinely test whether the camera has moved to a new position that warrants a change in LOD level. The benefits on the Rendering Pipeline are rather impressive, however. Dynamically rendering simpler meshes reduces the amount of vertex data we need to pass and potentially reduces the number of draw calls, Fill Rate, and memory bandwidth needed to render the object.

Due to the number of sacrifices needed for mesh-based LOD to function, developers should avoid preoptimizing by automatically assuming that mesh-based LOD will help them. Excessive use of the feature will lead to burdening other parts of our application's performance and chew up precious development time, all for the sake of paranoia. It should only be used if we start to observe problems in the Rendering Pipeline, and we've got CPU, RAM, and development time to spare.

Having said that, scenes that feature large, expansive views of the world and have lots of camera movement might want to consider implementing this technique very early, as the added distance and a massive number of visible objects will likely exacerbate the vertex count enormously. As a counterexample, scenes that are always indoors or feature a camera with a viewpoint looking down at the world will find little benefit in this technique since objects will tend to be at a similar distance from the camera at all times. Examples include **Real-Time Strategy (RTS)** and **Multiplayer Online Battle Arena (MOBA)** games.

Culling groups

Culling groups are a part of the Unity API that effectively allows us to create our own custom LOD system as a means of coming up with our own ways of dynamically replacing certain gameplay or rendering behaviors. Some examples of things we might want to apply LOD to include replacing animated characters with a version with fewer bones, applying simpler shaders, skipping Particle System generation at great distances, and simplifying AI behavior.

Since the culling group system at its most basic level simply tells us whether objects are visible to the camera and how big they are, it also has other uses in the realm of gameplay, such as determining whether certain enemy spawn points are currently visible to the player or whether a player is approaching certain areas. There is a wide range of possibilities available with the culling group system that makes it worth considering. Of course, the time spent to implement, test, and redesign scenes to exploit can be significant.

Check out the Unity documentation for more information on culling groups at `https://docs.unity3d.com/Manual/CullingGroupAPI.html`.

Making use of Occlusion Culling

One of the best ways to reduce both Fill Rate consumption and Overdraw is to make use of Unity's Occlusion Culling system. The system works by partitioning the world into a series of small cells and flying a virtual camera through the scene, making a note of which cells are invisible from other cells (are *occluded*) based on the size and position of the objects present.

 Note that this is different from the technique of Frustum Culling, which culls objects outside the current camera view. Frustum Culling is always active and automatic. Objects culled by this process are, therefore, automatically ignored by the Occlusion Culling system.

Occlusion Culling data can only be generated for objects properly labeled **Occluder Static** and/or **Occludee Static** under the **StaticFlags** drop-down menu. **Occluder Static** is the general setting for static objects we expect to be so large that they will both occlude and be occluded by other objects, such as skyscrapers or mountains, which can hide other objects behind them, as well as be hidden behind each other, and so on. **Occludee Static** is a special case for things, such as transparent objects that always require other objects behind them to be rendered, but they themselves need to be hidden if something large blocks their visibility.

> Naturally, because **Static** flags must be enabled for Occlusion Culling, this feature will not work for dynamic objects.

The following screenshot shows how effective Occlusion Culling can be at reducing the number of rendered objects from our scene from an external point of view for the sake of demonstration. From the point of view of the main camera, the two situations appear identical.

The Rendering Pipeline is not wasting time rendering objects that are obscured by closer ones:

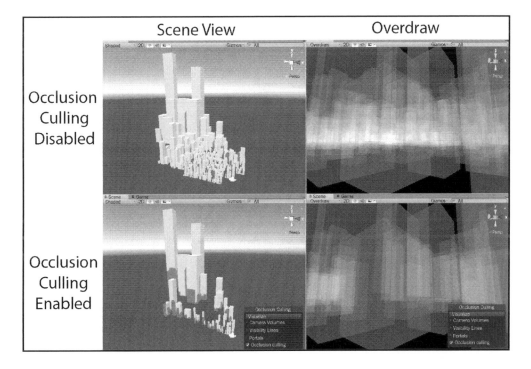

Enabling the Occlusion Culling feature will cost additional disk space, RAM, and CPU time. Extra disk space is required to store the occlusion data, extra RAM is needed to keep the data structure in memory, and there will be a CPU processing cost to determine which objects are being occluded in each frame. The Occlusion Culling data structure must be properly configured to create cells of the appropriate size for our scene, and the smaller the cells, the longer it takes to generate the data structure. However, if it is configured correctly for the scene, Occlusion Culling can provide both fill rate savings through reduced Overdraw and draw call savings by culling nonvisible objects.

 Note that even though an object may be culled by occlusion, its shadows must still be calculated, so we won't save any draw calls or fill rate from those tasks.

Optimizing Particle Systems

Particle Systems are useful for a huge number of different visual effects, and usually, the more particles they generate, the better the effect looks. However, we will need to be responsible about the number of particles generated and the complexity of shaders used since they can touch on all parts of the Rendering Pipeline; they generate a lot of vertices for the frontend (each particle is a quad) and could use multiple textures, which consume Fill Rate and memory bandwidth in the backend, so they can potentially cause an application to be bound anywhere if used irresponsibly.

Reducing Particle System density and complexity is fairly straightforward—use fewer Particle Systems, generate fewer particles, and/or use fewer special effects. Atlasing is also another common technique for reducing Particle System performance costs. However, there is an important performance consideration behind Particle Systems that is not too well known and happens behind the Scenes, and that is the process of automatic Particle System culling.

Making use of Particle System culling

The basic idea is that all Particle Systems are either predictable or not (deterministic versus non-deterministic), depending on various settings. When a Particle System is predictable and not visible to the main view, then the entire Particle System can be automatically culled away to save performance. As soon as a predictable Particle System comes back into view, Unity can figure out exactly how the Particle System is meant to look at that moment as if it had been generating particles the entire time it wasn't visible.

So long as the Particle System generates particles in a very procedural way, then the state is immediately solvable mathematically.

However, if any setting forces the Particle System to become unpredictable or nonprocedural, then it would have no idea what the current state of the Particle System needs to be, had it been hidden previously, and will hence need to render it fully every frame regardless of whether or not it is visible. Settings that break a Particle System's predictability include, but are not limited to, making the Particle System render in world-space; applying external forces, collisions, and trails; or using complex animation curves. Check out the blog post mentioned previously for a rigorous list of nonprocedural conditions.

Note that Unity provides a useful warning on Particle Systems when something would cause it to break automatic culling, as shown in the following screenshot:

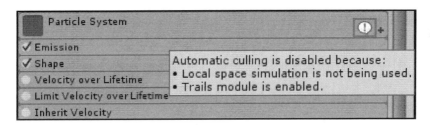

 Unity Technologies has released an excellent blog post covering this topic, which can be found at `https://blogs.unity3d.com/2016/12/20/` `unitytips-particlesystem-performance-culling/`.

Avoiding recursive Particle System calls

Many methods available to a `ParticleSystem` component are recursive calls. Calling them will iterate through each child of the Particle System, which then calls `GetComponent<ParticleSystem>()` on each child, and, if the component exists, it will call the appropriate method. This then repeats for each child `ParticleSystem` beneath the original parent, its grandchildren, and so on. This can be a huge problem with deep hierarchies of Particle Systems, which is sometimes the case with complex effects.

There are several `ParticleSystem` API calls affected by this behavior, such as `Start()`, `Stop()`, `Pause()`, `Clear()`, `Simulate()`, and `isAlive()`. We obviously cannot avoid these methods entirely since they represent the most common methods we would want to call on a Particle System. However, each of these methods has a `withChildren` parameter that defaults to `true`. Bypassing `false` in place of this parameter (for example, by calling `Clear(false)`, it disables the recursive behavior and will not call into its children. Hence, the method call will only affect the given Particle System, reducing the overhead cost of the call.

This is not always ideal since we do often want all children of the Particle System to be affected by the method call. Another approach, therefore is to, cache the `ParticleSystem` components in the same way we learned in Chapter 2, *Scripting Strategies*, and iterate through them manually ourselves (making sure that we pass `false` for the `withChildren` parameter each time).

 Note that there is a bug in Unity 2017.1 and older, where additional memory is allocated each time `Stop()` and `Simulate()` are called (even if the Particle System has already been stopped). This bug was fixed in Unity 2017.2.

Optimizing Unity UI

Unity's first few attempts at built-in UI systems were not particularly successful; it is often quickly supplanted by products on the Asset Store. However, the latest generation of their solution (simply called Unity UI) has become a much more popular solution, so many developers are starting to rely on it for their UI needs, so much so, in fact, that Unity Technologies bought the company behind the Text Mesh Pro asset in early 2017 and merged it into the Unity UI as a built-in feature.

Let's explore a few techniques we can use to improve the performance of Unity's built-in UI.

Using more Canvases

A `Canvas` component's primary task is to manage the meshes that are used to draw the UI elements beneath them in the **Hierarchy** window and issue the draw calls necessary to render those elements. An important task of the Canvas is to batch these meshes together (which can only happen if they share the same Material) to reduce draw calls. However, when changes are made to a Canvas, or any of its children, this is known as *dirtying* the Canvas.

When a Canvas is *dirty*, it needs to regenerate meshes for all of the UI elements beneath it before it can issue a draw call. This regeneration process is not a simple task and is a common source of performance problems in Unity projects because, unfortunately, many things can cause the Canvas to be made dirty. Even changing a single UI element within a Canvas can cause this to occur. There are so many things that cause dirtying, and so few that don't (and usually only in certain circumstances) that it's best to simply err on the side of caution and assume that any change will cause this effect.

Perhaps the only notable action that doesn't cause dirtying is changing a `Color` property of a UI element.

If we find that our UI causes a large spike in CPU usage any time something changes (or sometimes literally every frame if they're being changed every frame), one solution we can apply is to simply use more Canvases. A common mistake is to build the entire game's UI in a single Canvas and keep it this way as the game code, and its UI continues to become more complex.

This means that it will need to check every element every time anything changes in the UI, which can become more and more disastrous on performance as more elements are crammed into a single Canvas. However, each Canvas is independent and does not need to interact with other Canvases in the UI, and so by splitting up the UI into multiple Canvases, we can separate the workload and simplify the tasks required by any single Canvas.

Ensure that you add a `GraphicsRaycaster` component to the same `GameObject` as the child Canvas so that its own child elements can still be interacted with. Conversely, if none of the Canvas' child elements are interactable, then we can safely remove any `GraphicsRaycaster` components from it to reduce performance costs.

In this case, even though an element still changes, fewer other elements will need to be regenerated in response, reducing the performance cost. The downside of this approach is that elements across different Canvases will not be batched together, so we should try to keep similar elements with the same Material grouped together within the same Canvas, if possible.

It's also possible to make a Canvas a child of another Canvas, for the sake of organization, and the same rules apply. If an element changes in one Canvas, the other will be unaffected.

Separating objects between static and dynamic Canvases

We should strive to try and generate our Canvases in a way that groups elements based on when they get updated. We should think of our elements as fitting within one of three groups:

- **Static**: Static UI elements are those that never change; good examples of these are background images, labels, and so on
- **Incidental Dynamic**: Dynamic elements are those that can change, where Incidental Dynamic objects are those UI elements that only change in response to something, such as a UI button press or a hover action
- **Continuous Dynamic**: Continuous Dynamic objects are those UI elements that update regularly, such as animated elements

We should try to split UI elements from these three groups into three different Canvases for any given section of our UI, as this will minimize the amount of wasted effort during regeneration.

Disabling Raycast Target for non-interactive elements

UI elements have a **Raycast Target** option, which enables them to be interacted with by clicks, taps, and other user behavior. Each time one of these events takes place, the `GraphicsRaycaster` component will perform pixel-to-bounding box checks to figure out which element has been interacted with and is a simple iterative `for` loop. By disabling this option for non-interactive elements, we're reducing the number of elements that `GraphicsRaycaster` needs to iterate through, thereby saving performance.

Hiding UI elements by disabling the parent Canvas component

The UI uses a separate layout system to handle the regeneration of certain element types, which operates in a similar way as dirtying a Canvas. `UIImage`, `UIText`, and `LayoutGroup` are all examples of components that fall under this system. Many things can cause a layout system to become dirty, the most obvious of which are enabling and disabling such elements. However, if we want to disable a portion of the UI, we can avoid these expensive regeneration calls from the layout system by simply disabling the `Canvas` component they are children of. This can be done by setting the `Canvas` component's `enabled` property to `false`.

The drawback of this approach is that, if any child objects that have some Update(), FixedUpdate(), LateUpdate(), or coroutine code, then we would also need to disable them manually, otherwise they will continue to run. By disabling the Canvas component, we're only stopping the UI from being rendered and interacted with, and we should expect various update calls to continue to happen as normal.

Avoiding Animator components

Unity's Animator components were never intended to be used with the latest version of its UI System, and their interaction with it is a naive implementation. Each frame, the animator will change properties on UI elements that cause their layouts to be dirtied and cause regeneration of a lot of internal UI information. We should avoid using Animators entirely, and instead perform tweening ourselves or use a utility asset intended for such operations.

Explicitly defining the event camera for World Space Canvases

Canvases can be used for UI interactions in both 2D and 3D. This is determined by whether the Canvas has its **Render Mode** setting configured to **Screen Space** (2D) or **World Space** (3D). Any time a UI interaction takes place, the Canvas Component will check its eventCamera property (exposed as **Event Camera** in the **Inspector** window) to figure out which camera to use. By default, a 2D Canvas will set this property to the main camera, but a 3D Canvas leaves it set to null. This is unfortunate because, each time the event camera is needed, it will still use the main camera, but will do so by calling FindObjectWithTag(). Finding objects by tag isn't as bad of a performance cost as using the other variations of Find(), but its performance cost scales linearly with the more tags we use in a given project. To make matters worse, the event camera is accessed fairly often during a given frame for a **World Space** Canvas, which means that leaving this property null will cause a huge performance hit for no real benefit. We should manually set this property to the main camera for all of our **World Space** Canvases.

Don't use alpha to hide UI elements

Rendering a UI element with an alpha value of `0` in its `color` property will still cause a draw call to be issued. We should favor changing the `IsActive` property of a UI element to hide it when necessary. Another alternative is to use Canvas Groups via `CanvasGroup` Components, which can be used to control the alpha transparency of all child elements beneath them. Setting the `alpha` value of a Canvas Group to `0` will cull away its child objects, and, therefore, no draw calls will be issued.

Optimizing ScrollRects

`ScrollRect` Components are UI elements that are used to scroll through a list of other UI elements and are fairly common in mobile applications. Unfortunately, the performance of these elements scales very poorly with size since the Canvas needs to regenerate them regularly. There are several things we can do to improve the performance of our `ScrollRect` Components. Let's take a look at some of them in the following.

Make sure to use a RectMask2D

It's possible to create scrolling UI behavior by simply placing other UI elements with a lower `depth` value than the `ScrollRect` elements. However, this is bad practice since there will be no culling taking place in `ScrollRect`, and every element will need to be regenerated for each frame that `ScrollRect` is moving. If we haven't already, we should use a `RectMask2D` Component to clip and cull child objects that are not visible. This Component creates a region of space, whereby any child UI elements within it will be culled away if they are outside the bounds of the `RectMask2D` Component. The cost of determining whether to cull an object compared to the savings of rendering too many invisible ones is typically worth it.

Disable Pixel Perfect for ScrollRects

Pixel Perfect is a setting on a `Canvas` component that forces its child UI elements to be drawn with direct alignment to the pixels on the screen. This is often a requirement for art and design, as the UI elements will appear much sharper than if it was disabled. While this alignment behavior is a relatively expensive operation, it is effectively mandatory that it will be enabled for the majority of our UI to keep things crisp and clear. However, for animating and fast-moving objects, it can be somewhat pointless due to the motion involved.

Disabling **Pixel Perfect** for `ScrollRect` elements is a good way to make some impressive savings. However, since the **Pixel Perfect** setting affects the entire Canvas, we should make sure to enable the `ScrollRect` element as a child object beneath a separate Canvas so that other elements will maintain their pixel-aligned behavior.

 Different kinds of animated UI elements actually look better with **Pixel Perfect** disabled. Be sure to do some testing, as this can save quite a bit of performance.

Manually stop ScrollRect motion

The Canvas will always need to regenerate the entire `ScrollRect` element even if the velocity is moving by a fraction of a pixel each frame. We can manually freeze its motion once we detect that its velocity is below a certain threshold using `ScrollRect.velocity` and `ScrollRect.StopMovement()`. This can help to reduce the frequency of regeneration a great deal.

Using empty UIText elements for full-screen interaction

A common implementation in most UIs is to activate a large, transparent interactable element that covers the entire screen, forcing the player to handle a popup before proceeding, while still allowing the player to see what's going on behind it (as a means of not ripping the player out of the game experience entirely). This is often done with a `UIImage` element, but unfortunately, this can break batching operations, and transparency can be a problem on mobile devices.

A hacky way around this problem is to use a `UIText` element with no **Font** or **Text** defined. This creates an element that doesn't need to generate any renderable information and only handles bounding box checks for interaction.

Checking the Unity UI source code

If we're having significant problems with the performance of our UI, it is possible to look into the source code to figure out exactly what might be going on and hopefully discover ways to get around the problem.

A more drastic measure, but a potential option, could be to actually modify the UI code, compile it, and add it to our project manually.

Unity provides the code for its UI system in a Bitbucket repository, found at `https://bitbucket.org/Unity-Technologies/ui`.

Checking the documentation

The tips mentioned previously are some of the more obscure, undocumented, or critical performance optimization tips for the UI system. There are several great resources on the Unity website that explain how the UI system works and how best to optimize it, which is far too large to fit in this book verbatim.

Start with the following page and work your way through them for many more helpful UI optimization tips: `https://unity3d.com/learn/tutorials/temas/best-practices/guide-optimizing-unity-ui`.

Shader optimization

Fragment shaders are the primary consumers of Fill Rate and memory bandwidth. The costs depend on their complexity—how much texture sampling takes place, how many mathematical functions are used, and many more factors. The GPU's parallel nature (sharing small pieces of the overall job between hundreds of threads) means that any bottleneck in a thread will limit how many fragments can be pushed through that thread during a frame.

The classic analogy is a vehicle assembly line. A complete vehicle requires multiple stages of manufacture to complete. The critical path to completion might involve stamping, welding, painting, assembly, and inspection, where each step is completed by a single team. For any given vehicle, no stage can begin before the previous one is finished, but whatever team handled the stamping for the last vehicle can begin stamping for the next vehicle as soon as it has finished. This organization allows each team to become masters of their particular domain rather than trying to spread their knowledge too thin, which would likely result in less consistent quality in the batch of vehicles.

We can double the overall output by doubling the number of teams, but if any team gets blocked, then precious time is lost for any given vehicle, as well as all future vehicles that would pass through the same team. If these delays are rare, then they can be negligible in the grand scheme, but if not, and even if one stage takes several minutes longer than normal each and every time it must complete the task, then it can become a bottleneck that threatens the release of the entire batch.

The GPU parallel processors work similarly: each processor thread is an assembly line, each processing stage is a team, and each fragment is the thing that needs to be built. If the thread spends a long time processing a single stage, then time is lost on each fragment. This delay will multiply such that all future fragments coming through the same thread will be delayed. This is a bit of an oversimplification, but it often helps to paint a picture of how quickly some poorly optimized shader code can chew up our Fill Rate, and how small improvements in shader optimization provide big benefits in backend performance.

Shader programming and optimization is a very niche area of game development. Their abstract and highly specialized nature requires a very different kind of thinking to generate high-quality shader code compared to typical gameplay or Engine code. They often feature mathematical tricks and back-door mechanisms for pulling data into the shader, such as pre-computing values and putting them in texture files. Because of this, and the importance of optimization, shaders tend to be very difficult to read and reverse-engineer.

Consequently, many developers rely on prewritten shaders, visual shader creation tools from the Asset Store, such as Shader Forge or Amplify Shader Editor. This simplifies the act of initial shader code generation, but might not result in the most efficient form of shaders. Whether we're writing our own shaders, or we're relying on pre-written/pre-generated shaders, we might find it worthwhile to perform some optimization passes over them using some tried-and-true techniques, which we are going to see in the following sections.

Consider using shaders intended for mobile platforms

The built-in mobile shaders in Unity do not have any specific restrictions that force them only to be used on mobile devices. They are simply optimized for minimum resource usage (and tend to feature some of the other optimizations listed in this section).

Desktop applications are perfectly capable of using these shaders, but they tend to feature a loss of graphical quality. It only becomes a question of whether the loss of graphical quality is acceptable. So, consider doing some testing with the mobile equivalents of common shaders to check whether they are a good fit for your game.

Using small data types

GPUs can calculate with smaller data types more quickly than larger types (particularly on mobile platforms), so the first tweak we can attempt is replacing our `float` data types (32-bit, floating-point) with smaller versions such as `half` (16-bit, floating-point) or even `fixed` (12-bit, fixed point). The size of the data types listed previously will vary depending on what floating-point formats the target platform prefers. The sizes listed are the most common.

Optimization stems from the relative size between formats since there are fewer bits to process.

Color values are good candidates for precision reduction, as we can often get away with fewer precise color values without a noticeable loss in coloration. However, the effects of reducing precision can be very unpredictable for graphical calculations. So, changes such as these can require some testing to verify that the reduced precision is costing too much graphical fidelity.

 Note that the effects of these tweaks can vary enormously between one GPU architecture and another (for example, AMD versus Nvidia versus Intel) and even GPU brands from the same manufacturer. In some cases, we can make some decent performance gains for a trivial amount of effort. In other cases, we might see no benefit at all.

Avoiding changing precision while swizzling

Swizzling is the shader programming technique of creating a new vector (an array of values) from an existing vector by listing the components in the order in which we wish to copy them into the new structure.

Here are some examples of swizzling:

```
float4 input = float4(1.0, 2.0, 3.0, 4.0);  // initial test value (x, y, z, w)

// swizzle two components
float2 val1 = input.yz; // val1 = (2.0, 3.0)

// swizzle three components in a different order
float3 val2 = input.zyx; // val2 = (3.0, 2.0, 1.0)

// swizzle the same component multiple times
float4 val3 = input.yyy; // val3 = (2.0, 2.0, 2.0)

// swizzle a scalar multiple times
float sclr = input.w; // sclr = (4.0)
float3 val4 = sclr.xxx; // val4 = (4.0, 4.0, 4.0)
```

We can use both the `xyzw` and `rgba` representations to refer to the same components, sequentially. It does not matter whether it is a color or a vector; they just make the shader code easier to read. We can also list components in any order we like to fill in the desired data, repeating them if necessary.

Converting from one precision type to another in a shader can be a costly operation, but converting the precision type while simultaneously swizzling can be particularly painful. If we have mathematical operations that use swizzling, ensure that they don't also convert the precision type. In these cases, it would be wiser to simply use the high-precision data type from the very beginning or reduce precision across the board to avoid the need for changes in precision.

Using GPU-optimized helper functions

The shader compiler often performs a good job of reducing mathematical calculations down to an optimized version for the GPU, but compiled custom code is unlikely to be as effective as both the **Cg** library's built-in helper functions and the additional helpers provided by the Unity **Cg** included files. If we are using shaders that include custom function code, perhaps we can find an equivalent helper function within the **Cg** or Unity libraries that can do a better job than our custom code can.

These extra `include` files can be added to our shader within the CGPROGRAM block, as follows:

```
CGPROGRAM
// other includes
#include "UnityCG.cginc"
// Shader code here
ENDCG
```

Example **Cg** library functions to use are `abs()` for absolute values, `lerp()` for linear interpolation, `mul()` for multiplying matrices, and `step()` for step functionality. Useful `UnityCG.cginc` functions include `WorldSpaceViewDir()` for calculating the direction toward the camera and `Luminance()` for converting color into grayscale.

> Check out `http://http.developer.nvidia.com/CgTutorial/cg_tutorial_appendix_e.html` for a full list of Cg standard library functions. Check out the Unity documentation for a complete and up-to-date list of possible `include` files and their accompanying helper functions at `http://docs.unity3d.com/Manual/SL-BuiltinIncludes.html`.

Disabling unnecessary features

Perhaps we can make savings by simply disabling shader features that aren't vital. Does the shader really need transparency, Z-writing, alpha testing, and/or alpha blending? Will tweaking these settings or removing these features give us a good approximation of our desired effect without losing too much graphical fidelity? Making such changes is a good way of making Fill Rate cost savings.

Removing unnecessary input data

Sometimes, the process of writing a shader involves a lot of back and forth experimentation in editing code and viewing it in the Scene. The typical outcome of this process is that input data that was needed when the shader was going through early development is now surplus fluff once the desired effect has been obtained, and it's easy to forget what changes were made when/if the process drags on for an extended period. However, these redundant data values can cost the GPU valuable time, as they must be fetched from memory even if they are not explicitly used by the shader. So, we should double-check our shaders to ensure that all of their input geometry, vertices, and fragment data is actually being used.

Exposing only necessary variables

Exposing unnecessary variables from our shader to the accompanying Material can be costly, as the GPU can't assume these values are constant, which means the compiler cannot compile away these values. This data must be pushed from the CPU with every pass since they can be modified at any time through a Material object's methods such as `SetColor()` and `SetFloat()`. If we find that, toward the end of the project, we always use the same value for these variables, then they should be replaced with a constant in the shader to remove such excess runtime workload. The only cost is obfuscating what could be critical graphical effect parameters, so this should be done very late in the process.

Reducing mathematical complexity

Complicated mathematics can severely bottleneck the rendering process, so we should do whatever we can to limit the damage. It is entirely possible to store a map of complex mathematical function outputs by precalculating them and placing them as floating-point data in a texture file. A texture file is, after all, just a huge blob of floating-point values that can be indexed quickly with three dimensions: x, y, and color (`rgba`).

We can feed this texture into the shader and sample the pre-generated table in the shader at runtime instead of completing a complex calculation at runtime.

We may not see any improvement with functions such as `sin()` and `cos()` since they've been heavily optimized to make use of GPU architecture, but complex methods such as `pow()`, `exp()`, `log()`, and our own custom mathematical calculations can only be optimized so much and would be good candidates for simplification. This is assuming that we can easily index the result from the texture with *x* and *y* coordinates. If complex calculations are required to generate those coordinates, then it may not be worth the effort.

This technique will cost us additional graphics memory to store the texture at runtime and some memory bandwidth, but if the shader has already been receiving a texture (which they are, in most cases), but the alpha channel is not being used, then we could sneak the data in through the texture's alpha channel, costing us literally no performance since that data has already been passed through anyway. This will involve hand-editing our art assets to include such data in any unused color channel(s), possibly requiring coordination between programmers and artists, but is a very good way of saving shader processing costs with no runtime sacrifices.

Reducing texture sampling

Texture sampling is at the core of all memory bandwidth costs. The fewer textures we use, and the smaller we make them, the better. The more we use, the more cache misses we are likely to invoke, and the larger they are, the more memory bandwidth is consumed transferring them to the texture cache. Such situations should be simplified as much as possible to avoid severe GPU bottlenecks.

Even worse, sampling textures in a non-sequential order would likely result in some very costly cache misses for the GPU to suffer through. So, if this is being done, then the texture should be reordered so that it can be sampled in a more sequential order. For example, if we're sampling by inverting the x and y coordinates (for example, `tex2D(y, x)` instead of `tex2D(x, y)`), the texture lookup would iterate through the texture vertically, then horizontally, inflicting a cache-miss almost every iteration. A lot of performance could be saved by simply rotating the texture file data and performing a sample in the correct order (`tex2D(x,y)`).

Avoiding conditional statements

When conditional statements are run through a modern-day CPU, they undergo a lot of clever predictive techniques to make use of *instruction-level parallelism*. This is a feature where the CPU attempts to predict which direction a conditional statement will go in before it has actually been resolved and speculatively begins processing the most likely result of the conditional using any free cores that aren't being used to resolve the conditional (fetching some data from memory, copying some floating-point values into unused registers, and so on). If it turns out that the decision is wrong, then the current result is discarded, and the proper path is taken instead. So long as the cost of speculative processing and discarding false results is less than the time spent waiting to decide the correct path, and it is right more often than it is wrong, then this is a net gain for the CPU's speed.

However, this feature is less beneficial for GPU architecture because of its parallel nature. The GPU's cores are typically managed by some higher-level construct that instructs all cores under its command to perform the same machine code-level instruction simultaneously, such as a huge stamping machine that stamps sheets of metal in groups simultaneously. So, if the fragment shader requires `float` to be multiplied by 2, then the process will begin by having all cores copy data into the appropriate registers in one coordinated step. Only when all cores are finished copying to the registers will the cores be instructed to begin the second step: multiplying all registers by 2 all in a second simultaneous action.

Hence, when this system stumbles onto a conditional statement, it cannot resolve the two statements independently. It must determine how many of its child cores will go down each path of the conditional, grab the list of required machine code instructions for one path, resolve them for all cores taking that path, and repeat these steps for each path until all possible paths have been processed. So, for an `if-else` statement (two possibilities), it will tell one group of cores to process the `true` path, and then ask the remaining cores to process the `false` path. Unless every core takes the same path, it must process both paths every time.

So, we should avoid branching and conditional statements in our shader code. Of course, this depends on how essential the conditional is to achieving the graphical effect we desire. However, if the conditional is not dependent on per-pixel behavior, then we would often be better off absorbing the cost of unnecessary mathematics than inflicting a branching cost on the GPU.

Reducing data dependencies

The compiler will try its best to optimize our shader code into the more GPU-friendly low-level language so that it is not waiting on data to be fetched when it could be processing some other task. For example, the following poorly optimized code could be written in our shader:

```
float sum = input.color1.r;
sum = sum + input.color2.g;
sum = sum + input.color3.b;
sum = sum + input.color4.a;
float result = calculateSomething(sum);
```

This code has a data dependency such that each calculation cannot begin until the last finishes due to the dependency on the sum variable. However, such situations are often detected by the shader compiler and optimized into a version that uses instruction-level parallelism. The following code is the high-level code equivalent of the resulting machine code after the previous code is compiled:

```
float sum1, sum2, sum3, sum4;
sum1 = input.color1.r;
sum2 = input.color2.g;
sum3 = input.color3.b;
sum4 = input.color4.a;
float sum = sum1 + sum2 + sum3 + sum4;
float result = CalculateSomething(sum);
```

In this case, the compiler would recognize that it can fetch the four values from memory in parallel and complete the summation once all four have been fetched independently via thread-level parallelism. This can save a lot of time relative to performing the four fetches one after another.

However, long chains of data dependency that cannot be compiled away can absolutely murder shader performance. If we create a strong data dependency in our shader's source code, then it has no freedom to make any optimizations. For example, the following data dependency would be painful on performance, as one step literally cannot be completed without waiting on another to fetch data, since sampling each texture requires sampling another texture beforehand, and the compiler cannot assume that the data hasn't changed in the meantime.

The following code represents a very strong data dependency between instructions since each relies on texture data being sampled from the previous instruction:

```
float4 val1 = tex2D(_tex1, input.texcoord.xy);
float4 val2 = tex2D(_tex2, val1.yz); // requires data from _tex1
float4 val3 = tex2D(_tex3, val2.zw); // requires data from _tex2
```

Strong data dependencies such as these should be avoided whenever possible.

Surface Shaders

Unity's Surface Shaders are a simplified form of fragment shaders, allowing Unity developers to get to grips with shader programming in a more simplified fashion. The Unity Engine takes care of converting our Surface Shader code for us, abstracting away some of the optimization opportunities we have just covered. However, it does provide some miscellaneous values that can be used as replacements, which reduce accuracy but simplify the mathematics in the resulting code. Surface Shaders are designed to handle the general case fairly efficiently, but optimization is best achieved with a personal touch by writing our own shaders.

The `approxview` attribute will approximate the view direction, saving costly operations. The `halfasview` attribute will reduce the precision of the view vector, but beware of its effect on mathematical operations involving multiple-precision types.
The `noforwardadd` attribute will limit the shader to only considering a single directional light, reducing draw calls, since the shader will render in only a single pass, and lighting complexity. Finally, the `noambient` attribute will disable ambient lighting in the shader, removing some extra mathematical operations that we may not need.

Use shader-based LOD

We can force Unity to render distant objects using simpler shaders, which can be an effective way of saving Fill Rate, particularly if we're deploying our game onto multiple platforms or supporting a wide range of hardware capability. The LOD keyword can be used in the shader to set the onscreen size factor that the shader supports. If the current LOD level does not match this value, it will drop to the next fallback shader and so on until it finds the shader that supports the given size factor. We can also change a given shader object's LOD value at runtime using the `maximumLOD` property.

This feature is similar to the mesh-based LOD covered earlier and uses the same LOD values for determining object form factor, so it should be configured as such.

Check out `https://docs.unity3d.com/Manual/SL-ShaderLOD.html` in the Unity documentation for more information on shader-based LOD.

Using less texture data

This approach is simple, straightforward, and always a good idea to consider. Reducing texture quality, either through resolution or bit rate, is not ideal for graphical quality, but we can sometimes get away with using 16-bit textures without any noticeable degradation.

Mipmaps (explored in `Chapter 4`, *Optimizing Your Art Assets*) are another excellent way of reducing the amount of texture data being pushed back and forth between VRAM and the Texture Cache. Note that the **Scene** window has a **Mipmaps** shading mode, which will highlight textures in our scene blue or red, depending on whether the current texture scale is appropriate for the current **Scene** window's camera position and orientation. This will help identify what textures are good candidates for further optimization.

Testing different GPU texture compression formats

As you learned in `Chapter 4`, *Optimizing Your Art Assets*, there are different texture compression formats, which can reduce our application's disk footprint (executable file size), runtime CPU, and RAM usage. These compression formats are designed to support GPU architecture for the given platform. There are many different formats, such as DXT, PVRTC, ETC, and ASTC, but only a handful of these are available on a given platform.

By default, Unity will pick the best compression format determined by the **Compression** setting for a texture file. If we drill down into platform-specific options for a given texture file, then different compression type options will be available, listing the different texture formats the given platform supports. We may be able to find some space or performance savings by overriding the default choices for compression.

Although beware that if we're at the point where individually tweaking texture compression techniques is necessary, then hopefully we have already exhausted all other options for reducing memory bandwidth. By going down this road, we would be committing ourselves to support many different devices each in their own specific way. Many developers would prefer to keep things simple with a general solution instead of personal customization and time-consuming handiwork for small performance gains.

Check out the Unity documentation for an overview of all of the different texture formats available and which formats Unity prefers by default at `https://docs.unity3d.com/Manual/class-TextureImporterOverride.html`.

In older versions of Unity, all formats were exposed for **Advanced** texture types, but if the platform did not support the given type, it would be handled at the software level. In other words, the CPU would need to stop and recompress the texture to the desired format the GPU wants, as opposed to the GPU taking care of it with a specialized hardware chip. Unity Technologies decided to remove this capability in more recent versions so that we can't accidentally cause these problems.

Minimizing texture swapping

This one is fairly straightforward. If memory bandwidth is a problem, then we need to reduce the amount of texture sampling we're doing. There aren't really any special tricks to exploit here since memory bandwidth is all about throughput, so the primary metric under consideration is the volume of data we're pushing.

One way to reduce volume is to simply lower texture resolution and, hence, quality. This is obviously not ideal, so another approach is to find clever ways to reuse textures on different meshes, but using different Material and shader properties. For instance, a properly darkened brick texture may appear to look like a stone wall instead. Of course, this will require different Render States, and hence, we won't save on draw calls, but it could reduce memory bandwidth consumption.

Did you ever notice how clouds and bushes looked exactly the same in Super Mario Bros but with different colors? This is the same concept.

There could also be ways to combine textures into atlases to reduce the number of swaps needed. If there are a group of textures that are always used together at similar times, then they could potentially be merged together. This could save the GPU from having to pull in separate texture files over and over again during the same frame.

Finally, removing textures from the application entirely is always the last resort option we could employ.

VRAM limits

One last consideration related to textures is how much VRAM we have available. Most texture transfer from CPU to GPU occurs during initialization, but can also occur when a non-existent texture is first required by the current view. This process is normally asynchronous and will result in a blank texture being used until the full texture is ready for rendering (refer to `Chapter 4`, *Optimizing Your Art Assets*, to note that this assumes read/write access is disabled for the texture). As such, we should avoid introducing new textures at runtime too frequently.

Preloading textures with hidden GameObjects

The blank texture that is used during asynchronous texture loading can be jarring when it comes to game quality. We would like a way to control and force the texture to be loaded from disk to RAM and then to VRAM before it is actually needed.

A common workaround is to create a hidden `GameObject` that uses the texture and place it somewhere in the scene on the route that the player will take toward the area where it is actually needed. As soon as the player looks at that object, the texture is needed by the Rendering Pipeline (even if it's technically hidden), it will begin the process of copying the data from RAM to VRAM. This is a little clunky but easy to implement and works sufficiently well in most cases.

We can also control such behavior via Script code by changing a Material's `texture` property:

```
GetComponent<Renderer>().material.texture = textureToPreload;
```

Avoid texture thrashing

In the rare event that too much texture data is loaded into VRAM, and the required texture is not present, the GPU will need to request it from RAM and overwrite one or more existing textures to make room for it. This is likely to worsen over time as the memory becomes fragmented, and it introduces a risk that the texture just flushed from VRAM needs to be pulled again within the same frame. This will result in a serious case of memory thrashing and should be avoided at all costs.

This is less of a concern on modern consoles such as the PS4, Xbox One, and Wii U since they share a common memory space for both CPU and GPU. This design is a hardware-level optimization, given the fact that the device is always running a single application, and almost always rendering 3D graphics. However, most other platforms must share time and space with multiple applications, where a GPU is merely an optional device and is not always present. They, therefore, feature separate memory spaces for the CPU and GPU, and we must ensure that the total texture usage at any given moment remains below the available VRAM of the target hardware.

Note that this thrashing is not precisely the same as hard disk thrashing, where memory is copied back and forth between the main memory and the virtual memory (the swap file), but it is analogous. In either case, data is being unnecessarily copied back and forth between two regions of memory because too much data is being requested in too short a time period for the smaller of the two memory regions to hold it all.

 Thrashing such as this can be a common cause of dreadful rendering performance when games are ported from modern consoles to desktop platforms and should be treated with care.

Avoiding this behavior may require customizing texture quality and file sizes on a per-platform and per-device basis. Be warned that some players are likely to notice these inconsistencies if we're dealing with hardware from the same console or desktop GPU generation. As many of us will know, even small differences in hardware can lead to a lot of apples-versus-oranges comparisons, but hardcore gamers tend to expect a similar level of quality across the board.

Lighting optimization

We covered the theory of lighting behavior earlier in this chapter, so let's run through some techniques we can use to improve lighting costs.

Using real-time shadows responsibly

As mentioned previously, shadowing can easily become one of the largest consumers of draw calls and Fill Rate, so we should spend the time to tweak these settings until we get the performance and/or graphical quality we need.

There are multiple important settings for shadowing that can be found under **Edit | Project Settings | Quality | Shadows**. As far as the **Shadows** option is concerned, **Soft Shadows** are expensive, **Hard Shadows** are cheap, and **No Shadows** are free. **Shadow Resolution**, **Shadow Projection**, **Shadow Distance**, and **Shadow Cascades** are also important settings that affect the performance of our shadows:

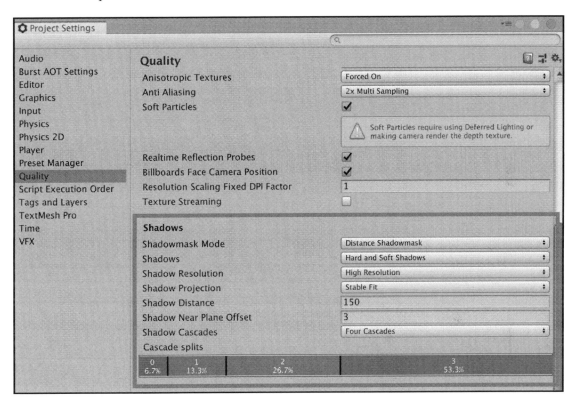

Shadow Distance is a global multiplier for runtime shadow rendering. There is little point in rendering shadows at a great distance from the camera, so this setting should be configured specific to our game and how much shadowing we expect to witness during gameplay. It is also a common setting that is exposed to the user in an options screen, so they can choose how far to render shadows to get the game's performance to match their hardware (at least on desktop machines).

Higher values of **Shadow Resolution** and **Shadow Cascades** will increase our memory bandwidth and Fill Rate consumption. Both of these settings can help to curb the effects of artifacts generated by shadow rendering, but at the cost of much larger shadow map texture sizes, costing increased memory bandwidth and VRAM.

The Unity documentation contains an excellent summary of the topic of the aliasing effect of shadow maps and how the **Shadow Cascades** feature helps to solve the problem at `http://docs.unity3d.com/Manual/DirLightShadows.html`.

It's worth noting that **Soft Shadows** do not consume any more memory or CPU overhead relative to **Hard Shadows**, as the only difference is a more complex shader. This means that applications with enough Fill Rate to spare can enjoy the improved graphical fidelity of **Soft Shadows**.

Using culling masks

A `Light` component's **Culling Mask** property is a layer-based mask that can be used to limit the objects that will be affected by the given light. This is an effective way of reducing lighting overhead, assuming that the layer interactions also make sense with how we are using layers for physics optimization. Objects can only be a part of a single layer, and reducing physics overhead probably trumps lighting overhead in most cases; hence, if there is a conflict, then this may not be the ideal approach.

Note that there is limited support for Culling Masks when using Deferred Shading. Due to the way it treats lighting in a very global fashion, only four Layers can be disabled from the mask, limiting our ability to optimize its behavior.

Using baked lightmaps

Baking lighting and shadowing into a scene is significantly less processor-intensive than generating them at runtime. The downside is the added application disk footprint, memory consumption, and potential for memory bandwidth abuse. Ultimately, unless a game's lighting effects are being handled exclusively through the legacy Vertex-Lit Shading format or through a single `DirectionalLight` instance, then it should probably include lightmapping somewhere to make some huge budget savings on lighting calculations. Relying entirely on real-time lighting and shadows is a recipe for disaster due to the performance costs they are likely to inflict.

Several metrics can affect the cost of lightmapping, however, such as their resolution, compression, whether we are using pre-computed real-time GI, and, of course, the number of objects in our scene. The lightmapper generates textures that span all of the objects marked **Lightmap Static** in the scene, and, hence, the more we have, the more texture data must be generated for them.

This would be an opportunity to make use of additive or subtractive scene loading to minimize how many objects need to be processed in each frame. This, of course, pulls in even more lightmap data while more than one scene is loaded, so we should expect a big bump in memory consumption each time this happens, only to have it freed once the old scene is unloaded.

Optimizing rendering performance for mobile devices

Unity's ability to deploy to mobile devices has contributed greatly to its popularity among hobbyist, small, and mid-size development teams. As such, it would be prudent to cover some approaches that are more beneficial for mobile platforms than for desktop and other devices. Let's take a look at a few of these approaches.

Note that any, or all, of the following approaches may eventually become obsolete, at least for newer devices. The capabilities of mobile devices have advanced blazingly fast, and the following techniques as they apply to mobile devices merely reflect conventional wisdom from the last half-decade or so. We should test the assumptions behind these approaches to check whether the limitations of mobile devices still fit the mobile marketplace.

Avoiding alpha testing

Mobile GPUs haven't quite reached the same levels of chip optimization as desktop GPUs, and alpha testing remains a particularly costly task on mobile devices. In most cases, it should simply be avoided in favor of alpha blending.

Minimizing draw calls

Mobile applications are more often bottlenecked on draw calls than on Fill Rate. Not that Fill Rate concerns should be ignored (nothing should, ever!), but this makes it almost necessary for any mobile application of reasonable quality to implement mesh combining, batching, and atlasing techniques from the very beginning. Deferred Rendering is also the preferred technique, as it fits well with other mobile-specific concerns, such as avoiding transparency and having too many animated characters, but of course, not all mobile devices and graphics APIs support it.

Check out the Unity documentation for more information on which platforms/APIs support Deferred Shading at `https://docs.unity3d.com/Manual/RenderingPaths.html`.

Minimizing Material count

This concern goes hand in hand with the concepts of batching and atlasing. The fewer Materials we use, the fewer draw calls required. This strategy will also help with concerns relating to VRAM and memory bandwidth, which tend to be very limited on mobile devices.

Minimizing texture size

Most mobile devices feature a very small texture cache relative to desktop GPUs. There are very few devices on the market still supporting OpenGL ES 1.1 or lower, such as the iPhone 3G, but these devices could only support a maximum texture size of 1024 x 1024. Devices supporting OpenGLES 2.0, such as everything from the iPhone 3GS to the iPhone 6S, can support textures up to 2048 x 2048. Finally, devices supporting OpenGLES 3.0 or greater, such as devices running iOS 7, can support textures up to 4096 x 4096.

 There are way too many Android devices to list here, but the Android developer portal gives a handy breakdown of OpenGLES device support. This information is updated regularly to help developers to determine supported APIs in the Android market at `https://developer.android.com/about/dashboards/index.html`.

Double-check the device hardware we are targeting to be sure that it supports the texture file sizes we wish to use. However, later-generation devices are never the most common devices in the mobile marketplace. If we wish our game to reach a wide audience (increasing its chances of success), then we must be willing to support weaker hardware.

Note that textures that are too large for the GPU will be downscaled by the CPU during initialization. This wastes valuable loading time and is going to leave us with unintended loss of quality due to an uncontrolled reduction in resolution. This makes texture reuse of paramount importance for mobile devices due to the limited VRAM and texture cache sizes available.

Making textures square and the power-of-two

We have already covered this topic in Chapter 4, *Optimizing Your Art Assets*, but it is worth revisiting the subject of GPU-level Texture Compression. The GPU will find it difficult, or simply be unable, to compress the texture if it is not in a square format, so make sure that you stick to the common development convention and keep things square and sized to a power-of-two.

Using the lowest possible precision formats in shaders

Mobile GPUs are particularly sensitive to precision formats in its shaders, so the smallest formats should be used, such as `half`. On a related note, precision format conversion should be avoided at all costs for the same reason.

Summary

If you've made it this far without skipping ahead, then congratulations are in order. That was a lot of information to absorb for just one subsystem of the Unity Engine, but then it is clearly the most complicated of them all, requiring a matching depth of explanation. Hopefully, you've learned a lot of approaches to help you to improve your rendering performance and enough about the Rendering Pipeline to know how to use them responsibly.

By now, we should be used to the idea that, except for algorithm improvements, every performance enhancement we implement will come with some related cost that we must be willing to bear for the sake of removing one bottleneck. We should always be ready to implement multiple techniques until we've squashed them all, and potentially spend a lot of additional development time to implement and test some performance-enhancing features.

In the next chapter, let's bring performance optimization into the modern era by exploring some performance improvements we can apply to VR and AR projects.

3
Section 3: Advance Optimizations

The reader will learn how to implement additional and more advanced/situational optimization techniques. The chapters in this section are as follows:

7
Optimizations for Virtual and Augmented Reality

Two whole new entertainment mediums have entered the world stage in the forms of **virtual reality** (**VR**), where users are transported into a virtual space through the use of a **head-mounted device** (**HMD**), and **augmented reality** (**AR**), where virtual elements are superimposed on top of a display showing the real world. For the sake of brevity, these two terms are often combined into the singular term – **extended reality** (**XR**). There is also **Mixed Reality** (**MR**) (also known as **Hybrid Reality** (**HR**)), where an application mixes the real and virtual worlds together; this encompasses all of the previously mentioned formats, while also including AR, where real-world objects are scanned and superimposed inside a mostly virtual world.

The markets for these media formats have sprung up very fast and are continuing to grow rapidly, with huge investments from the technology industry's biggest players. Naturally, game engines such as Unity jumped on the bandwagon quickly, providing ample support for most of the top contending platforms, such as Google's Cardboard, HTC's VIVE, Oculus Rift, Microsoft's HoloLens, and Samsung's Gear VR platforms, as well as the more recent entries, such as Apple's ARKit, Google's ARCore, Microsoft's Windows Mixed Reality platform, PTC's (originally Qualcomm's) Vuforia, and Sony's PlayStation VR.

Overview of XR technology

XR offers a whole new realm for developers and creatives to explore. This includes entertainment products such as games and 360-degree videos (or 360 video for short), where a series of cameras are bundled together, each facing a different direction—the various captures from those cameras are stitched together and later played back like a movie in a VR headset, with visibility in all directions. Creative industry tools are also common in XR, such as 3D-modeling software, workflow visualizations, and quality-of-life gadgets. There are very few rules that have been set in stone, so there are plenty of opportunities to innovate, contribute to this new wave of technology, and become the one to create those rules. This has led to a lot of buzz and excitement as people explore what is possible and try to make their mark on the future of entertainment and interactive experiences.

Of course, almost every new and budding technology goes through the **Hype Cycle** (from the Gartner Hype Cycle, which you can see at `https://www.gartner.com/technology/research/methodologies/hype-cycle.jsp`). The Hype Cycle starts with its honeymoon period of excessive hype, where early adopters will evangelize its benefits. Later, there is an eventual cooling of emotions as it enters the trough of disillusionment since it hasn't quite hit the mainstream, and its benefits are not taking hold just yet. This continues until either the technology fails to capture hearts and minds, thereby falling out of existence, or takes a firm hold and continues steady adoption. The following diagram shows the essentials of the Gartner Hype Cycle:

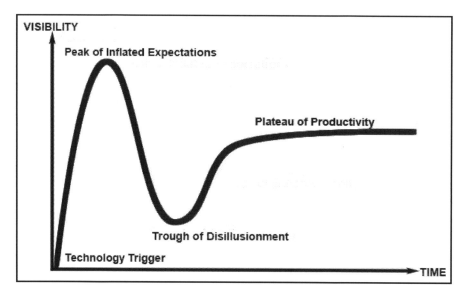

Arguably, XR has recently been passing through this final phase and is starting to enjoy much better support and much higher quality experiences than it did during the early days, although it is true that the adoption rate of XR has been slower than initially predicted. It remains to be seen whether XR will grow into a multibillion dollar industry or fade into a niche market of gadgets. Consequently, developing within this new medium is not without its risks, and we can find industry analysts who will agree with our opinions, regardless of where we stand on the future of XR. One thing is for certain, though: every time someone experiences firsthand what VR and AR are capable of, they're blown away by the level of immersion and the medium's ability to convincingly transport them into another world. This level of immersion and interactivity is unparalleled and teases many more possibilities as support for the platforms matures and technology continues to advance.

In this chapter, we will explore the following topics:

- The concerns to keep in mind when developing VR or AR projects in Unity and what must be avoided
- Performance enhancements specific to the XR medium

Developing XR products

Developing an XR product in Unity involves importing one of several XR **software development kits (SDKs)** into our Unity project and making some specialized API calls to configure and use the platform at runtime. Each SDK is different in its own way and offers a different set of features. For instance, the Oculus Rift and HTC VIVE SDKs provide APIs to control VR HMDs and their respective controllers, whereas Apple's ARKit provides utilities to determine spatial positioning and superimpose objects on the display. Unity Technologies have been working hard to create APIs that support all of these variations, so the APIs for XR development in Unity have changed a lot over the past few years.

The early days of Unity VR development meant dropping native plugins into our Unity projects, importing SDKs directly from an external developer portal (involving all kinds of annoying grunt work in the setup), and applying updates manually. Since then, however, Unity has incorporated several of these SDKs directly into the editor. In addition, since AR has become more popular recently, the main API has been renamed from `UnityEngine.VR` to `UnityEngine.XR` in Unity 2017.2.0 and later, and modified so that it can work with several AR SDKs.

The Unity XR system is currently transitioning from the legacy model to a new package-based model. By default, Unity supports a limited set of XR platforms. To import other XR SDKs and to configure them (such as ARKit or the Hololens), you need first to install them using **Package Manager** by going to **Window | Package Manager**.

The development experience of working on XR products is a bit of a mixed bag right now. It involves working on some top-of-the-line hardware and software, which means that there are constant changes, redesigns, breakages, patches, bugs, crashes, compatibility issues, performance problems, rendering artifacts, a lack of feature parity between platforms, and so on. All of these problems serve to slow down our progress, which makes gaining a competitive advantage extraordinarily difficult in the XR field. On the bright side, pretty much everyone is having the same issues, so they get a lot of attention from their developers, making them easier to develop with all the time. Lessons are learned, APIs are cleaned up, and new features, tools, and optimizations are made available with every passing update.

Performance problems limit an XR product's success, perhaps more so than non-XR projects because of the current state of the medium. Let's take a look at a few of these performance problems:

- Firstly, our users will be spending significant amounts of money to purchase VR HMDs and sensor equipment or AR-capable hardware. Both of these platforms can be very resource intensive, requiring similarly expensive graphics hardware to support them. This typically leads users to expect a much higher level of quality compared to typical games so that the investment feels worthwhile. To put it another way, this makes poor user experiences understandably less forgivable due to the monetary investment required by the user.
- Secondly, perhaps more so for VR projects than AR ones, poor application performance can lead to serious physical user discomfort, quickly turning even the staunchest advocate into a detractor. In particular, if the frame rate of the XR application is not enough, there will be a discrepancy between the motion the players feel (for example, by rotating the head) and what they see (we will learn about this in more detail later). This leads to the common issue of motion sickness that, in some cases, can last for hours.
- Thirdly, the XR platform's primary draw is its immersiveness, and nothing breaks that faster than frame drops, flickering, or any kind of application breakdown that forces the user to remove their headset or reboot the app.

Ultimately, we must be prepared to profile our XR applications early to make sure we aren't exceeding our runtime budget, as it will be stretched thin by the complex and resource-intensive nature of the technology behind these media.

User comfort

Unlike typical games and apps, VR apps need to consider user comfort as a metric to use to optimize themselves. Dizziness, motion sickness, eye strain, headaches, and even physical injuries from loss of balance have unfortunately been all too common for early VR adopters, and the onus is on us to limit these negative effects for users. In essence, content is just as important to user comfort as the hardware is, and we need to take the matter seriously if we are building for the medium.

Not everyone experiences these issues, and there are a lucky few who have experienced none of them; however, the overwhelming majority of users have reported these problems at one point or another. Also, just because our game doesn't trigger these problems in ourselves when we're testing them doesn't mean they won't trigger them in someone else. In fact, we will be the most biased test subject for our game due to familiarity. Without realizing it, we might start to predict our way around the most nauseating behavior our app generates, making it an unfair test compared to a new user experiencing the same situation. This, unfortunately, raises the costs of VR app development further, as a lot of testing with different unbiased individuals is required if we want to figure out whether our experience will cause discomfort, which may be needed each time we make significant changes that affect motion and frame rate.

 There are several things that users can do to improve their VR comfort, such as starting with small sessions and working their way up to get practice in balancing and training their brain to expect the mismatched motion. A more drastic option is to take motion sickness medication or drink a little ginger tea beforehand to settle the stomach. However, we will hardly convince users to try our app if we promise it'll only take a few sessions of motion sickness before it starts to get enjoyable.

There are three main kinds of discomfort that users can experience in VR:

- **Motion sickness**: The first problem, nausea caused by motion sickness, typically happens when there is a sensory disconnect between where the user's eyes think the horizon is and what their other senses are telling their brain, such as the inner ear's sense of balance.
- **Eye strain**: The second problem, eye strain, comes from the fact that the user is staring at a screen mere inches from their eyes, which tends to lead to a lot of eye strain and, ultimately, headaches after prolonged use.

- **Disorientation**: Finally, disorientation typically occurs because a user in VR is sometimes standing within a confined space, so if a game features any kind of acceleration-based motion, the user will instinctively try to offset that acceleration by adjusting their balance, which can lead to disorientation, falling over, and the user hurting themselves if we are not careful in ensuring that the user experiences smooth and predictable motion.

 Note that the term **acceleration** is used intentionally since it is a vector, which means it has both magnitude and direction. Any kind of acceleration can cause disorientation, which includes not only accelerating forward, backward, and sideways, but also an acceleration in a rotational fashion (turning around), falling, jumping, and so on.

Another potential problem for VR apps is the possibility of invoking seizures. VR is in the unique position of being able to blast images into the user's eyes at a close range, which opens up some risks that we might unintentionally trigger seizures in vulnerable users if rendering behavior breaks down and starts flickering. These are all things we need to keep in mind during development that need to be tested for and fixed sooner rather than later.

Perhaps the most important performance metric to reach in a VR app is having a high number of **frames-per-second (FPS)**, preferably 90 FPS or more, as this will generate a smooth viewing experience since there will be a very small disconnection between the user's head motion and the motion of the world. Any period of extended frame drops or having an FPS value consistently below this value is likely to cause a lot of problems for our users, making it critical that our application performs well at all times. Also, we should be very careful about how we control the user's viewpoint. We should avoid changing an HMD's field of view ourselves (let the user dictate the direction they are facing), generating acceleration over long periods, or causing uncontrolled world rotation and horizon motion, since these are extremely likely to trigger motion sickness and balance problems for the user.

A strict rule that is not up for debate is that we should never apply any kind of gain, multiplier effect, or acceleration effect to the positional tracking of an HMD in the final build of our product. Doing so for the sake of testing is fine, but if a real user moves their head two inches to the side, then it should feel like it moved the same relative distance inside the application and should stop the moment their head stops. Doing otherwise is not only going to cause a disconnect between where the player's head feels like it should be and where it is, but may also cause some serious discomfort if the camera becomes offset with respect to the player's orientation and the angle of their neck.

It is possible to use acceleration for the motion of the player character, but it should be incredibly short and rapid before the user starts to self-adjust too quickly. It would be wisest to stick to motion that relies on constant velocities and/or teleportation.

Placing banked turns in racing games seems to improve user comfort a great deal since the user naturally tilts their head and adjusts their balance to match the turn.

All of the previous rules apply just as well to 360 video content as they do to VR games. Frankly, there has been an embarrassing number of 360 videos released to the market that are not taking the aforementioned points into account—they feature too many jerking movements, a lack of camera stabilization, manual viewport rotation, and so on. These hacks are often used to ensure the user is facing in the direction we intend; however, we must spend more effort on doing this without hacking to avoid nausea-inducing behavior. Humans are naturally very curious about things that move. If they notice something moving in the corner of their eye, then they will most likely turn to face it. This can be used to great effect to keep the user facing in the direction we intend as they watch the video.

Laziness is not the way to go when generating VR content. Don't just slap a 360 camera on top of a dirt rally car and hack an unexpected camera rotation into the video to keep the action in the center. The motion needs to be smooth and predictable. During production, we need to constantly keep in mind where we expect the user to be looking so that we capture action shots correctly.

Fortunately, for the 360 video format, it seems as though industry-standard frame rates, such as 24 FPS or 29.97 FPS, do not have a disastrous effect on user comfort, but note that this frame rate applies to video playback only. Our rendering FPS is a separate FPS value and dictates how smooth positional head tracking will be. The rendering FPS must always be very high to avoid discomfort (ideally, 90 FPS).

Other problems arise when building VR apps—different HMDs and controllers support different inputs and behavior, making feature-parity across VR platforms difficult. A problem called **stereo fighting** can occur if we try to merge 2D and 3D content together, where 2D objects appear to be rendering deep inside 3D objects since the eyes can't distinguish the distance correctly. This is typically a big problem for the user interface of VR applications and 360 video playback, which tends to be a series of flat panels superimposed over a 3D background. Stereo fighting does not usually lead to nausea, but it can cause additional eye strain.

Although the effects of discomfort are not quite as pronounced in the AR platform, it's still important not to ignore it. Since AR apps tend to consume a lot of resources, low frame rate applications can cause some discomfort. This is especially true if an AR app makes use of superimposing objects onto a camera image (which is the majority of them), where there will probably be a disconnect in the frame rate between the background camera image and the objects we're superimposing over it. We should try to synchronize these frame rates to limit that disconnect.

Performance enhancements in XR

That's enough talk about the industry and XR development. In the next section, we will cover some performance enhancements that can be applied to XR projects, such as choosing between the different kinds of stereo rendering algorithms and how to apply antialiasing and other effects to VR games

The kitchen sink

Since AR and VR apps are built using the same engine, the same subsystems, assets, tools, and utilities as any other Unity game, literally every other performance enhancement mentioned in this book, can help VR and AR apps in some fashion, and we should try them all before getting too in-depth with XR-specific enhancements. This is reassuring, as there are a lot of potential performance enhancements we could apply. The downside is that we may need to apply many of them to reach the level of performance we need for our app.

The biggest threat to a VR app's performance is the GPU fill rate, which is already one of the more likely bottlenecks in any other game, but significantly more so for VR, since we will always be trying to render a high-resolution image to a much larger frame buffer (since we're effectively rendering the scene twice—once for each eye). AR apps are typically going to find extreme consumption in both the CPU and the GPU since AR platforms make heavy use of the GPU's parallel pipeline to resolve the spatial locality of objects and perform tasks such as image recognition, as well as requiring a lot of draw calls to support those activities.

Of course, certain performance-enhancing techniques are not going to be particularly effective in XR. **Occlusion Culling** in a VR app may be difficult to set up since the user can look under, around, and sometimes through objects in the scene (although it can still be enormously beneficial). Meanwhile, AR apps normally render objects at reachable distances; LOD enhancements – that is, using simpler meshes for objects far away – may be fairly pointless to set up.

We must use our better judgment to determine whether a performance optimization technique is worth implementing before we start implementing it, since many of them take a lot of time to implement and support.

Single Pass versus Multi Pass Stereo rendering

For VR apps, Unity provides three rendering modes: **Multi Pass**, **Single Pass**, and **Single Pass Instanced**. This can be configured under **Edit** | **Project Settings** | **Player** | **XR Settings** | **Stereo Rendering Method** (note that the checkbox of **Virtual Reality Supported** must be enabled for this to show up):

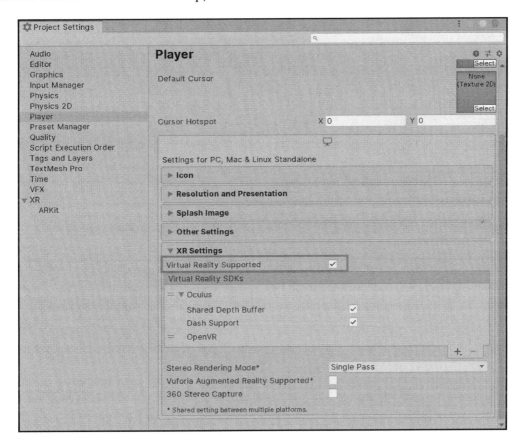

Multi Pass rendering will render the scene to two different images, which are displayed separately for each eye. Single Pass Stereo rendering combines both images into a single double-width render texture, where only the relevant half is displayed to each eye.

Note that **XR Settings** are enabled only for the legacy system. If you installed a new experimental **XR Managment** package, you will find the rendering modes by going to **Edit | Project Settings | XR Plugin Management**.

Multi Pass Stereo rendering is the default case. The advantage of **Single Pass** rendering is that it provides significant savings in the CPU work in the main thread (by reducing draw call setup) and in the GPU since less texture swapping needs to occur. Of course, the GPU will need to work just as hard to render the objects since each object is still rendered twice from two different perspectives (there are no freebies here). The disadvantage is that this effect can currently only be used when using OpenGL ES3.0 or higher, and so it is not available on all platforms.

In addition, its effects on the rendering pipeline require extra care and effort, particularly surrounding any shaders that are making use of screen-space effects (effects that only use data already drawn to the framebuffer). With Single Pass Stereo rendering enabled, shader code can no longer make the same assumptions about the incoming screen space information. The following image shows how screen space coordinates vary between **Multi-Pass Stereo Rendering** and **Single-Pass Stereo Rendering**:

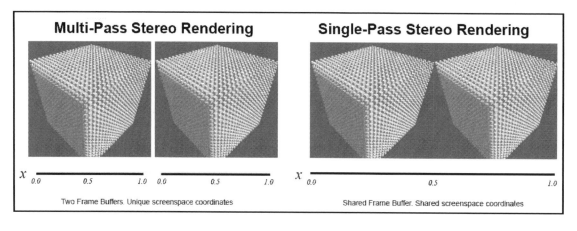

The shader is always informed of the screen space coordinates relative to the entire output render texture rather than just the portion it is interested in—for example, we would normally expect an **x** value of **0.5** to correspond to the horizontal halfway point of the screen, which would be the case when we use **Multi-Pass Stereo Rendering**; however, if we use **Single-Pass Stereo Rendering,** then an x value of **0.5** would correspond to the halfway point between the rendering of both eyes (the right edge of the left eye or the left edge of the right eye).

Unity provides some useful helper methods for screen space conversion for shaders, which can be found at `https://docs.unity3d.com/Manual/SinglePassStereoRendering.html`.

Another problem to worry about is post-processing effects. We essentially always pay double the cost for any post-processing effect applied to the scene in VR since it needs to be evaluated once for each eye. Single Pass Stereo rendering can reduce the draw calls needed to set up our effect, but we can't blindly apply a post-processing effect to both images simultaneously. Consequently, the post-processing effect shaders must also be adjusted to ensure that they render to the correct half of the output render texture. Without doing this, a post-processing effect will be stretched over both eyes twice, which might look incredibly bizarre for effects such as lens flares.

Single-Pass instancing (also known as **stereo instancing**), on the other hand, is an experimental rendering mode that has some advantages over the standard single pass. Instead of doubling draw calls by rendering the same object for the right and the left eye, single-pass instances makes heavy use of **GPU instancing**. In short, GPU instancing allows Unity to issue a single draw call to the GPU, but with the instruction that the mesh must be drawn in two different positions. Therefore, single-pass instances can offer a dramatic improvement compared with CPU performances; however, custom shaders need to be ready for GPU instantiation: this involves adding a position parameter to the shader (so that the GPU knows how to move the mesh) and several Unity utility functions.

 Enabling GPU instancing on a custom shader is a hard task, and it is not recommended unless you already have some experience with the Unity shading language. If you have, then the right place to start is `https://docs.unity3d.com/Manual/SinglePassInstancing.html`.

The single-pass rendering (both traditional and instanced) feature is not supported for all platforms. We can expect it to be rolled out to more platforms eventually, but for platforms supporting it, we will need to perform some profiling and sensible sanity checks on our screen space shaders to ensure that we are making positive gains from enabling this option.

Applying antialiasing

Applying antialiasing is less of a performance enhancement and more of a requirement. Antialiasing significantly improves the fidelity of XR projects since objects will blend better and appear less pixelated, improving immersion, which can cost a lot of fill-rate. We should enable this feature early and try to reach our performance goals with the assumption that it is simply always there, only disabling it as an absolute last resort.

Using forward rendering

The advantage of deferred rendering is the ability to resolve many light sources with minimal draw calls. Unfortunately, if we follow the preceding advice and apply antialiasing effects, then this must be done as a post-processing screen space shader when deferred rendering is used. This can cost a considerable amount of performance compared to how the same technique is applied as a multisampling effect in forward rendering, potentially making forward rendering the more performant of the two options.

Applying image effects in VR

The effects applied by normal maps tend to break down easily in VR, where the texture appears painted on to the surface instead of giving the illusion of depth. Normal maps normally break down very quickly with viewing angles that are very oblique (shallow) with the surface, which is not particularly common in a typical game; however, in VR, since most HMDs allow users to move their heads around in a 3D space via positional tracking (which, granted, not all of them do), they will quickly find positions that break the effect for any objects close to the camera. Normal maps have been known to improve the quality of high polygon count objects in VR, but it rarely provides a benefit for those with a low polygon count, so we should perform a little testing to make sure that any visual improvement is worth the costs in memory bandwidth.

Ultimately, we cannot rely on normal mapping to provide a quick and cheap increase in graphical fidelity for low polygon count objects that we might expect from a non-VR scene, so testing is required to establish whether the illusion is working as intended. Displacement maps, tessellation, and/or parallax mapping should be used instead to create a more believable appearance of depth. Unfortunately, all of these techniques are more expensive than a typical normal map, but it is a burden we must suffer in order to achieve good graphical quality in VR.

Other post-processing effects, such as depth of field, blurring, and lens flares, are effects that look good in a typical 3D game, but are generally not effects we witness in the real world, and will seem out of place in VR (at least until eye-tracking support is available), and so should generally be avoided.

Backface culling

Backface culling (removing faces from objects that will never be visible) can be tricky for VR and AR projects since the player's viewing angle could potentially come from any direction for objects near the camera. Assets near the camera should be a fully closed shape if we want to avoid immersion-breaking viewpoints. We should also think carefully about applying backface culling for distant objects, particularly if the user travels by teleportation since it can be tricky to restrict a user's location completely. Ensure that you test your game world's bounding volumes to ensure that the user cannot escape.

Spatialized audio

The audio industry is abuzz with new techniques to present audio experiences for VR (or, more accurately, old techniques that have finally found a good use) in the form of spatial audio. Audio data for these formats no longer represents audio data from specific channels, but instead contains data for certain audio harmonics that are merged at runtime to create a more believable audio experience depending on the current camera viewport, particularly vertical orientations. The key word from the previous sentence is runtime, meaning that this effect has a continuous nontrivial cost associated with it. These techniques will require CPU activity, but may also use GPU acceleration to generate their effects, so we should double-check the behavior of both devices if we're experiencing performance problems when we're making use of spatial audio.

Avoiding camera physics collisions

In VR and AR, the user can move the camera through objects, which can break their immersion. Although it may be tempting to add physics colliders to such surfaces to prevent the camera from moving through them, this will cause disorientation in VR since the camera will not move in unison with the user's movements. This could also break the positional-tracking calibration of an AR app. A better approach is to either allow the user to see into objects or to maintain a safe buffer zone between the camera and such surfaces. If we don't allow the player to teleport too close to them in the first place, then there's no risk of sticking their head through walls.

This will save on performance because of a reduced number of colliders, but should be followed as more of a quality-of-life issue. We shouldn't be too concerned about risking immersion-breaking behavior by doing this, as research has shown that users tend to avoid looking into objects once they realize they can do it. They may experience a moment of confusion or hilarity when it happens initially, but fortunately, people tend to want to remain in the immersive experience we've created and will tend to avoid putting their heads through walls. However, the ability to do so provides the gameplay advantage of seeing through a wall to observe where enemies are about to come from, so we should develop our scenes with that in mind.

Avoiding Euler angles

Avoid using Euler angles for any kind of orientation behavior. Quaternions are designed to be much better for representing angles (the only downside is that they are more abstract and harder to visualize when debugging) and maintaining accuracy whenever there are changes, while also avoiding the dreaded gimbal lock. Using Euler angles for calculations could eventually lead to inaccuracies after there are a lot of rotation changes, which is incredibly likely since the user's viewpoint will change by tiny amounts many times per second in both VR and AR.

Gimbal lock is a problem that can occur with Euler angles. Since Euler angles represent orientation via three axes, and there are overlaps when one of these axes is rotated 90 degrees, we could accidentally lock them together, becoming mathematically inseparable and causing future orientation changes to affect both axes simultaneously. Of course, a human being can figure out how to rotate the object to solve this problem, but gimbal lock is a purely mathematical problem. The classic example is the orientation bubble in a fighter jet. The pilot never has problems with gimbal lock, but the orientation instruments in their heads-up display could become inaccurate because of it. Quaternions solve this problem by including a fourth value that effectively allows overlapping axes to still be distinguishable from one another.

Exercise restraint

Performance targets for VR apps are very difficult to reach. It is, therefore, important to recognize when we are simply trying to cram too much quality into our app than is tolerable for the current generation of XR devices and typical user hardware. The last resort is always to cull objects from our scenes until we reach our performance goals. We should be more willing to do so for an XR app than a non-XR one since the costs of poor performance often far outweigh the gains of higher quality. We must refrain from adding more detail to our scenes if it has become apparent that the rendering budget has been exhausted. This can be difficult to admit with immersive VR content, where we want to create as much compelling immersion as we can, but until the technology catches up with our ambition, we need to remain frugal.

Keeping up to date with the latest developments

Unity provides a list of useful articles and tutorials containing VR design and optimization tips, which will likely get updated as the medium and market matures and new techniques are discovered. This list can be kept more up to date than this book ever could be, so check them out from time to time to catch the latest tips. As usual, the articles and tutorials in question can be found at `https://learn.unity.com`.

We should also keep an eye on Unity blogs to make sure that we don't miss anything important with regard to XR API changes, performance enhancements, and performance suggestions.

Summary

Hopefully, this brief guide will help you improve the performance of your XR applications. The reassuring news is that you have many performance optimization options to choose from since Unity XR apps are built on the same underlying platform we've been exploring throughout this book. Less reassuring is the fact that we might have to test and implement all of them in order to stand a chance of reaching our quality goals. We can expect hardware to get more powerful over time, prices to come down, and adoption to increase as a result; however, until then, we need to pull out all the stops if we're going to compete in the tech world's latest craze.

In the next chapter, we'll dig into Unity's underlying engine, along with the various frameworks, layers, and languages that it is built from. In essence, we will take a more in-depth look at our script code and investigate some methods to improve our CPU and memory management across the board.

Masterful Memory Management

8

Memory efficiency is an important element of performance optimization. It's possible for games of limited scope, such as hobby projects and prototypes, to get away with ignoring memory management. These games will tend to waste a lot of resources and potentially leak memory, but this won't be a problem if we limit its exposure to friends and coworkers. However, anything we want to release professionally needs to take this subject seriously. Unnecessary memory allocations lead to poor user experience due to excessive garbage collection (costing precious CPU time) and memory leaks, which will lead to crashes. None of these situations are acceptable in modern game releases.

Using memory efficiently with Unity requires a solid understanding of the underlying Unity engine, the Mono platform, and the C# language. Also, if we're making use of the new IL2CPP scripting backend, then it would be wise to become familiar with its inner workings. This can be a bit of an intimidating place for some developers since many pick Unity3D for their game development solution primarily to avoid the kind of low-level work that comes from engine development and memory management. We'd prefer to focus on higher-level concerns related to gameplay implementation, level design, and art asset management, but, unfortunately, modern computer systems are complex tools, and ignoring low-level concerns for too long could potentially lead to disaster.

Understanding what is happening with memory allocations and C# language features, how they interact with the Mono platform, and how Mono interacts with the underlying Unity engine are absolutely paramount to making high-quality, efficient script code. So, in this chapter, you will learn about all of the nuts and bolts of the underlying Unity engine: the Mono platform, the C# language, **Intermediate Language to C++ (IL2CPP)**, and the .NET Framework.

Fortunately, it is not necessary to become absolute masters of the C# language to use it effectively. This chapter will boil these complex subjects down to a more digestible form and is split into the following subjects:

- Overview of the Mono platform:
    - Native and managed memory domains
    - Garbage collection
    - Memory fragmentation
- Building a project using IL2CPP
- How to profile memory issues
- Implement various memory-related performance enhancements:
    - Minimizing garbage collection
    - Using value types and reference types properly
    - Using strings responsibly
    - A multitude of potential enhancements related to the Unity engine
    - Object and Prefab pooling

The Mono platform

Mono is a magical sauce mixed into the Unity recipe, which gives it a lot of its cross-platform capability. Mono is an open source project that built its own platform of libraries based on the API, specifications, and tools from Microsoft's .NET Framework. Essentially, it is an open source recreation of the .NET library, was accomplished with little-to-no access to the original source code, and is fully compatible with the original library from Microsoft.

The goal of the Mono project is to provide cross-platform development through a framework that allows code written in a common programming language to run against many different hardware platforms, including Linux, macOS, Windows, ARM, PowerPC, and more. Mono even supports many different programming languages. Any language that can be compiled into .NET's **Common Intermediate Language** (CIL) is sufficient to integrate with the Mono platform. This includes C# itself, but also several other languages, such as F#, Java, Visual Basic .NET, pythonnet, and IronPython.

A common misconception about the Unity engine is that it is built on top of the Mono platform. This is untrue, as its Mono-based layer does not handle many important game tasks such as audio, rendering, physics, and keeping track of time. Unity Technologies built a native C++ backend for the sake of speed and allowed its users control of this game engine through Mono as a scripting interface. As such, Mono is merely an ingredient of the underlying Unity engine. This is equivalent to many other game engines, which run C++ under the hood, handling important tasks such as rendering, animation, and resource management, while providing a higher-level scripting language for gameplay logic to be implemented. As such, the Mono platform was chosen by Unity Technologies to provide this feature.

 Native code is a common vernacular for code that is written specifically for the given platform. For instance, writing code to create a window object or interface with networking subsystems in Windows would be completely different to code performing the tasks for a macOS, Unix, PlayStation 4, Xbox One, and so on.

Scripting languages typically abstract away complex memory management through automatic garbage collection and provide various safety features, which simplify the act of programming at the expense of runtime overhead. Some scripting languages can also be interpreted at runtime, meaning that they don't need to be compiled before execution. The raw instructions are converted dynamically into machine code and executed the moment they are read during runtime; of course, this often makes the code relatively slow. The last feature, and probably the most important one, is that they allow simpler syntax of programming commands. This usually improves development workflow immensely, as team members without much experience using languages such as C++ can still contribute to the code base. This enables them to implement things such as gameplay logic in a simpler format at the expense of a certain amount of control and runtime execution speed.

Note that such languages are often called **managed languages**, which feature **managed code**. Technically, this was a term coined by Microsoft to refer to any source code that must run inside their **Common Language Runtime** (CLR) environment, as opposed to code that is compiled and run natively through the target OS.

However, because of the prevalence and common features that exist between the CLR and other languages that feature their own similarly designed runtime environments (such as Java), the term **managed** has since been hijacked. It tends to be used to refer to any language or code that depends on its own runtime environment, and that may or may not include automatic garbage collection. For the rest of this chapter, we will adopt this definition and use the term **managed** to refer to code that both depends on a separate runtime environment to execute and is being monitored by automatic garbage collection.

The runtime performance cost of managed languages is always greater than the equivalent native code, but it is becoming less significant every year. This is partly due to gradual optimizations in tools and runtime environments, and partly due to the computing power of the average device gradually becoming greater although the main point of controversy with using managed languages still remains their automatic memory management. Managing memory manually can be a complex task that can take many years of difficult debugging to be proficient at, but many developers feel that managed languages solve this problem in ways that are too unpredictable, risking too much product quality. Such developers might claim that managed code will never reach the same level of performance as native code, and hence it is foolhardy to build high-performance applications with them.

This is true to an extent, as managed languages invariably inflict runtime overheads, and we lose partial control over runtime memory allocations. This would be a deal-breaker for high-performance server architecture; however, for game development, it becomes a balancing act since not all resource usage will necessarily result in a bottleneck, and the best games aren't necessarily the ones that use every single byte to their fullest potential. For example, imagine a user interface that refreshes in 30 ms via native code versus 60 μs in managed code due to an extra 100% overhead (an extreme example). The managed code version is still fast enough that the user will never be able to notice the difference, so is there really any harm in using managed code for such a task?

In reality, at least for game development, working with managed languages often just means that developers have a unique set of concerns to worry about compared to native code developers. As such, the choice to use a managed language for game development is partly a matter of preference and partly a compromise of control versus development speed.

Let's revisit a topic we touched upon in earlier chapters but didn't quite flesh out: the concept of memory domains in the Unity engine.

Memory domains

Memory space within the Unity engine can be essentially split into three different memory domains. Each domain stores different types of data and takes care of a very different set of tasks. Let's take a look at each of them:

- The first memory domain—the managed domain—should be very familiar. This domain is where the Mono platform does its work, where any `MonoBehaviour` scripts and custom C# classes we write will be instantiated at runtime, and so we will interact with this domain very explicitly through any C# code we write. It is called the managed domain because this memory space is automatically managed by a **Garbage Collector (GC)**.

- The second domain—the native domain—is more subtle since we only interact with it indirectly. Unity has an underlying native code foundation, which is written in C++ and compiled into our application differently, depending on which platform is being targeted. This domain takes care of allocating internal memory space for things such as asset data (for example, textures, audio files, and meshes) and memory space for various subsystems such as the Rendering Pipeline, physics system, and user input system. Finally, it includes partial native representations of important gameplay objects such as GameObjects and components so that they can interact with these internal systems. This is where a lot of built-in Unity classes keep their data, such as the `transform` and `Rigidbody` components.

- The third and final memory domains are those of external libraries, such as DirectX and OpenGL libraries, as well as any custom libraries and plugins we include in our project. Referencing these libraries from our C# code will cause a similar memory context switch and subsequent cost.

The managed domain also includes wrappers for the very same object representations that are stored within the native domain. As a result, when we interact with components such as `transform`, most instructions will ask Unity to dive into its native code, generate the result there, and then copy it back to the managed domain for us. This is where the native-managed bridge between the managed domain and native domains derives from, which was briefly mentioned in previous chapters. When both domains have their own representations for the same entity, crossing the bridge between them requires a memory context switch that can potentially inflict some fairly significant performance hits on our game. Obviously, crossing back and forth across this bridge should be minimized as much as possible due to the overhead involved. We covered several techniques for this in Chapter 2, *Scripting Strategies*.

Memory in most modern OS splits runtime memory space into two categories.

The stack

The stack is a special reserved space in memory, dedicated to small, short-lived data values, which are automatically deallocated the moment they go out of scope, hence why it is called the stack. It literally operates as a stack data structure, pushing and popping data from the top. Allocation to the stack complies with the following properties:

- The stack contains any local variables we declare and handles the loading and unloading of functions as they're called. These function calls to expand and contract through what is known as the call stack. When the call stack is done with the current function, it jumps back to the previous point on the call stack and continues from where it left off.

- The start of the previous memory allocation is always known, and there's no reason to perform any clean-up operations since any new allocations can simply overwrite the old data. Hence, the stack is relatively quick and efficient.

- The total stack size is usually very small, usually on the order of MB. It's possible to cause a stack overflow by allocating more space than the stack can support. This can occur during exceptionally large call stacks (for example, an infinite loop) or having a large number of local variables, but in most cases, causing a stack overflow is rarely a concern despite its relatively small size.

The heap

The heap represents all remaining memory space, and it is used for the overwhelming majority of memory allocation.

- Since we want most of the memory allocated to persist longer than the current function call, we couldn't allocate it on the stack since it would just get overwritten when the current function ends. So, instead, whenever a data type is too big to fit in the stack or must persist outside the function it was declared in, it is allocated on the heap.

- There's nothing physically different between the stack and the heap; they're both just memory spaces containing bytes of data that exist in RAM, which have been requested and set aside for us by the OS. The only difference is in when, where, and how they are used.

In native code, such as code written in languages such as C++, these memory allocations are handled manually in that we are responsible for ensuring that all pieces of memory we allocate are properly and explicitly deallocated when they are no longer needed. If this is not done properly, then we could easily and accidentally introduce memory leaks since we are likely to keep allocating more and more memory space from RAM that is never cleaned up until there is no more space to allocate and the application crashes.

Meanwhile, in managed languages, this process is automated through the GC. During the initialization of our Unity app, the Mono platform will request a given chunk of memory from the OS and use it to generate a heap memory space that our C# code can use (often known as the **managed heap**). This heap space starts off fairly small, less than 1 MB, but will grow as new blocks of memory are needed by our script code. This space can also shrink by releasing it back to the OS if Unity determines that it's no longer needed.

Garbage collection

The GC has an important job, which is to ensure that we don't use more managed heap memory than we need, and that memory that is no longer needed will be automatically deallocated. For instance, if we create GameObject and then later destroy it, the GC will flag the memory space used by GameObject for eventual deallocation later. This is not an immediate process, as the GC only deallocates memory when necessary.

When a new memory request is made, and there is enough empty space in the managed heap to satisfy the request, the GC simply allocates the new space and hands it over to the caller. However, if the managed heap does not have room for it, then the GC will need to scan all of the existing memory allocations for anything that is no longer being used and cleans them up first. It will only expand the current heap space as the last resort.

The GC in the version of Mono that Unity uses is a type of tracing GC, which uses a **Mark-and-Sweep** strategy. This algorithm works in two phases: each allocated object is tracked with an additional bit. This flags whether the object has been marked or not. These flags start set to false to indicate that it has not yet been marked.

When the collection process begins, it marks all objects that are still reachable to the program by setting their flags to true. Either the reachable object is a direct reference, such as static or local variables on the stack, or it is an indirect reference through the fields (member variables) of other directly or indirectly accessible objects. In essence, it is gathering a set of objects that are still referenceable to our application. Everything that is not still referenceable would be effectively invisible to our application and can be deallocated by the GC.

The second phase involves iterating through this catalog of references (which the GC will have kept track of throughout the lifetime of the application) and determining whether or not it should be deallocated based on its **marked** status. If the object is marked, then it is still being referenced by something else, and so the GC leaves it alone. However, if it is not marked, then it is a candidate for deallocation. During this phase, all marked objects are skipped over, but not before setting their flag back to `false` for the first phase of the next garbage collection scan.

In essence, the GC maintains a list of all objects in memory, while our application maintains a separate list containing only a portion of them. Whenever our application is done with an object, it simply forgets it exists, removing it from its list. Hence, the list of objects that can be safely deallocated would be the difference between the GC's list and our application's list.

Once the second phase ends, all unmarked objects are deallocated to free space, and then the initial request to create the object is revisited. If the GC has freed up enough space for the object, then it is allocated within that newly-freed space and returned to the caller. However, if it is not, then we hit the last-resort situation and must expand the managed heap by requesting it from the OS, at which point the object space can finally be allocated and returned to the caller.

In an ideal world, where we only keep allocating and deallocating objects, but only a finite number of them exist at once, the heap would maintain a roughly constant size because there's always enough space to fit the new objects we need. However, all objects in an application are rarely deallocated in the same order they were allocated, and even more rarely do they all have the same size in memory. This leads to memory fragmentation.

Memory fragmentation

Fragmentation occurs when objects of different sizes are allocated and deallocated in alternating orders and if lots of small objects are deallocated, following by lots of large objects being allocated.

This is best explained through an example. The following shows four steps we take in allocating and deallocating memory in a typical heap memory space:

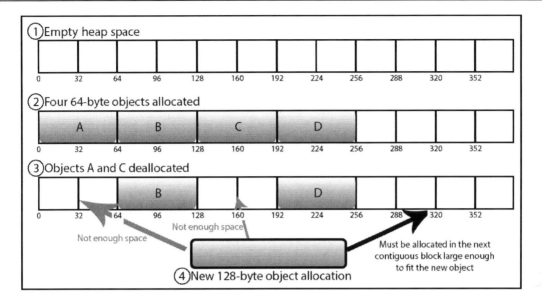

The memory allocation takes place as follows:

1. We start with an empty heap space
2. We then allocate four objects on the heap, **A**, **B**, **C**, and **D**, each 64-bytes in size
3. At a later time, we deallocate two of the objects, **A** and **C**, freeing up 128-bytes
4. We then try to allocate a new object that is 128-bytes in size

Deallocating objects **A** and **C** technically frees 128 bytes worth of space, but since the objects were not contiguous (adjoining neighbors) in memory, we cannot allocate an object larger than both individual spaces there. New memory allocations must always be contiguous in memory; therefore, the new object must be allocated in the next available contiguous 128-byte space available in the managed heap. We now have two empty 64-byte holes in our memory space, which will never be reused unless we allocate objects sized 64 bytes or smaller.

Over long periods of time, our heap memory can become riddled with more, smaller empty spaces such as these as objects of different sizes are deallocated, and then the system later tries to allocate new objects within the smallest available space that it can fit within, leaving some small remainder that becomes harder to fill. In the absence of background techniques that automatically clean up this fragmentation, this effect would occur in literally any memory space—RAM, heap space, and even hard drives—which are just larger, slower, and more permanent memory storage areas (this is why it's a good idea to defragment our hard drives from time to time).

Memory fragmentation causes two problems:

- Firstly, it effectively reduces the total usable memory space for new objects over long periods of time, depending on the frequency of allocations and deallocations. This is likely to result in the GC having to expand the heap to make room for new allocations.
- Secondly, it makes new allocations take longer to resolve due to the extra time it takes to find a new memory space large enough to fit the object.

This becomes important when new memory allocations are made in a heap since the location of available space becomes just as important as how much free space is available. There is no way to split an object across partial memory locations, so the GC must either continue searching until it finds a large enough space or the entire heap size must be increased to fit the new object, costing even more time after it just spent a bunch of time doing an exhaustive search.

Garbage collection at runtime

So, in a worst-case scenario, when a new memory allocation is being requested by our game, the CPU would have to spend cycles completing the following tasks before the allocation is finally completed:

1. Verify that there is enough contiguous space for the new object.
2. If there is not enough space, iterate through all known direct and indirect references, marking everything they connect to as reachable
3. Iterate through all of these references again, flagging unmarked objects for deallocation
4. Iterate through all flagged objects to check whether deallocating some of them would create enough contiguous space for the new object
5. If not, request a new memory block from the OS to expand the heap
6. Allocate the new object at the front of the newly allocated block and return it to the caller

This can be a lot of work for the CPU to handle, particularly if this new memory allocation is an important object such as a particle effect, a new character entering the scene, or a cutscene transition. Users are extremely likely to note moments where the GC is freezing gameplay to handle this extreme case. To make matters worse, the garbage collection workload scales poorly as the allocated heap space grows since sweeping through a few MBs of space will be significantly faster than scanning several GBs of space.

All of this makes it absolutely critical to control our heap space intelligently. The lazier our memory usage tactics are, the worse the GC will behave in an almost exponential fashion, as we are more and more likely to hit this worst-case scenario. So, it's a little ironic that, despite the efforts of managed languages to make the memory management problem easier, managed language developers still find themselves being just as, if not more, concerned with memory consumption than developers of native applications. The main difference is in the types of problems they're trying to solve.

Threaded garbage collection

The GC runs on two separate threads: the main thread and what is called the **finalizer thread**. When the GC is invoked, it will run on the main thread and flag heap memory blocks for future deallocation. This does not happen immediately. The finalizer thread, controlled by Mono, can have a delay of several seconds before the memory is finally freed and available for reallocation:

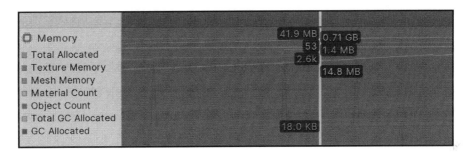

We can observe this behavior in the **Total Allocated** block (the green line, with apologies to that 5% of the population with deuteranopia/deuteranomaly) of the **Memory Area** within the **Profiler** window. It can take several seconds for the total allocated value to drop after a garbage collection has occurred. Owing to this delay, we should not rely on memory being available the moment it has been deallocated, and as such, we should never waste time trying to eke out every last byte of memory that we believe should be available. We must ensure that there is always some kind of buffer zone available for future allocations.

Blocks that have been freed by the GC may sometimes be given back to the OS after some time, which would reduce the reserved space consumed by the heap and allow the memory to be allocated for something else, such as another application. However, this is very unpredictable and depends on the platform being targeted, so we shouldn't rely on it. The only safe assumption to make is that as soon as the memory has been allocated to Mono, it's then reserved and is no longer available to either the native domain or any other application running on the same system.

In the next section, we will look at another essential element of the development process: code compilation. During code compilation, the C# code will be transformed into real instructions executed by the CPU. Surprisingly, there are multiple ways of performing this conversion; let's see how to choose among them.

Code compilation

When we make changes to our C# code, it is automatically compiled when we switch back from our favorite IDE (which is typically either MonoDevelop or the much more feature-rich Visual Studio) to the Unity Editor. However, the C# code is not converted directly into machine code, as we would expect static compilers to do if we are using languages such as C++.

Instead, the code is converted into an intermediate stage called **Common Intermediate Language** (**CIL**), which is an abstraction above the native code. This is how .NET can support multiple languages—each uses a different compiler, but they're all converted into CIL, so the output is effectively the same regardless of the language that we pick. CIL is similar to Java bytecode, upon which it is based, and the CIL code is entirely useless on its own, as CPUs have no idea how to run the instructions defined in this language.

At runtime, this intermediate code is run through the Mono **Virtual Machine** (**VM**), which is an infrastructure element that allows the same code to run against multiple platforms without the need to change the code itself. This is an implementation of the .NET CLR. If we're running on iOS, we run on the iOS-based VM infrastructure, and if we're running on Linux, then we simply use a different one that is better suited for Linux. This is how Unity allows us to write code once, and it works magically on multiple platforms.

Within the CLR, the intermediate CIL code will actually be compiled into the native code on demand. This immediate native compilation can be accomplished either by an **Ahead-Of-Time** (**AOT**) or **Just-In-Time** (**JIT**) compiler. Which one is used will depend on the platform that is being targeted. These compilers allow code segments to be compiled into native code, allowing the platform's architecture to complete the written instructions without having to write them ourselves. The main difference between the two compiler types is when the code is compiled.

AOT compilation is the typical behavior for code compilation and happens early (AOT) either during the build process or in some cases during app initialization. In either case, the code has been precompiled, and no further runtime costs are inflicted due to dynamic compilation since there are always machine code instructions available whenever the CPU needs them.

JIT compilation happens dynamically at runtime in a separate thread and begins just before execution (JIT for execution). Often, this dynamic compilation causes the first invocation of a piece of code to run a little (or a lot) more slowly because the code must finish compiling before it can be executed. However, from that point forward, whenever the same code block is executed, there is no need for recompilation, and the instructions run through the previously compiled native code.

A common adage in software development is that 90% of the work is being done by only 10 percent of the code. This generally means that JIT compilation turns out to be a net positive on performance than if we simply tried to interpret the CIL code directly. However, because the JIT compiler must compile code quickly, it is not able to make use of many optimization techniques that static AOT compilers can exploit.

Not all platforms support JIT compilation, but some scripting functionalities are not available when using AOT. Unity provides a complete list of these restrictions at `https://docs.unity3d.com/Manual/ScriptingRestrictions.html`.

A few years ago, Unity Technologies was faced with a choice to either continue to support the Mono platform, which Unity was finding more and more difficult to keep up with, or implement their own scripting backend. They chose the latter option, and multiple platforms now support IL2CPP.

The Unity Technologies' initial post about IL2CPP, the reasoning behind the decision, and its long-term benefits can be found at `https://blogs.unity3d.com/2014/05/20/the-future-of-scripting-in-unity/`.

IL2CPP

IL2CPP is a scripting backend designed to convert Mono's CIL output directly into the native C++ code. This leads to improved performance since the application will now be running native code. This ultimately gives Unity Technologies more control of runtime behavior since IL2CPP provides its own AOT compiler and VM, allowing custom improvements to subsystems such as the GC and compilation process. IL2CPP does not intend to replace the Mono platform completely, but it is an additional tool we can enable, which improves part of the functionality that Mono provides.

Note that IL2CPP is automatically enabled for iOS and WebGL projects. For other platforms that support it, **IL2CPP** can be enabled under **Edit** | **Project Settings** | **Player** | **Other Settings** | **Configure** | **Scripting Backend**:

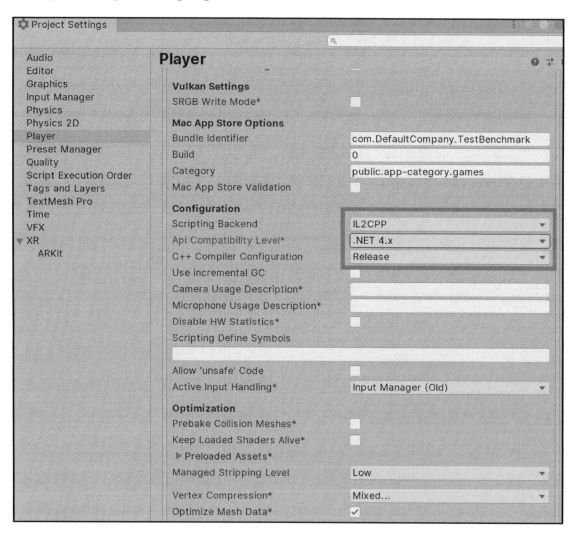

A list of platforms currently supporting IL2CPP can be found at `https://docs.unity3d.com/Manual/IL2CPP.html`.

Profiling memory

There are two issues we are concerned about when it comes to memory management: how much we're consuming and how often we're allocating new blocks. Let's cover each of these topics separately.

Profiling memory consumption

We do not have direct control over what is going on in the native domain since we don't have the Unity engine source code and hence can't add any code that will interact with it directly. We can, however, control it indirectly using various script-level functions that serve as interaction points between managed and native code. There are technically a variety of memory allocators available, which are used internally for things such as GameObjects, graphics objects, and the Profiler, but these are hidden behind the native-managed bridge.

However, we can observe how much memory has been allocated and reserved in this memory domain via the **Memory Area** of the **Profiler** window. Native memory allocations show up under the values labeled **Unity**, and we can even get more information using **Detailed** mode and sampling the current frame:

```
Used Total: 101.2 MB  Unity: 68.1 MB   Mono: 7.8 MB   GfxDriver: 15.8 MB   FMOD: 1.3 MB   Video: 224 B   Profiler: 9.5 MB
Reserved Total: 241.4 MB   Unity: 199.0 MB   Mono: 10.7 MB   GfxDriver: 15.8 MB   FMOD: 1.3 MB   Video: 224 B   Profiler: 16.0 MB
Total System Memory Usage: 0.78 GB
```

Under the **Scene Memory** section of breakdown view, we can observe that `MonoBehaviour` objects always consume a constant amount of memory, regardless of their member data. This is the memory consumed by the native representation of the object.

> Note that memory consumption in **Edit** mode is always wildly different from that of a standalone version due to various debugging and editor hook data being applied. This adds a further incentive to avoid using **Edit** mode for benchmarking and instrumentation purposes.

We can also use the `Profiler.GetRuntimeMemorySize()` method to get the native memory allocation size of a particular object.

Managed object representations are intrinsically linked to their native representations. The best way to minimize our native memory allocations is to simply optimize our managed memory usage.

We can verify how much memory has been allocated and reserved for the managed heap using the **Memory Area** of the **Profiler** window, under the values labeled **Mono**, as follows:

```
Used Total: 101.2 MB   Unity: 68.1 MB  [Mono: 7.8 MB]  GfxDriver: 15.8 MB   FMOD: 1.3 MB   Video: 224 B   Profiler: 9.5 MB
Reserved Total: 241.4 MB   Unity: 199.0 MB  [Mono: 10.7 MB]  GfxDriver: 15.8 MB   FMOD: 1.3 MB   Video: 224 B   Profiler: 16.0 MB
Total System Memory Usage: 0.78 GB
```

We can also determine the current used and reserved heap space at runtime using the `Profiler.GetMonoUsedSize()` and `Profiler.GetMonoHeapSize()` methods, respectively.

Profiling memory efficiency

The best metric we can use to measure the health of our memory management is simply watching the behavior of the GC. The more work it's doing, the more waste we're generating and the worse our application's performance is likely to become.

We can use both the **CPU Usage Area** (the **GarbageCollector** checkbox) and **Memory Area** (the **GC Allocated** checkbox) of the **Profiler** window to observe the amount of work the GC is doing and the time it is taking to do it. This can be relatively straightforward for some situations, where we only allocated a temporary small block of memory or we just destroyed a `GameObject` instance.

However, root-cause analysis for memory efficiency problems can be challenging and time-consuming. When we observe a spike in the GC's behavior, it could be a symptom of allocating too much memory in a previous frame and merely allocating a little more in the current frame, requiring the GC to scan a lot of fragmented memory, determine whether there is enough space, and decide whether to allocate a new block. The memory it cleaned up could have been allocated a long time ago, and we may only be able to observe these effects when our application runs over long periods of time and could even happen when our scene is sitting relatively idle, giving no obvious cause for the GC to trigger suddenly. Even worse, the Profiler can only tell us what happened in the last few seconds or so, and it won't be immediately obvious what data was being cleaned up.

We must be vigilant and test our application rigorously, observing its memory behavior while simulating a typical play session if we want to be certain we are not generating memory leaks or creating a situation where the GC has too much work to complete in a single frame.

Memory management performance enhancements

In most game engines, we would have the luxury of being able to port inefficient managed code into faster native code if we were hitting performance issues. This is not an option unless we invest serious cash in obtaining the Unity source code, which is offered as a license separate from the Free/Personal/Pro licensing system, and on a per case, per-title basis. We could also purchase a license of Unity Pro with the hope of using native plugins, but doing so rarely leads to a performance benefit since we must still cross the native-managed bridge to invoke function calls inside of it. Native plugins are normally used to interface with systems and libraries that are not built specifically for C#. This forces the overwhelming majority of us into a position of needing to make our C# script-level code as performant as possible ourselves.

With this in mind, we should now have enough understanding of Unity engine internals and memory spaces to detect and analyze memory performance issues and understand and implement enhancements for them. So, let's cover some performance enhancements we can apply.

Garbage collection tactics

One strategy to minimize garbage collection problems is concealment by manually invoking the GC at opportune moments when we're certain the player would not notice. Garbage collection can be manually invoked by calling `System.GC.Collect()`.

Good opportunities to invoke a collection may occur while loading between levels, when the gameplay is paused, shortly after a menu interface has been opened, during cutscene transitions, or any break in gameplay when the player would not witness, or care about, a sudden performance drop. We could even use the `Profiler.GetMonoUsedSize()` and `Profiler.GetMonoHeapSize()` methods at runtime to determine whether a garbage collection needs to be invoked soon.

We can also cause the deallocation of a handful of specific objects. If the object in question is one of the Unity object wrappers, such as a `GameObject` or `MonoBehaviour` component, then the finalizer will first invoke the `Dispose()` method within the native domain. At this point, the memory consumed by both the native and managed domains will then be freed. In some rare instances, if the Mono wrapper implements the `IDisposable` interface class (that is, it has a `Dispose()` method available from script code), then we can actually control this behavior and force the memory to be freed instantly.

There are a number of different object types in the Unity engine (most of which are introduced in Unity 5 or later), which implement the `IDisposable` interface class, as follows: `NetworkConnection`, `WWW`, `UnityWebRequest`, `UploadHandler`, `DownloadHandler`, `VertexHelper`, `CullingGroup`, `PhotoCapture`, `VideoCapture`, `PhraseRecognizer`, `GestureRecognizer`, `DictationRecognizer`, `SurfaceObserver`, and more.

These are all utility classes for pulling in potentially large datasets where we might want to ensure immediate destruction of the data it has acquired since they normally involve allocating several buffers and memory blocks in the native domain to accomplish their tasks. If we kept all of this memory for a long time, it would be a colossal waste of precious space. So, by calling their `Dispose()` method from script code, we can ensure that the memory buffers are freed promptly and precisely when they need to be.

All other asset objects offer some kind of unloading method to clean up any unused asset data, such as `Resources.UnloadUnusedAssets()`. Actual asset data is stored within the native domain, so the GC technically isn't involved here, but the idea is basically the same. It will iterate through all assets of a particular type, check whether they're no longer being referenced, and, if so, deallocate them. However, again, this is an asynchronous process, and we cannot guarantee exactly when the deallocation will occur. This method is automatically called internally after a scene is loaded, but this still doesn't guarantee instant deallocation. The preferred approach is to use `Resources.UnloadAsset()` instead, which will unload one specific asset at a time. This method is generally faster since time will not be spent iterating through an entire collection of asset data to figure out what is unused.

However, the best strategy for garbage collection will always be avoidance; if we allocate as little heap memory and control its usage as much as possible, then we won't have to worry about the GC inflicting frequent, expensive performance costs. We will cover many tactics for this throughout the remainder of this chapter.

Manual JIT compilation

If JIT compilation is causing a runtime performance loss, be aware that it is actually possible to force JIT compilation of a method at any time via reflection. Reflection is a useful feature of the C# language that allows our code base to explore itself introspectively for type information, methods, values, and metadata. Using reflection is often a very costly process. It should be avoided at runtime or, at the very least, only used during initialization or other loading times. Not doing so can easily cause significant CPU spikes and gameplay freezing.

We can manually force JIT compilation of a method using reflection to obtain a function pointer to it:

```
var method = typeof(MyComponent).GetMethod("MethodName");
if (method != null) {
  method.MethodHandle.GetFunctionPointer();
  Debug.Log("JIT compilation complete!");
}
```

The preceding code only works on `public` methods. Obtaining `private` or `protected` methods can be accomplished through the use of `BindingFlags`:

```
using System.Reflection;
// ...
var method = typeof(MyComponent).GetMethod("MethodName",
BindingFlags.NonPublic | BindingFlags.Instance);
```

This kind of code should only be run for very targeted methods where we are certain that JIT compilation is causing CPU spikes. This can be verified by restarting the application and profiling a method's first invocation versus all subsequent invocations. The difference will tell us the JIT compilation overhead.

 Note that the official method for forcing JIT compilation in the .NET library is `RuntimeHelpers.PrepareMethod()`, but this is not properly implemented in the current default version of Mono that comes with Unity (Mono version 2.6.5). Since Unity 2018.1, the .NET 4.x runtime is no longer considered experimental; however, it is not supported on all platforms, and it is still not the suggested one. The aforementioned workaround is not pretty, but it is still the best and most consistent way to proceed.

Value types and reference types

Not all memory allocations we make within Mono will go through the heap. The .NET Framework (and, by extension, the C# language, which merely implements the .NET specification) has the concept of value types and reference types, and only the latter needs to be marked by the GC while it is performing its Mark-and-Sweep algorithm. Reference types are expected to (or need to) last a long time in memory due to their complexity, their size, or how they're used. Large datasets and any kind of object instantiated from a `class` instance is a reference type. This also includes arrays (regardless of whether it is an array of Value types or reference types), delegates, all classes, such as `MonoBehaviour`, `GameObject`, and any custom classes we define.

Reference types are always allocated on the heap, whereas value types can be allocated either on the stack or the heap. Primitive data types such as `bool`, `int`, and `float` are examples of value types. These values are typically allocated on the stack, but as soon as a value type is contained within a reference type, such as `class` or an array, then it is implied that it is either too large for the stack or will need to survive longer than the current scope and must be allocated on the heap, bundled with the reference type it is contained within.

All of this can be best explained through examples. The following code will create an integer as a value type that exists on the stack only temporarily:

```
public class TestComponent {
  void TestFunction() {
    int data = 5; // allocated on the stack
    DoSomething(data);
  } // integer is deallocated from the stack here
}
```

As soon as the `TestFunction()` method ends, the integer is deallocated from the stack. This is essentially a free operation since, as mentioned previously, it doesn't bother doing any cleanup; it just moves the stack pointer back to the previous memory location in the call stack (back to whichever function called `TestFunction()` on the `TestComponent` object). Any future stack allocations simply overwrite the old data. More importantly, no heap allocation took place to create the data, so the GC does not need to track its existence.

However, if we created an integer as a member variable of the `MonoBehaviour` class definition, then it is now contained within a reference type (`class`) and must be allocated on the heap along with its container:

```
public class TestComponent : MonoBehaviour {
  private int _data = 5;
  void TestFunction() {
    DoSomething(_data);
  }
}
```

The `_data` integer is now an additional piece of data that consumes space in the heap alongside the `TestComponent` object it is contained within. If `TestComponent` is destroyed, then the integer is deallocated along with it, but not before then.

Similarly, if we put the integer into a normal C# class, then the rules for reference types still apply and the object is allocated on the heap:

```
public class TestData {
   public int data = 5;
}

public class TestComponent {
   void TestFunction() {
      TestData dataObj = new TestData(); // allocated on the heap
      DoSomething(dataObj.data);
   } // dataObj is not immediately deallocated here, but it will
      // become a candidate during the next GC sweep
}
```

So, there is a big difference between creating a temporary value type within a `class` method versus storing long-term value type as a member field of `class`. In the former case, we're storing it in the stack, but in the latter case, we're storing it within a reference type, which means it can be referenced elsewhere. For example, imagine that `DoSomething()` has stored the reference to `dataObj` within a member variable:

```
public class TestComponent {
   private TestData _testDataObj;

   void TestFunction() {
      TestData dataObj = new TestData(); // allocated on the heap
      DoSomething(dataObj.data);
   }

   void DoSomething (TestData dataObj) {
      _testDataObj = dataObj; // a new reference created! The referenced
      // object will now be marked during Mark-and-Sweep
   }
}
```

In this case, we would not be able to deallocate the object pointed to `dataObj` as soon as the `TestFunction()` method ends because the total number of things referencing the object would go from 2 to 1. This is not 0, and hence the GC would still mark it during Mark-and-Sweep. We would need to set the value of `_testDataObj` to `null` or make it reference something else before the object is no longer reachable.

Note that a value type must have a value and can never be `null`. If a stack-allocated value type is assigned to a reference type, then the data is simply copied. This is true even for arrays of value types:

```
public class TestClass {
  private int[] _intArray = new int[1000]; // Reference type
                                           // full of Value types
  void StoreANumber(int num) {
    _intArray[0] = num; // store a Value within the array
  }
}
```

When the initial array is created (during object initialization), 1000 integers will be allocated on the heap set to a value of 0. When the `StoreANumber()` method is called, the value of `num` is merely copied into the zeroth element of the array rather than storing a reference to it.

The subtle change in the referencing capability is what ultimately decides whether something is a reference type or a value type, and we should try to use value types whenever we have the opportunity so that they generate stack allocations instead of heap allocations. Any situation where we're just sending around a piece of data that doesn't need to live longer than the current scope is a good opportunity to use a value type instead of a reference type. Ostensibly, it does not matter if we pass the data into another method of the same class or a method of another class—it still remains a value type that will exist on the stack until the method that created it goes out of the scope.

Pass by value and by reference

Technically, something is duplicated every time a data value is passed as an argument from one method to another, and this is true whether it is a value type or a reference type. When we're passing the object's data, this is known as **passing by value**. When we're simply copying a reference to something else, it is called **passing by reference**.

An important difference between value types and reference types is that a reference type is merely a pointer to another location in memory that consumes only 4 or 8-bytes in memory (32 bit or 64 bit, depending on the architecture), regardless of what it is actually pointing to. When a reference type is passed as an argument, it is only the value of this pointer that gets copied into the function. Even if the reference type points to a humongous array of data, this operation will be very quick since the data being copied is very small.

Meanwhile, a value type contains the full and complete bits of data stored within a concrete object. Hence, all of the data of a value type will be copied whenever they are passed between methods or stored in other value types. In some cases, it can mean that passing a large value type as arguments around too much can be more costly than just using a reference type and letting the GC take care of it. For most value types, this is not a problem since they are comparable in size to a pointer, but this becomes important when we begin to talk about the `struct` type in the next section.

Data can also be passed around by reference using the `ref` keyword, but this is very different from the concept of value and reference types, and it is very important to keep them distinct in our mind when we try to understand what is going on under the hood. We can pass a value type by value or by reference, and we can pass a reference type by value or by reference. This means that there are four distinct data passing situations that can occur, depending on which type is being passed and whether the `ref` keyword is being used or not.

When data is passed by reference (even if it is a value type), then making any changes to the data will change the original. For example, the following code would print the value as 10:

```
void Start() {
    int myInt = 5;
    DoSomething(ref myInt);
    Debug.Log(String.Format("Value = {0}", myInt));
}

void DoSomething(ref int val) {
    val = 10;
}
```

Removing the `ref` keyword from both places would make it print the value 5 instead (and removing it from only one of them would lead to a compiler error since the `ref` keyword needs to be present in both locations or neither). This understanding will come in handy when we start to think about some of the more interesting data types we have access to, namely, structs, arrays, and strings.

Structs are value types

The `struct` type is an interesting special case in C#. A `struct` object can contain `private`, `protected`, and `public` fields; have methods; and be instantiated at runtime, just like a `class` type. However, there is a fundamental difference between the two: a `struct` type is a value type, and a `class` type is a reference type. Consequently, this leads to some important differences between the two, namely, that a `struct` type cannot support inheritance, their properties cannot be given custom default values (member data always defaults to values such as `0` or `null` since it is a value type), and their default constructors cannot be overridden. This greatly restricts their usage compared to classes, so simply replacing all classes with structs (under the assumption that it will just allocate everything on the stack) is not as easy as it sounds.

However, if we're using a class in a situation whose only purpose is to send a blob of data to somewhere else in our application, and it does not need to last beyond the current scope, then we might be able to use a `struct` type instead, since a `class` type would result in a heap allocation for no particularly good reason:

```
public class DamageResult {
  public Character attacker;
  public Character defender;
  public int totalDamageDealt;
  public DamageType damageType;
  public int damageBlocked;
  // etc.
}

public void DealDamage(Character _target) {
  DamageResult result = CombatSystem.Instance.CalculateDamage(this,
_target);
  CreateFloatingDamageText(result);
}
```

In this example, we're using a `class` type to pass a bunch of data from one subsystem (the combat system) to another (the UI system). The only purpose of this data is to be calculated and read by various subsystems, so this is a good candidate to convert into a `struct` type.

Merely changing the `DamageResult` definition from a `class` type to a `struct` type could save us quite a few unnecessary garbage collections since it would be allocated on the stack as a value type instead of the heap as a reference type:

```
public struct DamageResult {
  // ...
}
```

This is not a catch-all solution. Since structs are value types, the entire blob of data will be duplicated and provided to the next method in the call stack, regardless of how large or small it is. So, if a struct object is passed by a value between five different methods in a long chain, then five different stack copies will occur at the same time. Recall that stack deallocations are effectively free, but stack allocations (which involve copying of data) is not. This data copying is pretty much negligible for small values, such as a handful of integers or floating-point values, but passing around ridiculously large datasets through structs over and over again is obviously not a trivial task and should be avoided.

We can work around this problem by passing the struct object by reference using the ref keyword to minimize the amount of data being copied each time (just a single pointer). However, this can be dangerous since passing by reference allows any subsequent methods to make changes to the struct object, in which case it would be prudent to make its data values readonly. This means that the values can only be initialized in the constructor, and never again, even by its own member functions, which prevents accidental changes as it's passed through the chain.

All of the preceding is also true when structs are contained within reference types, as follows:

```
public struct DataStruct {
   public int val;
}

public class StructHolder {
   public DataStruct _memberStruct;
   public void StoreStruct(DataStruct ds) {
      _memberStruct = ds;
   }
}
```

To the untrained eye, the preceding code appears to be attempting to store a stack-allocated struct (ds) within a reference type (StructHolder). Does this mean that a StructHolder object on the heap can now reference an object on the stack? If so, what will happen when the StoreStruct() method goes out of scope and the struct object is (effectively) erased? It turns out that these are the wrong questions.

What's actually happening is that while a `DataStruct` object (`_memberStruct`) has been allocated on the heap within the `StructHolder` object, it is still a value type and does not magically transform into a reference type when it is a member variable of a reference type. So, all of the usual rules for value types apply. The `_memberStruct` variable cannot have a value of `null`, and all of its fields will be initialized to 0 or `null` values. When `StoreStruct()` is called, the data from `ds` will be copied into `_memberStruct` in its entirety. There are no references to stack objects taking place, and there is no concern about lost data.

Arrays are reference types

The purpose of arrays is to contain large datasets, which makes them difficult to be treated as a value type since there's probably not enough room on the stack to support them. Therefore, they are treated as a reference type so that the entire dataset can be passed around via a single reference (if it were a value type, we would need to duplicate the entire array every time it is passed around). This is true irrespective of whether the array contains value types or reference types.

This means that the following code will result in a heap allocation:

```
TestStruct[] dataObj = new TestStruct[1000];

for(int i = 0; i < 1000; ++i) {
  dataObj[i].data = i;
  DoSomething(dataObj[i]);
}
```

However, the following, functionally equivalent, code would not result in any heap allocations since the `struct` objects being used are value types, and hence, it would be created on the stack:

```
for(int i = 0; i < 1000; ++i) {
  TestStruct dataObj = new TestStruct();
  dataObj.data = i;
  DoSomething(dataObj);
}
```

The subtle difference in the second example is that only one `TestStruct` exists on the stack at a time, whereas the first example needs to allocate `1000` of them via an array. Obviously, these methods are kind of ridiculous as they're written, but they illustrate an important point to consider. The compiler isn't smart enough to automatically find these situations for us and make the appropriate changes. Opportunities to optimize our memory usage through value type replacements will be entirely down to our ability to detect them and understand why conversions from reference types to value types will result in stack allocations, rather than heap allocations.

Note that when we allocate an array of reference types, we're creating an array of references, which can provide each reference other locations on the heap. However, when we allocate an array of value types, we're creating a packed list of value types on the heap. Each of these value types will be initialized with a value of `0` (or equivalent) since they cannot be `null`, while each reference within an array of reference types will always initialize to `null` since no references have been assigned yet.

Strings are immutable reference types

We briefly touched upon the subject of strings in `Chapter 2`, *Scripting Strategies*, but now it's time to go into more detail about why proper string usage is extremely important.

Strings are essentially arrays of characters, and so they are considered reference types and follow all of the same rules as other reference types; they will be allocated on the heap, and a pointer is all that is copied from one method to the next. Since a string is effectively an array, this implies that the characters it contains must be contiguous in memory. However, we often find ourselves expanding, contracting, or combining strings to create other strings. This can lead us to make some faulty assumptions about how strings work. We might assume that because strings are such common, ubiquitous objects, performing operations on them is fast and cheap. Unfortunately, this is incorrect. Strings are not made to be fast. They are only made to be convenient.

The string object class is immutable, which means they cannot be changed after they've been allocated. Therefore, when we change a string, we are actually allocating a whole new string on the heap to replace it, where the contents of the original will be copied and modified as needed into a whole new character array, and the original string object reference now points to a completely new string object. In which case, the old string object might no longer be referenced anywhere, will not be marked during *Mark-and-Sweep*, and will eventually be purged by the GC. As a result, lazy string programming can result in a lot of unnecessary heap allocations and garbage collection.

A good example to illustrate how strings are different than normal reference types is the following code:

```
void TestFunction() {
   string testString = "Hello";
   DoSomething(testString);
   Debug.Log(testString);
}

void DoSomething(string localString) {
   localString = "World!";
}
```

If we were under the mistaken assumption that strings worked just like other reference types, then we might be forgiven for assuming that the log output of the following to be World!. It appears as though testString, a reference type, is being passed into DoSomething(), which would change what testString is referencing to, in which case, the Log statement will print out the new value of the string.

However, this is not the case, and it will simply print out Hello. What is actually happening is that the localString variable, within the scope of DoSomething(), starts off referencing the same place in memory as testString due to the reference being passed by value. This gives us two references pointing to the same location in memory as we would expect if we were dealing with any other reference type. So far, so good.

However, as soon as we change the value of localString, we run into a little bit of a conflict. Strings are immutable, and we cannot change them, so, therefore, we must allocate a new string containing the World! value and assign its reference to the value of localString; now, the number of references to the Hello string returns back to one. The value of testString, therefore, has not been changed, and that is still the value that will be printed by Debug.Log(). All we've succeeded in doing by calling DoSomething() is creating a new string on the heap that gets garbage-collected and doesn't change anything. This is the textbook definition of wasteful.

If we change the method definition of DoSomething() to pass the string by reference via the ref keyword, the output would indeed change to World!. Of course, this is also what we would expect to happen with a value type, which leads a lot of developers to incorrectly assume that strings are value types. However, this is an example of the fourth and final data-passing case, where a reference type is being passed by reference, which allows us to change what the original reference is referencing.

So, let's recap:

- If we pass a value type by value, we can only change the value of a copy of its data
- If we pass a value type by reference, we can change the value of the original data passed in
- If we pass a reference type by value, we can make changes to the object referenced by the original reference variable
- If we pass a reference type by reference, we can change to which object the original reference is pointing to

If we find functions that seem to generate a lot of GC allocations the moment they are called, then we might be causing undue heap allocations due to a misunderstanding of the preceding rules.

String concatenation

Concatenation is the act of appending strings to one another to form a larger string. As you've learned, any such cases are likely to result in excess heap allocations. The biggest offender in a string-based memory waste is concatenating strings using the + operator and += operators, because of the allocation chaining effect they cause.

For example, the following code tries to combine a group of string objects together to print some information about a combat result:

```
void CreateFloatingDamageText(DamageResult result) {
    string outputText = result.attacker.GetCharacterName() + "
            dealt " + result.totalDamageDealt.ToString() + " " +
            result.damageType.ToString() + " damage to " +
            result.defender.GetCharacterName() + " (" +
            result.damageBlocked.ToString() + " blocked)";
    // ...
}
```

An example output of this function might be a string that reads as follows:

```
Dwarf dealt 15 Slashing damage to Orc (3 blocked)
```

This function features a handful of string literals (hardcoded strings that are allocated during application initialization) such as " `dealt` "," `damage to` ", and " `blocked)` ", which are simple constructs for the compiler to pre-allocate for us. However, because we are using other local variables within this combined string, it cannot be compiled away at build time, and, therefore, the complete string is regenerated dynamically at runtime each time the function is called.

A new heap allocation will be generated each time a + or += operator is executed. Only a single pair of strings will be merged at a time, and it allocates a new string object each time. Then, the result of one merger will be fed into the next and merged with the next string and so on until the final string object has been built.

So, the previous example will result in nine different strings being allocated all in one statement. All of the following strings would be allocated to satisfy this instruction, and all would eventually need to be garbage collected (note that the operators are resolved from right to left):

```
"3 blocked)"
" (3 blocked)"
"Orc (3 blocked)"
" damage to Orc (3 blocked)"
"Slashing damage to Orc (3 blocked)"
" Slashing damage to Orc (3 blocked)"
"15 Slashing damage to Orc (3 blocked)"
" dealt 15 Slashing damage to Orc (3 blocked)"
"Dwarf dealt 15 Slashing damage to Orc (3 blocked)"
```

That's 262 characters being used, instead of 49. In addition, because a character is a 2-byte data type (for Unicode strings), that's 524 bytes of data being allocated when we only need 98 bytes. The chances are that if this code exists in the code base once, it exists all over the place; so, for an application that's doing a lot of lazy string concatenation like this, that is a ton of memory being wasted on generating unnecessary strings.

Note that big, constant string literals can be safely combined using the + and += operators. The compiler knows that you will eventually need the full string and pre-generates the string automatically. This helps us to make a huge block of text more readable within the code base, but only if they will result in a constant string.

Better approaches for generating strings are to use either the `StringBuilder` class or one of several string class methods for string formatting.

StringBuilder

Conventional wisdom says that if we roughly know the final size of the resultant string, then we can allocate an appropriate buffer AOT and save ourselves undue allocations. This is the purpose of the StringBuilder class. It is effectively a mutable (changeable) string-based object that works like a dynamic array. It allocates a block of space, which we can copy future string objects into, and allocates additional space whenever the current size is exceeded. Of course, expanding the buffer should be avoided as much as possible by predicting the maximum size we will need and allocating a sufficiently sized buffer AOT.

When we use StringBuilder, we can retrieve the resultant string object by calling the ToString() method. This still results in one additional memory allocation for the completed string, but, at the very least, we only allocated one large string as opposed to dozens of smaller strings, had we used the + or += operators.

For the previous example, we might allocate a StringBuilder buffer of 100 characters to make room for long character names and damage values:

```
using System.Text;
// ...
StringBuilder sb = new StringBuilder(100);
sb.Append(result.attacker.GetCharacterName());
sb.Append(" dealt " );
sb.Append(result.totalDamageDealt.ToString());
// etc.
string result = sb.ToString();
```

String formatting

If we don't know the final size of the resultant string, then using a StringBuilder class is unlikely to generate a buffer that fits the result size exactly. We will either end up with a buffer that's too large (wasted space) or, worse, a buffer that's too small, which must keep expanding as we generate the complete string. In this scenario, it might be best to use one of the various string class formatting methods.

There are three string class methods available for generating strings: string.Format(), string.Join(), and string.Concat(). Each operates slightly differently, but the overall output is the same. A new string object is allocated, containing the contents of the string objects we pass into them, and it is all done in a single action, which reduces excess string allocations.

Unfortunately, regardless of the approach we use, if we're converting other objects into additional string objects (such as the calls to generate the strings for `"Orc"`, `"Dwarf"`, or `"Slashing"` in the preceding example), then this will allocate an additional string object on the heap. There is nothing we can do about this allocation, except perhaps cache the result so that we don't need to recalculate it each time it's needed.

It can be surprisingly hard to say which one of these string generation approaches would be more beneficial in a given situation, as there are a lot of silly little nuances involved that tend to explode into religious debate (just do a Google search for `C# string concatenation performance`, and you'll see what I mean), so the simplest approach is to implement one or the other using the conventional wisdom described previously. Whenever we run into bad performance with one of the string-manipulation methods, we should also try the other to check whether it results in performance improvement. The best way to be certain is to profile them both for comparison and then pick the best options.

Boxing

Everything in C# is an object (caveats apply), meaning that they derive from the `System.Object` class. Even primitive data types such as `int`, `float`, and `bool` are implicitly derived from `System.Object`, which is itself a reference type. This is a special case, which allows them access to helper methods such as `ToString()` so that they can customize their string representation, but without actually turning them into reference types. Whenever one of these value types is implicitly treated in such a way that it must act as an object, the CLR automatically creates a temporary object to store, or *box*, the value inside so that it can be treated as a typical reference type object. As we should expect, this results in a heap allocation to create the containing vessel.

Note that boxing is not the same thing as using value types as member variables of reference types. Boxing only takes place when value types are treated as reference types via conversion or casting.

Check out these examples:

- The following code will cause the `i` integer variable to be boxed inside the `obj` object:

```
int i = 128;
object obj = i;
```

- The following code will use the `obj` object representation to replace the value stored within the integer, and unbox it back into an integer, storing it in `i`. The final value of `i` would be `256`:

```
int i = 128;
object obj = i;
obj = 256;
i = (int)obj; // i = 256
```

The preceding types can be changed dynamically.

- The following is perfectly legal C# code, where we override the type of `obj`, converting it into `float`:

```
int i = 128;
object obj = i;
obj = 512f;
float f = (float)obj; // f = 512f
```

- The following is also legal—conversion into `bool`:

```
int i = 128;
object obj = i;
obj = false;
bool b = (bool)obj; // b = false
```

- Note that attempting to unbox `obj` into a type that isn't the most recently assigned type would result in `InvalidCastException`:

```
int i = 128;
object obj = i;
obj = 512f;
i = (int)obj; // InvalidCastException thrown here since most recent
conversion was to a float
```

All of this can be a little tricky to wrap our head around until we remember that, at the end of the day, everything is just bits in memory and that we are free to interpret them any way we like. After all, data types such as `int`, `float`, and so on are just an abstraction over binary lists of `0` and `1`. What's important is knowing that we can treat our primitive types as objects by boxing them, converting their types, and then unboxing them into a different type at a later time, but each time we do this results in a heap memory allocation.

> Note that it's possible to convert a boxed object's type using one of the many `System.Convert.To...()` methods.

Boxing can be either implicit, as shown in the preceding examples, or explicit, by typecasting to System.Object. Unboxing must always be explicit by typecasting back to its original type. Whenever we pass a value type into a method that uses System.Object as arguments, boxing will be applied implicitly.

Methods such as String.Format(), which take System.Object as arguments, are one such example. We typically use them by passing in value types, such as int, float, and bool, to generate a string with. Boxing is automatically taking place in these situations, causing additional heap allocations that we should be aware of. Collections.Generic.ArrayList is another such example since ArrayList always contains converts its inputs into System.Object references, regardless of what types are stored within.

Any time we use a function definition that takes System.Object as arguments, and we're passing in value types, we should be aware that we're implicitly causing heap allocations due to boxing.

The importance of data layout

The importance of how our data is organized in memory can be surprisingly easy to forget about but can result in a fairly big performance boost if it is handled properly. Cache misses should be avoided whenever possible, which means that in most cases, arrays of data that are contiguous in memory should be iterated over sequentially as opposed to any other iteration style.

This means that data layout is also important for garbage collection since it is done in an iterative fashion, and if we can find ways to have the GC skip over problematic areas, then we can potentially save a lot of iteration time.

In essence, we want to keep large groups of reference types separated from large groups of value types. If there is even one reference type within a value type, such as struct, then the GC considers the entire object, and all of its data members, indirectly referenceable objects. When it comes time to Mark-and-Sweep, it must verify all fields of the object before moving on. However, if we separate the various types into different arrays, then we can make the GC skip the majority of the data.

For instance, if we have an array of `struct` objects that looks like the following code, then the GC will need to iterate over every member of every `struct`, which could be fairly time-consuming:

```
public struct MyStruct {
    int myInt;
    float myFloat;
    bool myBool;
    string myString;
}

MyStruct[] arrayOfStructs = new MyStruct[1000];
```

However, if we reorganize all pieces of this data into multiple arrays of each time, then the GC will ignore all of the primitive data types and only check the string objects. The following code will result in much a faster garbage collection sweep:

```
int[] myInts = new int[1000];
float[] myFloats = new float[1000];
bool[] myBools = new bool[1000];
string[] myStrings = new string[1000];
```

The reason this works is that we're giving the GC fewer indirect references to check. When the data is split into separate arrays (reference types), it finds three arrays of value types, marks the arrays, and then immediately moves on because there's no reason to mark the contents of an array of value types. It must still iterate through all of the string objects within `myStrings` since each is a reference type and it needs to verify that there are no indirect references within it. Technically, the string objects cannot contain indirect references, but the GC works at a level where it only knows whether the object is a reference type or value type and, therefore, can't tell the difference between a string and class. However, we have still spared the GC from needing to iterate over an extra 3,000 pieces of data (the 3,000 values in `myInts`, `myFloats`, and `myBools`).

Arrays from the Unity API

Several instructions within the Unity API result in heap memory allocations, which we should be aware of. This essentially includes everything that returns an array of data. For example, the following methods allocate memory on the heap:

```
GetComponents<T>(); // (T[])
Mesh.vertices; // (Vector3[])
Camera.allCameras; // (Camera[])
```

Each and every time we call a Unity API method that returns an array will cause a whole new version of that data to be allocated. Such methods should be avoided whenever possible or at the very least called once and cached so that we don't cause memory allocations more often than necessary.

There are other Unity API calls where we provide an array of elements to a method, and it writes the necessary data into the array for us. One such example is providing a `Particle[]` array to `ParticleSystem` to get its `Particle` data. The benefit of these types of API calls is that we can avoid reallocating large arrays, whereas the downside is that the array needs to be large enough to fit all of the objects. If the number of objects we need to acquire keeps increasing, then we may find ourselves reallocating larger arrays. In the case of `ParticleSystem`, we need to be certain we create an array large enough to contain the maximum number of `Particle` objects it generates at any given time.

 Unity Technologies have hinted in the past that they may eventually change some of the API calls that return arrays into the form that requires an array to be provided. The API of the latter form can be confusing for new programmers at first glance; however, unlike the first form, it allows responsible programmers to use memory much more efficiently.

Using InstanceIDs for dictionary keys

As mentioned in Chapter 2, *Scripting Strategies*, dictionaries are used to map associations between two different objects, which are very quick at telling us whether a mapping exists, and if so, what that mapping is. It's common practice to map `MonoBehaviour` or `ScriptableObject` reference as the key of a dictionary, but this causes some problems. When the dictionary element is accessed, it will need to call into several derived methods of `UnityEngine.Object`, which both of these object types derive from. This makes element comparison and mapping acquisition relatively slow.

This can be improved by making use of `Object.GetInstanceID()`, which returns an integer representing a unique identification value for that object that never changes and is never reused between two objects during the entire lifecycle of the application. If we cache this value in the object somehow and use it as the key in our dictionary, then the element comparison will be around two to three times faster than if we used the object reference directly.

However, there are caveats to this approach. If the instance ID value is not cached (we keep calling `Object.GetInstanceID()` each time we need to index into our dictionary) and we are compiling with Mono (and not IL2CPP), then element acquisition could end up being slow. This is because it will call some thread-unsafe code to acquire the instance ID, in which case, the Mono compiler cannot optimize the loop, and, therefore causes some additional overhead by comparison to caching the instance ID value. If we are compiling with IL2CPP, which doesn't have this problem, then the benefits are still not as great (only around 50% faster) than if we had simply cached the value beforehand. Therefore, we should aim to cache the integer value in some way so that we avoid having to call `Object.GetInstanceID()` too often.

foreach loops

The `foreach` loop keyword is a bit of a controversial issue in Unity development circles. It turns out that a lot of `foreach` loops implemented in Unity C# code will incur unnecessary heap memory allocations during these calls, as they allocate an `Enumerator` object as a class on the heap, instead of a `struct` on the stack. It all depends on the given collection's implementation of the `GetEnumerator()` method.

 Note that it is safe to use `foreach` loops on typical arrays. The Mono compiler secretly converts `foreach` over arrays into simple for loops.

Since Unity 2018.1, Unity uses an upgraded Mono runtime (4.0.30319) and some compiler fixes many of the previous issues with `foreach`. As a consequence, `foreach` is no more a big issue in the general case. Yet, `foreach` still has a bad reputation among developers. The fact that sometimes they can actually be problematic makes everything more complicated. As usual, there is only one way to be sure: use the Profiler and check whether `foreach` is actually creating problems in your specific situation.

In any case, even in the worst scenario—that is, your `foreach` loop is actually doing heap allocations—the cost is fairly negligible, as the heap allocation cost does not scale with the number of iterations. Only one `Enumerator` object is allocated and reused over and over again, which only costs a handful of bytes of memory overall. So, unless our `foreach` loops are being invoked for every update (which is typically dangerous in, and of, itself), the costs will be mostly negligible on small projects. The time taken to convert everything into a `for` loop may not be worth it.

Coroutines

As mentioned before, starting a coroutine costs a small amount of memory, to begin with, but note that no further costs are incurred when the method calls `yield`. If memory consumption and garbage collection are significant concerns, we should try to avoid having too many short-lived coroutines and avoid calling `StartCoroutine()` too much during runtime.

Closures

Closures are useful, but dangerous tools. Anonymous methods and lambda expressions are not always closures, but they can be. It all depends on whether the method uses data outside of its own scope and parameter list or not.

For example, the following anonymous function would not be a closure, since it is self-contained and functionally equivalent to any other locally defined function:

```
System.Func<int,int> anon = (x) => { return x; };

int result = anon(5); // result = 5
```

However, if the anonymous function pulled in data from outside itself, it becomes a closure, as it closes the environment around the required data. The following would result in a closure:

```
int i = 1024;
System.Func<int,int> anon = (x) => { return x + i; };
int result = anon(5);
```

In order to complete this transaction, the compiler must define a new custom class that can reference the environment where the `i` data value would be accessible. At runtime, it creates the corresponding object on the heap and provides it to the anonymous function. Note that this includes value types (as per the preceding example), which were originally on the stack, possibly defeating the purpose of them being allocated on the stack in the first place. So, we should expect each invocation of the second method to result in heap allocations and inevitable garbage collection.

The .NET library functions

The .NET library offers a huge amount of common functionalities that help to solve numerous problems that programmers may come across during day-to-day implementation. Most of these classes and functions are optimized for general use cases, which may not be optimal for a specific situation. It may be possible to replace a particular .NET library class with a custom implementation that is more suited to our specific use case.

There are also two big features in the .NET library that often become big performance hogs whenever they're used. This tends to be because they are only included as a quick-and-dirty solution to a given problem without much effort put into optimization. These features are **LINQ** and **regular expressions**.

LINQ provides a way to treat arrays of data as miniature databases and perform queries against them using a SQL-like syntax. The simplicity of its coding style and complexity of the underlying system (through its usage of closures) implies that it has a fairly large overhead cost. LINQ is a handy tool, but is not really intended for high-performance, real-time applications, such as games, and does not even function on platforms that do not support JIT compilation, such as iOS.

Meanwhile, regular expressions through the `Regex` class allow us to perform complex string parsing to find substrings that match a particular format, replace pieces of a string, or construct strings from various inputs. Regular expressions are very useful tools but tends to be overused in places where they are largely unnecessary or in so-called clever ways to implement a feature such as text localization, when straightforward string replacement would be far more efficient.

Specific optimizations for both of these features go far beyond the scope of this book, as they could fill an entire book by themselves. We should either try to minimize their usage as much as possible, replace their usage with something less costly, bring in a LINQ or regex expert to solve the problem for us or do some Googling on the subject to optimize how we're using them.

One of the best ways to find the correct answer online is to simply post the wrong answer. People will either help us out of kindness or will take such a great offense from our implementation that they will consider it their civic duty to correct us. Just be sure to do some kind of research on the subject first. Even the busiest of people are generally happy to help if they can see that we've put in our fair share of effort beforehand.

Temporary work buffers

If we get into the habit of using large, temporary work buffers for one task or another, then it just makes sense that we should look for opportunities to reuse them, instead of reallocating them over and over again, as this lowers the overhead involved in allocation and garbage collection (often called **memory pressure**). It might be worthwhile to extract such functionality from case-specific classes into a generic *God* class that contains a big work area for multiple classes to reuse.

Object pooling

Speaking of temporary work buffers, object pooling is an excellent way of both minimizing and establishing control over our memory usage by avoiding deallocation and reallocation. The idea is to formulate our own system for object creation, which hides away whether the object we're getting has been freshly allocated or has been recycled from an earlier allocation. The typical terms to describe this process are to spawn and despawn the object rather than creating and deleting them in memory. When an object is despawned, we're simply hiding it, making it lay dormant until we need it again, at which point it is respawned from one of the previously despawned objects and used in place of an object we might have otherwise newly allocated.

Let's cover a quick implementation of an object pooling system:

1. First, we define a common interface for the object we want to use in the object pool. An important feature of this system is to allow the pooled object to decide how to recycle itself when the time comes. The following interface class called `IPoolableObject` will satisfy this requirement nicely:

```
public interface IPoolableObject{
  void New();
  void Respawn();
}
```

This interface class defines two methods: `New()` and `Respawn()`. These should be called when the object is first created and when it has been respawned, respectively.

2. Now, we need to implement a class that manages the poolable objects. The following `ObjectPool` class definition is a fairly simple implementation of the object pooling concept:

```
using System.Collections.Generic;

public class ObjectPool<T> where T : IPoolableObject, new() {
  private Stack<T> _pool;
  private int _currentIndex = 0;

  public ObjectPool(int initialCapacity) {
    _pool = new Stack<T>(initialCapacity);
    for(int i = 0; i < initialCapacity; ++i) {
      Spawn (); // instantiate a pool of N objects
    }
    Reset ();
  }

  public int Count {
    get { return _pool.Count; }
  }

  public void Reset() {
    _currentIndex = 0;
  }

  public T Spawn() {
    if (_currentIndex < Count) {
      T obj = _pool.Peek ();
      _currentIndex++;
      IPoolableObject po = obj as IPoolableObject;
      po.Respawn();
      return obj;
    } else {
      T obj = new T();
      _pool.Push(obj);
      _currentIndex++;
      IPoolableObject po = obj as IPoolableObject;
      po.New();
      return obj;
    }
  }
}
```

This class allows `ObjectPool` to be used with any object type so long as it fits the following two criteria: it must implement the `IPoolableObject` interface class, and the derived class must allow for a parameter-less constructor (specified by the `new()` keyword in the class declaration).

3. Finally, we need to implement the `IPoolableObject` interface for any object we want to pool. An example poolable object would look like so: it must implement two `public` methods, `New()` and `Respawn()`, which are invoked by the `ObjectPool` class at the appropriate times:

```
public class EnemyObject : IPoolableObject {
  public void New() {
    // very first initialization here
  }
  public void Respawn() {
    // reset data which allows the object to be recycled here
  }
}
```

Now, just consider this usage example: we want to have a continuous wave of monsters. Obviously, we do not want to create new enemies continuously, instead, we want to recycle the enemies killed by the player. To do that, first we create a pool of 100 `EnemyObject` objects (we assume we never need to show more than 100 enemies on screen at the same time):

```
private ObjectPool<EnemyObject> _objectPool = new
ObjectPool<EnemyObject>(100);
```

The first 100 calls to `Spawn()` on `ObjectPool` will cause the enemy to be respawned, providing the caller with a unique instance of the object each time. If there are no more enemies to provide (we have called `Spawn()` more than 100 times), then we will allocate a new `EnemyObject` instance and push it onto the stack. Finally, if `Reset()` is called on `ObjectPool`, it will begin again from the start, recycling enemies and providing them to the caller.

Note that we are using the `Peek()` method on the `Stack` object so that we don't remove the old instance from the stack. We want `ObjectPool` to maintain references to all of the enemies we create.

Also, note that this pooling solution will not work for classes we haven't defined and cannot derive from `IPoolableObject`, such as `Vector3` and `Quaternion`. This is normally dictated by the `sealed` keyword in the class definition. In these cases, we would need to define a containing class:

```
public class PoolableVector3 : IPoolableObject {
  public Vector3 vector = new Vector3();
  public void New() {
    Reset();
  }
  public void Respawn() {
    Reset();
  }
  public void Reset() {
    vector.x = vector.y = vector.z = 0f;
  }
}
```

We could extend this system in a number of ways, such as defining a `Despawn()` method to handle destruction of the object, making use of the `IDisposable` interface class and `using` blocks when we wish to automatically spawn and despawn objects within a small scope, and/or allowing objects instantiated outside the pool to be added to it.

Prefab pooling

The previous pooling solution is useful for typical C# objects, but it won't work for specialized Unity objects, such as `GameObject` and `MonoBehaviour`. These objects tend to consume a large chunk of our runtime memory, can cost us a great deal of CPU usage when they're created and destroyed, and tend to risk a large amount of garbage collection at runtime. For instance, during the lifecycle of a small RPG game, we might spawn a thousand Orc creatures, but at any given moment, we may only need a maximum of 10 of them. It would be nice if we could perform similar pooling as before but, for Unity Prefabs, to save on a lot of unnecessary overhead creating and destroying 990 Orcs we don't need.

Our goal is to push the overwhelming majority of object instantiation to scene initialization rather than letting them get created at runtime. This can provide some big runtime CPU savings and avoids a lot of spikes caused by object creation/destruction and garbage collection at the expense of scene loading times and runtime memory consumption. As a result, there are quite a few pooling solutions available on the Asset Store to handle this task, with varying degrees of simplicity, quality, and feature sets.

It is often recommended that pooling should be implemented in any game that intends to be deployed on mobile devices, due to the greater overhead costs involved in the allocation and deallocation of memory compared to desktop applications.

However, creating a pooling solution is an interesting topic, and building one from scratch is a great way of getting to grips with a lot of important internal Unity engine behavior. Also, knowing how such a system is built makes it easier to extend if we wish it to meet the needs of our particular game, rather than to rely on a prebuilt solution.

The general idea of Prefab pooling is to create a system that contains lists of active and inactive GameObjects that were all instantiated from the same Prefab reference. The following diagram shows how the system might look after several spawns, despawns, and respawns of various objects derived from four different Prefabs (**Orc**, **Troll**, **Ogre**, and **Dragon**):

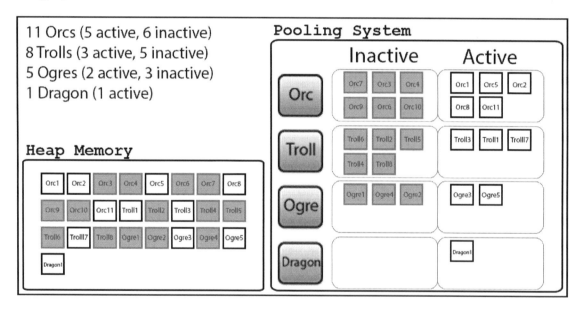

 Note that the **Heap Memory** area in the previous screenshot represents the objects as they exist in memory, while the **Pooling System** area represents the **Pooling System's** references to those objects.

In this example, several instances of each Prefab were instantiated (**11 Orcs, 8 Trolls, 5 Ogres**, and **1 Dragon**). Currently, only 11 of these objects are active, while the other 14 have been previously despawned and are inactive. Note that the despawned objects still exist in memory, although they are not visible and cannot interact with the game world until they have been respawned. Naturally, this costs us a constant amount of heap memory at runtime to maintain the inactive objects, but when a new object is instantiated, we can reuse one of the existing inactive objects rather than allocating more memory to satisfy the request. This saves significant runtime CPU costs during object creation and destruction and avoids garbage collection.

The following diagram shows the chain of events that needs to occur when **New Orc is spawned**:

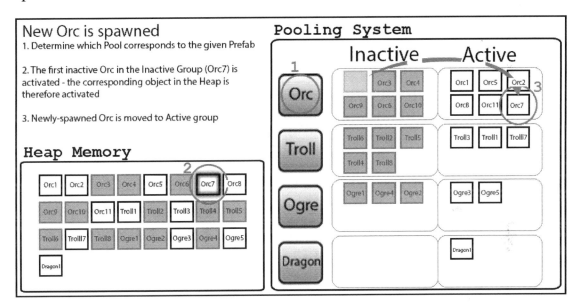

The first object in the **Inactive** Orc pool (**Orc7**) is reactivated and moved into the **Active** pool. We now have six active Orcs and five inactive Orcs.

The following diagram shows the order of events when an **Ogre** object is despawned:

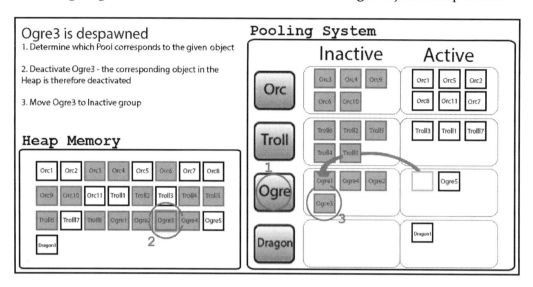

This time, the object is deactivated and moved from the **Active** pool into the **Inactive** pool, leaving us with one active **Ogre** and four inactive Ogres.

Finally, the following diagram shows what happens when a new object is spawned, but there are no inactive objects to satisfy the request:

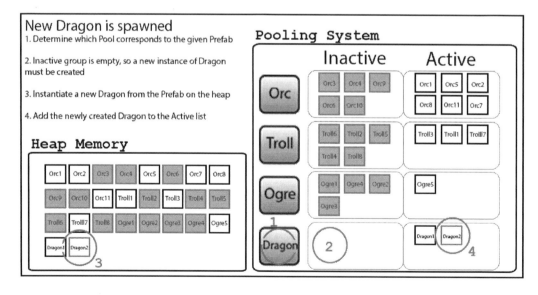

In this scenario, more memory must be allocated to instantiate the new **Dragon** object since there are no **Dragon** objects in its **Inactive** pool to reuse. Therefore, to avoid runtime memory allocations for our GameObjects, it is critical that we know beforehand how many we will need and that there is sufficient memory space available to contain them all at once. This will vary depending on the type of object in question and requires occasional testing and sanity checking to ensure that we have a sensible number of each Prefab instantiated at runtime.

With all of this in mind, let's create a pooling system for Prefabs.

Poolable components

Let's first define an interface class for a component that can be used in the pooling system:

```
public interface IPoolableComponent {
  void Spawned();
  void Despawned();
}
```

The approach for `IPoolableComponent` will be very different from the approach taken for `IPoolableObject`. The objects being created this time are GameObjects, which are a lot trickier to work with than standard objects because of how much of their runtime behavior is already handled through the Unity engine and how little low-level access we have to it.

GameObjects do not give us access to an equivalent `New()` method that we can invoke any time the object is created, and we cannot derive from the `GameObject` class to implement one. GameObjects are created either by placing them in a scene or by instantiating them at runtime through `GameObject.Instantiate()`, and the only inputs we can apply are an initial position and rotation. Of course, their components have an `Awake()` callback that we can define, which is invoked the first time the component is brought to life, but this is merely a compositional object—it's not the actual parent object we're spawning and despawning.

So, because we have control over only a `GameObject` class's components, it is assumed that the `IPoolableComponent` interface class is implemented by at least one of the components that is attached to the `GameObject` class we wish to pool.

The `Spawned()` method should be invoked on every implementing component each time the pooled `GameObject` class is respawned, while the `Despawned()` method gets invoked whenever it is despawned. This gives us entry points to control the data variables and behavior during the creation and destruction of the parent `GameObject` class.

The act of despawning GameObject is trivial: turn its active flag to false through SetActive(). This disables Collider and Rigidbody for physics calculations, removes it from the list of renderable objects, and essentially takes care of disabling all interactions with all built-in Unity engine subsystems in a single stroke. The only exception is any coroutines that are currently invoking on the object since, as you learned in Chapter 2, *Scripting Strategies*, coroutines are invoked independently of any Update() and GameObject activity. We will, therefore, need to call StopCoroutine() or StopAllCoroutines() during the despawning of such objects.

Also, components typically hook into our own custom gameplay subsystems as well, so the Despawn() method allows our components to take care of any custom cleanup before shutting down. For example, we would probably want to use Despawn() to deregister the component from the messaging system we defined in Chapter 2, *Scripting Strategies*.

Unfortunately, successfully respawning the GameObject is a lot more complicated. When we respawn an object, there will be many settings that were left behind when the object was previously active, and these must be reset to avoid conflicting behaviors. A common problem with this is the Rigidbody's linearVelocity and angularVelocity properties. If these values are not explicitly reset before the object is reactivated, then the newly respawned object will continue moving with the same velocity the old version had when it was despawned.

This problem becomes further complicated by the fact that built-in components are sealed, which means that they cannot be derived from. So, to avoid these issues, we can create a custom component that resets the attached Rigidbody instance whenever the object is despawned:

```
public class ResetPooledRigidbodyComponent : MonoBehaviour,
IPoolableComponent {
  [SerializeField] Rigidbody _body;
  public void Spawned() {  }
  public void Despawned() {
    if (_body == null) {
      _body = GetComponent<Rigidbody>();
      if (_body == null) {
        // no Rigidbody!
        return;
      }
    }
    _body.velocity = Vector3.zero;
    _body.angularVelocity = Vector3.zero;
  }
}
```

Note that the best place to perform the cleanup task is during despawning, because we cannot be certain in what order the GameObject class's IPoolableComponent interface classes will have their Spawned() methods invoked. It is unlikely that another IPoolableComponent will change the object's velocity during despawning, but it is possible that a different IPoolableComponent attached to the same object might want to set the Rigidbody's initial velocity to some important value during its own Spawned() method. Ergo, performing the velocity reset during the ResetPooledRigidbodyComponent class's Spawned() method could potentially conflict with other components and cause some very confusing bugs.

In fact, creating poolable components that are not self-contained and tend to tinker with other components like this is one of the biggest dangers of implementing a pooling system. We should minimize such design and routinely verify them when we're trying to debug strange issues in our game.

For the sake of illustration, here is the definition of a simple poolable component making use of the MessagingSystem class we defined in Chapter 2, *Scripting Strategies*. This component automatically handles some basic tasks every time the object is spawned and despawned:

```
public class PoolableTestMessageListener : MonoBehaviour,
IPoolableComponent {
  public void Spawned() {
    MessagingSystem.Instance.AttachListener(typeof(MyCustomMessage),
                                     this.HandleMyCustomMessage);
  }

  bool HandleMyCustomMessage(BaseMessage msg) {
    MyCustomMessage castMsg = msg as MyCustomMessage;
    Debug.Log (string.Format("Got the message! {0}, {1}",
                       castMsg._intValue,
                       castMsg._floatValue));
    return true;
  }

  public void Despawned() {
    if (MessagingSystem.IsAlive) {
      MessagingSystem.Instance.DetachListener(typeof(MyCustomMessage),
                                       this.HandleMyCustomMessage);
    }
  }
}
```

The Prefab pooling system

Hopefully, we now have an understanding of what we need from our pooling system, so all that's left is to implement it. The requirements are as follows:

- It must accept requests to spawn a GameObject instance from a Prefab, an initial position, and an initial rotation:
  - If a despawned version already exists, it should respawn the first available one
  - If it does not exist, then it should instantiate a new GameObject instance from the Prefab
  - In either case, the Spawned() method should be invoked on all IPoolableComponent interface classes attached to GameObject
- It must accept requests to despawn a specific GameObject instance:
  - If the object is managed by the pooling system, it should deactivate it and call the Despawned() method on all IPoolableComponent interface classes attached to GameObject
  - If the object is not managed by the pooling system, it should send an error

The requirements are fairly straightforward, but the implementation requires some investigation if we wish to make the solution performance-friendly. Firstly, a typical singleton would be a good choice for the main entry point since we want this system to be globally accessible from anywhere:

```
public static class PrefabPoolingSystem {}
```

The main task for object spawning involves accepting a Prefab reference and figuring whether we have any despawned GameObjects that were originally instantiated from the same reference. To do this, we will essentially want our pooling system to keep track of two different lists for any given Prefab reference: a list of active (spawned) GameObjects and a list of inactive (despawned) objects that were instantiated from it. This information would be best abstracted into a separate class, which we will name PrefabPool.

To maximize the performance of this system (and hence make the largest gains possible, relative to just allocating and deallocating objects from memory all of the time), we will want to use some fast data structures in order to acquire the corresponding PrefabPool objects whenever a spawn or despawn request comes in.

Since spawning involves being given a Prefab, we will want a data structure that can quickly map Prefabs to the `PrefabPool` that manages them. Also, since despawning involves being given `GameObject`, we will want another data structure that can quickly map spawned GameObjects to the `PrefabPool` instance that originally spawned them. A pair of dictionaries would be a good choice for both of these needs.

Let's define these dictionaries in our `PrefabPoolingSystem` class:

```
public static class PrefabPoolingSystem {
    static Dictionary<GameObject,PrefabPool> _prefabToPoolMap = new
Dictionary<GameObject,PrefabPool>();
    static Dictionary<GameObject,PrefabPool> _goToPoolMap = new
Dictionary<GameObject,PrefabPool>();
}
```

Next, we'll define what happens when we `Spawn` an object:

```
public static GameObject Spawn(GameObject prefab, Vector3 position,
Quaternion rotation) {
    if (!_prefabToPoolMap.ContainsKey (prefab)) {
      _prefabToPoolMap.Add (prefab, new PrefabPool());
    }
    PrefabPool pool = _prefabToPoolMap[prefab];
    GameObject go = pool.Spawn(prefab, position, rotation);
    _goToPoolMap.Add (go, pool);
    return go;
}
```

The `Spawn()` method will be given a `prefab` reference, an initial `position`, and an initial `rotation`. We need to figure out which `PrefabPool` the `prefab` reference belongs to (if any), ask it to spawn a new `GameObject` instance using the data provided, and then return the spawned object to the requestor. We will first check our Prefab-to-pool map to check whether a pool already exists for this Prefab. If not, we immediately create one. In either case, we then ask `PrefabPool` to spawn us a new object. `PrefabPool` will either end up respawning an object that was despawned earlier or instantiate a new one (if there aren't any inactive instances left).

This class doesn't particularly care how `PrefabPool` creates the object. It just wants the instance generated by the `PrefabPool` class so that it can be entered into the GameObject-to-pool map and returned to the requestor.

For convenience, we can also define an overload that places the object at the world's center. This is useful for GameObjects that aren't visible and just need to exist in the scene:

```
public static GameObject Spawn(GameObject prefab) {
    return Spawn (prefab, Vector3.zero, Quaternion.identity);
}
```

 Note that no actual spawning and despawning are taking place, yet. This task will eventually be implemented within the PrefabPool class.

Despawning involves being given GameObject and then figuring out which PrefabPool is managing it. This could be achieved by iterating through our PrefabPool objects and checking whether they contain the given GameObject instance. However, if we end up generating a lot of Prefab pools, then this iterative process can take a while. We will always end up with as many PrefabPool objects as we have Prefabs (at least, so long as we manage all of them through the pooling system). Most projects tend to have dozens, hundreds, if not thousands, of different Prefabs.

So, the GameObject-to-pool map is maintained to ensure that we always have rapid access to PrefabPool that originally spawned the object. It can also be used to quickly check whether the given GameObject instance is even managed by the pooling system to begin with. Here is the method definition for the despawning method, which takes care of these tasks:

```
public static bool Despawn(GameObject obj) {
    if (!_goToPoolMap.ContainsKey(obj)) {
        Debug.LogError (string.Format ("Object {0} not managed by pool
system!", obj.name));
        return false;
    }

    PrefabPool pool = _goToPoolMap[obj];
    if (pool.Despawn (obj)) {
        _goToPoolMap.Remove (obj);
        return true;
    }
    return false;
}
```

 Note that the Despawn() method of both PrefabPoolingSystem and PrefabPool returns a Boolean that can be used to check whether the object was successfully despawned.

As a result, thanks to the two maps we're maintaining, we can quickly access the `PrefabPool` instance that manages the given reference, and this solution will scale for any number of Prefabs that the system manages.

Prefab pools

Now that we have a system that can handle multiple Prefab pools automatically, the only thing left is to define the behavior of the pools. As mentioned previously, we will want the `PrefabPool` class to maintain two data structures: one for active (spawned) objects that have been instantiated from the given Prefab and another for inactive (despawned) objects.

Technically, the `PrefabPoolingSystem` class already maintains a map of which Prefab is governed by which `PrefabPool`, so we can actually save a little memory by making the `PrefabPool` class dependent upon the `PrefabPoolingSystem` class to give it the reference to the Prefab it is managing. Consequently, the two data structures would be the only member variables `PrefabPool` needs to keep track of.

However, for each spawned `GameObject`, it must also maintain a list of all of its `IPoolableComponent` references to invoke the `Spawned()` and `Despawned()` methods on them. Acquiring these references can be a costly operation to perform at runtime, so it would be best to cache the data in a simple struct:

```
public struct PoolablePrefabData {
  public GameObject go;
  public IPoolableComponent[] poolableComponents;
}
```

This `struct` will contain a reference to `GameObject` and the precached list of all of its `IPoolableComponent` components.

Now, we can define the member data of our `PrefabPool` class:

```
public class PrefabPool {
  Dictionary<GameObject,PoolablePrefabData> _activeList = new
Dictionary<GameObject,PoolablePrefabData>();
  Queue<PoolablePrefabData> _inactiveList = new
Queue<PoolablePrefabData>();
}
```

The data structure for the active list should be a dictionary to do a quick lookup for the corresponding `PoolablePrefabData` component from any given `GameObject` reference. This will be useful during object despawning.

Meanwhile, the inactive data structure is defined as Queue, but it will work equally well as List, Stack, or really any data structure that needs to regularly expand or contract, where we only need to pop items from one end of the group, since it does not matter which object it is. It only matters that we retrieve one of them. Queue is useful in this case because we can both retrieve and remove the object from the data structure in a single call to Dequeue().

Object spawning

Let's define what it means to spawn GameObject in the context of our pooling system: at some point, PrefabPool will get a request to spawn GameObject from a given Prefab, at a particular position and rotation. The first thing we should check is whether or not we have any inactive instances of the Prefab. If so, then we can dequeue the next available one from Queue and respawn it. If not, then we need to instantiate a new GameObject from the Prefab using GameObject.Instantiate(). At this moment, we should also create a PoolablePrefabData object to store the GameObject reference and acquire the list of all MonoBehaviours that implement IPoolableComponent that are attached to it.

Either way, we can now activate GameObject, set its position and rotation, and call the Spawned() method on all of its IPoolableComponent references. Once the object has been respawned, we can add it to the list of active objects and return it to the requestor.

The following is the definition of the Spawn() method that defines this behavior:

```
public GameObject Spawn(GameObject prefab, Vector3 position, Quaternion
rotation) {
  PoolablePrefabData data;

  if (_inactiveList.Count > 0) {
    data = _inactiveList.Dequeue();
  } else {
    // instantiate a new object
    GameObject newGO = GameObject.Instantiate(prefab, position, rotation)
as GameObject;
    data = new PoolablePrefabData();
    data.go = newGO;
    data.poolableComponents = newGO.GetComponents<IPoolableComponent>();
  }

  data.go.SetActive (true);
  data.go.transform.position = position;
  data.go.transform.rotation = rotation;

  for(int i = 0; i < data.poolableComponents.Length; ++i) {
```

```
      data.poolableComponents[i].Spawned ();
   }
   _activeList.Add (data.go, data);

   return data.go;
}
```

Instance prespawning

Since we are using `GameObject.Instantiate()` whenever the `PrefabPool` has run out of despawned instances, this system does not completely rid us of runtime object instantiation, hence heap memory allocation. It's important to prespawn the expected number of instances that we will need during the lifetime of the current scene so that we minimize or remove the need to instantiate more during runtime.

Note that we shouldn't prespawn too many objects. It would be wasteful to prespawn 100 explosion particle effects if the most we will ever expect to see in the scene at any given time is three or four. Conversely, spawning too few instances will cause excessive runtime memory allocations, and the goal of this system is to push the majority of allocation to the start of a scene's lifetime. We need to be careful about how many instances we maintain in memory so that we don't waste more memory space than necessary.

Let's define a method in our `PrefabPoolingSystem` class that we can use to quickly prespawn a given number of objects from a Prefab. This essentially involves spawning N objects and then immediately despawning them all:

```
public static void Prespawn(GameObject prefab, int numToSpawn) {
   List<GameObject> spawnedObjects = new List<GameObject>();

   for(int i = 0; i < numToSpawn; i++) {
     spawnedObjects.Add (Spawn (prefab));
   }

   for(int i = 0; i < numToSpawn; i++) {
     Despawn(spawnedObjects[i]);
   }

   spawnedObjects.Clear ();
}
```

We would use this method during scene initialization to prespawn a collection of objects to use in the level. Take, for example, the following code:

```
public class OrcPreSpawner : MonoBehaviour
  [SerializeField] GameObject _orcPrefab;
  [SerializeField] int _numToSpawn = 20;

  void Start() {
    PrefabPoolingSystem.Prespawn(_orcPrefab, _numToSpawn);
  }
}
```

Object despawning

Finally, there is the act of despawning the objects. As mentioned previously, this primarily involves deactivating the object, but we also need to take care of various bookkeeping tasks and invoking Despawned() on all of its IPoolableComponent references.

Here is the method definition for PrefabPool.Despawn():

```
public bool Despawn(GameObject objToDespawn) {
    if (!_activeList.ContainsKey(objToDespawn)) {
      Debug.LogError ("This Object is not managed by this object pool!");
      return false;
    }

    PoolablePrefabData data = _activeList[objToDespawn];

    for(int i = 0; i < data.poolableComponents.Length; ++i) {
      data.poolableComponents[i].Despawned ();
    }

    data.go.SetActive (false);
    _activeList.Remove (objToDespawn);
    _inactiveList.Enqueue(data);
    return true;
}
```

First, we verify that the object is being managed by the pool and then we grab the corresponding PoolablePrefabData instance to access the list of IPoolableComponent references. Once Despawned() is invoked on all of them, we deactivate the object, remove it from the active list, and push it into the inactive queue so that it can be respawned later.

Prefab pool testing

The following class definition allows us to perform a simple hands-on test with the `PrefabPoolingSystem` class; it will support three Prefabs and prespawn five instances of each during application initialization. We can press the *1, 2, 3,* or *4* keys to spawn an instance of each type and then press *Q, W, E,* and *R* to despawn a random instance of each type, respectively:

```
public class PrefabPoolingTestInput : MonoBehaviour {
  [SerializeField] GameObject _orcPrefab;
  [SerializeField] GameObject _trollPrefab;
  [SerializeField] GameObject _ogrePrefab;
  [SerializeField] GameObject _dragonPrefab;

  List<GameObject> _orcs = new List<GameObject>();
  List<GameObject> _trolls = new List<GameObject>();
  List<GameObject> _ogres = new List<GameObject>();
  List<GameObject> _dragons = new List<GameObject>();

  void Start() {
    PrefabPoolingSystem.Prespawn(_orcPrefab, 11);
    PrefabPoolingSystem.Prespawn(_trollPrefab, 8);
    PrefabPoolingSystem.Prespawn(_ogrePrefab, 5);
    PrefabPoolingSystem.Prespawn(_dragonPrefab, 1);
  }

  void Update () {
    if (Input.GetKeyDown(KeyCode.Alpha1)) {SpawnObject(_orcPrefab, _orcs);}
    if (Input.GetKeyDown(KeyCode.Alpha2)) {SpawnObject(_trollPrefab,
_trolls);}
    if (Input.GetKeyDown(KeyCode.Alpha3)) {SpawnObject(_ogrePrefab,
_ogres);}
    if (Input.GetKeyDown(KeyCode.Alpha4)) {SpawnObject(_dragonPrefab,
_dragons);}
    if (Input.GetKeyDown(KeyCode.Q)) { DespawnRandomObject(_orcs); }
    if (Input.GetKeyDown(KeyCode.W)) { DespawnRandomObject(_trolls); }
    if (Input.GetKeyDown(KeyCode.E)) { DespawnRandomObject(_ogres); }
    if (Input.GetKeyDown(KeyCode.R)) { DespawnRandomObject(_dragons); }
  }

  void SpawnObject(GameObject prefab, List<GameObject> list) {
    GameObject obj = PrefabPoolingSystem.Spawn (prefab,
                                                5.0f *
Random.insideUnitSphere,
                                                Quaternion.identity);
    list.Add (obj);
  }
```

```
    void DespawnRandomObject(List<GameObject> list) {
      if (list.Count == 0) {
        // Nothing to despawn
        return;
      }

      int i = Random.Range (0, list.Count);
      PrefabPoolingSystem.Despawn(list[i]);
      list.RemoveAt(i);
    }
  }
```

Once we spawn more than five instances of any of the Prefabs, it will need to instantiate a new one in memory, costing us some memory allocation. However, if we observe the **Memory Area** in the **Profiler** window, while we only spawn and despawn instances that already exist, then we will notice that absolutely no new allocations take place.

Prefab pooling and scene loading

There is one important caveat to this system that has not yet been mentioned: the PrefabPoolingSystem class will outlast the scene's lifetime since it is a static class. This means that when a new scene is loaded, the pooling system's dictionaries will attempt to maintain references to any pooled instances from the previous scene, but Unity forcibly destroys these objects regardless of the fact that we are still keeping references to them (unless they were set to DontDestroyOnLoad()), and so the dictionaries will be full of null references. This would cause some serious problems for the next scene.

We should, therefore, create a method in PrefabPoolingSystem that resets the pooling system in preparation for this likely event. The following method should be called before a new scene is loaded so that it is ready for any early calls to Prespawn() in the next scene:

```
public static void Reset() {
  _prefabToPoolMap.Clear ();
  _goToPoolMap.Clear ();
}
```

Note that if we also invoke a garbage collection during scene transitions, there's no need to explicitly destroy the PrefabPool objects these dictionaries were referencing. Since these were the only references to the PrefabPool objects, they will be deallocated during the next garbage collection. If we aren't invoking garbage collection between scenes, then the PrefabPool and PooledPrefabData objects will remain in memory until that time.

Prefab pooling summary

This pooling system provides a decent solution to the problem of runtime memory allocations for GameObjects and Prefabs, but, as a quick reminder, we need to be aware of the following caveats:

- We need to be careful about properly resetting important data in respawned objects (such as `Rigidbody` velocity)
- We must ensure that we don't prespawn too few, or too many, instances of a Prefab
- We should be careful of the order of execution of `Spawned()` and `Despawned()` methods on `IPoolableComponent` and not assume that they will be called in a particular order
- We must call `Reset()` on `PrefabPoolingSystem` when loading a new scene to clear any `null` references to objects, which may no longer exist

There are several other features that we could implement. These will be left as academic exercises if we wish to extend this system in the future:

- Any `IPoolableComponent` added to the `GameObject` after initialization will not have their `Spawned()` or `Despawned()` methods invoked since we only collect this list when `GameObject` is first instantiated. We could fix this by changing `PrefabPool` to keep acquiring `IPoolableComponent` references every time `Spawned()` and `Despawned()` are invoked at the cost of additional overhead during spawning/despawning.
- Any `IPoolableComponent` attached to children of the Prefab's root will also not be counted. This could be fixed by changing `PrefabPool` to use `GetComponentsInChildren<T>` at the cost of additional overhead if we're using Prefabs with deep hierarchies.
- Prefab instances that already exist in the scene will not be managed by the pooling system. We could create a component that needs to be attached to such objects and that notifies the `PrefabPoolingSystem` class of its existence in its `Awake()` callback, which passes the reference along to the corresponding `PrefabPool`.
- We could implement a way for `IPoolableComponent` to set a priority during acquisition and directly control the order of execution for their `Spawned()` and `Despawned()` methods.

- We could add counters that keep track of how long objects have been sitting in the Inactive list relative to total scene lifetime and print out the data during shutdown. This could tell us whether or not we're prespawning too many instances of a given Prefab.

- This system will not interact kindly with Prefab instances that set themselves to `DontDestroyOnLoad()`. It might be wise to add a Boolean to every `Spawn()` call to say whether the object should persist or not and keep them in a separate data structure that is not cleared out during `Reset()`.

- We could change `Spawn()` to accept an argument that allows the requestor to pass custom data to the `Spawned()` function of `IPoolableObject` for initialization purposes. This could use a system similar to how custom message objects were derived from the `Message` class for our messaging system in `Chapter 2`, *Scripting Strategies*.

IL2CPP optimizations

Unity Technologies have released a few blog posts on interesting ways to improve the performance of IL2CPP in some circumstances, but they can be difficult to manage. If you're using IL2CPP and need to eke out the last little bit of performance from our application that we can, then check out the blog series at the following links:

- https://blogs.unity3d.com/2016/07/26/il2cpp-optimizations-devirtualization/

- https://blogs.unity3d.com/2016/08/04/il2cpp-optimizations-faster-virtual-method-calls/

- https://blogs.unity3d.com/2016/08/11/il2cpp-optimizations-avoid-boxing/

WebGL optimizations

Unity Technologies have also released several blog posts covering WebGL applications, which includes some crucial information about memory management that all WebGL developers should know. These can be found at the following links:

- https://blogs.unity3d.com/2016/09/20/understanding-memory-in-unity-webgl/

- https://blogs.unity3d.com/2016/12/05/unity-webgl-memory-the-unity-heap/

Summary

We've covered a humongous amount of theory and language concepts in this chapter, which have hopefully shed some light on how the internals of the Unity engine and C# language work. These tools try their best to spare us from the burden of complex memory management, but there is still a whole host of concerns we need to keep in mind as we develop our game. Between the compilation processes, multiple memory domains, the complexities of value types versus reference types, passing by value versus passing by reference, boxing, object pooling, and various quirks within the Unity API, you have a lot of things to worry about. However, with enough practice, you will learn to overcome them without needing to keep referring to giant tomes such as this!

With this chapter, we have covered all of the possible optimization areas in classic Unity. However, with the 2019.1 release, Unity officially introduced the **Data-Oriented Technology Stack (DOTS)**, a set of new fundamental APIs to access a completely new optimization level, especially in modern massively multi-threading systems. Follow me to the next chapter, where we will explore this new frontier.

The Data-Oriented Technology Stack

9

In recent years, we have seen a big push toward multithreading programming. The reason is obvious: while we have reached a technological limit on how fast a single core can go, we have discovered how to efficiently put thousands of cores into our hardware and run each piece of code in parallel to obtain a massive performance boost.

However, moving from single-thread programming to multithreading programming is not straightforward. Not every algorithm can easily be split into pieces and, even if it can, there are several details you need to take into account so as to avoid strange and unpredictable behaviors.

When the first version of Unity was released, back in 2005, massive multithreading was almost a futuristic scenario. However, fourteen years are the equivalent of a geological era in game development, and a game engine needs to adapt itself to stay on track with cutting-edge technology.

Unity is currently going through a massive effort to adapt its core design into a world dominated by massive multithreading. This effort takes the name of the **Data-Oriented Technology Stack (DOTS)**.

In this chapter, we will explore the components of DOTS:

- The Job System
- The **Entity Component System (ECS)**
- The Burst Compiler

 The DOTS stack in Unity is exceptionally experimental and, while public, all its components are still in an early preview state, meaning that their use should be avoided for serious projects. They also change very fast. The official tutorial on ECS on `https://learn.unity.com` is now unusable because it is out of date. I will not be surprised if even this chapter, some months from now, were to contain many deprecated functions and procedures. Do not worry; I will provide a link at the end for where to obtain fresh news on DOTS.

The problem of multithreading

Video games have great multithreading potential. In theory, every `GameObject` can be seen as a separate entity with its own life cycle and its own computation path. This would instantaneously increase your game performance with a lot of `GameObject` instances. Suppose that processing all the updates in the `GameObject` takes 1 ms. If you could have one thousand similar `GameObject` instances, that would take a full second but, if you can assign each update to a separate core, all the updates could run in parallel, and your total computation time would be exactly 1 ms. That represents a 100,000% speed boost!

Unfortunately, it is not so easy. As we said before, you cannot just assign a piece of code to a core and expect that everything keeps working. A big problem with writing multithreaded code is the risk of race conditions, deadlock, and bugs that are notoriously difficult to reproduce and debug.

 Race conditions are where two or more calculations are racing toward completion, but the actual outcome depends on the order in which they finish. Imagine one thread trying to add three to a number, whereas another thread multiplies it by four. The result will be different, depending on which operation happens first. Deadlock is a problem where two or more threads are competing for shared resources, where each requires the full resource collection to complete its task, but each has reserved a separate small portion of resources and refuses to relinquish control of them to another thread, in which case, none of the threads can get any work done because neither has the complete set it needs.

For this reason, traditionally, Unity APIs are not thread-safe, meaning that they cannot be invoked by different threads running in parallel. As a consequence, almost all Unity code runs in the main thread, and that includes every GameObject and MonoBehaviour (and that's why if you block a single update, you may end up freezing the entire Unity Editor).

Because multithreading is a complex topic, we will go over an example step by step.

A small example

Imagine you want to have thousands of similar items in your scene. This is not a strange request; there may be many valid reasons for that: you may wish to render thousands of ships in a gigantic galactic battle, or you may want to animate thousands of units for a **Real-Time Strategy (RTS)** game, or you may want to handle a massive number of particles.

For simplicity, in our demo, we want a scene with 10,000 spinning cubes. So let's begin:

1. Each cube will have a single MonoBehaviour instance that executes a very simple rotation cube:

```
using UnityEngine;

namespace Classic
{
  public class Rotator : MonoBehaviour
  {

    public float rotationSpeed;

    void Update()
    {
      transform.Rotate(0f, rotationSpeed * Time.deltaTime, 0f);
    }
  }
}
```

The script is self-explanatory: we have a public variable, rotationSpeed, storing the rotation speed of the cube. Then, in Update, we simply rotate the cube.

2. Now, we do not want to insert 10,000 cubes into the scene manually. So, we will create a **game manager** that will do the following:
    1. Spawn 10,000 cubes in the scene
    2. Set a random rotation speed for each one of them

3. So, we create an empty `GameObject`, and we attach to it a game manager script, as follows:

```
using UnityEngine;
using System;

namespace Classic {

    public class ClassicCubeManager : MonoBehaviour
    {

        #region COMMON_GAME_MANAGER_DATA
        public float cubeSpacing = 0.1f;
        public int width = 10;
        public int height = 10;

        public GameObject cubePrefab;
        #endregion

        void Start()
        {
            SpawnCubes();

        }

        private void SpawnCubes()
        {
            Debug.Log(String.Format("Spawning {0} cubes", (width /
cubeSpacing) * (height / cubeSpacing)));
            Vector3 position = new Vector3();
            while (position.x < width)
            {
                while (position.y < height) {
                    var newCube =
GameObject.Instantiate(cubePrefab);
                    newCube.transform.position = position;
                    newCube.GetComponent<Rotator>().rotationSpeed =
UnityEngine.Random.Range(25.0f, 50.0f);
                    position = new Vector3(position.x, position.y +
cubeSpacing, 0f);
                }
                position = new Vector3(position.x + cubeSpacing,
0f, 0f);
            }
        }

    }
}
```

The script simply takes a `cubePrefab` and spawns a certain number of them into a *width x height* rectangle of space. The exciting part is the `SpawnCubes` function. The function starts with `position` in the origin and starts spawning cubes until we reach the opposite corner. This is a pretty standard script.

4. Now we can run it, and we should see something like this:

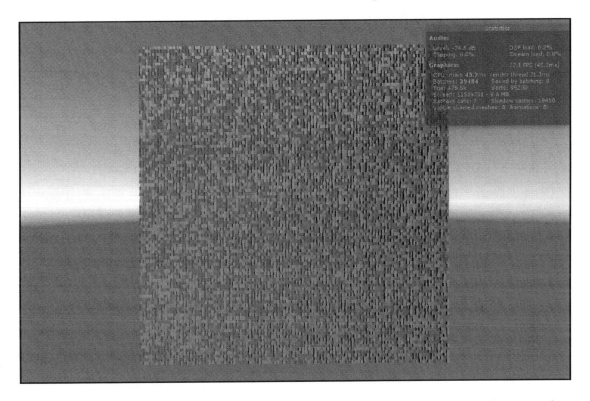

As you can see, the frame rate is not optimal. Looking at the stats in the top-right corner, you can see that the game is running at ~22 FPS.

Note that these values are taken from my non-optimal machine. You may find different values. If your computer is so fast that the demo is running perfectly, try to increase the number of cubes to 20,000 or more.

5. This FPS value is not optimal. However, we can open the **Profiler** window (**Window** | **Analysis** | **Profiler**) and try to understand how the application behaves:

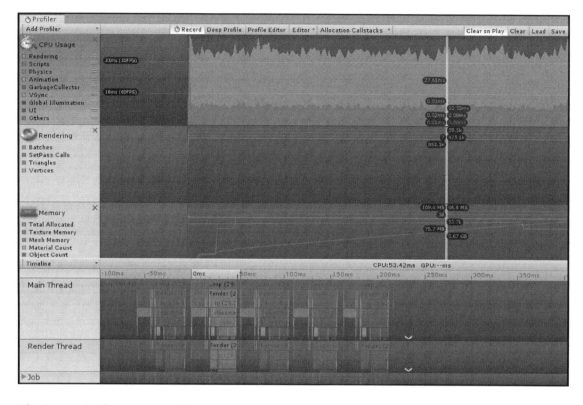

The image is clear: we are allocating almost 1 GB of RAM and spending 45 ms per frame, 10 ms of which are used just for the scripts. That's wrong. The update script is straightforward: we are just rotating a cube by a few degrees each frame.

We should do better. And we will.

The Unity Job System

The big block in the DOTS that can provide us with a huge performance-enhancing feature is the **C# Job System**. Like all the other DOTS components, the feature is still in active development, but has been made public since Unity 2019.1, so it would be wise to start becoming familiar with it sooner rather than later, as it will introduce considerable changes to how Unity developers will be writing high-performance code:

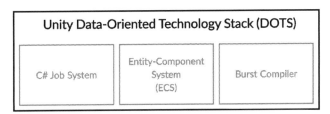

As we will see, the difference in the quality of a game that uses this system versus one that doesn't might become very noticeable, which may cause some fragmentation within the Unity development community. It is in our best interests to understand and exploit the benefits of the new Job System so that our application will have the greatest potential for success.

The idea of the C# Job System is to be able to create simple tasks that run in background threads to offload work from the main thread. The C# Job System will be ideal for tasks that are embarrassingly parallel, such as having hundreds of thousands of simple AI agents operating in a scene simultaneously and any problem that can be boiled down to thousands of small, independent operations. Of course, it can also be used for typical multithreading behavior as well, where we perform a number of calculations in the background that are not needed immediately. The Job System also introduces some compiler technology improvements to get an even greater performance boost than just moving the tasks to separate threads.

A basic job

In essence, a job is just a function running on a separate thread:

```
using Unity.Collections;
using Unity.Jobs;
using UnityEngine;

public struct SimpleJob : IJob
{
    // Put here a bunch of data...
```

```
        public float number;

        public NativeArray<float> data;

        // Write your Execute() function.
        public void Execute()
        {
            data[0] += number;
        }
    }
```

Every job is a struct extending the `IJobinterface` interface. The struct contains any data we want for the job to use and a function named `Execute` for the operation we want to execute in the job. The previous example, for instance, just adds a certain number to the first element of an array.

Because, as we said before, multithreading is a very tricky business, Unity offers some limitations in terms of the way in which you can pass and receive data to a job (or a set of jobs). The primary constraint is that the `Execute` function does not accept any argument and cannot return any value. All the data that the job needs must be copied in the struct, and the result must be written in the struct as well.

The fact that we need to copy stuff into the struct seems a significant limitation: you cannot pass a reference to a `MonoBehaviour` instance or a reference to `List`. Luckily, Unity offers a way to access shared memory in a job using a set of thread-safe wrappers using native containers.

The native containers include the following:

- `NativeArray`: A simple collection of data (the thread-safe equivalent of base C# arrays)
- `NativeList`: Similar to `NativeArray`, but resizable (the thread-safe equivalent of `List`)
- `NativeHashMap`: The thread-safe version of `HashMap`
- `NativeMultiHashMap`: Similar to `NativeHashMap`, but with multiple values per key
- `NativeQueue`: A thread-safe version of a **First In, First Out (FIFO)** queue

So, in our job, we use a one-sized `NativeArray` variable to store input and output data.

Now, we want to run the job. To do that, we need to use MonoBehaviour to initialize and run it:

```
using Unity.Collections;
using Unity.Jobs;
using UnityEngine;

public class SimpleJobRunner : MonoBehaviour
{

    public float numberToAdd = 5;

    private NativeArray<float> theData;

    private JobHandle simpleJobHandle;

    void Start()
    {
        theData = new NativeArray<float>(1, Allocator.Persistent);
        theData[0] = 2;

        SimpleJob simpleJob = new SimpleJob
        {
            number = numberToAdd,
            data = theData
        };

        simpleJobHandle = simpleJob.Schedule();

        JobHandle.ScheduleBatchedJobs();

        simpleJobHandle.Complete();

        if (simpleJobHandle.IsCompleted)
        {
            Debug.Log(simpleJob.data[0]);
        }

                theData.Dispose();
    }
}
```

In `Start`, we first create an empty `NativeArray`. The first argument of `NativeArrayconstructor` is the size; the second argument is `Allocator`. There are actually three allocators:

- `Allocator.Temp`: This is the fastest one, but its life span must be under a frame. In fact, Unity forces you to call `Dispose` on such an array before the function returns. For this reason, we cannot use `Allocator.Temp` for native containers passed as an argument to jobs. Jobs are not guaranteed to complete in the same frame in which they start.
- `Allocator.TempJob`: This is slower than `Allocator.Temp` and its lifetime is restricted to under four frames. This is the perfect type of `Allocator` for passing data to simple jobs that run and return quickly, such as the one in our example.
- `Allocator.Persistent`: This is the slower of the three, but its lifetime is unbounded. This is the type of `Allocator` where you want to store persistent data or data that jobs need to access for an extended period.

After that, we create a new `SimpleJob` instance, passing `number` and `data` to it. Then, we schedule and run the job with the `Schedule` function. This will return a `jobHandle` instance, which we can use to control the job execution. Finally, we wait for the job to be completed and then print the result. Everything looks like standard C# code, but the job runs in a separate thread!

 Remember to be nice C# citizens and always dispose of native containers manually! You do not want to pollute your memory in the same way that you do not want to pollute our world.

At this point, if you attach `SimpleJobRunner` to an empty object, you should see the result printed in the debug console. Everything is effected in a multithreading style.

A more complex example

Spawning a job just to sum two numbers is definitely not an example of optimal programming. Unity created jobs to run thousands of them to lift hard work into the multithreading domain.

Therefore, we will now modify our previous spinning cubes example so that the actual spinning is performed by jobs. The first thing we want to do is to create our job, as follows:

```
using System.Collections;
using System.Collections.Generic;
```

```
using Unity.Collections;
using UnityEngine;
using UnityEngine.Jobs;


namespace JobSystem
{

    public struct RotatorJob : IJobParallelForTransform
    {

        [ReadOnly]
        public NativeList<float> speeds;

        [ReadOnly]
        public float deltaTime;

        public void Execute(int index, TransformAccess transform)
        {
            Vector3 currentRotation = transform.rotation.eulerAngles;
            currentRotation.y += speeds[index] * deltaTime;
            transform.rotation = Quaternion.Euler(currentRotation);
        }
    }
}
```

This job is a bit more complicated, but do not worry. First, it extends
IJobParallelForTransform; this is a specialized job interface for running parallel
transformations of GameObject instances. You can do the same by extending IJob, but,
because this is a very common use case, Unity wrote most of the code for us. As you can
see, the main difference is the fact that Execute now has two parameters. In our demo, we
want to run the same job on every one of our 10,000 cubes. In this case, the parameters are
as follows:

- index represents the indexth cube in our scene
- transform is a reference to the Transform of the indexth cube

Our job takes two inputs:

- speeds: It is an array containing all the random speeds for every cube.
  Remember, we cannot get a reference to some data of a specific GameObject, so
  we need to write all the speeds into shared memory. Note that the field is
  [ReadOnly]; we do not want the ith cube to be able to change the speed of
  another cube.

- `deltaTime`: Because a job is completely disconnected from the Unity engine, it cannot access `Time` and other thread-unsafe parts of Unity. Therefore, we need to pass `deltaTime` ourselves.

The `Execute` function is straightforward; we just rotate the cube.

Now, we need to call these jobs on every cube, and we need to use a game manager for this:

```
namespace JobSystem
{
    public class JobCubeManager : MonoBehaviour
    {

        #region COMMON_GAME_MANAGER_DATA
        public float cubeSpacing = 0.1f;
        public int width = 10;
        public int height = 10;

        public GameObject cubePrefab;
        #endregion

        TransformAccessArray transformAccessArray;
        Unity.Jobs.JobHandle jobHandle;
        NativeList<float> speeds;


            . . .
```

We start by defining the underlying data as in the classic example. The first attributes are the same; the interesting ones are the final three:

- `transformAccessArray` is the array in which we will store `transform` instance references of all of our cubes. That's how our job can access them.
- `jobHandle` is the handle we will use to query the Job System for the state of the job.
- `speeds` is the list of random speeds as described before:

```
void Start()
{
    transformAccessArray = new TransformAccessArray(0, -1);
    speeds = new NativeList<float>(1, Allocator.Persistent);
    SpawnCubes();
}
```

In `Start`, we just initialize all the native containers, and then we spawn the cubes. Note that we use the `Allocator.Persistent` allocator because we want to initialize the speed on `Start` and then use the same list for the application's entire lifetime:

```
private void SpawnCubes()
{
    Debug.Log(String.Format("Spawning {0} cubes", (width /
cubeSpacing) * (height / cubeSpacing)));
    Vector3 position = new Vector3();
    while (position.x < width)
    {
        while (position.y < height)
        {
            var newCube = Instantiate(cubePrefab);
            newCube.transform.position = position;
            position = new Vector3(position.x, position.y +
cubeSpacing, 0f);
            transformAccessArray.Add(newCube.transform);
            speeds.Add(UnityEngine.Random.Range(25.0f, 50.0f));
        }
        position = new Vector3(position.x + cubeSpacing, 0f, 0f);
    }

}
```

The `SpawnCubes` function is very similar to the previous one. However, there are two crucial lines that differ:

1. After we instantiate a cube, we add its `transform` to `transformAccessArray`.
2. Instead of setting the random speed in the `Rotator MonoBehaviour` of the cube, we set it in the speeds array. In fact, we should not have the `Rotator` component in the Prefab!

Now, every frame, we need to run the job in parallel on every cube:

```
void Update()
{
    jobHandle.Complete();

    if (jobHandle.IsCompleted)
    {
        var rotatorJob = new RotatorJob()
        {
            deltaTime = Time.deltaTime,
            speeds = speeds
        };
```

```
        jobHandle = rotatorJob.Schedule(transformAccessArray);
        JobHandle.ScheduleBatchedJobs();
    }

}
```

We use the same pattern as before. We check whether the previous jobs are now complete, we instantiate a new job, we set the data, and then we schedule the job over the entire `transformAccessArray`.

If everything is correct, we can run the game and see the same scene as before. Now, however, we can enjoy ~35 FPS:

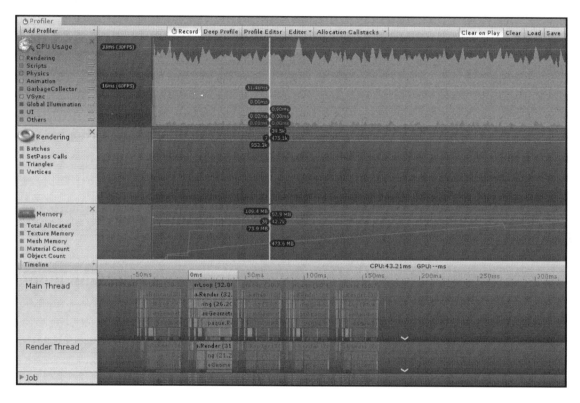

Looking at **Profiler**, we can see that, now, the time used by scripts (the lower blue one) is almost invisible. It dropped from 10 ms to 1 ms. That's a 90% improvement!

However, we still have a problem. Our scene is filled by 10,000 GameObject instances, 10,000 Transforms, 10,000 MeshRenderers, and another 10,000 copies of different components. MonoBehaviour and GameObject are heavy data structures, and they are consuming a sensible amount of memory and CPU cycles.

Can we do better? Yes, we can.

The new ECS

The ECS is a brave and ambitious attempt to redesign the core foundation of Unity's design: the GameObject-MonoBehaviour paradigm. As you can imagine, changing the base design pattern of every object in the game is not an easy task. So you may ask: Why?

There are several reasons for that. Let's look at some of them objectively:

- First, as we said before, GameObject and MonoBehaviour are heavy objects; they carry a lot of internal code and data structures. The overhead introduced by GameObject instances and MonoBehaviour is large enough to limit the number of objects you can have on the screen more than the resources needed to render them. That's not a good thing for an abstraction model.
- Second, MonoBehaviour instances are scattered in memory. This means that GameObject needs to look around in memory to retrieve all the MonoBehaviour instances it is connected to, and that the system relies on references. This has two problems: it makes caches very inefficient and, more important, it is a problem when we want to use GameObject instances in a massive multithreading application, for instance, by using jobs (we have seen that jobs cannot use references safely).
- Last, but not least, MonoBehaviour instances have a problem from a code design point of view: they store both data and behavior. This is not a huge problem. After all, a lot of amazing games have been shipped using this paradigm. However, it is common in software architecture to separate the data (often called the **model**) and the algorithm that uses the data (often called the **controller***).

The ECS, on the other hand, goes in the direction of separating the data from the behavior. It is based on three different components:

- An **entity** is just defined by its set of components. There is literally zero abstraction here.

- A **component** is purely data. A `Health` component contains only the life points; a `Shield` component contains only the number of shields; a `Rotation` component contains only the object orientation, and so on.

- A **system** defines the behavior of entities. A system applies a specific behavior to every entity containing a particular set of components. For instance, `MoveAndRotateEnemy` may apply translation and rotation to every entity with the `Rotation`, `Translation`, and `Enemy` components.

Everything is now in its own place.

Mixing ECS and jobs

It is time to apply ECS to our 10,000 spinning cubes. Before we start, we need to install the packages:

1. Open **Window | Package Manager**. Click on **Advanced** and make sure that **Show preview packages** is enabled.

2. Then, from the list, install the **Entities** package and the **Hybrid Renderer** package:

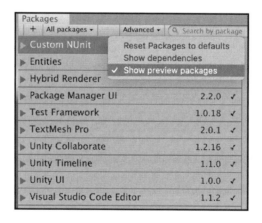

As mentioned previously, ECS is changing rapidly. We tested the code in this book with version 0.1.1-preview. If you, as a future reader, have a more recent version, there is a big chance that there will be some incompatibility. In that case, I encourage you to compare the code with the latest examples of ECS contained in this official repository: `https://github.com/Unity-Technologies/EntityComponentSystemSamples`. I apologize for my lack of forecasting ability.

3. Now we are ready to write the first component. Our cube needs to spin, so we need to have a certain `RotationSpeed`. That will be the name of our component:

```
[Serializable]
public struct RotationSpeed : IComponentData
{
    public float Value;
}
```

See how simple that is. As we have said before, a component is just data. The rotation speed is represented by a single float; therefore, we just need to store a simple float.

You may ask: how do I attach this component to an entity? Can I still use the inspector to set the values? How about all the goodies I love in Unity? Sadly, components cannot be attached to `GameObject` (after all, `GameObject` is not part of the ECS). Entities do not show up in the scene editor and components do not appear in the inspector.

Fortunately, there is a solution if we want to keep some functionality of the Editor, such as, for instance, defining a Prefab that we can spawn 10,000 times. Mixing the `GameObject-MonoBehaviour` paradigm with ECS is called **hybrid ECS** and is the perfect way to keep the best of both worlds.

4. To enable it for our component, we need to write an `IConvertGameObjectToEntity` implementation. `IConvertGameObjectToEntity` is a piece of code that automatically converts a standard `MonoBehaviour` to the correspondent component:

```
using System.Collections;
using System.Collections.Generic;
using UnityEngine;
using Unity.Entities;
using System;
using Unity.Mathematics;

[RequiresEntityConversion]
public class RotationSpeedAuthoring : MonoBehaviour,
IConvertGameObjectToEntity
{

    public float rotationSpeed = 35f;

    public void Convert(Entity entity, EntityManager
dstManager, GameObjectConversionSystem conversionSystem)
    {
```

```
            var data = new RotationSpeed { Value =
math.radians(rotationSpeed) }; // Convert to speed in radians
            dstManager.AddComponentData(entity, data);
        }
    }
```

In the preceding code, `RotationSpeedAuthoring` is an `IConvertGameObjectToEntity` **implementation and a** `MonoBehaviour` **(so that we can attach it to a** `GameObject`**). The core of the conversion lies in the** `Convert` function. The signature is confusing; it changed a lot in the past, and it will probably change again in the future. What is important is the content: the function takes the data of the `MonoBehaviour`, adds it to a new component (in our case, `RotationSpeed`), applies some processing (in our case, we convert degrees per second into radians per second), and finally attaches the component to the entity.

5. We now create `cubePrefab` as before and add the `RotationSpeedAuthoring` `MonoBehaviour` to it and, at runtime, `GameObject` will be converted to an entity.

6. Now that we have everything we need, we just need to write our game controller:

```csharp
using System;
using UnityEngine;
using Unity.Entities;
using Unity.Transforms;
using Unity.Mathematics;

namespace ECSJob
{
    public class ECSJobManager : MonoBehaviour
    {

        #region COMMON_GAME_MANAGER_DATA
        public float cubeSpacing = 0.1f;
        public int width = 10;
        public int height = 10;

        public GameObject cubePrefab;
        #endregion

        EntityManager entityManager;

        void Start()
        {
            entityManager = World.Active.EntityManager;
```

```
            SpawnCubes();
    }

    private void SpawnCubes()
    {
        int amount = Mathf.FloorToInt(width / cubeSpacing) *
Mathf.FloorToInt(height / cubeSpacing);
        Debug.Log(String.Format("Spawning {0} cubes", amount));

        Vector3 position = new Vector3();

        var entityPrefab =
GameObjectConversionUtility.ConvertGameObjectHierarchy(cubePrefab,
World.Active);

        while (position.x < width)
        {
            while (position.y < height)
            {
                var instance =
entityManager.Instantiate(entityPrefab);

                position = new Vector3(position.x, position.y +
cubeSpacing, 0f);
                entityManager.SetComponentData(instance, new
Translation() { Value = position });
                entityManager.SetComponentData(instance, new
RotationSpeed() { Value =
math.radians(UnityEngine.Random.Range(25.0f, 50.0f)) });
            }
            position = new Vector3(position.x + cubeSpacing,
0f, 0f);
        }

    }
}
```

This is a pretty standard game manager, but let's go over the exciting parts. First, we have a new attribute: entityManager. This is just a reference to the primary entity manager. An entity manager, as the name suggests, is a data structure where you can perform basic operations on entities, such as checking whether an entity is still alive, or creating and editing entities.

You do not need to create an entity manager. Unity will provide one for you. As you can see in `Start`, you just need to reference the main global one.

7. It is now time to spawn the cubes. The first interesting line is this one:

```
var entityPrefab =
GameObjectConversionUtility.ConvertGameObjectHierarchy(cubePrefab,
World.Active);
```

With this one, we take the Prefab we built, and we convert it to an entity. Every `MonoBehaviour` in the Prefab gets converted into a component and, sometimes, more than one. We already know that `RotationSpeedAuthoring` gets converted into `RotationSpeed`, but Unity provides conversions for many standard `MonoBehaviour` subclasses, such as the following:

- Each `Transform` is converted into `Translation`, `Rotation`, and `Scale` components (and some less common ones, such as `NonLocalScale`)
- Each `MeshRenderer` is converted into the `RenderMesh` component

8. Now, for each cube position, we need to instantiate a new entity. This is similar to how we instantiate a `GameObject`, but we invoke `Instantiate` on `entityManager`, as shown in the following code block:

```
var instance = entityManager.Instantiate(entityPrefab);
```

9. Then, we set the `Translation` and `RotationSpeed` components on the entity.

The first is to set the cube position to the computed position, and the latter to set the random rotation speed. Note that the component uses radian per second, so we need to convert the value:

```
entityManager.SetComponentData(instance, new Translation() { Value
= position });
entityManager.SetComponentData(instance, new RotationSpeed() {
Value = math.radians(UnityEngine.Random.Range(25.0f, 50.0f)) });
```

At this point, we have the components, and we have a way to instantiate the entities. We are still missing a system to actually move the cubes. We want to build a system that takes every entity with `RotationSpeed` and a `Rotation` component and make them spin. Not only this, but we also want to use C# jobs so that all 10,000 cubes spin in parallel. This is a typical pattern and, therefore, Unity has a class for us.

However, we first need to write our job:

```
public struct RotatorJob : IJobForEach<Rotation, RotationSpeed>
        {

            [ReadOnly]
            public float deltaTime;

            public void Execute(ref Rotation rotation, [ReadOnly] ref
    RotationSpeed rotationSpeed)
            {
                rotation.Value = math.mul(math.normalize(rotation.Value),
    quaternion.AxisAngle(math.up(), rotationSpeed.Value * deltaTime));
            }
        }
```

This is similar to the previous job, but with a number of differences. First, we extend IJobForEachinstead of IJobParallelForTransform because entities have no Transforms. You may note that we pass two type parameters to the IJobForEach interface. These are the types of components we want to use in our job, namely, Rotation and RotationSpeed. We may put any number of components in there; the important thing is that we add the same component, in the same order, as the parameters of Execute.

For example, if we extend IJobForEach<Rotation, RotationSpeed>, then Execute will take as parameters a reference to a Rotation and a RotationSpeed component. However, if we extend IJobForEach<Scale>, then Execute will only take as a parameter a reference to a Scale component; and so on. This acts as a filter over all the entities and makes sure that this job is applied only on entities containing Rotation and RotationSpeed components.

Finally, you may note that we are using some strange types for rotation: quaterion, with a lower case *q*. This is because Unity developed some new types for vectors and quatrains in the ECS that have the advantage of being more optimized for jobs and components.

 There are a lot of them but, as usual, they are a work in progress. To find up-to-date info on them, check the documentation of the Unity.Mathematics module here: https://docs.unity3d.com/ Packages/com.unity.mathematics@1.0/manual/index.html

Now that we have a job, we need to create a component system that takes advantage of it:

```
public class RotationSystem : JobComponentSystem
    {
        protected override JobHandle OnUpdate(JobHandle inputDeps)
        {
```

```
RotatorJob rotatorJob = new RotatorJob()
{
    deltaTime = Time.deltaTime
};

return rotatorJob.Schedule(this, inputDeps);
}
}
```

`JobComponentSystem` is a class designed to build a system that can run using C# jobs.

We start by defining a new class called `RotationSystem`, which extends the `JobComponentSystem` class. Inside this class, we override the `OnUpdate` (note: `OnUpdate`, not `Update`) method, inside which we just create a new `RotatorJob` job and schedule it.

Now, we just need to attach the `ECSJobManager` to an empty `GameObject` and run the application and see all the cubes spinning as normal. With these changes, we finally reach more than 100 FPS! Let's look at **Profiler**:

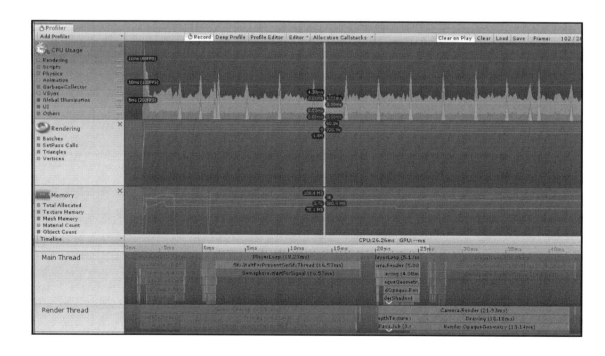

The time is so fast that we can see the small spikes of v-sync. Every frame takes less than 10 ms; this is less than the time we spend only on scripts using the classical non-DOTS approach! That's an incredible speeding up, and the application contains less than half the memory.

But guess what. We can still do better.

The burst compiler

The last component of the DOTS is the burst compiler. The burst compiler is a compiler that can compile a subset of C# into optimized native code. The main goal of Burst is to compile jobs so that they can be as fast and lightweight as possible.

The cool thing is that using the burst compiler is extremely easy. First, you need to install the Burst package from **Window | Package Manager**. Then, the only thing you need to change is to add the [BurstCompile] decorator on top of the job definitions as follows:

```
[BurstCompile]
public struct RotatorJob : IJobForEach<Rotation, RotationSpeed>
    {

        [ReadOnly]
        public float deltaTime;

        public void Execute(ref Rotation rotation, [ReadOnly] ref
RotationSpeed rotationSpeed)
        {
            rotation.Value = math.mul(math.normalize(rotation.Value),
quaternion.AxisAngle(math.up(), rotationSpeed.Value * deltaTime));
        }
    }
```

That's it! Now the job is compiled with Burst, and this will squeeze a bit more performance from our application. Our demo is straightforward, and the Burst compilation effect is limited—on my machine, I can reach 110 FPS, but for more complex jobs, the impact is more significant.

Summary

The DOTS is the peak of Unity's effort to push Unity into the future of gaming. I firmly believe that in the future, DOTS will be a core component of any optimization effort, and this chapter will definitely grow into several ones while DOTS becomes more stable and is supported by the community.

Unfortunately, at this stage, C# jobs and ECS are still very unstable, their APIs are changing rapidly and, therefore, I do not advise using them in big, important, commercial games. However, I believe it is important to start experimenting with them so as to be ready for when their time comes.

This chapter merely scratches the surface of the DOTS. There are many more details, configurations, and optimizations that can be implemented both in jobs and ECS. For more information, the main Unity Hub for DOTS (`https://unity.com/dots`) is your best friend.

This chapter effectively concludes all of the techniques we can bestow that explicitly aim to improve application performance. However, optimizing your workflow is also enormously beneficial. As mentioned previously, the one constant cost of performance optimization work is development time. However, if you can speed up our development working, saving some time during the more tedious parts of the job, then hopefully, you can save yourself enough time to actually implement as many optimization techniques we've talked about through this entire book as you can. There are a lot of neat little nuances to the Unity Engine that aren't well known or clearly documented, and that only become apparent through experience with the engine or by involving ourselves in its community. As such, the next chapter will be full of hints and tips for improving how to manage your project and scenes more effectively and how to make the most of the Unity Editor.

10
Tactical Tips and Tricks

Software engineers are an optimistic bunch and, as such, we often underestimate the amount of work it takes to fully implement new features or make changes to an existing code base. A common mistake is to only consider how long it will take to write the code that's required to create that feature. In such cases, we forget to include the time it takes for several important tasks. We often need to spend time refactoring other subsystems to support the changes we're making. This can happen either because we didn't think it would be necessary at the time, or because we thought of a better way to implement it halfway through, which can quickly turn into a rabbit hole dive of redesign and refactoring if we don't plan far ahead. We should also consider the time that's needed for testing and documentation. Even if a QA team does a testing pass against the change after it has been implemented, we still need to run through some scenarios on our own system during implementation in order to ensure that the change actually does what it's intended to do.

The one constant cost that's included in all performance optimization work is time. So, with limited time at our disposal to implement our features and keep everything working, an important skill for any developer to learn about is workflow optimization. Having a better understanding of the tools we use will save us more time in the long run, and hopefully provide the extra time we need to implement everything we want to, which applies not only to the Unity engine, but to every tool we use—IDEs, build systems, analytics systems, social media platforms, app stores, and so on.

There are a lot of little nuances to using the Unity engine that can help improve our project workflow. However, quite a lot of the Editor's functionality is not well documented, well-known, or just not something we think about until after quite some time—we realize the fact that it could have been applied perfectly to solve a particular problem we were having 6 months ago.

The internet is crammed full of blogs, tweets, and forum posts that try to help other Unity developers learn about these useful features, but they only tend to focus on a handful of tips at a time. There doesn't seem to be any online resources that group many of them in one place. As a result, the internet browsers of intermediate and advanced Unity developers are probably bursting at the seams with links to these tips that we bookmark for later and then completely forget about.

So, because this book is primarily for such users, I felt like it was worth including a short chapter to pool many of these tips and tricks together into one location. This chapter serves as a reference list in the hope of saving us time during future development efforts.

In this chapter, we'll cover the following topics:

- Editor hotkey tips
- Editor UI tips
- Scripting tips
- Custom Editor scripts and menu tips
- External tips
- Other tips

Editor hotkey tips

The Editor is rife with hotkeys that can aid rapid development, and it's worth checking out the documentation. However, let's be honest—nobody reads the manual until they need something specific from it. In this section, we will go over some of the most useful, yet less well-known, hotkeys that are available when we're playing with the Unity Editor.

 For each case we'll be looking at, the Windows hotkey is listed. If the macOS hotkey requires a different set of keystrokes, then it will be shown in parentheses.

Working with GameObjects

GameObjects can be duplicated by selecting them in the **Hierarchy** window and pressing *Ctrl + D (cmd + D)*. New, empty GameObjects can be created by pressing *Ctrl + Shift + N (cmd + shift + N)*.

Press *Ctrl* + *Shift* + *A* (*cmd* + *shift* + *A*) to quickly open the **Add Component** menu. From there, you can type in the name of the component you wish to add.

Scene window

Pressing *Shift* + *F* will lock the camera on an object in the **Scene** window (assuming that the **Scene** window is open and visible), which can be helpful for tracking high-velocity objects or figuring out why objects may be falling out of our scene.

Holding *Alt* and left-click and dragging with the mouse in the **Scene** window will make the **Scene** window's camera orbit the currently selected object (as opposed to looking around it). Holding *Alt* and right-click and dragging with the mouse in the **Scene** window will zoom the camera in/out (*Alt* + *Ctrl* + left-drag).

Holding *Ctrl* and left-click and dragging will cause the selected object to snap to the grid as it moves. The same can be done for rotation by holding *Ctrl* as we adjust the rotation widgets around the object. In the **Scene** window, you can click on the arrow near the grid icon (see the following screenshot) to open a window where we can edit the grid that objects snap to on a per-axis basis:

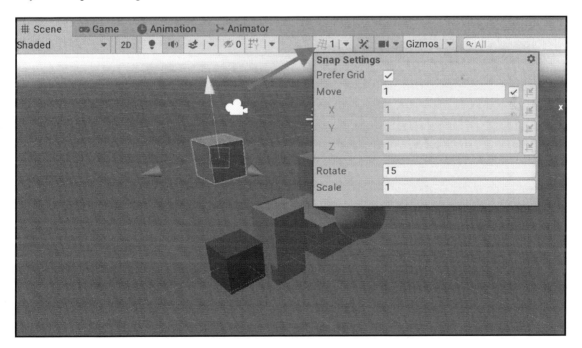

In Unity 2020.1, the snap to grid setting has been moved from the **Scene** view toolbar to the main window toolbar (where the **Play/Pause/Step** buttons are):

We can force objects to snap to each other through their vertices by holding down the *V* key as we move an object around in the **Scene** window. By doing so, the selected object will automatically snap its vertices to the nearest vertex of the nearest object. This is very useful for aligning scene pieces, such as floors, walls, platforms, and other tile-based systems, without needing to make small manual position adjustments.

Arrays

We can duplicate array elements that have been exposed in the **Inspector** window by selecting them and pressing *Ctrl + D* (*cmd + D*). This will copy the element and insert it into the array immediately after the current selection.

We can remove entries from an array of references (for example, an array of GameObjects) by selecting the element, right-clicking on it, and selecting **Delete Array Element**. This will strip the element and condense the array. Removing elements from arrays of primitive types (`int`, `float`, and so on) can be accomplished by simply pressing *delete* without the *shift* key (*cmd*) modifier being held down:

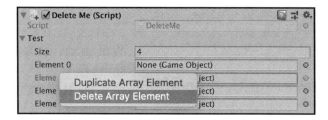

While holding down the right mouse button in the **Scene** window, we can use the *W, A, S,* and *D* keys to fly around with the camera in a typical first-person camera control style. The *Q* and *E* keys can also be used to fly up and down, respectively.

Interface

We can press *Alt* and click on any **Hierarchy** window arrow (the small gray arrow to the left of any parent object's name) to expand the object's entire hierarchy, rather than just the next level in the **Hierarchy** window. This works on GameObjects in the **Hierarchy** window, folders and Prefabs within the **Project** window, lists in the **Inspector** window, and so on.

We can save and restore object selections in the **Hierarchy** or **Project** windows much like a typical RTS game. Make the selection and press *Ctrl + Alt + <0-9> (cmd + alt + <0-9>)* to save the selection. Press *Ctrl + Shift + <0-9> (cmd + shift + <0-9>)* to restore it. This is exceptionally useful if we find ourselves selecting the same handful of objects over and over again while we're making adjustments. You can also find the save/load selections commands in **Edit | Selection**:

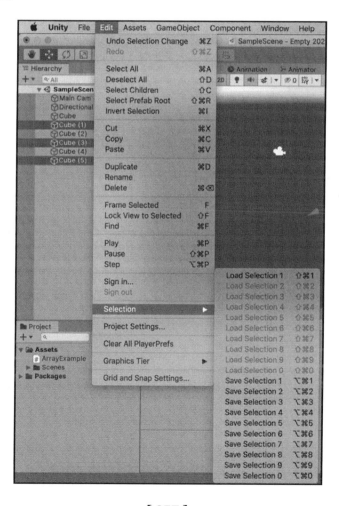

Pressing *Shift* + spacebar will expand the window under the mouse cursor so that it fills the entire Editor screen. Pressing it again will shrink the window and restore it to its previous location.

Pressing *Ctrl* + *Shift* + *P* (*cmd* + *shift* + *P*) will toggle the **Pause** button while in **Playmode**. This is usually an awkward key combination to press if we're trying to pause in a hurry, so it often helps to create a custom hotkey for pausing:

```
void Update() {
    if (Input.GetKeyDown(KeyCode.P)) {
        Debug.Break();
    }
}
```

In-editor documentation

We can quickly access the documentation of any Unity keyword or class by highlighting it in Visual Studio Community and pressing *Ctrl* + ' (*cmd* + '). This will open the default browser and perform a search on the Unity documentation for the given keyword or class.

Note that users with European keyboards may also need to hold down the *Shift* key for this feature to work.

The same can be done in Visual Studio by pressing *Ctrl* + *Alt* + *M*, followed by *Ctrl* + *H*.

Editor UI tips

The Editor's default behavior is designed to be efficient and satisfy every user; however, each of us is different, just like beautiful snowflakes, and so are our working preferences. Fortunately, Unity allows us to customize many aspects of the Editor's workflow. Let's see how with the following collection of tips.

Script Execution Order

We can prioritize which scripts will have their `Update()` and `FixedUpdate()` callbacks called before others by navigating to **Edit | Project Settings | Script Execution Order**. If we find ourselves trying to solve complex problems using this feature (with the exception of time-sensitive systems, such as audio processing), it implies that we've got some very fragile and tight coupling going on between our components. From a software design perspective, this can be a warning sign that we may need to approach the problem from another angle. However, this can be helpful to use as a quick fix.

Editor files

Integrating Unity projects with a source control solution can be a little tricky. The first step is to include the `.meta` files that Unity generates for various assets; if we don't do this, then anyone pulling data into their local Unity project must regenerate their own metadata files. This could potentially cause conflicts, so it is essential that everyone uses the same versions. This can be enabled by navigating to **Edit | Project Settings | Editor | Version Control | Mode | Visible Meta Files**.

It can also be helpful to convert certain asset data into text-only format, rather than into binary data, to allow data files to be manually edited. This turns many data files into the much more human-readable YAML format. For instance, if we're using ScriptableObjects to store custom data, we can use a text editor to search for and edit these files without having to do it all through the Unity Editor and serialization system. This can save a lot of time, especially when we're searching for a particular data value or performing multi-editing across different derived types. This option can be enabled by navigating to **Edit | Project Settings | Editor | Asset Serialization | Mode | Force Text**.

The Editor has a log file that can be accessed by opening the **Console** window (where log messages are printed), left-clicking on the hamburger icon in the top right corner (which looks like three thin horizontal lines), and selecting **Open Editor Log**. This can help us get more information about build failures.

Alternatively, if we successfully built our project, it will contain a breakdown of the compressed file sizes of all of the assets that were packed into the executable, ordered by size. This is an extremely helpful way of figuring out which assets consume the majority of our application's footprint (hint: it's almost always texture files) and which files take up more space than we would expect:

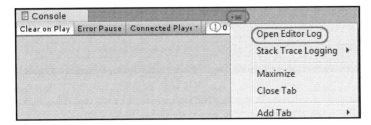

Additional windows can be added to the Editor by right-clicking on the title of an existing window and selecting **Add Tab**. This also allows us to add duplicate windows, such as having more than one **Project** window or **Inspector** window open at a time. This can be particularly useful for moving files between different locations via multiple **Project** windows:

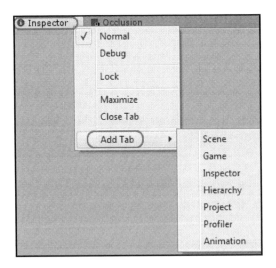

Having duplicate **Inspector** windows can be virtually redundant, since they'll show the exact same information when we click on a new object. However, by making use of the *lock icon*, we can lock the given **Inspector** window to its current selection. When we select an object, all the **Inspector** windows will be updated to show the object's data, except for any locked **Inspector** windows, which continue to show the data of the object they were locked to:

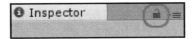

Some common tricks that make use of window locking include the following:

- Using two of the same window (**Inspector, Animation,** and so on) to compare two objects side by side or to easily copy data from one object to another
- Watching what happens to any dependent object if an object is tweaked during **Playmode**
- Selecting multiple objects in the **Project** window and then dragging and dropping them into a serialized array in the **Inspector** window without losing the original selection

The Inspector window

We can enter calculations into numeric **Inspector** window fields. For example, typing `4*128` into an `int` field will resolve the value to `512`, sparing us from having to pull out a calculator or do the math in our head.

Array elements can be duplicated and deleted from a list (in the same fashion as hotkeys can) by right-clicking on the root element and selecting **Duplicate Array Element** or **Delete Array Element**.

A component's context menu can be accessed by clicking on the small *cog* icon in the upper right corner or by right-clicking on the name of the component. Every component's context menu contains a **Reset** option, which resets all of the values back to their default states, sparing us from having to reset values manually. This is useful when we're working with `Transform` components as this option will set the object's position and rotation to `(0,0,0)` and its scale to `(1,1,1)`.

It's commonly known that, if `GameObject` was spawned from a Prefab, then the entire object can be reverted back to its initial Prefab state using the **Revert** button at the top of the **Inspector** window. However, it's less well-known that individual values can be reverted by right-clicking on the name of the value and selecting **Revert Value to Prefab**. This restores the selected value while leaving the rest untouched.

The **Inspector** window has a **Debug** mode that can be accessed by left-clicking on the hamburger icon next to the lock icon and selecting **Debug**. This will disable all custom **Inspector** window drawing from Editor scripts and instead reveal all the pieces of raw data within the given GameObject and its components. Even private data fields become visible. Although they are grayed out and cannot be modified through the **Inspector** window, this still gives us a useful way of examining the private data and other hidden values during **Playmode**. The **Debug** mode of the **Inspector** window also reveals internal ObjectIDs, which can be useful if we're doing interesting things with Unity's serialization system and want to resolve conflicts. Since Editor scripts are also disabled in this mode, it can be useful to debug such scripts by comparing its internal data to what we are trying to reveal in our Editor script.

If we have an array of data elements serialized in the **Inspector** window, then they are typically labeled **Element N**, where N represents the array index of that element, starting from 0. This can make it tricky to find a specific element if our array elements are a series of serialized classes or structs, which tend to have multiple children themselves. However, if the very first field in the object is a string, then the elements will be named after the value of the string field:

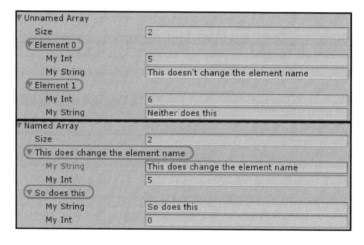

When a mesh object is selected, the **Preview** subsection at the bottom of the **Inspector** window is often fairly small, which makes it hard for us to look at the details in the mesh and what it will look like when it appears in our scene. However, if we right-click on the top bar of the **Preview** subsection, it will be detached and enlarged into a separate **Preview** window, making it much easier for us to see our mesh. We don't have to worry about setting the detached window back to its original home because if the detached window is closed, then the **Preview** subsection will return to the bottom of the **Inspector** window.

The Project window

The **Project** window's search bar allows us to filter for objects of a particular type by clicking on the small icon to the right of the search bar. This provides a list of different types that we can filter by revealing all the objects of that type within the entire project. However, selecting these options simply fills the search bar with a string of the t:<type> format, which applies the appropriate filter.

Thus, we can simply type the equivalent strings into the search bar for the sake of speed. For instance, typing t:prefab will filter for all Prefabs, no matter where they are in the **Hierarchy** window. Similarly, t:texture will reveal textures, t:scene will reveal scene files, and so on. Adding multiple search filters to the search bar will include objects of all types (it doesn't reveal objects that only satisfy both filters). These filters are modifiers in addition to name-based filtering, so adding a plain text string will cause a name-based search to occur through the filtered objects. For example, t:texture normalmap will find all the texture files that include the word normalmap in their name.

If we're making use of Asset Bundles and the built-in labeling system, the **Project** window's search bar also allows us to hunt down bundled objects by their label using l:<label type>.

If a MonoBehaviour script contains serialized references (using [SerializeField] or public) to Unity assets, such as meshes and textures, then we can assign default values to the script directly. Select the script file in the **Project** window; the **Inspector** window should contain a field for the asset so that we can drag and drop the default assignment into it:

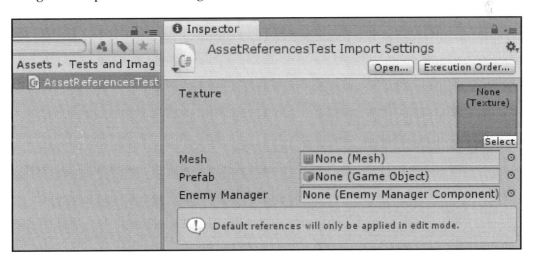

By default, the **Project** window splits files and folders into two columns and treats them separately. If we prefer the **Project** window to have a typical hierarchical folder and file structure, then we can set it to **One Column Layout** in its context menu (the hamburger icon at the top right). This can be a great space saver in some Editor layouts.

Right-clicking on any object in the **Project** window and selecting **Select Dependencies** will reveal all the objects that this asset relies on so that it can exist, such as textures, meshes, and `MonoBehaviour` script files. For scene files, it will list all the entities that are referenced within that scene. This is helpful if we're trying to perform asset cleanup.

The Hierarchy window

A less well-known feature of the **Hierarchy** window is its ability to perform component-based filtering within the currently active scene. This can be accomplished by typing `t:<component name>`. For example, typing `t:light` inside the **Hierarchy** window search bar will reveal all the objects in the scene that contain a Light component.

This feature is not case-sensitive, but the string we input must match the full component name for the search to be completed. Components that derive from the given type will also be revealed, so typing `t:renderer` will reveal all the objects with derived components, such as `MeshRenderer` and `SkinnedMeshRenderer`.

The Scene and Game windows

The **Scene** window camera is not visible from the **Game** window, but it is generally a lot easier to move around and place through the use of the hotkeys we mentioned previously. The Editor allows us to align the selected object to the same position and rotate the **Scene** window camera by navigating to **GameObject | Align with View** or pressing *Ctrl + Shift + F* (*cmd + shift + F*). This means that we can use the camera controls to place the **Scene** window camera where we would like our object to be and place the object there by aligning it with the camera.

Similarly, we can align the **Scene** window camera to the selected object by selecting **GameObject | Align View to Selected** (note that there is no hotkey for this on either Windows or macOS). This is useful for checking whether the given object is pointing in the right direction.

We can perform similar component-based filtering on the **Scene** window, just like we can with the **Hierarchy** window, by using the t:<component> syntax within its search bar. This will cause the **Scene** window to only render objects containing the given component (or those that derive from it). Note that this textbox is linked to the same textbox in the **Hierarchy** window, so anything we type in one will automatically affect the other, which is very helpful when we're searching for elusive objects.

At the very top right of the Unity Editor is a dropdown menu labeled **Layers**. This contains a layer-based filtering and locking system for the **Scene** window. Enabling the eye icon for a given layer will show/hide all the objects of that layer within the **Scene** window. Toggling the lock icon will allow or prevent objects of the given layer from being selected or modified (through the Editor UI, at least).

This is helpful when we wish to prevent someone from accidentally selecting and moving background objects that have already been placed correctly:

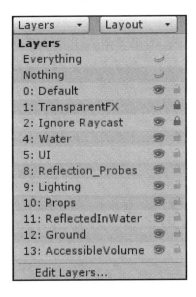

A well-known and useful feature of the Editor is that GameObjects can be given special icons or labels to make them easier to find in the **Scene** window. This is particularly helpful for objects with no renderer but that we wish to find easily. For instance, objects such as Lights and cameras have built-in icons that identify them in our **Scene** window more easily. However, the same gizmos can be revealed within the **Game** window by clicking on the **Gizmos** button at the top right of the **Game** window. The dropdown for this option determines what gizmos will be visible when this option is enabled.

Playmode

Since **Playmode** changes are not automatically saved, it is wise to modify the tint color that's applied during **Playmode** to make it blatantly obvious which mode we're currently working with. This value can be set by navigating to **Edit | Preferences | Colors | Playmode tint**.

Changes can be saved from **Playmode** simply using the clipboard. If we're tweaking an object in **Playmode** and we're happy with its settings, then we can copy the object into the clipboard using *Ctrl + C (cmd + C)* and paste it back into the scene once **Playmode** ends via *Ctrl + V (cmd + V)*.

All of the settings that have been applied to the object at the time of the copy will be kept. The same can be done with individual values of entire components if we use the **Copy Component** and **Paste Component** options in the component's context menu. However, the clipboard can only contain data for one GameObject, component, or value at a time.

Another approach, which allows us to save the data of multiple objects during **Playmode**, is to create Prefabs from them by dragging and dropping them into the **Project** window at runtime once we're happy with the settings. If the original object was derived from a Prefab, and we wish to update it across all instances, then we only need to overwrite the old Prefab with the new one we created by dragging and dropping the copy on top of the original. Note that this also works while **Playmode** is active, but it can be dangerous since there is no dialog popup to confirm the overwrite. Be very careful not to overwrite the wrong Prefab.

We can use the **Frame Skip** button (the button to the right of the **Pause** button in the Editor) to iterate one frame at a time. This can be useful for watching frame by frame physics or gameplay behavior. Keep in mind that this causes one FixedUpdate and one Update to be called per iteration, in equal counts, which may not reflect the actual runtime behavior, where we tend to have an unequal number of calls to these callbacks.

If the **Pause** button is enabled when **Playmode** begins, then the game will be paused just after the very first frame, giving us a chance to observe any anomalies that occurred during the initialization of our scene.

Scripting tips

If you are a developer, you will spend a lot of time editing code. While artists and designers are playing with colorful images and visual effects, you may find yourself stuck in the black and white code editor domain. Coding may be hard sometimes, but it doesn't need to be tedious. In the following tips, we will learn how to simplify some of the most boring parts of the job.

General

We can modify various templates of the new script, as well as shader and compute shader files. This can be helpful if we want to remove the empty Update stubs which, as we covered in `Chapter 2`, *Scripting Strategies*, can cause unnecessary runtime overhead. These files can be found in the following locations:

- Windows: `<Unity install>\Editor\Data\Resources\ScriptTemplates\`
- macOS: `/Applications/Unity/Editor/Data/Resources/ScriptTemplates/`

The `Assert` class allows for assert-based debugging, which some developers are more comfortable with, as opposed to exception-based debugging. Check out the Unity documentation for more information on `Assert`: `http://docs.unity3d.com/ScriptReference/Assertions.Assert.html`.

Attributes

Attributes are very useful meta-level tags that can be given to almost any target in C#. They are commonly used on fields and classes, allowing us to flag them with special properties so that they can be processed differently. Intermediate and advanced Unity developers will find it worthwhile to read the C# documentation on attributes and use their imagination to come up with their own attributes that help accelerate their workflow. There are quite a few attributes built into the Unity engine that can be exceptionally useful when used in the right place.

> Advanced users will note that attributes can also be given to enums, delegates, methods, parameters, events, modules, and even assemblies.

Variable attributes

The [Range] attribute can be added to an integer or floating-point field to convert it into a slider in the **Inspector** window. We can provide minimum and maximum values, thus limiting the range that the value can contain.

Normally, if a variable is renamed, even if we do a refactor through our IDE, then the values are lost as soon as Unity recompiles the MonoBehaviour and makes the appropriate changes to any instances of the component. However, the [FormerlySerializedAs] attribute is incredibly helpful if we want to rename a variable that has been previously serialized, since it will copy the data from the variable that was named within the attribute into the given variable at compile time. No more lost data due to renaming stuff!

Note that it isn't safe to remove the [FormerlySerializedAs] attribute after the conversion is completed unless the variable has been manually changed and resaved into every relevant Prefab since the attribute was included. The .prefab data file will still contain the old variable name, and so it still needs the [FormerlySerializedField] attribute to figure out where it should place the data the next time the file is loaded (for example, when the Editor is closed and reopened). Thus, this is a helpful attribute, but extended use does tend to clutter up our code base a lot.

Class attributes

The [SelectionBase] attribute will mark any GameObject the component is attached to as the root of selection for the **Scene** window. This is especially useful if we have meshes that are children of other objects since we may want the parent object to be selected with the first click, instead of the object with the MeshRenderer component.

If we have components with a strong dependency, we can use the [RequireComponent] attribute to force level designers to attach vital components to the same GameObject. This ensures that any dependencies that our code base relies on will be satisfied by designers, without us having to write out a whole bunch of documentation for them.

The [ExecuteInEditMode] attribute will force the object's Update(), OnGUI(), and OnRenderObject() callbacks to be called during **Edit Mode**. However, there are some caveats to this, as follows:

- The Update() method is only called if something changes in the scene, such as moving the camera around or changing an object property

- OnGUI() is only called during **Game** window events and not for other window events, such as the **Scene** window
- OnRenderObject() is called during any repaint event for the **Scene** and **Game** windows

However, this attribute gives such objects a different set of event hooks and entry points compared to typical Editor scripts, so it still has its uses.

Logging

We can add rich text tags to debug strings. Tags such as `<size>`, `<b>` (bold), `<i>` (italics), and `<color>` work on debug strings. This can help us differentiate between the different kinds of log messages and allows us to highlight specific elements, as follows:

```
Debug.Log ("<color=red>[ERROR]</color>This is a <i>very</i>
<size=14><b>specific</b></size> kind of log message");
```

The error message we will obtain is as shown as follows:

The MonoBehaviour class has a print() method for convenience, which does the same thing as Debug.Log().

It can help to create a custom logger class, which automatically appends \n\n to the end of every log message. This will push away the unnecessary UnityEngine.Debug:Log(Object) clutter that tends to fill the **Console** window.

Useful links

Unity provides many useful tutorials on the usage of various scripting features, which primarily target beginner- and intermediate-level developers. These tutorials can be found at https://unity3d.com/learn/tutorials/topics/scripting.

There's a helpful post on Unity Answers that provides a reference list that covers many of the different scripting and compilation errors we may run into during development. This can be found by searching for Scripting at https://learn.unity.com/.

Nested coroutines is an interesting and useful area of scripting that is not well documented. However, the following old but still valid third-party blog post, which covers a lot of the interesting details, should be considered when working with nested coroutines: http://www.zingweb.com/blog/2013/02/05/unity-coroutine-wrapper.

Custom Editor scripts and menu tips

While it's common knowledge that we can create an Editor menu item in an Editor script with the [MenuItem] attribute, a less well-known ability is being able to set custom hotkeys for menu items. For example, we can make the *K* key trigger our menu item method by defining that the [MenuItem] attribute ends with _k, as follows:

```
[MenuItem("My Menu/Menu Item _k")]
```

We can also include modifier keys such as *Ctrl (cmd)*, *Shift*, and *Alt* using the %, #, and & characters, respectively.

[MenuItem] also has two overloads, which allow us to set two additional parameters: a Boolean that determines whether the menu item requires a validation method and an integer that determines the menu item's priority in the **Hierarchy** window.

Check out the documentation for [MenuItems] for a complete list of available hotkey modifiers, special keys, and how to create validation methods: http://docs.unity3d.com/ScriptReference/MenuItem.html.

It is also possible to *ping* an object in the **Hierarchy** window, similar to what happens when we click on a GameObject reference in the **Inspector** window and call EditorGUIUtility.PingObject().

The original implementation of the Editor class, and the way that most people learned how to write Editor scripts, originally involved writing all the logic and content drawing in the same class. However, the PropertyDrawer class is an effective way of delegating **Inspector** window drawings to a different class from the main Editor class. This effectively separates input and validation behavior from display behavior, thus allowing for more fine-tuned control of rendering on a per-field basis and more effective reuse of code. We can even use PropertyDrawer to override default Unity drawings for built-in objects, such as Vector and Quaternion.

`PropertyDrawer` makes use of the `SerializedProperty` class to accomplish the serialization of individual fields, and they should be preferred when writing Editor scripts since they make use of built-in undo, redo, and multi-edit functionality. Data validation can be a little problematic, and the best solution is to use `OnValidate()` calls in the *setter* properties. A session at Unite 2013, by Unity Technologies developer Tim Cooper, explains the benefits and pitfalls of various serialization and validation approaches in great detail (`https://www.youtube.com/watch?v=Ozc_hXzp_KU`).

We can add entries to component context menus and even the context menus of individual fields with the `[ContextMenu]` and `[ContextMenuItem]` attributes. This allows us to customize the **Inspector** window's behavior for our components without needing to write broad `Editor` classes or custom **Inspector** windows.

Advanced users may find it useful to store custom data within Unity metadata files through the `AssetImporter.userData` variable. There's also a multitude of opportunities to make use of Reflection in the Unity code base. Ryan Hipple's session at Unite 2014 outlines a huge number of neat little hacks and tricks we can use with Reflection in the Unity Editor (`https://www.youtube.com/watch?v=SyR4OYZpVqQ`).

External tips

The following tips and tricks are related to topics outside the Unity Editor itself but can help Unity development workflow enormously.

The Twitter hashtag `#unitytips` is a great resource for useful tips and tricks for Unity development and is, in fact, where many of the tips in this chapter originate from. However, hashtags are difficult to filter for tips you haven't seen before, and it tends to be abused for marketing. A great resource that pulls together a bundle of weekly tips from `#unitytips` can be found at `http://devdog.io/blog`.

Googling Unity-related problems or concerns can be made a lot faster if we start the search with `site:unity3d.com`, which will filter all the results so that only those under the `unity3d.com` domain will appear.

If the Unity Editor crashes, for whatever reason, then we can potentially restore our scene by renaming the following file to include the `.unity` extension (for scene files) and copying it into our `Assets` folder:

```
\<project folder>\Temp\_EditModeScene
```

There is a great resource for game programming patterns (or, rather, typical programming patterns explained in a way that is pertinent to game development), and it's completely free and available online. The following guide includes more information on several of the design patterns and game features we explored in this book, such as the Singleton pattern, the Observer pattern, the Game loop, and doubling-up on frame buffers: `http://gameprogrammingpatterns.com/contents.html`.

Keep an eye on any session videos that come from Unite conferences whenever they happen (or better yet, try to attend them). A couple of panels at each conference are usually held by Unity employees and experienced developers who will share lots of cool and interesting things they've been able to accomplish with the Engine and Editor. In addition to this, make sure that you involve yourself in the Unity community through the forums on `https://unity3d.com`, Twitter, Reddit, Stack Overflow, Unity Answers, or at whatever social gathering places pop out of the woodwork in the coming years.

Every single tip that was included in this book wasn't conjured out of thin air. It started out as an idea or tidbit of knowledge that someone shared, somewhere, at some point, and somehow eventually found its way into this book. So, the best way to keep up to date on the best tips, tricks, and techniques is to keep our fingers on the pulse of where Unity is heading by staying involved in its community.

Other tips

Finally, this section contains tips that didn't quite fit into the other categories.

It's always a good idea to organize our scenes using empty GameObjects and use them as parents for a group of objects while naming them something sensible for that group. The only drawback to this method is that the empty object's transform is included during position or rotation changes and is included during recalculations. As we know, reparenting `GameObject` to another transform has its own costs. Proper object referencing, transform change caching, and/or use of `localPosition`/`localRotation` can be used to solve some of these problems adequately. In almost all cases, the benefits of having a workflow from scene organization are significantly more valuable than such trivial performance losses.

Animator Override Controllers were introduced way back in Unity v4.3 but tend to be forgotten or rarely mentioned. They are an alternative to standard Animation Controllers, which allow us to reference an existing Animation Controller and then override specific animation states so that we can use different animation files. This allows for much faster workflows since we don't need to duplicate and tweak Animation Controllers multiple times; we only need to change a handful of animation states.

The amazing customizability of the Unity Editor and its ever-growing feature set means that there are tons of little opportunities to improve workflows, and more are being discovered or invented every single day. The asset store marketplace is absolutely rife with different products that try to solve some kind of problem that modern developers are having trouble with, which makes it a great place to browse if we're looking for ideas or, if we're willing, drop some money to save us a ton of hassle.

Since these assets tend to sell to a broad audience, this keeps prices low, and we can pick up some amazingly useful tools and scripts for little to no cost. In almost all cases, it would take us a significant number of hours to develop the same solution ourselves. If we consider our time as valuable, then scanning the asset store once in a while can be a very cost-effective approach to development.

Summary

This brings us to the end of this book. Hopefully, you have enjoyed the ride. To reiterate, perhaps the most important tip in this book is to always make sure that you verify the source of the performance bottleneck via benchmarking before making a single change. The last thing we want to waste time on is chasing ghosts in the code base when 5 minutes of Profiler testing can save us an entire day of work. In a lot of cases, the solution requires a cost-benefit analysis to determine whether we're not sacrificing too much in any other area at the risk of adding further bottlenecks. Make sure that you have a reasonable understanding of the root cause of the bottleneck to avoid putting other performance metrics at risk. To also reiterate the second most important tip in this book, always profile and test after making changes to ensure they had the intended effect.

Performance enhancement is all about problem-solving, which can be a lot of fun since, due to the complexity of modern computer hardware, small tweaks can yield big rewards. There are many techniques that can be implemented to improve application performance or speed up our workflows. Some of these are hard to fully realize unless we have the necessary experience, skills, and time to implement them. In most cases, these fixes are relatively simple if we simply take the time to find and understand the source of the problem. So, go forth and use your repository of knowledge to make your games the best they can be!

Other Books You May Enjoy

If you enjoyed this book, you may be interested in these other books by Packt:

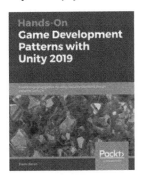

Hands-On Game Development Patterns with Unity 2019
David Baron

ISBN: 978-1-78934-933-7

- Discover the core architectural pillars of the Unity game engine.
- Learn about software design patterns while building gameplay systems.
- Acquire the skills to recognize anti-patterns and how to avoid their adverse effect in your codebase.
- Enrich your design vocabulary so you can better articulate your ideas on how to better your game's architecture.
- Gain some mastery over Unity's API by writing well-designed code.
- Get some game industry insider tips and tricks that will help you in your career.

Hands-On Deep Learning for Games
Micheal Lanham

ISBN: 978-1-78899-407-1

- Learn the foundations of neural networks and deep learning.
- Use advanced neural network architectures in applications to create music, textures, self driving cars and chatbots.
- Understand the basics of reinforcement and DRL and how to apply it to solve a variety of problems.
- Working with Unity ML-Agents toolkit and how to install, setup and run the kit.
- Understand core concepts of DRL and the differences between discrete and continuous action environments.
- Use several advanced forms of learning in various scenarios from developing agents to testing games.

Leave a review - let other readers know what you think

Please share your thoughts on this book with others by leaving a review on the site that you bought it from. If you purchased the book from Amazon, please leave us an honest review on this book's Amazon page. This is vital so that other potential readers can see and use your unbiased opinion to make purchasing decisions, we can understand what our customers think about our products, and our authors can see your feedback on the title that they have worked with Packt to create. It will only take a few minutes of your time, but is valuable to other potential customers, our authors, and Packt. Thank you!

Index

Made in the USA
Las Vegas, NV
09 May 2021